DISABILITY IN TRANSLATION

This volume explores how disability is seen, written about, read and understood through literature and translation. Foregrounding the asymmetrical world of power relations, it delves into the act of translation to exhibit how disability is constructed and deployed in language and culture.

The essays in the volume reflect and theorise on experiences of translating various Indian-language stories (into English) which have disability as their subject. They focus on recovering and empowering marginal voices, as well as on the mechanics of translating idioms of disability. Furthermore, the book goes on to engage the reader to demonstrate how disability, and the space it occupies in our lives, can be reinforced or deconstructed in translation.

A major intervention in translation and disability studies, this volume will be of great interest to scholars and researchers of literature, culture, and sociology.

Someshwar Sati is Associate Professor at the Department of English, Kirori Mal College, University of Delhi, India. His research interests encompass Postcolonial Studies and the Indian English Novel, Disability Studies, and Translation Studies. Dr Sati has edited three critical volumes on postcolonial theory and literature, *Warble of Postcolonial Voices, Volume I and II* and *Writing the Postcolonial: Poetics, Politics and Praxis*.

G.J.V. Prasad is Professor of English at Jawaharlal Nehru University (JNU), India, and former Director of the Jawaharlal Nehru Institute of Advanced Study, JNU, India. His major research interests are Indian English Literature, Contemporary Theatre, Dalit Writings, Australian Literature, and Translation Theory. He has co-edited with Sara Rai a collection of stories from Indian languages, *Imaging the Other*. His academic publications include *Continuities in Indian English Poetry: Nation Language Form*, and *Writing India, Writing English*, along with five other edited volumes of critical essays, *Vikram Seth: An Anthology of Recent Criticism*, *The Lost Temper: Essays on Look Back in Anger*, *Translation and Culture: Indian Perspectives*, *"Violets in a Crucible": Translating the Orient* (along with Madhu Benoit and Susan Blattes), and *Indian English and Vernacular India* (along with Makarand Paranjape). Professor Prasad is also a poet and a novelist, and has most notably received the Katha Award for translation from Tamil.

DISABILITY IN TRANSLATION

The Indian Experience

Edited by Someshwar Sati and G.J.V. Prasad

Routledge
Taylor & Francis Group

LONDON AND NEW YORK

First published 2020
by Routledge
2 Park Square, Milton Park, Abingdon, Oxon OX14 4RN

and by Routledge
52 Vanderbilt Avenue, New York, NY 10017

Routledge is an imprint of the Taylor & Francis Group, an informa business

British Library Cataloguing-in-Publication Data
A catalogue record for this book is available from the British Library

Library of Congress Cataloging-in-Publication Data
A catalog record has been requested for this book

ISBN: 978-0-8153-6984-4 (hbk)
ISBN: 978-0-367-33387-4 (pbk)
ISBN: 978-0-429-31957-0 (ebk)

Typeset in Bembo
by Apex CoVantage, LLC

Someshwar Sati's Dedication:
to
My teachers, especially the Late Professor Meenakshi Mukherjee
My parents Professor Rameshwar Sati and Dr Uma Sati
My brother Amreshwar
and
My wife Arti and my son Praneel

G.J.V. Prasad's Dedication:
to
Poonam Natarajan and Vidya Sagar
Ambika Kameshwar and RASA
and
Shubha and Kamala, as always

CONTENTS

List of figures   *x*
List of contributors   *xi*
Acknowledgements   *xvi*

Introduction   1
Someshwar Sati and G.J.V. Prasad

1 A different idiom: translation and disability   25
   Radha Chakravarty

2 Translation as social action: the counter-discourse on the
   literary representation of disability   37
   Chitra Harshvardhan

3 Gitopadesha on wheelchairs and crutches:
   an alternative aesthetic   55
   Himani Kapoor

4 Disabling normalcy in 'Thakara': a comparative reading of
   P. Padmarajan's short story and its film adaptation   72
   Sanju Thomas

5 Disability, translation and curriculum: a case study of
   Rangeya Raghav's 'Goongey'   84
   Shubhra Dubey

6 Translation as 're-presentation': the disability spectrum in
   selected Urdu short stories   97
   Deeba Zafir

7 Translating desires of the *undesired*: re-reading Tagore's
   different women in 'Subha' and 'Drishtidaan'   107
   Somrita Ganguly

8 'Blind' fate and the disabled genius: postcoloniality and
   'translation' in Saurabh Kumar Chaliha's 'Beethoven'   119
   Rajashree Bargohain

9 Fighting against multiple bodies! Translating 'Nāri o
   Nāgini' and 'Tamoshā' by Tarashankar Bandyopadhyay and
   'Bonjhi Gunjomālā' by Jagadish Gupta   133
   Subhadeep Ray

10 Negotiating disability in/and translation: a reading of two
   Tamil short stories   146
   B. Mangalam

11 Reading interrupted: translating dis*ability* in 'Subha'   159
   Ananya Ghoshal

12 'Lohini Sagai': translating disability, literature and culture   173
   Shilpa Das

13 Gendering disability in Dharamvir Bharti's 'Gulki Banno':
   'The Hunchback Bride'   186
   Mukul Chaturvedi

14 The politics of translation: disability, language and
   the in-between   198
   Ritwick Bhattacharjee

15 'Viklang': performing language and cripping modernity
   through translation   211
   Shefalee Jain

16 Translating stigma in the postcolonial context: an analysis
   of Bharat Sasne's short story 'Mai Dukh Ki Lambi Raat'   220
   Rohini Mokashi-Punekar

17 Translating rhetoricity and everyday experiences of
   disablement: the case of Rashid Jahan's 'Woh'   231
   Shilpaa Anand

18 Disability and the call for prayer: translating Khalid Jawed's
   short story 'Koobad'   243
   Sania Hashmi

Index   *254*

FIGURES

3.1 Shakuni from *Mahabharata* production by The Katkatha Puppet
Arts Trust, New Delhi   60
3.2 Wheelchairs being put to an innovative aesthetic use in
'Bharatnatyam on Wheels'   62
3.3 A scene from 'Bharatnatyam on Wheels', wheelchairs hanging
from the top   63
3.4 Representation of Vishnu in the centre and the seven heads of the
Shesha Naga around him   64
3.5 Krishna's *Vishvarupa*   65
3.6 Narasimha   66
3.7 Ramavtar   66

CONTRIBUTORS

Shilpaa Anand is at the Department of Humanities and Social Sciences BITS Pilani – Hyderabad Campus, India. She has an MA in English from the University of Hyderabad, India, and a PhD in the interdisciplinary programme of Disability Studies from the University of Illinois at Chicago, US. In her doctoral work she explored the conceptual history of disability in the Indian context. More recently, her research has focused on culturally distinct notions of corporeality and corporeal difference.

Rajashree Bargohain obtained her PhD degree from the Department of Humanities and Social Sciences at the Indian Institute of Technology, Guwahati, India. Her thesis is titled "Echoes from the Hills: Poetry in English from Northeast India". She obtained an MPhil degree from the Department of English, Gauhati University, in 2012. Her broader research interests include contemporary literature of North-East India in English, literature from North-East India in translation, women's writings from North-East India, cultural and political histories of North-East India, Assamese history and literature and folk literature from Northeast India. She is currently working as an assistant professor in Sonapur College, Assam, India.

Ritwick Bhattacharjee is an assistant professor at the Department of English, SGTB Khalsa College, University of Delhi, India. He has done his MPhil from the Department of English, University of Delhi. His research interests are in fantasy studies, phenomenology, continental philosophy, Indian English novels, and graphic novels.

Radha Chakravarty is a writer, critic and translator. She has co-edited *The Essential Tagore*, nominated Book of the Year 2011 by Martha Nussbaum, and edited *Shades of Difference: Selected Writings of Rabindranath Tagore* (2015). She is the author of *Feminism and Contemporary Women Writers* (2008) and *Novelist Tagore: Gender and*

Modernity in Selected Texts (2013). Her translations of Tagore include *Gora, Chokher Bali, Boyhood Days, Farewell Song: Shesher Kabita* and *The Land of Cards: Stories, Poems and Plays for Children.* Other works in translation are Bankimchandra Chatterjee's *Kapalkundala, In the Name of the Mother* by Mahasweta Devi, *Vermillion Clouds: Stories by Bengali Women,* and *Crossings: Stories from Bangladesh and India.* She has edited *Bodymaps: Stories by South Asian Women* and co-edited *Writing Feminism: South Asian Voices and Writing Freedom: South Asian Voices.* Her poems have appeared in *Journal of the Poetry Society of India, The Fib Review, The Skinny Poetry Journal* and *Indian Poetry Through the Passage of Time.* She is currently translating the memoirs of Mahasweta Devi. She was nominated for the Crossword Translation Award, 2004. She is a professor of Comparative Literature & Translation Studies and is dean of the School of Letters, at Ambedkar University Delhi, India.

Mukul Chaturvedi is an associate professor in the Department of English, Zakir Husain College, University of Delhi, India. Her doctoral thesis was on women's testimonies. She has published widely on testimonial writing. Her current areas of interest are oral narratives, autobiography, literature from conflict zones, and bio fiction.

Shilpa Das teaches in and heads the departments of Interdisciplinary Design Studies, PhD Research, and the Science and Liberal Arts Studies at National Institute of Design (NID), India. Her doctoral research is on the sociocultural impact of stigma on women with disabilities in Gujarat. She has published several papers on disability in India, in general, and women with disabilities, in particular. Her papers on design pertain to social issues particularly the need to bring in universal design solutions and inclusive practices. She is on the board of advisors to the Bill and Melinda Gates Foundation, US, working on projects of global public health. Shilpa is the founding editor of two prominent publications brought out by the Research and Publications department of NID – *The Trellis,* a research-based journal on design, and a magazine called *D/signed.* A notable outreach project she was part of had NID partnering with Handicap International, India and the Department of Health and Family Welfare, Government of Gujarat. The project titled 'Strategic Behaviour Change-Communications Campaign on Disability Prevention and Care in Rural Areas of Gujarat' was a two-year project (2005–2007) where NID carried out field research; designed a media strategy; created content including audio, video and print; did field testing; finalised the content; and made extensive recommendations.

Shubhra Dubey has completed her master's in English from University of Delhi, India. She has an MPhil from Centre for English Studies, Jawaharlal Nehru University, Delhi, and is currently working on her doctoral degree. Her interests at present include literacy and pedagogical practices.

Somrita Ganguly is a poet, and literary translator, presently affiliated with Brown University, Rhode Island, as a Fulbright Doctoral Research Fellow. She has taught

British literature to undergraduate students in Delhi and Calcutta and translates from Bengali and Hindi to English. She was selected by the Writers' Centre Norwich as an emerging translator in 2016. She has been invited as translator-in-residence at Cove Park, Scotland, in October 2017, and in December 2017 she was invited as poet-in-residence at Arcs of a Circle, Mumbai, an artists' residency organised by the US Consulate in Bombay. Somrita's work has been showcased at the 2017 London Book Fair. She has presented research papers at various national and international conferences in India, Singapore, the UK, and the US. She has thirteen academic publications to her credit and is a recipient of the Jawaharlal Nehru Memorial Fund Award (2013) and the Sarojini Dutta Memorial Prize (2011). Somrita has recently completed translating a political biography, an anthology of lyrical verses, a five-volume novel-in-verse, and a modern retelling of the *Mahabharata*. She is currently translating a novel on the Russian Revolution from Bangla to English.

Ananya Ghoshal is an assistant professor in the Discipline of English at Indian Institute of Technology (ITT) Indore, India. Ananya received her doctorate from the Department of English Literature at the English and Foreign Languages University (formerly CIEFL), Hyderabad, on the influence of music in postcolonial literature (2016). Her pre-doctoral research was conducted in the Department of English at the University of California, Berkeley, on a Fulbright–Nehru Fellowship. Her primary areas of interest are word and music studies, narratives of the Anthropocene, performance studies, digital humanities and visual culture. Her research also intersects with graphics, poetry, photography and filmmaking in relation to the discourses of emerging media technologies. Before coming to IIT Indore, she was an academic fellow at the Forum on Contemporary Theory, Baroda. Her latest publication is *An Anthropocene Primer* (http://anthropoceneprimer.org/). Edited by Jason M. Kelly and Fiona P. McDonald, the *Primer* is an innovative open-access, open peer-review publication that guides learners through the complex concepts and debates related to the Anthropocene.

Chitra Harshvardhan teaches translation theory and simultaneous and consecutive interpretation at the Centre of German Studies, Jawaharlal Nehru University, New Delhi, India. Her research interests include issues of globalisation, transculturation, identity and power relations in translation. She has published articles in the preceding areas and has translated and co-translated books and articles from German into English from the fields of anthropology and political science. Recently, she has translated the Hindi short story 'Goonge' by Rangeya Raghava into English. She is currently engaged in researching on Dalit self-narratives in English translation.

Sania Hashmi is a research scholar at the Centre for English Studies, Jawaharlal Nehru University, New Delhi, India. Her areas of interest include Indian writings in English, literary theory, 19th- and 20th-century British literature, translation studies, disability studies, literature and psychoanalysis. Her forthcoming publications include the book *Tolerant Indians With Muslim Friends* (2019).

Shefalee Jain is an artist based in New Delhi, India. She is currently teaching as an assistant professor in the Visual Art at the School of Culture and Creative Expressions, Ambedkar University Delhi (AUD), India. Her research interests are in the area of visual culture, critical history and philosophy and, particularly, in the examination of the imagery of ability, self-sufficiency and wellness in contexts such as modern medicine, advertisement, educational material for children and art. She has submitted her practice-based PhD in Visual Art at AUD in November 2018 which comprises submissions in the form of an installation accompanied by a thesis. The title of her installation is Landscape and Fall (February 2018), and that of her thesis is *The Phantasmagoria of Normalcy: Art Practice as an Exploration of Modern Visual Imagery of Self-sufficiency and Ability*. She occasionally writes and illustrates for children and has co-founded Blue Jackal, a platform for exploring visual storytelling.

Himani Kapoor is a PhD student at Department of English, Delhi University, India. Her research interests include religion and culture studies.

B. Mangalam is an associate professor, in the Department of English at Aryabhatta College, University of Delhi, India. Her research work pertains to gender and caste intersectionality in Tamil Dalit fiction. She has published critical editions *of Pride and Prejudice* (1999*), Paradise Lost* Bk 9 (2000), *The Balcony* (2001) and *The Book of Vanci, Cilappatikaram* (2015). She has published articles on translation studies and Dalit writings in various journals and critical volumes. She translates from Hindi and Tamil to English.

Rohini Mokashi-Punekar is a professor at the Department of Humanities and Social Sciences, Indian Institute of Technology Guwahati, India. She is a translator and works on the interstices between literary history, political change and social interrogation. Besides several papers in books and journals, she is the author of *On the Threshold: Songs of Chokhamela* (2005, 2002); *Untouchable Saints: An Indian Phenomenon* (2005), which she co-edited with Eleanor Zelliot; and *Vikram Seth: An Introduction* (2009). She is currently engaged in two translation projects. The first is an anthology of medieval Varkari poetry in translation. The second is a translation of Phule's *Tritiya Ratna*.

Subhadeep Ray teaches at the Department of English (Postgraduate and Undergraduate), Bidhan Chandra College, Kazi Nazrul University, Asansol, India. Having a doctoral degree for his thesis on Joseph Conrad's fiction, Ray is presently working on the comparative analysis of European and Bengali modernism, postcolonial studies, translation studies and disability studies. He is a contributor to the Maria Curie-Skłodowska University (Poland) – Columbia University Press (US) Conrad Project, and he presented his research paper on Bengali disability narratives at an international conference on "Disability Histories" at the University of Sheffield, UK. Ray is also engaged in translating mid-twentieth century Bengali literature, particularly fiction of Tarashankar Bandyopadhyay, into English.

Sanju Thomas is an assistant professor in the School of Letters at Ambedkar University Delhi, India. Her areas of interest are literatures of the Indian subcontinent, translation studies, Malayalam fiction and cinema and women's writing. Her publications include the English translation of the memoir of Ajitha (Kerala's Naxalbari, 2008) and an edited anthology of Malayalam short stories by women writers (Myriad Mirrors, 2003).

Deeba Zafir teaches in the Department of English, Lakshmibai College, University of Delhi, India. She has translated critical material, fiction and poetry from Hindi and Urdu. Her most recent translation is the autobiography of the well-known Dalit writer in Hindi Sheoraj Singh Bechain's *My Childhood on My Shoulders*, co-translated by Tapan Basu (2018). Her other publications include articles on disability, Dalit and partition studies.

ACKNOWLEDGEMENTS

We must acknowledge with thanks the support from the International Association for Translation and Intercultural Studies and of Jawaharlal Nehru Institute of Advanced Study (JNIAS), JNU, New Delhi. Dr. Hephzibah Israel was an early believer and backed the workshop and the book that resulted all the way. We must also thank the participants in the workshop for their invaluable contributions and incisive interactions.

We would like to also acknowledge the unflinching support and invaluable input given by Ritwick Bhattacharjee, Sania Hashmi, Shubhra Dubey, Himani Kapoor and Shilpaa Anand while editing the volume. We are also thankful for the cheerful assistance generously offered by Ankita Juyal, Poorvi Ahuja, Utkrishta Sharma, Shambhavi Sinha, Ritika Mishra, Simran Bhagat, Sakshi Sharma and Anukriti Bajpai.

INTRODUCTION

Someshwar Sati and G.J.V. Prasad

> The 'problem' is not the person with disabilities; the problem is the way that
> normalcy is constructed to create the 'problem' of the disabled person . . . one of
> the tasks for a developing consciousness of disability issues is the attempt, then, to
> reverse the hegemony of the normal and to institute alternative ways of thinking
> about the abnormal.
>
> – Davis (1995: 24, 49)

When we first announced our intention to organise a workshop on translating
disability short stories, even our so-called liberal colleagues greeted the announcement with puzzled looks that seemed to question the state of our sanity, looks that
seemed to hint at the futility of the project. 'What is the point?' they seemed to ask.
Are there enough disability short stories within the canon of Indian Literature to
merit such an exercise? Would the workshop be in any way viable? To our pleasant
surprise, soon we had a list with more than 80 disability short stories from 12 different Indian languages. The abundant number of texts that the workshop uncovered
was enough to silence the sceptics and put our worst apprehensions to rest.

Many of us have been studying and even teaching Indian literature for quite
some time now, little suspecting that this corpus of literature abounds in representations of disability. Rabindranath Tagore, Saadat Hasan Manto, Vaikom Mohd Bashir
and Dharamvir Bharti have all produced little gems on the subject. Obviously the
social marginalisation of disabled people has not resulted in their representational
erasure, at least not within the pages of the Indian short story. While Indian literary artists seem conscious of disability being a prime structuring category of social
relations, the puzzled looks that greeted our announcement suggested that the
phenomenon has yet to become a part of our academic consciousness. While the
so-called progressive minds in their critical practice appear to be invested in issues
related to race, gender, caste and ethnic biases and prejudices, they simply seem

unable to recognise and identify a disability text even when confronted with one. Rasheed Jahan's Urdu short story 'Woh', for example, narrates Sufiya's encounter with a prostitute who has a disfigured face. Although its plot revolves around a wide range of social responses to the prostitute's facial disfigurement, never has her diseased condition been a subject of animated discussion within our classroom, nor has 'Woh' been discussed in academic circles across the country as a disability text. Nobody seems interested in using the text to reflect on the experience of disablement or evolve with its help a theory of corporeal difference. The pedagogical and critical practice in India is, to say the least, not inclusive of disability. This is a matter of great concern and a manifestation of what Michael Bérubé calls 'the politics of disavowal' which is associated with 'the psychological distance most people put between themselves and disability' (1996: 85).

The present volume seeks to bridge this distance. Many contributors to the present volume, who unmistakably have an open and sensitive mind towards matters of disability, confess that they had revisited narratives that they had previously translated without even being conscious of them being disability texts. The workshop had simply given them an alternative frame of reference of which they had until then been blissfully unaware. While these confessions were a source of great pleasure and satisfaction for us, it had also simultaneously left us deeply disturbed. Why does it take a workshop to make translators who are never tired of flagging feminist and Dalit concerns recognise disability as a potential conceptual paradigm for textual analysis and acknowledge the phenomenon as a materially embodied experience of oppression? Disability is indeed a form of marginalisation that has been most marginalised in academia.

In society at large, disability has yet to be recognised as a discursive political entity, remaining for the most part associated with a medical condition. The essays anthologised herewith try to outline the role that translation studies can play in releasing Disability Studies from the confines of hospital hallways and therapeutic table and transform it into a more than acceptable conceptual paradigm for theorising and articulating from within the academia a resistance and political struggle against the dominant structures of power. In the process of doing so, we hope that Translation Studies will also enable Disability Studies to interrogate received conventions of representing the experience of disablement and critically unravel in all its complexities the processes of identity formation through which the subjectivity of disabled people has been discursively constituted over the ages. As a new line of academic enquiry within the disciplinary field of Translation Studies, Disability Studies must claim a space for itself in a highly contested terrain, argue for its existence and justify its inclusion.

Towards a politics of disablement

The presence of characters with disabilities in Indian narrative discourses is a literary phenomenon as old as the earliest oral narratives. The blind king Dhritarashtra and his 'orthopedically disabled' brother-in-law Shakuni in the *Mahabharata* and the 'mentally unstable' Mantra and the blind parents of Shravan Kumar in the *Ramayana* are only a few examples that immediately come to mind. Curiously, however, a civilisation with a 3,000-year-old history of disability narrative is yet to evolve a discursive category that can go by the name of Indian disability literature. Nor have issues related to disabilities and to the aesthetics and politics surrounding their representation been accorded a legitimate academic space in mainstream discussions of Indian culture. By identifying disability short stories in various Indian languages and then translating them to English and then subsequently reflecting on the act of translation, the present volume seeks to build a brief for the incorporation of a disability perspective within critical approaches to the Indian short story and within contemporary translational practices.

Even within the Western academic circles, it was not until the publication in 1995 of Lennard Davis's *Enforcing Normalcy* that one comes across a serious attempt to incorporate a disability perspective into an ideologically nuanced reading of the literature. What follows is a brief and therefore wholly inadequate outline of the intellectual lineage of literary Disability Studies. This has been presented not as a comprehensive or conclusive history of the field – such histories do already exist – but, rather, as a means of conveying to the reader the general understanding of the field that we as editors have relied on in compiling the volume.

The publication of *Enforcing Normalcy* signalled the arrival within the humanities of a new line of academic enquiry. Since then, this line of academic enquiry, which goes by the name of literary and cultural Disability Studies, has expanded and developed. From its early interest in revealing the constructed nature of normalcy and denaturalising the concept, the discipline today dwells on the impact of exclusionary literary and cultural practices on the constitution of the subjectivity and identity of disabled people. Like Davis, Rosemarie Garland-Thomson, Ato Quayson and other Disability Studies scholars in their works began to recognise disability as a discursively constituted phenomenon deeply imbricated in the structures of power in which normalcy had been elevated to the status of an assumed ideal within an ableist social order. Their works strike at the very root of this order and unsettle structures of ableist thinking, critically outlining and unpacking the various cultural processes of categorical Othering through which the disabled subject is denigrated.

Prior to these scholars, research in Disability Studies had been carried out primarily within the auspices of social sciences. The genesis of the discipline, however, can be traced back to the 1960s and to the voices of organisations of disabled people who inspired by the political campaign for rights by other marginalised groups, like those based on race and gender, began to push for the respect, recognition and dignity of their community. Predictably, early scholarship in the field had been produced in close association with disability activism, the Independent Living Movement (ILM) in the United States and the Union for the Physically Impaired against Segregation (UPIS) in Britain. For this reason, Disability Studies scholars in this period had a clear political orientation and were primarily interested in forging and consolidating a coherent sense of collective identity for the disabled community and projecting it as a disadvantaged group. Accordingly, their research was characterised by a materialist analysis of the impact of an exclusionary society on disabled people, and evaluative studies of state policies and practices. With Davis's treatise, Disability Studies began to move beyond purely sociological, economist, and rights-based arguments to engage itself with disability as a discursively produced and socially contextualised ontological phenomena.

Enforcing Normalcy is no doubt a seminal text in the field of literary Disability Studies, but the primary concern of this book is not the phenomenon of disability per se; it is, rather, the historical and ideological constitution of the idea of the normal human body in 18th- and 19th-century Europe. Nevertheless, this central concern provides Davis with a productive point of access into an intellectually engaging discussion of disability. *Enforcing Normalcy* had for the first time brought to bear on the understanding of normalcy and, by extension, of its deviant other disability post-structuralist notions of cultural history arguing that the cultural characterisation of those labelled as 'disabled' is less a matter of physical and medical limitations and more the outcome of regulatory practices and sociopolitical decisions associated with the 18th-and 19th-century Western factory system and eugenic policies, both of which required uniformly disciplined and statistically 'normal' bodies to achieve their respective goals. Davis, thus, exposes the cultural contingencies with which, at a particular moment in history and in a specific social context, some bodily differences or impairments become disabling. The ideological gesture exposes and even potentially subverts the fallacious and self-interested reasoning that seeks to marginalise those whose bodies are regarded as deviating from the norm. 'In an able-ist society', he writes, 'the 'normal' people have constructed the world physically and cognitively to reward those with like abilities and handicap those with unlike abilities (Davis 1995: 10). Clearly, disability is to Davis not a mere matter of body and medicine. It is much more. It is also a matter of social and cultural power differentiation wrought by the hegemonic operation of the rhetoric of normalcy.

Rosemarie Garland-Thomson, in *Extraordinary Bodies*, carries the preceding emphasis on the constructedness of the experience of disablement forward and lays stress on the centrality of the figure of the disabled in processes of American self-fashioning. Her ideologically nuanced reading of the American freak show, the mid-19th-century sentimental narrative by white women novelists and the representation of empowered deformed characters that, by black American authors of the 20th century reveal that in American culture, which promotes the liberal ideology of individualism and the Puritan sanctification of labour, the figure of the disabled, deformed and crippled functions as the image of the other in relation to which the ideal American self is defined. For this reason, to Garland-Thomson, '[d]isability is . . . the attribution of corporeal deviance-not so much a property of bodies as a product of cultural rule about what bodies should be or do'(1997: 6). She therefore argues that disability is the reading of bodily difference in the context of social-powered relations. The prime objective of her book as she herself confesses is to interrogate the convention of representation and unravel the complexities of identity formation within social narratives of bodily difference as 'to move disability from the realm of medicine to that of political minority, to recast disability as form of pathology into a form of ethnicity'(Garland-Thomson 1997: 6). But above all, extraordinary bodies is an attempt to evolve a politics of collision against the dominant structures of power. According to her gender, ethnicity, sexuality and disability are related products of the same social processes and practices that shake bodies according to ideological structures. This emphasis on the connection amongst the various marginalised groups enables Garland-Thomson to theorise and simultaneously deconstruct the experience of disablement, pushing the Disability Studies to move beyond the essentialism that had hitherto defined the discipline particularly during the 1970s, 1980s and early 1990s. Garland-Thomson to her great credit also draws attention to the failure of Disability Studies to theorise the phenomenon of disablement from a gendered perspective. Similarly, O. Stuart, Tom Shakespeare, D.J. Gallagher and D. Skidmore draw attention to the discipline's disregard to the categories of ethnicity, sexuality and social class, respectively. While all these Disability Studies scholars underscore the contested nature of laying claims to disability as an identity marker, Tobin Seibers, in *Disability Theory*, moves from a social construction to a new realism of the body and its identity and embarks on a vigorous defence of the relevance of identity politics and the academic discourse on it in today's world:

> My argument here takes issue with those who believe that identity politics either springs from disability or disables people for viable political action. I offer a defense of identity politics and a counterargument to the idea, embraced by the Right and Left, that identity politics cannot be justified because it is linked to pain and suffering. The idea that suffering produces weak identities both enforces the ideology of ability and demonstrates a profound misunderstanding of disability: disability is not a pathological condition, only analysable via individual psychology, but a social location complexly embodied.
>
> (2008: 14)

Seibers envisions identity politics, that which has become more material in recent years, as a wider category which necessarily includes disability along with race, gender, ethnicity and sexuality as elements of identity.

Michael Davidson, in *Concerto for the Left Hand: Disability and the Defamiliar Body*, carries this emphasis on identity politics forward and focuses on the various aesthetic and social implications of disability. He evolves a critical disability aesthetics, the enjoyment of which is implicitly linked with issues of social justice. This engagement with disability aesthetics develops a kind of an alternative narrative envisaged by Seibers and enacts the importance of disability and identity:

> Which is why a poetics – as much as a politics – of disability is important: because it theorises the ways that poetry defamiliarises not only language but the body normalised within language. A poetics of disability might unsettle

the thematics of embodiment as it appeared in any number of literary and artistic movements of the 1960s.

(Davidson 2008: 118)

In their own respective ways, both Seibers and Davidson dissolve the fractured postmodern self that Disability Studies had been grappling with around the turn of the century into a coherent, crisp identity.

Disability Studies is thus both an area of academic enquiry as well as a field of political struggle. Interestingly this volume makes an appearance at a time when disability as a form of materially embodied experience of discrimination and oppression is gaining a non-medicalised and a right-oriented positive legitimacy. On the 16 December 2016, the Indian parliament passed the right of persons with disability bill. Thanks to this historic legislation, disability in India today is a thriving developmental category – one that speaks the emancipatory global language of human rights and empowerment. This makes us wonder whether there exists a political praxis between the struggle of disabled people and the academic pursuit of Disability Studies, particularly in the current context, where the discipline is yet to be institutionalised within our Indian universities as a legitimate line of critical enquiry.

What makes the present moment in history even more interesting is the political heat generated by an almost endless debate about the naming of disabled people. During the past year and a half, with the professed benevolent intention of changing the social attitude towards persons with disability, the Indian government has left no stone unturned to promote and legitimise, both in official and casual usage, the term *Divyang* to refer to the disabled population of this country. The underlying suggestion here is that disabled people literally have divine body parts and are bestowed with divinity as compensation for their impairment. But underlying such a discourse of religiosity, there lurks a fatalistic acceptance of the 'condition' of disabled people as divinely ordained, diverting attention from the social structures that create and sustain exclusion. This obscures the fact that the experience of disablement is produced by social barriers and remedied through adequate policy intervention, absolving the government and society at large of complicity in its perpetration. Many disability scholars and activists locate in such diversionary strategies 'a complete denial of the struggles that disabled people have been engaged in, for their socio-economic and political rights as well as for non discrimination, respect, and dignity'(Ghosh 2017). Ironically, the idea of a social schism, a binary between non-disabled and disabled people is being produced and proactively disseminated to deny disabled people equal access to the rights of the citizens at the very time when the Indian parliament has been promulgating the Rights for Persons with Disability Act, 2015, with the intention of promoting this very access.

It is within this historical conjuncture that the present volume would like to locate itself and decode the poetics of previously mentioned politics with the hope that the essays collected herewith will cover the key debates in the field and provide a fresh perspective for future research.

The poetics of the politics

'Much of literature', Davis poignantly observes,

> is part of a national project in which representative character types are
> emplotted into narrative situations. These characters . . . are embodied in
> specific bodies . . . [which] are seen through the lens of normality as either
> disabled or non-disabled . . . When characters have disabilities, the novel is
> usually exclusively about those qualities.
>
> (1999: 510)

What Davis is hinting at here is a form of discursive violence inflicted by an ableist
literary establishment on disabled people cancelling and reducing their complex
personality to a single attribute: that of their impairment. Interestingly, all this takes
place, as Davis suggests, as a part of the national project of consolidating the hegemony and bolstering the subject position of the normative non-disabled self. It is perhaps in this sense and for this purpose that literary narratives are indelibly marked by
the inescapable presence of the norm. The implication of the centrality of this norm
is profound, and as this volume shall demonstrate, it extends into the very heart of
cultural production, ceaselessly transforming a physical difference into disabilities.
For this reason, Davis further proposes, the academic engagement with the literary
representation of disability should be premised on the need to trace the ideological
moorings of these representations to the all-pervasive proliferation of the hegemony
of normalcy and interrogate the national tendency of producing templates for the
body and according specific meanings and significations to them. If *Enforcing Normalcy*, following such a dictum, examines the role that the genre of the novel played
in promulgating, dissipating and consolidating the hegemony of normalcy in Britain, the present volume, through its focus on translation, recognises the inescapable
presence of the norm within the canon of the Indian short story and systematically
deconstructs its undisputed centrality in the representations of disability.

The literary artist undoubtedly has the licence to create an aesthetic universe
in which the wrongs and injustices of the real world are redressed. But while such
artistic rendering may apparently provide correctives and compensation for the
deformities and defects of the real world and encourage those reeling under and
struggling against oppressive structures of power, a fundamental question remains
unanswered: Can the transformative needs of the real world be met by the fancied
and rather simplistic resolutions of the imagined universe? Interestingly, none of
the stories analysed herewith create within their narratives a utopian space where
the hierarchies of the material world are put in abeyance. They show no interest
in ideologically massaging the cold reality of oppression and exclusion that define
disabled existence. Nor do they display a propensity towards presenting images
of sentimental amelioration through the depiction of improbable goodness. Nor
do they invoke a portrayal of the world that could or ought to be. They instead
prefer to focus on a cold, matter-of-fact, fateful representation of the world as it

is reflecting in the process the dominant attitudes towards disability and disabled people. It is in this sense that these stories are necessarily marked by the inescapable presence of the norm. It may then be argued that the centrality of the norm in the representation of disability in the Indian short story makes this canon of literature a proliferator of ideology. If this is indeed the case, then how should a reader/translator sensitive to issues pertaining to disability read and translate these texts? This is a question that lies at the heart of most, if not all, the essays collected herewith.

David Mitchell and Sharon Snyder point out that 'since texts provide us access to perspectives that filter disability through the reigning ideologies of their day, their analysis turns social beliefs into objects of investigation'(Mitchell and Snyder 2005: 633). In other words, a text, being inevitably bound to its historical moment, shortcomings, idiosyncrasies and obsessions, automatically offers transparency into these social contexts for critical scrutiny. The reading of a text from a disability perspective, in a sense then, engages all these social functions which mediate cultural realities. This engagement is necessary as it allows for an intervention in the propagation of the cultural images of disability which are responsible for the 'normal' responses to disability, disabled people and the imagination of human differences. Stories like Ishwar Petlikar's 'Lohi Ni Sagai'(Gujarati) and Khalid Jawed's 'Koobad'(Urdu), for example, draw the readers' attention to the social structures of control and exclusion – medicine and religion, respectively – that narratively shape and even define the figure of the 'disabled'. But the linguistic sign that surrounds their operations, when decoded through the act of reading/translation, gives rise to a new and radical conceptualisation of disability that questions the dominant morbid perception of the phenomena as an abstract nothingness. What follows is the collection of essays that outline how even the text marked by the inescapable presence of the norm can in its own quiet way disrupt the dominant power hierarchy and how a translator as an activist can rally against oppressive narrative structures and intervene and mediate in the process of literary production.

Within the wide spectrum of Indian short story, Saadat Hasan Manto's 'Toba Tek Singh' is often remembered for its masterly use of madness as a metaphor for evoking the senselessness of the violence that accompanied the partition of India. What we find compelling about such a figurative deployment of the experience of disablement is that Manto is not alone in rendering the phenomenon metaphorically. N. Masood, P. Padmarajan, Anjum Usmani, Sunil Kaushik and Agha Sohail and others have all revealed in their narratives a discursive dependency on the symbolic potency of disability to evoke a state of lack, inadequacy, helplessness, destitution and depravity. In fact, literary cultures across the globe have over the years deployed the phenomena in their narratives as 'an opportunistic metaphorical device'(Mitchell and Snyder 2000: 47) to figuratively capture 'a condition of social or individual collapse' (Mitchell and Snyder 2000: 47). Among the literary artists who have deployed disability metaphorically, we could name the works of William Faulkner, J.D. Salinger, Harper Lee, Ken Kesey, John Steinbeck, Herman Melville and the list goes on. This worldwide propensity to narratively evoke disability metaphorically has been fruitfully theorised by Mitchell and Snyder. In *Narrative*

Prosthesis, they recognise disability as the 'crutch' on which narratives 'lean for their representational power, disruptive potentiality, and analytical insight (Mitchell and Synder 2000: 49). In our capacity as editors of the current volume, we have noticed that many, if not most, submissions brought for our consideration explored and fleshed out the preceding theoretical formulation. But such reading practices say little about the materially embodied experience of disability and as Clare Barker in her illuminating study of the representation of disability in postcolonial fiction points out, 'effectively erases disability from view precluding its analysis as a socially significant phenomen[on] or a politicised aspect of identity' (2012: 3).

Perhaps, the most apt illustration of the above is the way disability has been widely used in common parlance as a metaphor. When the Bharatiya Janata Party (BJP) was the opposition party in India prior to 2014, it often referred to the United Progressive Alliance (UPA) government of Dr Manmohan Singh as an administration of the 'the government of the deaf and dumb'(*gunge behre ki sarkar*). While such an expression evokes the dysfunctionality of the government and denigrates its identity by linking it to the lack and inadequacy generally associated with disability, it simultaneously bolsters the subjectivity of those who can speak and listen. Precious little is conveyed in the expression about the materially embodied experience of disabled persons.

Disability here is objectified and placed within a medical narrative that evokes the supposed lack and dysfunctionality of disabled people bolstering the subject position of the non-disabled. When talking about bolstering the subject position of the non-disabled and erasing that of the disabled, how can we forget that disabled people have been almost left out of the Indian constitution? Few are aware that the Constitution of India, the foundational political document of the newly independent nation, literally erases disability and disabled people from view. They have been mentioned only once as a part of the Directive Principles which is not even legally binding. While it recognises other minority groups formed along the axis of race, gender, ethnicity, class, caste and religion as potentially oppressed, deprived and disenfranchised categories in need of state support and protection, the constitution does not even acknowledge the marginality or, for that matter the existence, of disabled people within the social fabric of postcolonial India. Disability and disabled people are indeed conspicuous by their absence from the pages of this sacred political document. The official omission of this section of society from the foundational political document of the newborn nation is quite troubling, raising disturbing questions about the identity of the disabled population and their validity and relevance in postcolonial India. The vows of this section of society were further confounded when during the 1950s, 1960s and 1970s, the Indian government revealed a marked unwillingness to recognise and include them within the national census. It was not until 1996, that is 48 years after country's independence, that disabled people were, with the passing of The Persons with Disabilities (Equal Opportunities, Protection of Rights and Full Participation) Act, 1995, made a subject of a major legislative measure. It further took another 21 years for this service delivery legislation to become a rights-oriented legal scripture through the promulgation of

Rights of Persons with Disabilities Bill, 2016. Nor have they ever been made the rallying point of a national protest movement which, more often than not, came to revolve around issues pertaining to untouchability, the exploitation of labour, the predicament of women, Dalit and tribals. In other words, disabled people within the postcolonial political ethos of India have simply been 'invisible, both literally and metaphorically' (Ghai 2002: 89–90).

People with disabilities in India may have been invisible in the political sphere; curiously, however, this invisibility has been matched by a hyper-visibility in works of literature. Yet there is little doubt that disability and disabled people inhabit the fringes of India's national consciousness and reside in a state that lies well beyond the experiential realm of postcolonial non-disabled Indian sensibility. It is this discursive location that unfortunately defines the general attitudinal orientation towards disability and disabled people in India today. For this reason, the encounter between the two worlds is defined by what David Bolt called 'critical avoidance'. While theoretically analysing the encounter between a person without impairment and a person with impairment and the influence that cultural representation has on this encounter, Bolt poignantly observes,

> Given this unawareness of (or disregard for) experiential knowledge and agency, it is perhaps not surprising that when normate thoughts do turn to impairment it is often associated with a story, placed in a narrative. Thus in an encounter between a person who has an impairment and a person who does not have an impairment . . . impairment may be rendered a part of Bakhtinian chronotope, that is to say, it becomes embedded in a story as a part of a time-sequenced narrative.
>
> (2012: 291)

In other words, when a person without impairment evokes a person with impairment in his thoughts or conversation, precious little is said about a materially embodied experience of disablement per se.

Of course, the wide metaphorical usage of the phenomenon of disablement is a perfect example of a critical avoidance or the previously mentioned politics of disavowal. Davis locates its operation in the

> social constructions such as 'the stare,' that telling glance directed towards people with physical differences; in the omission of disability culture from anthologies, curricula, and conference topics; in the barriers placed before Deaf and disabled scholars who do attempt to attend academic conferences that make no provision for them.
>
> (1999: 502)

Few have thought of the oppression perpetrated through the figurative deployment of disability. Consequently, one of the major tasks of this volume is to determine why this rather rampant form of discursive oppression exists, is easily acceptable and is unhesitatingly promulgated. Translators, through their very act of translation, we argue, should critically unpack this narrative practice, expose the arbitrariness of the apparently natural association between the experience of disablement and its metaphorical referent and thereby unsettle the privileged status granted to metaphor in disability narratives.

Bolt's concept of critical avoidance draws heavily on a rich intellectual tradition of disability thought that goes back to Erving Goffman (1983) who recognises all forms of human difference as been potentially stigmatisable. This, according to Bolt, leads to the creation of a divided ethos of social exclusion that both reflects the value judgement and bolsters the subject position of the dominant group. If Goffman's concept of stigma is carried over wholesale into the disciplinary terrain of Disability Studies, then we could argue that a narrative of stigma in the context of disability would obviously be marked by the hegemony of the non-disabled subject promoting and shoring up its identity and symbolically reproducing ableist structures of thinking. Many of the articles anthologised in the present collection dwell on the narrative of stigma arising out of a chance meeting between a non-disabled subject and its stigmatised other, the disabled. These anonymous encounters are obviously structured by the hegemony that the former exercises over the latter. Bharat Sasanein's Marathi short story, 'Mai Dukh Ki Lambi Raat' ('The Dark Night of Sorrow' in its English translation), and Suraj Sanim's Urdu short story 'Apahijh' ('Crippled' in its English translation) are cases in point. But as the plot of these stories unfolds a gradual melting of this hegemonic old is generally discerned as traces of extreme anxiety within the normate subject and its easy acceptance of stigmatised otherness of the world of the 'subaltern' begins to surface. Bharat Sasanein's Marathi short story, 'Mai Dukh Ki LambiRaat' ('The Dark Night of Sorrow') and Suraj Sanim's Urdu short story 'Apahijh' ('Crippled') are cases in point.

While elaborating productively on Goffman's concept of stigma, Rosemarie Garland-Thomson coins a particularly useful term to decipher the subject position of the dominant group. According to her, the normate is the composite identity position held by those unmarked by stigmatised identifiers of disability. However, its subject position is, to say the least, precarious. In fact, she uses the term to uncover the constructed identity of the cultural self who by virtue of othering, the marked deviant bodies 'step into a position of authority and wield the power it grants them'. The normate, according to her, refers to 'the veiled subject position of the cultural self' whose identity is defined and shored up in relation to the marked bodies of its deviant other (Garland-Thomson 1997: 8). In *Aesthetic Nervousness* (2007), Ato Quayson carries this line of thought forward and suggests that the subject position of the normate is necessarily insecure. According to him every individual is subject to contingency and the impaired body is merely a reminder of this contingency. Therefore, the tendency to read the impulse to 'other' disabled people, associate them with disorder and deem them socially deviant as the normate will to power must be re-evaluated. The instinct to categorise in this case should instead be seen as symptoms of extreme anxiety. Following the reliable lead of Quayson, translators could recover within the encounter between a non-disabled and a disabled person the traces of 'aesthetic nervousness' that destabilises the subject position of the normate unsettling the binary mode of thinking that lies at the heart of ableist structures of power. Such critical practices, according to Margrit Shildrick, 'challenge every one of us to rethink the relations between disabled and non-disabled designations – not just ethically as has long been the demand, but also ontologically, right at the heart of the whole question of self and other' (2012: 30).

Given the hegemonic sway that English as a world language holds over the political economy of the publication and, by extension, over the processes of the dissemination of knowledge, the principal traditions of scholarship available in the field of Disability Studies in India today are the British and American ones. Indian disability scholars have had for quite some time now easy access to the pioneering studies of Lionel Davis, Rosemarie Garland-Thomson, Michelle Snyder, Ato Quayson and others. The ready availability of their work has tempted our scholars to conveniently assimilate Western conceptual paradigms into their attempt to theorise the Indian experience of disablement.

Many may look upon and even celebrate the previously mentioned research practice as reflecting the universalisation or should we rather say the globalisation of Disability Studies as a legitimate line of academic enquiry. True there is a momentum already in place within Disability Studies to globalise its outlook and methodology, M. Miles and James Beckford, however, prefer to exercise caution about an uncritical transfer of theory and methodologies developed within the Western academy to other current location. They, in their respective historical enquiries into the conceptualisation of disability in non-Western society, argue that Western theories of disability have emerged within a cultural and epistemological context exclusive to the West and that one therefore should not assume their universality across time, space and culture. The two are questioning the wisdom of deploying Western conceptual paradigms to theorise the experience of disability in non-Western societies. Both of them, in a sense, build a case for affecting an epistemological shift in the way we understand and engage with disability in these societies – one that goes beyond metropolitan theories of disability to accommodate other culturally sensitive and context-specific non-universal and non-Western modes of knowing and engaging with the experience of disablement.

After all, as a socially produced phenomenon, corporeal difference intermingles with a variety of highly particularised cultural elements to produce heterogeneous forms of experience in different temporal, special and cultural locations. In postcolonial India, the category of disability not only coexists with other forms of marginality structured along the access of race, ethnicity, religion, gender, class and caste, it also intersects and overlaps with them creating complex configurations of identity. It is within these complex configurations of identity that the experience of disablement within the Indian context needs to be placed and decoded. Predictably, rather than restricting itself to the confines of disablement which would be a rather simplistic academic gesture, the volume embraces the interplay of various other marginalised groups like those based on gender, class and caste. Many of the stories analysed in the current volume bring the discourse of disability into a productive dialogue with feminist, Dalit and post-structuralist debate on postcolonial Indian identity and, in doing so, repositions disability as a central term in the process of postcolonial Indian self-fashioning.

The current volume seeks to effect an epistemological shift in the way postcolonial processes of Indian self-fashioning are approached by placing the figure of the disabled Indian subjects at the centre of these processes. It is in this context that the worldwide emphasis on the self-articulation of disabled people, in general, and Abilash Chandran's Tamil short story 'Maadippadigal' ('Steps and Stairs' in English translation), in particular, gathered significance. This self-portrayal foregrounds the struggle of an 'orthopedically disabled' author against a social system that fails to understand and accommodate his needs and aspirations. Yet he aspires to be a part of the mainstream.

According to Mitchell and Snyder, when persons with disabilities move from passive, silenced objects of discourse to active producers of knowledge about the social, political and phenomenological understanding of disability, they destabilise any number of objectifying practices. This change alone will prove monumental not because people with disabilities inherently know the truth of their own social and biological lives but because their visible entry into the discourse of their bodies makes all speaking positions in the field shift and grow necessarily self-conscious and, we hope, increasingly self-reflexive (Mitchell and Snyder 2005: 633). Even while asserting agency and taking control of his own life, the polio-stricken protagonist of Chandran's story evolves a narrative of self-affirmation that revolves around the trauma and anxiety experienced by him in a callous and unfriendly disability hostile society. This brings us a full circle back to the cold and matter-of-fact depiction of the structures of oppression and exclusion that define disabled existence, to the inescapable presence of the norm and its centrality in Indian representations of disability. We have nevertheless come a long way from the days when 'those who live with disabilities have been defined by the gaze and the needs of the non disabled world' (Fries 2000:1).

Translating the poetics and the politics

Translation is an 'enabling' act, one which directly addresses a 'disability', the readers' lack of reading ability in a particular language so that they can read the text in another. However, if you think about it, it is the lack of translation that is actually disabling, like other acts of society as for example the denial of universal education which is disabling to and marginalises and oppresses the poor or those denied such an opportunity. Thus, the fundamental reason for the existence of translation is overcoming the disability enforced by sociopolitical systems, linguistic chauvinisms and national pride and borders. One can argue that all articulation is translation, that all languages are translations and that what we think of translation is only one further step in a world of incomplete articulations since it is never easy to translate what we think, never easy to convey to others exactly what we mean and since we, each one of us, speaks a language unique to us, that while language gives us the hope of communication, it is impossible to ever communicate perfectly all that we intend. However, we don't need to adopt that position: that each language is unique and untranslatable, that each person's articulation is unique and never completely communicable. If we adopt that view, we are all born and raised 'disabled'(and we are, for we are forever being told to speak more clearly or write more clearly or use our body language more clearly as if the fault lies in only ourselves as communicators, not in the others who are unable or unwilling to receive), for we are social animals and communication is essential to us. We may agree with the view expressed or we may not. However, it is true that translation is an essential activity if we have to assert everyone's membership of humanity at large.

Having said that, one must explore what translation theory has to say about disability. Translation is a field that has been theorised and been written about and talked about and practised for millennia in many cultures. Human disability is as old as human beings. One of the first things you note is that the language of disability has changed over the centuries. Old census records in the archives in the UK refer to disability in these terms: *deaf, dumb, blind, lunatic, imbecile, idiot, asylum, inmate* and *patient*. The terminology used over centuries has constructed exclusion, labelled and marginalised person with disabilities. The change in terminology over the second half of the 20th century has not been fully accepted yet, or specific terms have been rejected and changed very often, since many terms seem to be euphemisms that normalise disability and undermine the gravity of the rights struggle and many others are simply ableist and used as negative terms that other and oppress persons with disability.

There is a parallel to this struggle to change the way we think of the language we use, including the language we translate into, whether in terms of race, class, caste or gender. From the mid-20th century onwards, the feminist movement has ensured that '[w]omen's language, women's writings, women's views about the world we live in, have all been the focus of much debate and study.' (Kamala 2009: XI) The sexist nature of language and the fact that 'most terms designating women have derogatory resonances while their masculine counterparts have positive overtones' (Kamala 2009: XII) are wellknown. There have been well-known and effective ways in which our sexist language has been challenged and changed. Canadian feminist translation practices went a step further to ensure they show us the biases inherent in the two languages at play. This has been the case with racial rights, and those of caste as well in India, and can thus be seen now in the articulation and translation of rights of the disabled in the ways in which we evolve terms to make for a more inclusive society based on rights.

To take the example of a term that had early acceptability and later criticism, one of the most significant of the new terms for persons with disabilities was and is *differently abled*. For a very long time, people used to be 'handicapped' in the US and 'disabled' in the UK and India. Perhaps the first use of the new term was by the US Democratic National Committee in the early 1980s as a more acceptable term than handicapped (or disabled). To many this seemed only a weird manifestation of political correctness. It seemed grammatically absurd to call people 'differently abled'. However, the term caught on and came into use immediately in India. It is obvious that the term *differently abled* would be so attractive to people who wanted to force society to see the disabled in terms of their abilities, just as all people look at each other. People are born with different abilities – the term forces us to recognise it. It took a while for activists to accept that the term doesn't work.

It is clear that each one of us is different from the other; we are different from our parents, who, in turn, are different from each other and different from our siblings, other relatives, and our friends. We are different not just in terms of our looks but our physical abilities as well – to begin with the most obvious difference. Some of us can see more sharply than others – the cline on vision will go from these really sharp-sighted people to people who can't see at all. There are people who can hear a pin drop in the next room, there are those who can't hear it drop from their own hands, and there are those who can't hear at all. There are those who have such a heightened sense of smell that there are professions tailor-made for them, and there are those of us who can't smell anything. There are people who ensure their tongues because they can discern tastes so clearly, and some of us can eat anything. If we were not each one differently abled, all of us would be athletes capable of winning Olympic track-and-field events just depending on our mood and wellness on a particular day. It is a truth we don't need to express, let alone emphasise, that we are all differently abled from each other in terms of our physical abilities. So are we mentally and in terms of other skills as well? Can we cook as well as our mother or father, the one who cooks better? Do all of us have the same IQ? Are we all equally good at drawing or writing or understanding science? Again, it is quite obvious that we are all differently abled. There is no group anywhere in which people will all be the same in ability in every sphere. We are all differently abled.

But *differently abled* was invented to refer to the handicapped, to the disabled. It was a politically correct, less hurtful way of referring to persons with disabilities by making the world focus on their abilities and not their handicaps. To call people disabled cloaked them with an identity based on their inability to carry out some activity, extending to thinking of them as incapable of doing anything of use, anything desired by themselves or others. However, what the term *differently abled* often did was to shut down any discussion on disability – including what it means to be disabled. This is actually profoundly 'disabling' to society at large while ensuring further marginalisation of persons with disabilities. All it does is to reinforce the difference – there are the abled, and there are the differently abled. We don't even see that different abilities also includes different disabilities, even while using the term to define the abled, the so-called normal! Instead of working to include the disabled into the community at large, it is again a term of exclusion, furthermore reinforcing a false divide, a divide that is the sociocultural cause of disability.

The term normalises disability as something that the disabled individual has to work on to showcase his or her different abilities. The world has, by the invention of this term, equalised the playing field, and now it is up to individuals to rise above their disabilities, thus in one stroke denying that society plays a role in marginalising, in constructing, the disabled. Disability is an attitude, an attitude in the disabled; it seems to say, 'Get over it; you are just differently abled!' So, we came back to *disabled*, to *persons with disabilities*. To say someone is disabled is not an insult, not a cuss word. It only highlights a factor that is important to that person, not something that expresses his or her complete identity but something that is important to the construction of that identity. It highlights a factor that influences the attitudes and behaviour of others towards the person with disability and the impact it has on his or her self-worth, sense of identity. Including every person in your imagination of society, even when calling someone disabled in a particular way, is possible so long as we consider all of us as full members of our community, our society and don't make false binaries. We must be constantly aware of the ableist nature of language we use and, through such reflexivity, evolve constantly towards an equitable society.

Hence, when translating literary or mythical or religious texts which represent disabled characters or the world of disability in a negative manner, we must take care to historicise their world view as well as ensure that we find ways to make the translation itself free of those negative values.

As Kerry Wynn, writing as a preacher of the need to be sensitive to offensive terms used in Bible translation to describe the disabled, said in 2001, '[t]he negative image of disability is virtually universal' (402). In the article, Wynn tries to develop some guidelines for translating terms for physical disabilities. His aim is to 'show that disability sensitive terminology . . . creates a more positive attitude towards people with disabilities', and this is done so that disabled people do not view the bible as hostile to them (*ibid.*). He identifies four strategies or guidelines for translating references to disability in the Bible (404):

1   Use "people first" terminology
2   Use language acknowledged as appropriate by those who have the disability
3   Don't use euphemistic language
4   Avoid clinical terminology

The first guideline is based on sound foundations – the human being's identity is not disability-based. He or she is a person first; the disability, while significant in various ways, does not define the person and is not the sole factor in the construction of identity. Hence, there is more acceptability for the usage of *person with disability* rather than *disabled person*. We will come back to this later. However, this can lead to many awkward phrases, but the awkwardness is worth it so long as it is acceptable to those who have the disability.

This leads us to the second of Wynn's guidelines. Obviously, this will change with time. As we have argued, the term *differently abled* was embraced quite enthusiastically once, in the recent past, and, indeed, is still in use, but *disabled* has come back into favour as a more useful term. The acceptability of terms is not just in terms of time period but also in terms of cultures and languages, as Wynn acknowledges. So if you know which country you are translating for, you should ask representatives of that group with the particular disability what term they would prefer. This is sensible advice, since you always translate for contemporaries. The third guideline is self-explanatory. Do not make disability equivalent to Voldemort in the Harry Potter series, something so threatening that it cannot be named or something to be so ashamed of that it cannot be talked about directly in polite company. People need to acknowledge and engage with disability, not turn their faces away from it. The final guideline is crucial, since if translators use medical terms while translating literary representations (unless the text specifically uses medical terminology), it moves the representation to the medical model, seeing disability as a medical condition, an illness and that which needs to be seen is in terms of treatment and curable, rather than in political terms of human rights and social terms of exclusion and inclusion.

To go back to the first guideline, the term for disabled people was once again debated in 2016 when the government of India began to propagate the Hindi term *Divyang* to represent the disabled. *Persons with Disability*, or 'PWD', is the accepted official term, and has been used by the Government of India, which was one of the first to sign and ratify the UN Convention on Persons with Disabilities (UNCRPD). This is the term in force in India since 2007. *Divyang* means 'divine body'. So religion is used to give a 'positive' spin to disability, normalising it as a God-given condition, something therefore to be accepted along with all it entails. This is much like the terms *Harijan*, children of God, which was used by Gandhi to mainstream the lowest castes. It is almost as if a term can make oppressive values and systems acceptable. This takes the focus away from the rights-based approach to disability. Because of much opposition from persons with disabilities, the Hindi term, *Divyang*, has not been translated and used officially in other Indian languages. However, it leads us to consider how various religions speak of disability and how we can and must move away from a language of retribution and sin to explain disability and to move it to a rights issue rather than a divine test or result issue.

Translation is not easy even if you wish to proselytise, to preach, as Wynn wishes to, to the disabled community. A preacher would not want to change the cosmology that looks at persons with disabilities in a particular religiously sanctioned manner, but the preacher would not want to use terms that persons with disabilities would see as insulting and oppressive. In an interesting paper on translating disability in the Muslim community of Israel, Nissim Mizrachi points attention to what he calls 'modular translation' (2014). In an earlier essay, he defines this strategy as 'the selective translation and adjustment of meaning components from one network of meaning into another.' (Mizrachi 2012: 198) What this implies is that when you translate a passage about the rights of people with disabilities, you do so without giving up the language of religion. Thus, persons with disabilities would not be seen as marginalised by an oppressive society but by misguided faith; thus, the rights of the people with disabilities are spoken in the language of divine test and communal support, individual acceptance of divine justice and the community's responsibility to take care of fellow humans; thus, both the whole community and the people with disabilities would work towards deeper faith in order for the people with disabilities to be fully integrated in society, to find the space to realise their potential (not to be independent, since no one is independent in divine cosmology; Table 1 in Mizrachi 2014: 156). Thus, translating for the faithful, in the project that Mizrachi analyses, imams used 'Islamic theology as the most valuable cultural resource for promoting the hope for change in public attitudes towards disability' (156). Mizrachi concludes further that this 'strategy allowed them to advocate public norms and attitudes in line with the . . . notion of disability rights while ignoring their liberal underlying justifications' (156). This modular translation allowed them to manage 'to initiate change while leaving religious cosmology intact and reinforcing its underlying justifications'(Mizrachi 2014: 156). Thus, modular translation is one way in which to re-present the disabled and the need for societal self-reflexivity and reform when your audience is firmly entrenched in a certain religious cosmology, be it Muslim or Hindu or Christian or any other. Both Wynn and Mizrachi seem to say the same thing finally, that you must make disability speak within the discourse of religion. The language can be altered, but the belief has to be kept intact. One is writing as a preacher, and the other is analysing the strategies of preachers.

Know your audience is a well-accepted mantra in Translation Theory; knowing who you are translating for – meaning who has commissioned you, for what purpose and who is your target audience – will help you devise your translation strategy. In the Hindu view of life, every birth is a rebirth to live out the causal effects of one's previous lives, to be punished or rewarded in various ways in a form of divine justice. Hence, in all religions, you have to bear your disability, see it as part of a divine cosmology, keep faith and overcome your circumstances by without anger or frustration, simply accepting it as God's will. This is easy to reinforce when you are a believer and are translating texts into the languages of belief to other fellow believers. Translating into languages of other beliefs is always tricky, since you don't want your text to be read in terms of other belief systems. However, it is easy enough for translations to insert the religious into the secular discourse of rights, show different ways of speaking of disabilities. A visualisation of Hindu gods will show how what would seem odd to another culture has been included in the divine. To speak of religious community-based inclusiveness and a world view that encompasses all may also help contest the liberal-Western negative reading of society and social construction of disabilities, as both Wynn and Mizrachi argue (Wynn 2001; Mizrachi 2014).

Interestingly, when you translate from Indian languages into English, you can secularise the terminology, make the text one of human rights and not of divine retribution and testing, individual forbearance and societal exclusion or sympathy. This is easier than trying to retain Indian religious languages and world views in English even if the text is Christian, since Christianity itself has undergone different translations in India. Translating from other Indian languages into English can thus result in specific gains, helping bring out the intent of the writer without the entanglements of sociocultural (read religious) discourse and worldview. When language comes in the way of expression, translation can help retrieve the text. In any case, societies change and many such changes are best reflected in translations. The translator has to be careful either that the pejorative is erased from the translation, that terms are carefully employed so that the translation speaks of and to persons with disabilities as full members of society whose rights have to be respected, or retain the pejorative terms to show how a particular story is completely ableist. As said before, it is important for a translator to be clear why he or she is translating, for whom and the strategies to be employed.

The practice of translation

This collection of essays addresses a gap in our understanding of translation, of translating disability. All of them arose from the experience of translating stories from various Indian languages into English to form a corpus of stories on disability easily available to interested readers. As translators, they struggled with many issues; most of them have been engaged with or written about by many translation theorists and practitioners. What was unique about these stories was the way they addressed disability and what the translators began to see as their duty, not just to the target audience but to the characters in the stories themselves, not just to the authors but also the issues raised by the stories about the ways in which we construct the world of the disabled, in the ways in which we represent them. The translators began to see themselves as activists, trying hard to de-construct the contexts of oppression and furthering the cause of persons with disabilities.

As Radha Chakravarty points out, the same social context gives rise to both the prejudiced views of disability and the writer's consciousness that critiques such attitudes. The translation of progressive literary texts allows disruptive, radical textual practices, which 'demonstrate that, along with creative writing and literary criticism, translating disability also represents a way of addressing the gaps in our awareness of the significance of disability in literary studies, a lacuna that we urgently need to address' (p. 35). Taking the short stories of four writers that she had translated before becoming aware of the relationship between Translation and Disability Studies, she explores the way the double lens of Translation and Disability Studies makes one realise that disability has to be read in India in terms of its intersections with caste, class and gender. The translator has to be an activist.

Chitra Harshvardhan takes this issue of translational activism, speaking of the translation ethics and translation practice as empowering, an act that can restore agency to the marginalised. Looking at issues of disability and literary representation, she tries to evolve an alternative aesthetics. Using Walter Benjamin's concept to 'afterlife' and Paul Ricoeur's concept of 'linguistic hospitality', she posits the act of translation as one that bridges discourses and contexts and thus at translation as a transformative act. She looks closely at the language employed by writers and how writers and readers (translators) have to challenge and subvert language to create an emancipatory space.

Himani Kapoor raises interesting issues of how we re-present persons with disabilities. After reading the way in which the two major Indian epics, the *Ramayana* and the *Mahabharatha*, exploit the widespread negative attitudes towards persons with disabilities, she explores later, more positive re-representations of the same character Sakuni (from the *Mahabharatha*) in two Indian languages, Odiya and Kannada, the first in a translation of the epic and the second in a performative interpretation. This opens the possibility of translational counter-readings of hegemonic texts and positions. She then explores how a contemporary performance of dancers with limb and hearing impairment, 'Bhagavad Gita on Wheels', showcases and creates a foundation for an alternative aesthetics of disability. In a nuanced reading, Himani Kapoor shows us how the performance puts an entirely different spin on the view of the 'disabled' body.

In her chapter on the cinematic adaptation of a Malayalam short story, 'Thakara', Sanju Thomas shows how the writer constructs the world of social exclusion. She looks at the role of language (Thakara is the name of the character with some kind of mental impairment, but the name itself refers to a troublesome weed) in marginalisation, in the prevalent attitudes to persons with disabilities, where they can at best be exotic specimens to be constantly observed and experimented on and, are in terms of caste hierarchy, outside caste, the lowest of the low. She demonstrates how a story that could and should have been translated from a Disabled Studies perspective, is turned into a sexy potboiler by the film director, where the focus shifts away from social marginalisation to the ableist male gaze that objectivises and oppresses women and misrepresents persons with disabilities.

Shubhra Dubey brings her reading of a short story in Hindi, Rangeya Raghav's 'Goongey', which is taught to school students to examine how it is taught as a text on disability, enforcing ableist perspectives, instead of a text on all kinds of marginalisation which it is. She sees it as a missed opportunity for flagging ableist language while staying true to the writer's intention, which is to speak of an inclusive nation in terms of communities of marginalised people. She goes on to show how it could be translated into English to play a role in the 'depoliticised' English classroom as obtains now in the senior secondary schools which follow the curriculum of the Central Board of Secondary Education. Such a translation would aim to be disruptive, to show up the biases of the first text and to facilitate a radical understanding of disability based on 'difference and alterity'.

In a similar vein, Deeba Zafir looks at the task of translating three Urdu short stories. She argues that translation takes the stories to a wider audience, and a wider field of reception, and contributes to the understanding of what constitutes an exclusionist world. The translator's task is then that of an activist who can act as a collaborator to a sensitive author or offer resistance to an antagonistic text or uncover silences to offer a subversive reading, she says. The translator is a consciousness raiser, Deeba Zafir concludes.

Somrita Ganguly analyses existent translations of two short stories by Rabindranath Tagore to go on to explain why she felt the need to attempt her own translations. She reflects on the choices she made in light of her position that translators need to be accountable in terms of both aesthetics and politics. Both stories are about desire, and hence, Somrita Ganguly explores the notion of 'desirable' and 'undesirable' in the normative world of ableist culture. She concludes with a set of five important questions, which could help to contribute to a theory of translation for Disability Studies.

On a different note, Rajashree Borgohain examines an Asamiya short story on hearing impairment and the creation of art (specifically music) to explore social attitudes and understanding of 'disability' and to see how language hierarchy plays a crucial role in translation. Rajashree Borgohain posits that the first text in Asamiya is already a translation since it is a result of the colonial experience and Western culture. A translation of such a text carries its own challenges, especially if it proceeds from the perspective of Disability Studies. Rajashree Borgohain concludes that such a project helps to understand the history of Asamiya literature, the changes in attitudes to 'disability', as also the history of Assam in general.

Subhadeep Ray examines three Bengali short stories that feature persons with disabilities and reads them on the axes of nationality, caste, religion, gender and sexuality. He argues that social exclusions and oppressions have a major role to play in these texts and that the translator has to tease these out, inhabiting the space between individual consciousness and the sociocultural material space of power and hierarchy. He argues for the significance of translation to take across every nuance, every register of the first text to ensure that regionalism is translated along with hierarchy and power relations to an understanding of mutual dependency of all humanity.

Conscious of the need to sensitise society at large through an intercultural and interlingual dissemination, B. Mangalam argues that the act of negotiating disability narrative encompasses the process of translation as a strategy of reading which takes into account the target audience – the non-disabled reader whose relationship, is, for the most part, defined by a first-hand experiential unfamiliarity with the cultural otherness of the world of the disabled. 'While the otherness of language and culture is widely recognised in the domain of translation,' she points out, 'the otherness of the subject experience or the experience of the protagonist who is differently abled in mainstream society and therefore less accessible to the ["able"] translator's imaginative or lived experience is hardly accounted for or conceded'(p. 147). The 'able' translator's task therefore would be to act as a bridge between the two worlds in a continuous process of mirroring the other, accommodating the other and negotiating and grappling with the dynamics of alterity embedded in the relationship between the two worlds. The translator in this sense not only becomes a mediator of the source and the target language reader but also moves beyond to fit the gap of unfamiliarity between the non-disabled reader and the experiential reality of the disabled world. Translation therefore is an enabling enterprise that opens a dialogue between two languages and two cultures, as well as two worlds divided along the axis of ability.

Ananya Ghoshal in her incisive essay on Tagore's classic Bengali story 'Subha' uses translation as a tool to confront non-disabled anxieties and stereotyped beliefs about the experience of disablement. Her reading uncovers the various structures of control and exclusion that shape and even define the figure of the mute girl. She argues that the act of translation can help us systematically deconstruct these structures and evolve a narrative that destabilises conventional beliefs about disability and disabled people.

Shilpa Das, however, while translating disability texts from Gujarati to English, finds herself helplessly caught between the highly medicalised representation of disability in the original text and the need to problematise it within her translation. She reflects on the viability of non-disabled translation theories, questioning the notions of equivalence for such translations. More important, her essay teases out the classic concerns of Disability Studies, that is the definition, experience, stratification, marginalisation, oppression and politics of disability, and places them within the feminine experience of disablement, drawing parallels between the two marginalised categories of disability and gender. While women, she argues, are subjected to the gaze, disabled persons are to the stare. Both, according to her, have a damaging, dehumanising effect.

The experience of disablement obviously overlaps with other marginalised categories like those of gender, and these present specific challenges to the translator which have been explored by many contributors to the current volume. Mukul

Chaturvedi in her reading of Dharamvir Bharati's 'Gulki Banno', for example, addresses the challenges of translating the gendered experiences of disability and contends that a text chronicling this experience confronts the translator not only with the physical aspects of disability but also with preconceived cultural notions of ableism, womanhood and the female body. Using feminist translation theories, she argues that feminist translation strategies can highlight the gendered agency of the disabled protagonist and construct her as an active social subject. To her, the larger purpose of translation is to make the feminine and the disabled visible in language and make the language speak for the disabled woman.

With a fundamental comprehension of language as a phenomenon that is directly related to existence and experience, Ritwick Bhattacharya tries to see how translation can become a political act to overcome the marginalising tendencies that language incurs by creating categories. His essay situates the translated body as a third physical space in which two different bodies interact without taking over each other and allowing the political aspects of each to assert in themselves as they are. Disability, in this schema, becomes a catalytic phenomenon which exposes how language creates divisions and, through the construction of metaphors, favours one existential category over another. Translating a disability narrative, according to him, destroys the marginalising tendencies of the non-disabled body while maintaining the two experiences as different.

Following the reliable lead of Gayatri Spivak, Shefalee Jain carries the preceding line of thought forward and suggests that the task of the translator is not to follow the mere logic of language but, rather, to facilitate the 'fraying to pry open' the gaps already present in the text, thereby creating new configurations of meaning. She uses Spivak's concept of 'reader as translator' to examine the use of metaphor, gaze and silence in the context of disability within Suraj Samin's 'Viklang'. The story shows how the universal narrative of modernity and capitalist development tends to muffle the subjectivity of those on the margins by evoking pity for both the poor and the disabled. Jain, however, through her reading and translation of the text, disrupts the overarching tone of pity that structures the narrative by locating moments of silence in the text that problematises the narrator's middle-class subjectivity and any easy association that the logic of the text may establish between disability and economic and social destitution.

In her retrospective reflection of having translated Bharat Sasne's short story 'Mai Dukh Ki Lambi Raat', Rohini Mokashi-Punekar, however, locates the subjectivity of their disabled characters in Indian disability narratives literally on the edges of society where they routinely face stigma and acute economic deprivation. These experiences generally lie outside the realm of postcolonial middle-class Indian sensibility and are generally documented in fiction in the language spoken on the streets, overlaced with frequent code-switching and code-mixing amongst various class, caste and regional registers of several languages. The principal challenge faced by the translator of such a text is therefore, according to her, to convey the stigma and acute deprivation faced by the marginalised disabled subject and translate the multilingual working-class idiom into the elite metropolitan register of English without detaching the original narrative from the material and polyglot reality in which it is originally anchored. Punekar's chapter explores the preceding challenges from a multiplicity of disciplinary locations – Disability Studies, Urban Studies and Translation Studies. In her chapter, she strives to evolve a translation practice that can enable the translator to recuperate the material reality and subjectivity of a disabled person's marginalised existence and preserve in the English language the fascinating cosmopolitan linguistic and cultural fabric of the original text.

Shilpaa Anand's reflections on the translation and representation of disability in Rashid Jahan's Urdu short story 'Woh', which forms the penultimate chapter of the current volume, is a progression of the kind of thinking espoused by Miles and Beckford into the interlingual and intercultural disciplinary field of translation studies. In her chapter, she critically examines the role that the translation of a literary text can play in decoding and conceptualising context-specific experiences of disablement. 'Context-sensitive examination and translation of literary narrative,' she observes, 'would reveal or, at least, enable us to become acquainted with other ways of knowing and engaging with corporeal difference that are specific to distinct ways of knowing and going about the world' (p. 232).

Anand's essay, in fact, jostles with the need to articulate a culturally sensitive and context-specific, non-universal and non-Western theory of corporeal difference. Studies of this kind are indeed a rarity in academia whose intellectual climate is largely conditioned by theoretical frameworks that are predominantly Western. Predictably, such studies are yet to attain wide circulation in the departments of humanities across the country. Their visibility in the academia and the influence that they exercise on research produced at these institutional sites are sadly limited. There is, however, little doubt that other non-universal and non-Western conceptions of corporeal difference are still in the process of being uncovered, and it is in the uncovering of these culturally sensitive and context-specific conceptualisations of the phenomenon that the way forward and the future of translating disability text lies.

Sania Hashmi's chapter, with which the current volume concludes, is a positive step in this direction as it situates disability in the theological framework of Islam to understand the place accorded to the disabled subject in the larger Islamic codes of conduct mandating ways to attain salvation in the Hereafter, and what role that inclusion/exclusion plays in the propagation of ideas of condemnation and guilt that the disabled protagonist seeks forgiveness for. By situating these signifiers in the source and target languages of Urdu and English, respectively, she highlights the liminality of disability in their respective chains of signification. The chapter articulates the conundrum of the translator in communicating the disablement rooted in the specific cultural context of the Indian Muslim community from the highly restricted vocabulary of Urdu to the wide biological taxonomy of English while also retaining the amused texture of the narratorial tone that seeks to provide psychological support sans logical justification.

Delicately poised on the cusp of Disability Studies and Translation Studies, this book will, we hope, raise provocative questions and create new spaces for academic exploration of great interest to both disability and translation scholars. This book aims to make an intervention in both Translation Studies and Disability Studies and to present an understanding of various Indian texts and contexts. If the book generates an awareness of how language is inherently ableist and encourages translators and translation scholars to reflect on the translation of 'disability' texts and to evolve theoretical positions and strategies for translation, it will have succeeded in its major aim.

References

Barker, Clare. 2012. *Postcolonial Fiction and Disability: Exceptional Children, Metaphor and Materiality*. Basingstoke: Palgrave Macmillan.

Bérubé, Michael. 1996. *Life as We Know It: A Father, a Family, an Exceptional Child*. New York, NY: Pantheon.

Bolt, David. 2012. 'Social Encounters, Cultural Representation and Critical Avoidance', in Nick Watson, Alan Roulstone and Carol Thomas (eds) *Routledge Handbook on Disability Studies*, pp. 287–297. Oxon: Routledge.

Davidson, Michael. 2008. *Concerto for the Left Hand: Disability and the Defamiliar Body*. Ann Arbor, MI: University of Michigan Press.

Davis, Lennard J. 1995. *Enforcing Normalcy: Disability. Deafness and the Body*. London and New York: Verso.

———.1999. 'Crips Strike Back: The Rise of Disability Studies', *American Literary History*, 11(3): 500–512.

Fries, Kenny. 2000. *Staring Back: The Disability Experience from the Inside out*. New York, NY: Plume.

Garland-Thomson, Rosemarie, ed. 1997. *Extraordinary Bodies: Figuring Physical Disability in American Culture and Literature*. New York, NY: New York University Press.

Ghai, Anita. 2002. 'Disability in the Indian Context: Postcolonial Perspectives', in Mirian Corker and Tom Shakespeare (eds) *Disability/Postmodernity: Embodying Disability Theory*, pp. 88–100. London and New York: Continuum.

Ghosh, Nandini. 2017. 'Divyang: The Latest Frontier', *Cafe Dissensus*, https://cafedissensus.com/2017/08/15/divyang-the-latest-frontier/ (accessed on 15 September 2017).

Goffman, Erving. 1963. *Stigma: Notes on the Management of Spoiled Identity*. Middlesex: Penguin.

Kamala, N., ed. 2009. *Translating Women: Indian Interventions*. New Delhi: Zubaan.

Mitchell, David T. and Sharon L. Snyder. 2000. *Narrative Prosthesis*. Ann Arbor, MI: University of Michigan Press.

———.2005. 'Compulsory Feral-ization: Institutionalizing Disability Studies', *PMLA*, 120(2): 627–634.

Mizrachi, Nissim. 2012. 'On the Mismatch Between Multicultural Education and Its Subjects in the Field', *British Journal of Sociology of Education*, 33(2): 185–201.

———.2014. 'Translating Disability in a Muslim Community: A Case of Modular Translation', *Culture Medicine and Psychiatry*, 38: 133–159.

Seibers, Tobin. 2008. *Disability Theory*. Ann Arbor, MI: University of Michigan Press.

Shildrick, Margrit. 2012. 'Critical Disability Studies: Rethinking the Conventions for the Age of Postmodernity', in Nick Watson, Alan Roulstone and Carol Thomas (eds) *Routledge Handbook on Disability Studies*, pp. 287–297. Oxon: Routledge.

Wynn, Kerry. 2001. 'Disability in Bible Translation', *The Bible Translator*, 52(4): 402–414.

1

A DIFFERENT IDIOM

Translation and disability

Radha Chakravarty

Translation, as an intercultural, interlingual practice, draws attention to the role that language plays in the organisation of social relations. Such a 'worlded' view also prevails in disability studies today, for it is increasingly recognised that disability is not so much a physiological or biological condition but, rather, a socially and culturally produced idea.[1] To examine the convergence of these two discourses in the practice of translating disability is to open a space for transformative textual radicalism. The idiom in which we speak or write determines the way we perceive and represent our world. To change the idiom therefore is to transform our perspective on the world, in our representations as well as social relations. The present chapter seeks, via a retrospective reflection on my own practice as a translator, to change the idiom in which one thinks about the relationship between translation and disability.

Here I revisit some stories I have previously translated in order to dwell upon the implications of resituating these narratives at the cusp between translation and disability studies. The stories chosen for analysis are Rabindranath Tagore's 'Mahamaya', Mahasweta Devi's 'Sindhubala', Debes Ray's 'Ranju's Blood' and Rizia Rahman's 'Irina's Picture'. When translating these stories, I did not think of them as narratives of disability. I must thank the coordinators of the present project for providing the impulse to rethink my own work in this altered frame of reference. In these rereadings of my work, an epistemic shift is involved, demanding that the selected stories move beyond the discourse of literary traditions and readerships, into the apparently unrelated discourse of disability studies. Recasting the idiom of this new discursive field, these narratives acquire alternative resonances that give rise to a host of pressing questions. Can the forms of so-called dysfunctionality represented in these stories – disfigurement, childlessness and mental impairment – be classified as forms of disability? Who determines such classifications, and by what principles? What conceptual advances and emancipatory potential can we locate in the practice of translating disability? What are the special challenges of translating disability in an Indian context?

Thinking about these questions made me recognise a parallel between translation and disability: both face a discriminatory attitude from the mainstream on account of their perceived deviation from a predetermined norm. In the field of translation, the original or source text is held to be supreme, and conventional criticism tends to focus on what is 'lost' in the translated version. Likewise, it is commonplace to think of disability as an 'impairment' or 'lack' that sets one apart from the world of 'normalcy'. There is thus a form of hierarchical thinking implicit in the binaries usually invoked, between original/translation in literary discourse and normal/disabled in disability studies. To translate disability therefore is to confront a double binary and a double hierarchy.

The call then seems to be for a double radicalism: to displace the supremacy of the original above the translation and, simultaneously, to destabilise the conventional understanding of the 'norms' in relation to which disability is commonly defined. Even this dualistic model of emancipatory socio-literary practice proves inadequate, however, for it remains premised on abstractions rather than grounded cultural realities. As a socially produced phenomenon, disability intersects with other culture-specific elements to acquire heterogeneous forms of significance in diverse contexts and locations. According to Anita Ghai (2009), '[d]isability in the Indian context is often understood as a "lack" or "deficit" as well as a "difference"'. She points out that most people refuse to accept that disability, like other markers of identity, can be a social construct.

> Since the normative culture in India and the world over carries existential and aesthetic anxieties about differences of any kind, be it caste, class, gender, race or disability, people who are impaired in any way have to live with labels such as 'disabled', 'handicapped', 'crippled', 'differently-abled' and 'special'. This results in an existence marked by acute marginalisation, discrimination and stigmatisation, and disability appears more as a personal quest and tragedy to be borne alone.
>
> (Ghai 2009)

Ghai places disability within a list of other forms of social difference, such as gender, caste, class, race, ethnicity and nationality, but we also need to understand that these forms of difference not only coexist but also often intersect or overlap in constructions of identity. Keeping in mind the complex relationships between disability and other axes of discrimination, we can frame a new question. How can translating disability in South Asia function as a distinctive form of literary activism or textual radicalism premised on a recognition of heterogeneity? This question is central to my rereading of the selected texts.

Revisiting these works also made me aware of the truth in what David Bolt (2007) says: 'regarding disability a conspicuous absence exists in literary studies. I'll identify a series of interrelated absences, the most fundamental being that disability is implicitly and/or explicitly present in all literary works, but too frequently absent from literary criticism'. In other words, while creative writers have always been conscious of disability as a factor in social relations, critical discourse has remained largely silent on this and other related issues. Bolt claims to have introduced what he calls a 'post-disability' approach to literary studies. He explains: 'a post-disability reading is one that is critical of the way in which society disables people who have impairments, a reading that is critical of the way in which impairment is depicted as tragic, disabling, abnormal and so on' (Bolt 2004). While some people may be impaired, it is social perceptions and practices that make them disabled. Hence, Bolt (2004) insists, '[i]t follows that in a progressive society disability is not a necessity, that impairment need not result in disability, which is the conceptual basis for post-disability criticism'. While Bolt's argument against regarding impairment as tragic and disabling is persuasive, it is important to recognise that different modes of oppression also generate their own forms of resistance. The same social contexts which give rise to such prejudices also provide the frame for literary texts that critique these discriminatory attitudes. These forms of radical literary practice can be located in creative writing as well as critical analysis. The present chapter addresses both possibilities, for while the selected literary texts are progressive in their representations of impairment, translating them for other readerships also invokes a 'post-disability' potential.

Reconsidering Tagore's 'Mahamaya' through the double lens of translation and disability studies, for instance, one becomes aware of the ways in which disability in our part of the world is connected with other axes of marginalisation based on caste, class and gender. Mahamaya, the eponymous protagonist of Rabindranath Tagore's story, is a high-caste *kulin*[2] woman of forty who enters into a forbidden relationship with Rajiv, who belongs to a lower caste. When their friendship is discovered, she is forced by her guardian to marry a dying Brahmin at the cremation ground. When her husband dies immediately after the marriage, she is forced to enter his funeral pyre in a ritual act of sati but manages to escape when a heavy storm breaks out. She seeks shelter in Rajiv's house and offers to live with him but only on one condition: he must never ask her to lift the veil that hides her face. '"I had promised that I would come to your house," she says. "I have come here to keep my vow. But Rajib, I'm not quite the same person anymore I'm a different person altogether"' (Tagore 2011: 523). Rajib accepts, and the two leave the place to set up their home elsewhere. Over time, however, the veil creates an unbearable block in their relationship. 'Separating the two of them was just her head covering, no more. But that mere veil was as permanent as death, yet more agonizing than death itself' (Tagore 2011: 524). One night, when she is asleep, Rajib feels impelled to go up to the sleeping Mahamaya to see her face revealed. To his horror and revulsion, he discovers that the flames of the funeral pyre have left half her face hideously disfigured. 'But alas, what was this! Where was that well-known face! The flames of the funeral pyre, with their cruel, greedy tongue, had licked off an entire portion of Mahamaya's left cheek, leaving only a mark of their hunger' (Tagore 2011: 525). The moment of exposure is also the moment of tragedy: Mahamaya storms out of

Rajiv's home and his life, never to be heard of again. 'Without saying a word and without looking back for a single instant, Mahamaya left the house. . . . No trace of her could be found again after that. The silent, angry fire of that unforgiving, eternal goodbye branded Rajib's entire life with a very long scar' (Tagore 2011: 526).

In this narrative, the woman's facial disfigurement works as a powerful trope for the 'difference' that makes her unacceptable to her husband and to society. Although not a conventional form of disability, her scarred face signals an 'impairment' which marks her as a woman who is un-beautiful, undesirable and, hence, socially unacceptable. The veil represents her utter isolation: even to her husband she cannot reveal her face. Disfigurement-as-disability here combines with caste and gender discrimination, to generate a narrative of multiple marginalities. Mahamaya's disfigurement functions as a metaphorical representation of her otherness, as well as a literal, physical form of impairment that renders her social relations dysfunctional. She is 'disabled' by her caste status as a *kulin* woman, which condemns her to long-term spinsterhood followed by forced marriage to a dying man. She is also 'disabled' by her gendered identity as a woman in a patriarchal society, for it renders her vulnerable to the domination of her brother and to collective social malpractices such as sati. To translate 'Mahamaya' is to translate a culture and the complex configuration of prejudices that disable the woman marked as 'different' or aberrant. The removal of the veil that covers Mahamaya's face can be read as a figurative unmasking of the truth about these prejudices.

It is worth reflecting on the range of cultural, social, psychological and linguistic border crossings involved in translating this story. We encounter here a male-authored narrative of a woman's trauma; a high-caste writer's critique of caste divides and related social malpractices; a sympathetic representation of disfigurement as physical, social and psychological disablement; and, at the level of translation, a linguistic transformation that is also a cultural transfer involving a change of readership and reception. Each border crossed here constitutes an act of reaching out to the other. It also signals the need to address the marginalisation of those perceived as 'different' through a collective awareness of responsibility. Yet such emancipatory moves are neither smooth nor simple. For the problem of representation acquires a double resonance for the translator: in translating the authorial voice of the original and in 'speaking for' the subaltern protagonist (in Spivak's terms), does a double silencing take place? Does it reconfirm Mahamaya's banishment into oblivion because society is still not ready to 'see', or confront, the reality of her predicament? The question cannot but haunt us. The choice before the translator is to either abjure translation because it might imply usurping the voices of those already silenced or to translate with the purpose of expressing solidarity with those cast in the shade by mainstream discourse, in order to give their narratives wider visibility. To me, the latter appears a more enabling alternative.

Sindhubala, in Mahasweta Devi's story of the same name, is a simple village girl whose lack of beauty becomes a liability for her family. Her own mother complains: 'Seen the girl's face? Bulging forehead, snub nose, black skin?' (Devi 2004: 34). Although she is eventually married off to a man called Sanneshi, he soon loses interest in her, and she fails to bear children. Instigated by his mother, Sanneshi rejects her and marries again, while Sindhu is left to languish in her mother's home. In a clever ploy, her mother, with the connivance of the midwife Manudasi, spreads the story that Sindhu is *devangshi*, part divine, and that because she entered the world feet first, the touch of her 'auspicious' feet can cure ailing children. Sindhu is forced to participate in this charade. Her feet with their healing powers attract a steady stream of clients, and her mother's trade in charlatanism begins to flourish. Sindhu walls herself into a world of delusion and detachment: 'The supernatural is as destructive a drug as power. Sindhu has spent many years of her life addicted to this drug. The addiction is an invisible enchanted wall. 'A wall that stands between Sindhu and all of life's realities' (Devi 2004: 40). But inwardly, she begins to feel lonely, bitter and frustrated. The turning point comes when she is asked to cure Sanneshi's son, born of his second marriage. She also learns that ten years ago, San-neshi had come to take her back, but her mother had sent him away because she did not want to lose the profits of Sindhu's practice as a healer. Inwardly, Sindhu begins to seethe with anger and bitterness. 'Sindhu was angry, saddened, offended, and then angry again. But was Sindhu an ordinary person, to be so quick to show her rage?' (Devi 2004: 41). This time, Sindhu's powers fail, and Sanneshi loses his child. A change now comes over Sindhu. Her illusions fall away, she rebels against her exploiters and refuses to 'cure' children anymore.

> Sindhu didn't listen to any of them. If you're human, you must burn. If you're holy, then too you must burn. If life has the same end for both, then why should the woman Sindhu spend her days pretending to be a goddess?
>
> (Devi 2004: 44)

The narrative challenges the discourse of the body and the conventional identifica-tion of women with beauty and the reproductive function. In its questioning of normative hierarchies, it also draws attention to the parallels between the discourses of gender and disability. In *Extraordinary Bodies*, Garland-Thomson says,

> Many parallels exist between the social meanings attributed to female bodies and those assigned to disabled bodies. Both the female and the disabled body are cast as deviant and inferior; both are excluded from full participation in public as well as economic life; both are defined in opposition to a norm that is assumed to possess natural physical superiority.
>
> (Garland-Thomson 1997: 19)

Sindhubala's story marks the convergence of these two discourses, tracking a process of double marginalisation within a specific social context. As Nandini Ghosh says, '[t]he gender regimes that operate in the cultural context of Bengal draw heavily on the concept of bhalo meye – an ideological construct of the ideal woman'(Ghosh 2010). Sindhu's 'difference', her otherness, is measured in relation to this norm. In Mahasweta's story, therefore, the discourses of gender and disability come together.

Sindhu's marginalisation stems from her perceived dysfunctionality as a woman. In terms of traditional wisdom, it is her lack of beauty which has led to her 'failure' to fulfil the woman's destiny of becoming a desirable wife and the mother of male offspring. This leads to a further stage of objectification and exploitation when her own mother markets Sindhu's supposedly 'auspicious' feet as an exploitable commodity.

The story marks the successive stages in Sindhu's psychological development, from acceptance of patriarchal norms to a recognition that her own bodily experiences bely conventional wisdom to a realisation that she has been duped and exploited by her own people and then to her final rebellion against societal expectations. 'This sterile, barren body. This body that flourishes like a fruitless tree. No sons, no daughters, no birthing pains to break this body. With this body, unmarred and throbbing, Sindhu doesn't always enjoy sitting around as a *devangshi* woman' (Devi 2004: 39). Sindhu's mental and emotional journey can also be read as a paradigm for the successive stages through which approaches to translation have evolved, from the subordination of the translation to the source text, through a questioning of this power equation, to an assertion of the distinctive identity of the translated work. In disability studies too, life writing often marks successive stages, including a recognition of being different, the trauma of marginalisation, followed in some instances by a break with internalised social perceptions and a challenge to discriminatory labels and attitudes.

In Debes Ray's story 'Ranju's Blood', the protagonist is an eighteen-year-old youth with the mind of a wayward child. His mental condition is not medically defined but seems to conform to common descriptions of autism. Difference is the defining feature in the representation of Ranju in the story:

> [E]ighteen year old Ranju has the nature of an animal. When Ranju laughs, flinging out both arms and both legs, he wounds those around him. When Ranju cries, he stamps wildly about the courtyard like a lamb whose throat has been slit. In his studies, Ranju is almost like the sage Valmiki; he can't even pronounce Rama's name the correct way.
>
> (Ray 2003: 162)

In the 'present' of the story, Ranju vomits a 'rainbow' of blood as he lies on his deathbed attended by his family. The blood, and the insistent figurations of violence in the language of the narrative, signify the trauma of his existence in a hostile world. 'From Ranju's throat the blood flows as if from a slaughtered lamb' (Ray 2003: 161). The language underscores his alterity: 'On the shore of this stream of thick blood stand Ma-Didi-Mintu-Bintu and at the source of the same stream is Ranju's wide-open mouth, like the coiled locks of Shiva at Gangotri' (Ray 2003: 162).

While such alienation is represented as a form of collective social prejudice, Ranju, throughout the story, is shown as a person with special powers who is mentally beyond the reach of all the humiliations inflicted on him. The reference to Shiva is one such instance. The narrative on several occasions breaks away from the traditional linear mode to resort to lists and catalogues that highlight the extraordinariness of Ranju's character and predicament. One list, for instance, tells us about the 'lore' that has accumulated around Ranju's antics. We are told of the time he is imprisoned for 'misdemeanour' and found to have 'carved his own name on his thigh with a blunt razor-blade', much to his own amusement (Ray 2003: 163). The list mentions the occasion when he returns from a film to cut the sleeves of all his shirts before hemming the edges with purple thread, 'stamped with that purple seal' (Ray 2003: 163). When he feels attracted to a girl in the neighbourhood, he grabs and kisses her. Once, when he is tied to a post and beaten on all his joints by his elder brother, he fails to shed a single tear. It becomes second nature for Ranju to feel like an unwanted outsider amongst his own people. He develops 'the aspect of a strange dog from a different area, when it finds itself surrounded by local dogs from the neighbourhood' (Ray 2003: 164). The animal metaphor graphically expresses the alienation experienced by those marked as 'other' by mainstream society.

As he lies dying, Ranju's singularity is highlighted by another list which describes the 'stream of blood as lonely as

> The blood that flows from the suddenly severed head of a Muslim in a Hindu locality . . .
> The blood that flows down both thighs of a raped woman . . .
> In a silent and desolate curfew-bound city, the sudden sound of Vande Mataram or Allah-o-Akbar;
> Our own nation, like the emptiness of the sky after some tall tree is ripped apart;
> A married woman's severed hand, naked encircled in a conch-shell bangle.
>
> (Ray 2003: 170)

This list of similes lifts Ranju's narrative out of the personal realm into the public, political domain, asserting the links between different forms of prejudice that fragment our society. At the end of the story, the description of Ranju's death explicitly reasserts the same correspondence, and the blood-red tide becomes a sign of the waves of hatred that sweep away the desired integrity of a nation in the making: 'Ranju floats away in a wave-churned sea – torn away from the shore land of food-sleep-kisses, just like his own nation' (Ray 2003: 170).

Ranju's story becomes the occasion for a powerful, sweeping commentary on divisive politics based on prejudice and exclusivist attitudes. The story moves beyond the private realm to make a strong political comment on the state of the public sphere. To reread this narrative as an interrogation of prevalent notions of 'normal/abnormal' or 'able/disabled' adds a further dimension to this critique. The link between private and public domains underscores the collective culpability of a whole society in the ostracisation and victimisation of those perceived as 'different'. The rhetoric of the narrative indicates that such forms of discrimination set in motion a cycle of violence that harms not only the victim but also the perpetrators. To translate such a narrative therefore is to summon up the power of the written word to draw wider public attention to the connection between the discourse of disability and the larger structures of dominance and exclusion within our society.

Rizia Rahman's 'Irina's Picture' presents the plight of Mahboob ul-Hasan, a professor of English who loses his mental balance after the breakup of his marriage and the death of his beloved mother. Before her death, his mother leaves him the keys to her house and bequeaths to him the power of attorney to dispose of her property and personal effects. Branded a lunatic and alienated from his siblings and their spouses, he secludes himself in his room and distances himself from their bickering over the inheritance. But he refuses to part with the keys to the house. He submits unwillingly to the medical treatment meted out to him in the name of psychiatric care but feels misunderstood by the world at large. He withdraws into an imaginary world where he feels his mother's presence and carries on a regular dialogue with her spirit. Another cherished memory is of a picture from his childhood days: a newspaper photograph of Irina, a young Russian girl, who stands before an advancing army holding out a bunch of white flowers, crying out for an end to the war. Constantly pressured by his relatives to part with the keys, and tormented about his so-called lunacy, Mahboob remains non-compliant and hostile. Ultimately, he flings away his mother's keys as a gesture of defiance against those who seek to isolate and oppress him.

In this story, mental illness is viewed as a disability by the members of the protagonist's family. For as Rosemarie Garland-Thomson says in *Freakery: Cultural Spectacles of the Ordinary Body*, disability is 'always an interpretive occasion' (Garland-Thomson 1996: 1). Mahboob is marginalised and treated with contempt because he is labelled as mentally dysfunctional. His Mejo Apa declares, 'You're an infirm person, of course. That's why Mejo Bhaiya was saying that it is not possible to grant a lunatic the power of attorney in property matters. That will have to be cancelled' (Rahman 2003: 109).[3] Despite such constant attempts to label and stigmatise, Mahboob resists internalising this form of identification. 'With the speed of lightning, I spin around to face Mejo Apa: "Who says I'm a lunatic?"' (Rahman 2003: 109). He realises that this labelling stems from the disjuncture between his own 'unworldly' values of love, compassion and creativity, imbibed from his mother, and the greed and aggression that drives the world around him. 'The doctor gives me medicines meant for crazy people. Once a week, I have to visit a psychiatrist. Of course, everybody would consider me crazy' (Rahman 2003: 107). He feels trapped by the treatment meted out to him in the name of therapy. 'Boro Apa and my three bhabhis – sisters-in-law – come, and stand before me. As if they hold my arrest warrant in their hands. I know they will now force me to take tranquillizers and sedatives' (Rahman 2003: 107). Eventually, the war within his family and the memories of his mother and of Irina's picture prompt him to create in his private inner world a counter-discourse that prioritises love and empathy above violence and mercenary motives. At the end of the story, with the rediscovery of Irina's picture and his mother's poem scribbled behind it, the public discourse of war converges with the private trauma of family battles. The message of Irina, articulated in his mother's lines, acquires for Mahboob a new resonance:

> Come.
> Stand here.
> Throw down your arms and take in your hands
> These white roses.
>   (Rahman 2003: 111)

Against the discourse of violence, a strong cry breaks forth. 'Stop! My mother's powerful cry of protest makes the entire house tremble. It shakes towns. Cities. The whole world' (Rahman 2003: 111). It is really Mahboob's voice that rings out in protest. 'Clutching Irina's picture in my fist, banging my head against the wall, I keep screaming: "Stop! Stop all of you. Stop this." I keep on banging my head against the wall' (Rahman 2003: 111). Mahboob's rage, pain and despair emerge not only through his cry but also in his body language. The wall against which he beats his head is the wall of social prejudice against those who are condemned to marginality on account of their perceived aberrance from a norm. To translate this narrative is also to communicate this gesture of protest to a wider audience.

This story, too, can be read as paradigmatic of changing dimensions of translation and disability studies. Throwing away the key, in relation to translation, can signify a break with the codes of the past that prioritise the authority of the source text, and an assertion of the freedom to recode the text in a transformative way. In relation to disability studies, it can signal a similar recoding of social values and attitudes and a gesture of self-empowerment.

All four stories analysed here confront us with protagonists positioned beyond the mainstream as outsider figures on account of their perceived deviation from societal norms. In each story, submission to these norms is followed by a questioning of them and, ultimately, by an act of rejection or defiance. The narratives demand of the reader a similar self-questioning, and a realignment of values and attitudes, to accommodate the 'others' of society. To the translator, they also present the possibility of a radical, emancipatory practice that will carry these narratives across cultural borders to potentially generate awareness of the need for collective responsibility.

The narratives also problematise the question of agency, demonstrating the need to examine what it really implies. They remind us of Amartya Sen's definition of agency as a form of empowerment that goes beyond mere 'control' over decisions. He says: 'The fuller sense of "agency" must, *inter alia*, involve the freedom to question established values and traditional priorities' (Sen 2005: 240). The protagonists of these stories claim this deeper form of agency for themselves. Translating these narratives involves, likewise, a challenge to conventional attitudes and a call to destabilise entrenched prejudices.

To be sure, translation brings us up against the incommensurable, but such elements of intractability prove to be, not a 'disabling' feature of the project of translation, but a potentially enabling one, for they compel the courageous translator to imagine into being creative bridges between self and other, between that which is familiar and that which is removed from our own experience. When translating 'Mahamaya' for instance, a major challenge was to convey the caste implications of the Bengali term *kulin* to readers from non-Indian backgrounds. One could, of course, italicise the word to defamiliarise it and add a detailed explanation in a footnote or glossary. Instead, I chose to leave the term un-italicised and described Mahamaya as 'an unwed woman from an exclusive, high-caste kulin family' (Tagore 2011: 519). The aim was to communicate the isolating effect of the caste factor without disrupting the flow of the narrative or resorting to pedantic use of paratext. Likewise, in 'Sindhubala', the narrative hinges on a culture-specific idea, the local superstition that identifies Sindhu, born feet-first, as *devangshi* or part divine. Instead of trying to find an English equivalent, I retained the Bengali word in my translation, letting the sense emerge through dialogue as in the expression: '[b]orn divine, a *devangshi* girl, so you're touching a brahman's granddaughter with your feet' (Devi 2004: 37). In this text, italics were used as part of the 'house rules' of Seagull, the publishing house authorised to serialise the works of Mahasweta Devi in successive volumes. Such circumstances can limit the translator's freedom to an extent, but an imaginative translator finds scope for experimentation even within formal constraints. In the same translation, I tried out colloquial speech rhythms in translating doggerel:

> Work hard never rest
> Your fortunes will prosper
> Your home'll be blest
> (Devi 2004: 36)

I also let names of local items of food and clothing go untranslated to create the flavour of a particular place, time and language: *khoi, muri, gamchha*. This has, in fact, been my general practice as a translator. In 'Irina's Picture', kinship terms left untranslated – such as *Boro Apa, Mejo Bhaiya* and *Sejo Bhabhi* – not only signal a specific Bengali context but also linguistically and culturally differentiate this Bangladeshi narrative from its Indian Bengali counterparts. 'Ranju's Blood' includes references to popular Hindi cinema – *Dil Tera Diwana* and the song 'Chahe Koi Mujhe Junglee Kahe' – that I make no attempt to render in Bengali, because the import would be immediately clear to my Indian readers, while offering readers from elsewhere a flavour of the linguistic and cultural hybridity that characterises the day-to-day life of young people in modern India (Ray 2003: 165).

For experiments of this kind there are no formulae: the role of the translator resembles that of the explorer or inventor who, when faced with unfamiliar circumstances, must imagine new strategies to negotiate the situation. To claim such creative liberty entails, of course, the risk of a further level of 'deviance' from social and literary norms, but in this case, *deviance* becomes not a pejorative term but one that denotes openness to change and innovation. It is the norm itself that is destabilised in the process, for it now emerges as precisely the obstacle to under-standing that needs to be overcome.

Such disruptive, radical textual practices demonstrate that, along with creative writing and literary criticism, translating disability also represents a way of address-ing the gaps in our awareness of the significance of disability in literary studies, a lacuna that we urgently need to address. To focus our gaze on disability in literature with the aim of changing the idiom in which we think and write about it can prove to be an enabling endeavour. Doing so with a collective will to transform language, mental attitudes and social relations is the need of the hour.

Notes

1 According to David Bolt (2004), '[t]he social model of disability holds that many persons are impaired in many ways, but that it is only by society that they become disabled. People are impaired, but society disables'.
2 The term *kulin* refers to Bengali Brahmans at the top of the caste hierarchy. Women of *kulin* families often remained unmarried due to orthodox concerns about caste purity. The system of kulinism came to be associated with practices such as polygamy, age dispar-ity in marriages and sati.
3 It is easy for the marginalised to internalise a socially ascribed subject position. Katie Aubrecht (2016) recounts, for instance, 'My being named mentally ill led me to view myself as a problem, my histories and experiences as deficient, defective, and the products of an unfortunate chain of events, and my perceptions as delusional'.

References

Aubrecht, Katy. 2016. 'Disability Studies and the Language of Mental Illness', *Review of Disability Studies: An International Journal*, 8(2). www.rdsjournal.org/index.php/journal/article/view/98 (accessed on 9 October 2017).

Bolt, David. 2004. 'A Brief Introduction to Post-Disability Literary Criticism'. Lecture presented at Keele University on 21 September. http://pf7d7vi404s1dxh27mla5569. wpengine.netdna-cdn.com/files/library/bolt-Keele-Presentation-Archive.pdf (accessed on 9 October 2017).

———. 2007. 'Literary Disability Studies: The Long Awaited Response'. Paper presented at the Inaugural Conference of the Cultural Disability Studies Research Network, Liverpool John Moores University, 26 May. http://pf7d7vi404s1dxh27mla5569.wpengine.netdna-cdn. com/files/library/bolt-Long-Awaited-Response.pdf (accessed on 9 October 2017).

Devi, Mahasweta. 2004. 'Sindhubala', in Radha Chakravarty (trans. and ed) *In the Name of the Mother: Four Stories*, pp. 33–44. Kolkata: Seagull.

Garland-Thomson, Rosemarie. 1996. *Freakery: Cultural Spectacles of the Extraordinary Body*. New York, NY: New York University Press.

———. 1997. *Extraordinary Bodies: Figuring Physical Disability in American Culture and Litera-ture*. New York, NY: Columbia University Press.

Ghai, Anita. 2009. 'The Women's Movement Must Do More for Disabled Women', *Info Change News and Features*, 24 June. https://disabilitynewsworldwide.wordpress. com/2009/06/24/the-womens-movement-must-do-more-for-disabled-women/ (accessed on 9 October 2017).

Ghosh, Nandini. 2010. 'Embodied Experiences: Being Female and Disabled', *Eco-nomic and Political Weekly*, 45(17), 24 April: 58–63. www.epw.in/journal/2010/17/

review-womens-studies-review-issues/embodied-experiences-being-female-and disabled?0=ip_login_no_cache%3D44a828c855e26d105efd3f4ffc70fab3 (accessed on 9 October 2017).

Rahman, Rizia. 2003. 'Irina's Picture', in Radha Chakravarty (trans and ed), *Crossings: Stories from Bangladesh and India*, pp. 94–111. New Delhi: Indialog.

Ray, Debes. 2003. 'Ranju's Blood', in Radha Chakravarty (trans and ed), *Crossings: Stories from Bangladesh and India*, pp. 160–171. New Delhi: Indialog.

Sen, Amartya. 2005. *The Argumentative Indian: Writings on Indian History, Culture and Identity*. London: Allen Lane.

Tagore, Rabindranath. 2011. 'Mahamaya', in Radha Chakravarty (trans), Fakrul Alam and Radha Chakravarty (eds) *The Essential Tagore*, pp. 518–526. Cambridge, MA: Harvard University Press.

2

TRANSLATION AS SOCIAL ACTION

The counter-discourse on the literary representation of disability

Chitra Harshvardhan

This chapter focuses on the issue of translation and representation of disability in literary works, with particular reference to India, in a possible anthology of Indian texts in translation. The assumption is that translation will engender a richer and more nuanced understanding of an inclusive otherness, of the diversity amongst human beings both across cultures and within cultures and the need to ensure equality and a life of dignity for all regardless of difference rather in celebration and mutual respect of difference. It is expected that translation will facilitate a dialogue that disturbs, provokes and challenges inherited stereotypes or worldviews, hierarchies and binary oppositions and highlights prevalent phobias, entrenched ignorance, perceived superiority and accepted notions and norms of able-bodiedness, 'inscribing subtle counter-voices to trouble the reader's consciousness' (Davison 2014: 18) and resulting in a reflected engagement with and reconstruction of the image of self and other. The chapter is broadly divided into three parts: the first focuses on the ethos and ethics of translation and on translation as an instrument to foster cultural alterity, the second on issues of disability and literary representation and the third on the alternate aesthetics to drive a counter-discourse to sustain diversity.

The ethos and ethics of translation

All translation is communication and action rooted in culture. However, translation today is itself a contested site. No longer viewed merely as an objective substitution of the signs of one language by those of another, increasingly it has come to be accepted as not only a linguistic transfer but also equally a cultural engagement that is not neutral. The cultural transmission involved in the act of translation seeks to represent and convey the 'reality' of thought and perception as reflected in the language and text of the original. The cultural conception of reality is never static or universal and is subject to constant change. This dynamic of change is inherent to the original, which, while remaining linguistically 'fixed' or unchanged, is subject to and informed by cultural alterity. Thus, the text 'changes' in its own culture as well whilst remaining linguistically 'fixed'. This is not and cannot be the case in translation. No translation is ever final, linguistically, nor is it exhaustive in its 'excavated' rendering of the source text.[1] Translation, therefore, attempts to lay the foundation for an understanding that would necessarily transform the hitherto perceived reality and the norms of its construction in the culture and tradition of both the original and the translation. Translation not only seeks to convey the concepts, worldview, mindset, imaginary and values that are woven into the texture of the source text but is, of necessity, a re-articulation and re-contextualisation of this represented 'reality', through the lens of the translator, involving choices. As Gentzler and Tymoczko point out, translators select

> aspects or parts of a text to transpose and emphasize. Such choices in turn serve to create representations of their source texts, representations that are also partial. This partiality is not to be considered a deficit, a lack or an absence in a translation.
>
> (2002: XVIII)

The boundedness of a specific translation is determined by the preferred approach of the translator. This, in turn, shapes the reception of the translated text, opening or foreclosing the myriad possibilities of reading and interpreting the text. The privileging of a particular aspect provides the translated text with an identity that is singular in comparison to all other translations of the same text. Thus, multiple translations of the same original are unique moments in its 'afterlife',[2] brought alive by the relevance and significance of the translation to the time and space which it is to inhabit. The choices made by the translator throw light onto the translation strategy applied and illuminate the ideological positioning and subjectivity of the translator and/or of the receiving culture, if a pattern in time and space of such preferred translation strategies can be established.[3]

Translation is constitutive of the acts of both reading and writing that go beyond transcoding. Yet the writing self of the translator is dissimilar from that of the author as has been argued in various approaches to translation, and equally, been reflected in a variety of translation practices, each generating its own discursive strategy that seeks to affect and shape the consciousness of the reader and may in some cases even contribute to the spawning of identities and solidarity, intended or not. Thus, Walter Benjamin makes the distinction between the original being spontaneous and graphic whereas the translation is derivative and ideational (1979a: 76–77). Benjamin highlights the constraints within which the translator functions by drawing on the analogy of language as forest where the original is located in the 'centre of the language forest' whereas the translation is 'on the outside facing the wooded ridge' with the task of the translator being to produce 'the echo of the original' in translation (1979a: 76). The work of the translator is predicated on the source text and is ideational, unlike that of the author, who can draw unrestrainedly on his or her language to translate his or her abstract thoughts into graphic language, pointing, in some cases, in the direction of a circumstantial discourse. The translation is an offshoot that creatively follows and flows from the source text. The translator writes but writes differently. The original cannot be duplicated, nor does the translator strive for the impossibility of identity with the original. This is what Ricoeur terms the 'work of mourning', which is the renunciation by the translator of achieving 'the ideal of the perfect translation', a replication of the source text (Ricoeur 2006: 4ff.). No translator seeks to replace the source text. Every translation is a representation of the source text in the receiving culture. It is as André Lefevere asserts a form of rewriting, embedded in the intricate web of patronage, ideology and poetics of the receiving culture (Lefevere 1992). The translator is caught in a double bind, seeking to carry across the singularity of the source text into the translation in the language of the receiving culture. In translation, the act of writing is necessarily preceded by the act of close reading of the source text, the insightful appropriation of the 'protocols of the text' (Spivak 2005: 94) that inform the recasting of the source into the product that the translated text is. The translator negotiates an understanding of the source text, initiating a dialogue between the text and the reader. Reading is, to quote Paul Ricoeur, 'a linking together of a new discourse to the discourse of the text' (1971: 144). Ricoeur also writes that 'reading is like the performance of a musical score: it betokens the fulfillment, the actualization of the semantic virtualities of the text' (Ricoeur 1971: 145). Every translation is one possible reading of the source text within a historical context. This is amply borne out by the existence of multiple variant translations of one and the same work. The translated text, which mutates into a new text in the receiving language and culture, has to be viewed in the context of the polysystem existing in the receiving culture, as it addresses a perceived need in that culture and may indeed be filling a gap,[4] as evidenced from the translational priority. The translation has to create a place for itself within the web of texts that constitute the cosmos of the receiving culture. Its significance in the receiving system accrues from the difference, the added value it brings to the system as a whole, in its relationship to other texts, disturbing the existing equilibrium. The translated text can sharpen the gaze, inspire a different reading, stimulate the intellect to envisage a different world, convince the reader of the plausibility and necessity of creating this new world, nurture both hope and conviction in the need to question and unlearn inherited, received norms and structures of dominance, authority, discrimination and exclusion. 'It is the transforming process of translation that allows this reimagining of the givens of cultural and ideological identity . . . it allows us to transcend the static vision' (O'Brien Fall 2001-Spring 2002: 34). The transformative potential of translation is thus intrinsic to its very being.

There is no one single universally correct method of translating; just as writers in most societies have the freedom to write in the manner they desire, so, too, do translators exercise with responsibility the same autonomy in the pursuit of their profession and choice of their preferred translation strategy and practice. Benjamin once wrote that 'writers are really people who write books not because they are poor, but because they are dissatisfied with the books which they could buy but do not like' (1979b: 61). Similarly, many translators undertake translations of works of which at least one or more translations already exist, because of perceived discontentment with these, or they are commissioned by publishers who believe that existing translations can be improved on or augmented. The multiple possible readings and understanding of the text engender multiple versions in translation. However, all translations represent in distinct ways the relationship between the self and the other. As O'Brien posits, 'in bringing the texts of one culture before the readership of another, the aesthetic experience, by definition, has the ethical function of leading self and other into some form of interaction' (Fall 2001–Spring 2002: 22).[5]

There are broadly two approaches that facilitate such interaction: one is to strive for the universality of experience and apparent equivalence of meaning and values. Such an approach would transfer the otherness in terms of sameness, familiarity, the known and would, thus, deliberately or inadvertently, deny the possibility of conveying similarity with difference. It would, in fact, efface difference and otherness. As Ricoeur so aptly states, 'recaptured universality would try to abolish the memory of the foreign' (2006: 9). The second approach is to strive to reclaim and affirm heterogeneity and diversity by questioning the 'self-sufficiency' (Ricoeur 2006: 4) of the receiving language, 'de-provencialising' (Ricoeur 2006: 9) it, 'broadening' (Ricoeur 2006: 21) its horizon as well as being mind-expanding, contributing to new insights by extending what Ricoeur calls 'linguistic hospitality', which he defines as 'where the pleasure of dwelling in the other's language is balanced by the pleasure of receiving the foreign word at home, in one's own welcoming house' (2006: 10). This would spur a rethinking, a scrutiny of the known resulting perhaps in the transformation of self and other and the dawning realisation that 'the self is not defined in simplistic contradistinction to the other, but rather is marked with traces of that other, is seen as a painful and self-alienating experience' (O'Brien Fall 2001–Spring 2002: 28).

Instrumentalising translation in a counter-discourse of otherness

Translations can reflect otherness through a number of techniques. The use of paratexts (preface, forward, afterword or epilogue) is one such possibility, especially when the translated text remains within the normative frame of the source text, choosing to analogously retain the corresponding norms of the receiving language, culture and literary tradition. The consciousness raising, understanding and insights that paratexts provide influence the reception of the text, leading to a critical engagement with the translated text. The situatedness of the translated text within a critical discourse would likely provoke a reconsideration of the received and accepted norms revealing the ideology and power relations underpinning the source text and the transmission of these in the translated text.

The use of 'thick translation' (Appiah 1993: 808–819; Hermans 2003: 380–389) is also a possibility. Thick translation is viewed as a scholarly annotated translation for pedagogic purposes, where there is a thick contextualisation of the source text. The term is drawn from Clifford Geertz's concept of 'thick description' (1993: 3–30). The intent is to embed and contextualise the translation within the frame of reference of the source culture, making it difficult if not impossible for the reader to be judgemental of the source by applying the received and accepted frame of reference of the receiving culture. In transporting the reader to another world, the reader is nudged into questioning the absoluteness of the inherited worldview into which he or she has been socialised. This is translation as 'writing culture', creating a new sensibility and awareness. Theo Hermans adds another dimension to thick translation through the notion of self-reflexivity of the translator. From the above, it is clear that the otherness of the source text would be refracted in the translated text.

Another possibility is to subvert the dominant, mainstream usage of language by deliberately using a disruptive style: the unconventional usage of orthography or the use of neologisms, the innovative use of images and metaphors, of archaisms, changing the syntax a little, compounding words innovatively, infusing a word with an entirely different meaning, code-switching. The idea is to experiment with language, challenging the hegemony of the dominant norm in language usage to signal resistance, what Lawrence Venuti terms as 'foreignising translation'.

The more radical technique in carrying across otherness is the feminist translation technique that David Homel labelled as 'hijacking', which, according to him, was a 'deliberate appropriation by feminist translators of non-feminist texts' (Santaemilia 2011: 71) but which is differently defined by feminist translators. Luise von Flotow defines it as 'the deliberate intervention in a text in order to incorporate contemporary feminist politics, where there are none, or nothing very visible, in the source text' (Santaemilia 2011: 71). In other words, it is the visible, overt intervention by the translator reflecting a particular ideology, with the intent to subvert the source text and highlight the discriminatory and oppressive practices of the dominant group.

Finally, another radical option is that of a collaborative translation, visibly becoming the co-author of the translated text, modifying it to suit the time, space and taste of the culture into which the source text is being transplanted. It has been asserted by several, including Harish Trivedi (Bassnett and Trivedi 1999: 8–9) and G.N. Devy (1995: 135), that the claim to single authorship of a text is a Western concept, collective authorship being the tradition of India with the many versions of the Ramayana (Bassnett and Trivedi 1999: 9–10; Dharwadkar 1999: 133ff.) being cited as proof of this. This notion of collaborative authorship has been described as transcreation, amongst others by P. Lal (1996). According to Lal, immersion in the text, values and traditions of the source text was essential for transcreation. The transcreator had to be able to think and feel in the language of the source text. Lal differentiates between imaginative and creative writing: 'the first is esthetically organic, the second esthetically and morally unified' (Lal 1996: 36). The activity involves editing, reconciling and transmuting (Lal 1996: 37). The transcreator 'must divine, discover, or guess the effect [the author] was trying to create, and then attempt to recreate it with the resources of the English language' (Lal 1996: 44). However, this did not mean conforming to the norms and conventions of English usage. The accepted degree of change of the source text in this process remains a contentious issue. Sujit Mukherjee mentions that the fifth edition of the *Oxford Advanced Learners Dictionary* carried a supplement of Indian English, which defined *transcreation* as 'creative translation seen as producing a new version of the original work' (2004: 43). Mukherjee observed that 'when we admired a literary text in one language, we used it as a take-off point and composed a similar text in another language. P. Lal's use of the term "transcreation" may well be most appropriate for such a situation' (2004: 45). Under the rubric of transcreation the source text is transformed in translation.

Another extreme form of a translation transformed is the example of the translation/rewriting of Ibsen's *A Doll's House* by Eleanor Marx and Israel Zangwill in 1896, where the ending was changed and the translation appeared under the changed title *A Doll's House Repaired*. Eleanor Marx is stated to have 'promoted the recessive character Christina Linden, elevating her into a model of the independent, self-supporting female wage earner' (Apter 2007: 1405). So the interventionist 'repairing' of a text to achieve the desired degree of otherness, and acknowledging having done so, is a practice in translation, which could be categorised as an extension of feminist practices of translation. In other contexts, it could be viewed as a form of collaborative translation. All the preceding translation techniques reflect overt ownership of the text by the translator.

Locating disability

Disability is a social and cultural construct that stigmatises bodily variations as 'deviant', or 'abnormal', from the norm of the able-bodied. As Rosemarie Garland-Thomson declares, 'disability, like femaleness, is not a natural state of corporeal inferiority, inadequacy, excess, or a stroke of misfortune. Rather, disability is a culturally fabricated narrative of the body, similar to what we understand as the fictions of race and gender' (2002: 5). The embodied persons are perceived as inferior beings, who are at best passive objects of concern, lacking subjectivity and agency, dependent on others for their care. The disabled community has actively and successfully fought back to establish the distinction between biological impairment (physical, sensory or cognitive) and socially constructed disability. The disabled have wrested back control over their lives.

As in most fields, in the area of Disability Studies, too, there is a plurality of theories and agendas for achieving an alternative non-normative, non-able nationalist world. While challenging the absoluteness of the medical model, theories and their advocates differ in the degree to which embodiment should play a role in securing rights and carving out identities. Consequently, the social model of disability highlights the fact that it is not the impairment in itself that is disabling but, rather, the milieu, including the psychosocial and institutional reaction to impairment that is disabling and which restricts access to opportunities and spawns social discrimination, and exclusion. This also contributes to the ossifying of stereotypes and the cultural construction of disability. By turning the spotlight on the devaluing of a certain section of human beings and their stigmatisation as deficient, lacking in ability and therefore inferior, monstrous, deviant and, in some cases, as even evil, it was shown that people with impairments came to be willfully marginalised, segregated, disenfranchised and oppressed. The social disability model, therefore, aimed to return agency to persons thus vilified and to empower them by restoring subjectivity, dignity and humanity by fighting for their human rights. This eventually had an impact on the shaping of public policy, resulting in awareness and recognition of diversity in human lives and greater access to jobs, income and education, which paved the path towards apparent societal integration and inclusiveness.

While not diminishing the material gains, especially legislative, won through such advocacy in many countries, particularly of the global North, the Critical Disability Studies (CDS) model critiqued the social model of disability for universalising all forms of impairment with a view to creating a singular identity and thus fostering the binary of normative versus the other in order to achieve structural social reform. It was contended that internal differences, plural singularities and diverse identities within the disability community were disregarded, the different bodily impairment and the varying severity of these erased and issues of subjectivity and sexuality either ignored or downplayed. The CDS approach highlights the notion 'of multiple irreducible differences' and is centred on understanding why inequitable conditions and discrimination persist despite apparent advances towards achieving an integrative and inclusive society. Its focus lies on critiquing stable notions of selfhood and personhood. This approach also includes the critical examination and interrogation by the non-disabled of the relationship between the able-bodied and the disabled. CDS views both the lived experience of the disabled and the engagement of the non-disabled, with their complicity or otherwise, in the creation and sustaining of normative assumptions to be equally important to transforming our ways at looking at corporeality (Shildrick 2012: 30, 37).

The minority model focuses on the notion of full citizenship based on equal access, premised on the concept of disabled bodies being 'natural human variations'. Although social and cultural accommodation is a goal, there is an awareness of the need to negotiate this without actually succumbing to becoming compliant 'abled-disabled' by accepting the normalising strategies of assimilation.[6] Given the plurality of theories, texts depicting disability can also be read variously.

Academic research and public awareness on disability issues in India is a fairly recent phenomenon. The discourse on disability and the disabled in India assumes importance, due to the continued marginality of the disabled (Ghai 2002: 50ff.). In contrast to the West, 'the developing world continues to agonize over securing the very basic elements that disabled people need to survive.' (Ghai 2002: 51). This is echoed by Reddy, who contends that 'if . . . in the West, the matters of identity, dignity, access, and inclusion are of critical importance, then in India, the matters of survival, poverty, exclusion, and despair become critical' (2011: 304). Nilika Mehrotra, too, opines that in India, disability issues need to be viewed from the development perspective given the numbers of rural disabled living in poverty with poor access to education, health and employment. Like Ghai, Mehrotra, also advocates an intersectional approach. Mehrotra further draws attention to the fact that in India the gender perspectives dominate the studies on disability (2012: 6). In addition, Ghai notes that disability activists in India, belonging to the elite, educated classes, have not substantively engaged with such issues.

Reading and writing disability

Disability has been configured in literary representations across time and space, from ancient times to the present, substantively corroborating Mitchell and Snyder's concept of 'narrative prosthesis', which they define as the perpetual discursive dependency of literary narratives upon disability, in the form of characterisation and/or as metaphor, because of its 'disruptive potentiality, and analytical insight' (2011: 49). They, however, lament that despite the widespread representation of disability in literary texts, these do not focus on the social and political dimensions thereof (Mitchell and Snyder 2011: 47ff.).[7] Literary representations are internalised and shape the perception of disability, often re-enforcing stereotypes in the mind of the reader. Such representations 'often serve to mobilize pity or horror in a moral drama that has nothing to do with the actual experience of disability' (Bérubé 2005: 570). It is through language that meanings are generated and transferred. In seeking to understand the text, the reader delves into the meaning-making process of images that is rooted in both the subjectivity of the writer and reader and in the cultural framework of received traditions and practices. The socialisation through reading inures the reader at a young age to often associate images of disability with charity, ridicule, fear, deficiency and incapacity. Elizabeth Altieri, citing Kriegel and Margolis and Shapiro, makes the point that stories and grand epics in 'classical literature are rife with devalued representations of disability' (2003: 120). Such portrayals can ultimately feed biases that result in viewing the disabled as expendable and in the pursuit of practices that are discriminatory. The power of representation is not to be underestimated for 'discriminatory practices are legitimated by systems of representation, by collective cultural stories that shape the material world, underwrite exclusionary attitudes, inform human relations, and mold our senses of who we are' (Garland-Thomson 2002: 9).

There are commonalities, as well as differences, in the cultural imaginary of the literary representation of disability. Disability across cultures has, however, been predominantly negatively constructed. In India, the cultural construct of disability is marked by negativity, projecting disabled persons as being inauspicious, flawed and of diminished capability. Disability is often associated with evildoing and deceit. Figures in mythology also point to the disabled embodying demonic and diabolic traits. Often, being disabled is considered to be the divine retribution for misdeeds committed in an earlier life by the disabled person him- or herself or by his or her parents – the result of *karma*. In some parts of India, disability is conceived of as eternal childhood, which, in turn, activates images of dependence and the need for protection, perpetuating the belief in performing 'one's dharmic (religious) duty toward the needy, in the same spirit as one would give alms to beggars.' (Ghai 2002: 51). This generates an attitude of charity and pity, the objectification of the disabled person.[8]

Conventionally, in most cultures, including India, the portrayal of disability in literary texts can be broadly summed up in the following categories: as upholding the norms of the able-bodied and as depicting disability as unwanted and undesirable, what Garland-Thomson terms as 'the narrative of abjection that identifies disability as that which one can and must avoid at all costs' (2005: 1568)[9] and as Shapiro, Margolis and Anderson, quoting Baskin and Harris, write, '"deformed" outer body' used to 'reflect the "de-formed" inner quality' of the characters (December 1989–January 1990: 90). There is the narrative of cure where the disability registers as an impairment that can be cured fully or at least overcome with assistive technologies, a problem in need of a solution. Then there is the narrative that trains the normate to tolerate and perform charity vis-à-vis the disabled, what Garland-Thomson describes as 'sentimental narratives' that see the disabled as 'occasions for narcissistic pity or lessons in suffering for those who imagine themselves as nondisabled' (2005: 1568). Finally, there is the narrative of the 'supercrip' who overcomes all odds. Shapiro, Margolis and Anderson have critiqued this as '"overcomer" or "super-hero" depictions of disabled persons who excel after conquering virtually impossible obstacles creat[ing] similarly distorted and destructive images. They make the average person with disabilities feel inadequate' (December 1989–January 1990: 87). A slightly less oppressive narrative is the so-called inspirational one which reflects the achievements of the central character, who is disabled and whose life is being chronicled. It records the emergence of disability and the success achieved by the disabled person, serving as an inspiration for others. Thus, most representations of disability in literary texts are able-bodied-reader-specific, meeting clichéd expectations, not niggling at the readers' minds to spur them on to revisit and perhaps reconfiguring long-held impressions of disability and the disabled.

Looking at some short stories in the Indian languages, including Indian English, some of the preceding features are reflected. *Viklang Vibhutiyonki Jeevangathayan* (Mishra 2005) is a collection in Hindi of 'inspirational' stories of persons with an impairment, from mythical figures to living persons from across the world who are viewed as 'achievers' having managed to overcome their impairment where the criteria for success remain ableist, which is viewed by Lennard Davis as the 'hegemony of the normal' (Davis 2014: 12). Thus, while intended, on one hand, to be inspirational for the differently abled, to encourage them to strive for similar success, and, on the other, to sensitise the non-disabled to the travails of the disabled, the collection could actually serve to discourage some since the stories are not sensitive to the differing intensity of disability making it impossible for some to achieve similar progress. At the same time, the stories, having all been written by Vinod Kumar Mishra, lack the depiction of lived experience that is crucial for purposes of activism. Most of those portrayed are from middle-class homes with access to resources and a very supportive family – Ved Mehta, Rajender Yadav, Satish Gujral,

Sudha Chandran, and Anjali Arora are some of those included in this collection. In most cases, it is a case of acquired disability. The stories are all written in the third person. The style is also extremely impersonal, and the emphasis is on facts, shorn of emotion. Standard Hindi has been used.

Two children's books in English brought out by Tulika Publishers, supported under the Parag initiative of the Navajbai Ratan Tata Trust, *Kanna Panna* (Whitaker 2015) and *Wings to Fly* (Rajendran 2015) are very differently written. Both books are recommended for readers in the age group 5 and older. *Wings to Fly* would fall into the category of both narratives of cure and of supercrip. It reflects the bio-medical model and narrates lived experiences of the much-awarded international para-athlete, Malathi Hola, who had polio as an infant. She has won more than 300 medals. The story highlights the fact that she spent nearly 15 years away from her family in a medical centre, following instructions diligently, to become the 'overa-chiever' that she is, having, early in her career as sportsperson, won medals even in a race with men who were army veterans. She is also shown to be excellent at her work in a bank. The story does show the wheelchair as being emancipative. In contrast, *Kanna Panna* is about a visually impaired child, but the reader only learns of this towards the end of the story in a very natural way. Nowhere is the word 'blind' or the term 'visually impaired' used in the story. The interaction with the parents is shown to be lacking in communication beyond instructions regarding posture or neat appearance with reference to clothes. However, a visit by Kanna's maternal aunt leads to an invitation to visit her and spend time with his cousins. The family, along with Kanna, visits some cave temples, and there is a power failure. Everybody panics, but Kanna leads them out calmly, used as he is to finding his way in darkness. This gives him a great deal of confidence as he realises that everyone has been totally dependent on him, making him aware of his ability and capability. He returns home, joins school and becomes friends with a boy who, at their first meet-ing, asks him in irritation, when he stumbles against him, unbalancing the boy, if he could not see. The interaction in the story is natural. It is an integrative approach from which both the non-disabled and the disabled can learn without making a fetish of the impairment. The social nature of disability is also touched on in passing through the comparison with life at home and at the aunt's home.

A final example is of a Hindi short story 'Goonge' by Rangeya Raghava,[10] where the protagonist, Chameli, a homemaker, out of pity for a mute man decides to employ him. The mute man is very communicative through gestures and tries very hard to articulate meaningfully but can only bring out a variety of crude noises despite all his efforts, noises that sound fearful and dreadful to the ears of Cha-meli, who then sees the mute man more as savage than as human. In the course of the story, on the surface there appears to be a bonding between Chameli and the nameless mute man, and she occasionally feels a maternal instinct vis-à-vis the man, but the moment her son unjustly accuses the mute man of trying to hit him, Chameli finds herself, at first, torn between meting out justice or siding with her son, especially when the mute servant communicates that he expects justice from her and is disappointed at not receiving it. In the end, she turns out the mute man, who returns bloodied and injured after a fight with children on the street who had taunted him. Looking at him, she feels that there are several in the world who are mute despite having a voice because they do not raise it in protest against injustice because they find themselves helpless lacking the courage to take a position. This story seems to be, at one level, one of arousing pity, compassion and charity, Garland-Thomson's sentimental narrative, and, at another, through the depiction of the feelings and emotions of the disabled man, a critique of a callous society, forcing introspection and at yet another level it seeks to touch on a kind of self-critique by the temporarily able-bodied person, inviting self-reflexivity.

Celebrating diversity: an alternative aesthetics of disability

In maintaining diversity and otherness, it is necessary to use language differently, to experiment, to see 'beauty' in a usage that is not standard, that goes against the norm. Language that has been used to shame, humiliate and exclude must be forged anew to liberate, emancipate and empower. It must become a space of bonding and creating solidarity. In the context of black empowerment, bell hooks contends that the black enslaved people created a counter-language by the incorrect use of words and syntax to create a 'site of resistance' and, in so doing, 'also forge[d] a space for alternative cultural production and alternative epistemologies – different ways of thinking and knowing that were crucial to creating a counterhegemonic worldview' (1996: 298).

The disability movement also has sought to reclaim power by creating an equally effective alternative aesthetics. To quote Lennard Davis, 'disability studies demands a shift from the ideology of normalcy, from the rule and hegemony of normates, to a vision of the body as changeable, unperfectable, unruly, and untidy' (1999: 505). Similarly, Garland-Thomson draws attention to the need for using a convoluted syntax that, according to her, is more precise. She writes that she prefers to

> use phrases such as 'the traits we think of as disability,' for example, rather than words like 'deformities' or 'abnormalities.' We say things like 'bodies that violate the normative standards and expectations of bodily form and function' not to obfuscate but rather to clarify by insisting that readers do not fall back on essentialist definitions of disability as inferior embodiment.
>
> (Garland-Thomson 2005: 1558)

Nancy Mairs, as quoted in Garland-Thomson's article, prefers not to use euphemisms when discussing impairment. '"Cripple", Mairs declares, evokes a "wince" from those who imagine themselves as nondisabled. "As a cripple," she avers, "I swagger"' (Garland-Thomson 2005: 1569). There are others who object to phrases such as 'confined to the wheelchair' or 'wheelchair-bound' since *wheelchair* has positive associations for the disabled community. Julie Allan speaks of an '"aesthetics of disability," a type of kynicism formed by disabled people, in which the body is used as a weapon to subvert and undermine disabling barriers' (2004: 33).

The idea is to discomfit the non-disabled to make them introspect on their 'normalising and disablist attitudes' (Allan 2004: 41).

Translational subversion and disruption in 'Goonge'[11]

It is in this context that the title of the Hindi short story 'Goonge' throws up multiple possibilities in translation, among them dumb, mute and voice-less. The negative and pejorative meanings linked to the word *dumb* make it unsuitable; on the other hand, *dumb* might be more subversive as it would draw attention to the intelligence and smartness of the disabled figure in contrast with the attribute of not being capable of sensible thought and being labelled as stupid by virtue of not being able to articulate speech sounds. The usage of *dumb* then would underline the culture's underlying bias against the disabled by highlighting that language does indeed discriminate against those with disabilities; *mute* is perhaps objective, neutral and politically correct and can perhaps be recuperated just as *cripple* has been, but given the context of the story, a more likely though unusual, non-standard choice would be *voice-less* since this creates ambiguity, permitting wordplay, alluding, on one hand, to the silence of those with voices – and thus provoking introspection – and, on the other, to being mute due to impairment. Furthermore, the unconventional compounding of the word by hyphenating the suffix –*less* in *voice-less* is intended to provoke reflection on the different forms of not having a voice, so while impairment could be one such form, perhaps the more damning form is the voluntary surrender, the loss of agency due to fear of repercussions or sheer indifference. Thus, although all three choices reflect the subversive technique of translation, the last option viz *voice-less* was the preferred choice in translation.

The mute figure in the short story remains nameless and is addressed by the generic term *mute*, which, on one hand, reflects the uncritical societal acceptance of negative and derogatory attitudes embedded in language, further entrenching these and, on the other, the indifference of society, erasing the identity of the 'other', devaluing him as merely an object of pity, calling attention to what is perceived as a defect, objectifying the disabled figure as deviating from the norm and subscribing to Davis's hegemony of normalcy. Consequently, in translation the word *mute* was privileged over the less commonly used *speech-less-one*, which would have partially resounded with empathy and sensitivity towards one lacking the ability to make speech sounds and his plight, viewing him not as an object of pity but as 'an other', and would perhaps have been critical of those endowed with speech, but this is not immediately the case in the story, for as mentioned earlier Chameli's bonding with him is an apparent one and not genuine. *Mute* is also thus used to make the reader wince as stated by Mair. It is therefore disruptive.

The translation also seeks to explicitly bring out the implication in the text that the deaf-mute also speak and talk, that is they communicate, only differently. Hence, they speak the language of gestures, of hand movements, of signals: they show; they demonstrate; they mime and very effectively use facial expressions. They, thus have a language, a mother tongue of their own, viz. the non-speech-sounds-tongue. This multi-hyphenated word might sound clumsy, but it is intended to do just that – the convoluted style recommended by Garland-Thomson with a view to fostering deeper engagement with the issue of muteness resulting in the breakdown of existing prejudices and the realisation that speech is not only of one kind and that persons with speech are more often the ones without a voice, not exercising their agency. The phrase 'the non-speech-sounds-tongue' is not there in the original. It has been deliberately inserted into the translation to provoke discomfiture and facilitate a re-imagining of the stereotype of the deaf-mute as a thinking 'other' capable of communicating and exercising agency.

To further accentuate self-reflexivity and introspection by the so-called able-bodied, the translation deliberately makes use of idiomatic phrases that are related to hearing and speech disability to underline the fact that those with speech-sounds can also for one reason or other become speech-less and equally that the deaf-mute can indeed speak. Thus, for example, the onlookers are said to be 'struck dumb' and not that they were at a loss for words or speechless; again love for her son made Chameli 'turn a deaf ear' and not turn a blind eye or ignore or pay no heed; again Chameli's anger leaves the mute 'dumbfounded', not astonished or bewildered. Again, at the beginning of the story the mute gesticulates in front of his mouth and not in front of his face which is literally the case – in order to emphasise that he is speaking despite being non-verbal. Similarly, at the beginning of the story the challenge is to see whether Shakuntala can get the mute 'to hear' and not to just come or react.

The story in the original compares the mute and his abortive efforts at making speech sounds consistently with animals, dogs, in particular, or with a caveman. The translation, too, has reproduced this, again even in places where a neutral phrase could have been used – thus, he 'doggedly' tries to speak, or the phrase can a 'leopard change his spots' is used. This is to emphasise the cultural discrimination and prejudice already embedded in the language.

Similarly, the original time and again reiterates the pity that engulfs most people when confronted with disability. This emotion is extremely negative as it focuses on what is perceived as deficient and strips the individual of value and worth. But the original philosophises on this attitude, making for self-critique, highlighting the frustration of the inability of the non-disabled which results in the expression of pity. This is effected through the thoughts of Chameli's husband, where it is said that the 'feeling of pity in human beings is a reflection of their own muteness, when there are so many things they want to do but are unable to do so' (my translation).

Finally, there are two instances in the story where in translation there is a conscious non-standard usage of words that are central to debates and discussions on disability and the disabled. The intent is to make the reader stumble in the act of reading, to pause and reflect so as to sensitise the reader to the inherent discriminations against the disabled in our societies and, particularly, to make readers engage with the question of who is the one who is really dis-abled in society. The word *stigmatised* occurs here in an unconventional surrounding or co-text: 'If he wants to stay, he had better abide by the rules, if not he can spend the rest of his life on the streets surviving like a dog on left-overs, constantly being insulted and stigmatised'. Normally, in such a context the word that would have been appropriate would be *humiliated*, which should strike every thinking reader and make him or her wonder why it has not been used. *Stigmatised* is a much stronger word than *humiliated*. To humiliate someone would be to hurt a person's feelings or injure his or her sense of dignity, whereas *stigmatise* has the additional connotation of demeaning another to such a degree that the person feels devalued and marked as a lesser being, which is what societal prejudices and discrimination do to persons with impairments making them disabled.

Prosthetic is the other non-standard usage of a word. This is normally used as a collocation with limb and in that context denotes the artificial body part. Here in the translation it is stated that 'yet not even the illusion of prosthetic happiness is enticing, because he yearns above all for love and equality' (my translation). There is, on one hand, a wordplay on the word *prosthetic* here – on the fact that medical solutions alone are not the harbingers of true happiness, – and on the other it is meant to indicate that unless there is love and equality, all else is but a semblance of happiness that is not fulfilling. False or artificial happiness would have been the conventional choice in this context. The unconventional use of words and phrases is, as already mentioned, a source of subversion and disruption in translation – a form of resistance, creating a counter-discourse.

The fact that societal prejudice and discrimination against the impaired is the genesis of disabledness is brought out in the original itself in the wordplay on *arth* (meaning or sense) and *asamarth* (helpless, of no consequence) which has been retained in the translation through *en-able*, *in-cap-able* and *dis-abled*:

> And the mute . . . they are very diverse, spread across the world in very different forms, those who want to speak out, yet are un–able to; who despite their desire for justice after weighing right and wrong are still un–able to challenge oppression and tyranny, because even though they have a voice, the voice does not empower and en–able because they are in–cap–able, dis–abled.
>
> (my translation)

The translation plays with the root word *able* and uses prefixes to transform the meaning of the root word to provoke engagement on part of the reader with the text and to encourage self-reflection as to who is really the dis-abled, resulting in a re-definition and a deeper understanding of the phenomenon of disabledness. *Un-able* indicates the lack of agency and courage and therefore the lack of ability to voice a position promoting justice, despite not being mute or deaf. Again *en-able* reflects that voice alone cannot overcome deficiency. The *cap* in *in-cap-able* highlights the limited ability; the prefix *in*–articulates the negation of capable, therefore again deficient in competence and ability which makes for such persons even without any impairment being, in fact, the real 'dis-abled', that is not able, not capable of acting with agency. The word *dis-abled* at the end of the paragraph is not in the original. This translational intervention is to drive home the fact that, very often, it is those with a voice and not the mute who are the truly disabled. Again, the prefixes are combined with the root word through a hyphen, hence using a non-standard compounding of words to disrupt and subvert.

Conclusion

Translation anthologies should strive to keep alive the rich diversity of literary representations of disability. For this, the selection of texts is crucial. The bouquet of texts selected should cover a wide spectrum of positions and sensibilities to provoke debate and dialogue. For the anthology to be effective, it would be worthwhile to include a selection of theoretical texts reflecting the debates in the field. This would contribute strongly to the effort of raising consciousness on the issue as well as towards self-reflexivity and to the opening of an imaginative space. An anthology focusing on disability would necessarily be a collection of texts by different authors and, in the case of India, of different *bhasas*. The choice of translation strategies and techniques should be left to the concerned translators. Although transmitting otherness with the intent to subvert is extremely important, and here the application of alternative aesthetics would be fruitful, yet equally it is important to allow all shades of translation to find a voice. Different readings and differing voices, too, will generate debate and drive a dialogue, all of which is indispensable in achieving integration and promoting solidarity amongst all, disabled and non-disabled.

Notes

1 See Walter Benjamin, 'The Task of the Translator', where he elaborates on the temporary and provisional nature, the non-permanence of translation: 'While a poet's words endure in his own language, even the greatest translation is destined to become part of the growth of its own language and eventually to be absorbed by its renewal. Translation is so far removed from being the sterile equation of two dead languages that of all literary forms it is the one charged with the special mission of watching over the maturing process of the original language and the birth pangs of its own' (1979a: 73). The notion of translation being unfinished, incomplete or not perfect is echoed by, amongst others, George Steiner and Georges Mounin, as quoted in D. Gareth Walters (2002: 863) and in Ricoeur (2006: 7).

2 Afterlife, as explained by Walter Benjamin, constitutes transformation and renewal, wherein the original undergoes a change. See Benjamin (1979a: 73).

3 James Holmes, as early as 1972, wrote of establishing a new discipline of Translation Studies that would record the history of translation practices in diverse cultures. He described the approach suggested by him as descriptive translation studies that would engage with the analysis of translation as product and from the analysis would emerge the translation strategy applied, from which a theory of translation could be derived. He also spoke of function of translation, not as the text function as discussed by Skopus theoreticians but, rather, as the role of translation in the receiving culture. See James S. Holmes, 1987, 'The Name and Nature of Translation Studies', in Gideon Toury (ed) *Translation Across Cultures*, pp. 9–24, New Delhi: Bahri Publications.

4 Even-Zohar distinguishes between translations that occupy either a central or a peripheral position by the influence they exercise on the subsequent production of texts in the receiving culture. Translated texts that occupy central positions are innovative in their impact. They challenge existing hierarchies, supplying cultural gaps, be it in terms of giving voice to the marginalised, questioning dominant norms or contributing to greater

diversity including in terms of literary genres, themes or poetics. The polysystem locates literature and translation within a complex network of relations, social, historical, political and economic, constituting a cultural system that determines the production and consumption of texts (Even-Zohar 1987: 107–115).

5 See also Sandra Bermann, who wrote that 'translations emphasize the play of other and self, different and same, stranger and host' (2010: 84).

6 For the preceding discussion see Nick Watson, Alan Roulstone and Carol Thomas (eds), 2012, *Routledge Handbook of Disability Studies*, London and New York: Routledge, especially chapters 2, 3 and 4; Colin Barnes, 'Understanding the Social Model of Disability: Past, Present and Future', pp. 12–29; MargritShildrick, 'Critical Disability Studies: Rethinking the Conventions for the Age of Postmodernity', pp. 30–41; and David Mitchell and Sharon Snyder, 'Minority Model: From Liberal to Neoliberal Futures of Disability', pp. 42–50.

7 David T. Mitchell and Sharon L. Snyder, 2011, *Narrative Prosthesis: Disability and the Dependencies of Discourse*, Ann Arbor, MI: University of Michigan Press, pp. 47ff. – see chapter 2: 'Narrative Prosthesis and the Materiality of Metaphor'.

8 For the preceding discussion see Anita Ghai, 2002, 'Disabled Women: An Excluded Agenda of Indian Feminism', *Hypatia*, Special Issue on Feminism and Disability, Part II, 17(3): 49 – 66, www.jstor.org/stable/3810795, accessed on 15 October 2016; NilikaMehrotra, 2004, 'Women, Disability and Social Support in Rural Haryana', *Economic and Political Weekly*, 39(52): 5640–5644, www.jstor.org/stable/4415982, accessed on 10 December 2016; 'Chapter 2: Attitudes Towards Disability and People with Disabilities', http://siteresources.worldbank.org/INDIAEXTN/Resources/295583-1171456325808/Chapter02.pdf, accessed on 12 October 2016.

9 Garland-Thomson categorises five narratives of disability: the biomedical, the sentimental, that of overcoming, of catastrophe and of abjection.

10 Rangeya Raghava, 1945, 'Goonge', http://gadyakosh.org/gk (accessed on 2 November 2016).

11 All examples of translation referred to in this section are my translation unless otherwise stated.

References

Allan, Julie. 2004. 'Chapter 2: The Aesthetics of Disability as a Productive Ideology', *Counterpoints, Ideology and the Politics of (In)Exclusion*, 270: 32–45. www.jstor.org/stable/42978584 (accessed on 25 August 2016).

Altieri, Elizabeth. 2003. 'Chapter 4: Seeing Disability in New Ways', *Counterpoints, Image, Inquiry, and Transformative Practice: Engaging Learners in Creative and Critical Inquiry Through Visual Representation*, 203: 109–154. www.jstor.org/stable/42978099 (accessed on 25 November 2016).

Appiah, Kwame Anthony. 1993. 'Thick Translation', *Callaloo*, 16(4): 808–819. www.jstor.org/stable/2932211 (accessed on 18 April 2010).

Apter, Emily. 2007. 'Taskography: Translation as Genre of Literary Labor', *PMLA*, 122(5): 1403–1415. www.jstor.org/stable/25501793 (accessed on 26 November 2016).

Barnes, Colin. 2012. 'Understanding the Social Model of Disability: Past, Present and Future', in Nick Watson, Alan Roulstone and Carol Thomas (eds) *Routledge Handbook of Disability Studies*, pp. 12–29. London and New York: Routledge.

Bassnett, Susan and Harish Trivedi, eds. 1999. *Post-colonial Translation: Theory and Practice*. London and New York: Routledge.

Benjamin, Walter. 1979a. 'The Task of the Translator', in Harry Zohn (trans), Hannah Arendt (ed) *Illuminations*, pp. 69–82. Glasgow: Fontana/Collins.

————. 1979b. 'Unpacking My Library: A Talk About Book Collecting', in Harry Zohn (trans), Hannah Arendt (ed) *Illuminations*, pp. 59–67. Glasgow: Fontana/Collins.

Bermann, Sandra. 2010. 'Teaching in – and About –Translation', *Profession*, 82–90. www. jstor.org/stable/41419864 (accessed on 28 November 2016).

Bérubé, Michael. 2005. 'Disability and Narrative', *PMLA*, 120(2): 568–576. www.jstor.org/ stable/25486186 (accessed on 25 August 2016).

Chapter 2: Attitudes Towards Disability and People with Disabilities. http://siteresources. worldbank.org/INDIAEXTN/Resources/295583-1171456325808/Chapter02.pdf (accessed on 12 October 2016).

Davis, Lennard J. 1999. 'Crips Strike Back: The Rise of Disability Studies', *American Literary History*, 11(3): 500–512. www.jstor.org/stable/490130 (accessed on 25 September 2016).

————. 2014. 'Introduction: Disability, Normality, and Power', in Lennard J. Davis (ed) *The Disability Studies Reader*, pp. 1 – 14. New York and London: Routledge.

Davison, Claire. 2014. *Translation as Collaboration: Virginia Woolf, Katherine Mansfield and S. S. Koteliansky*. Edinburgh: Edinburgh University Press.

Devy, Ganesh Narayandas. 1995. *In Another Tongue: Essays on Indian Literature in English*. Madras: Macmillan India.

Dharwadkar, Vinay, ed. 1999. *The Collected Essays of A. K. Ramanujan*. New Delhi: Oxford University Press.

Even-Zohar, Itmar. 1987. 'The Position of Translated Literature Within the Literary Poly-system', in Gideon Toury (ed) *Translation Across Cultures*, pp. 107–115. New Delhi: Bahri Publications.

Garland-Thomson, Rosemarie. 2002. 'Integrating Disability, Transforming Feminist Theory', *NWSA Journal*, 14(3): 1–32. www.jstor.org/stable/4316922 (accessed on 15 October 2016).

————. 2005. 'Feminist Disability Studies', *Signs*, 30(2):1557–1587. www.jstor.org/ stable/10.1086/423352 (accessed on 25 May 2016).

Geertz, Clifford. 1993. *The Interpretation of Cultures: Selected Essays*. London: Fontana.

Gentzler, Edwin and Maria Tymoczko, eds. 2002. *Translation and Power*. Boston and Amherst: University of Massachusetts Press.

Ghai, Anita. 2002. 'Disabled Women: An Excluded Agenda of Indian Feminism', *Hypatia*, Special Issue on Feminism and Disability, Part II, 17(3):49–66. www.jstor.org/ stable/3810795 (accessed on 15 October 2016).

Hermans, Theo. 2003. 'Cross-Cultural Translation Studies as Thick Translation', *Bulletin of the School of Oriental and African Studies, University of London*, 66(3): 380–389. www.jstor.org/ stable/4146100 (accessed on 14 November 2016).

Holmes, James S. 1987. 'The Name and Nature of Translation Studies', in Gideon Toury (ed) *Translation Across Cultures*, pp. 9–24. New Delhi: Bahri Publications.

hooks, bell. 1996. '"This Is the Oppressor's Language/ Yet I Need It to Talk to You": Language, a Place of Struggle', in Anuradha Dingwaney and Carol Maier (eds) *Between Language and Cultures: Translation and Cross-cultural Texts*, pp. 295–301. Delhi, Bombay, Calcutta and Madras: Oxford University Press.

Lal, Purushottama. 1996. *Transcreation: Seven Essays on the Art of Transcreation*. Calcutta: A Writer's Workshop Publication.

Lefevere, André. 1992. *Translation, Rewriting and the Manipulation of Literary Fame*. London and New York: Routledge.

Mehrotra, Nilika. 2004. 'Women, Disability and Social Support in Rural Haryana', *Economic and Political Weekly*, 39(52): 5640–5644. www.jstor.org/stable/4415982 (accessed on 10 December 2016).

————. 2012. 'Methodological Issues in Disability Research: An Introduction', *Indian Anthropologist*, 42(1): 1–10. www.jstor.org/stable/41922004 (accessed on 15 October 2016).

Mishra, Vinod Kumar. 2005. *Viklang Vibhutiyonki Jeevangathayan*. New Delhi: Kitabghar.

Mitchell, David T. and Sharon L. Snyder. 2011. *Narrative Prosthesis: Disability and the Dependencies of Discourse*. Ann Arbor, MI: University of Michigan Press.

————. 2012. 'Minority Model: From Liberal to Neoliberal Futures of Disability', in Nick Watson, Alan Roulstone and Carol Thomas (eds) *Routledge Handbook of Disability Studies*, pp. 42–50. London and New York: Routledge.

Mukherjee, Sujit. 2004. *Translation as Recovery*. New Delhi: Pencraft International.

O'Brien, Eugene. Fall 2001–Spring 2002. 'Seamus Heaney and the Ethics of Translation', *The Canadian Journal of Irish Studies*, 27(2)/28(1): 20–37. www.jstor.org/stable/25515374 (accessed on 4 November 2016).

Rajendran, Sowmya. 2015. *Wings to Fly*. Chennai: Tulika.

Rangeya Raghava. *Goonge*. http://gadyakosh.org/gk (accessed on 2 November 2016).

Reddy, C. Raghava. 2011. 'From Impairment to Disability and Beyond: Critical Explorations in Disability Studies', *Sociological Bulletin*, 60(2): 287–306. www.jstor.org/stable/23620921 (accessed on 14 October 2016).

Ricoeur, Paul. 1971. 'What Is a Text? Explanation and Interpretation', pp. 135–150. www.uni-trier.de/fileadmin/fb1/prof/PHI/003/Bilddateien/Text_6.pdf (accessed on 4 November 2016).

————. 2006. *On Translation*. Trans. Eileen Brennan. London and New York: Routledge.

Santaemilia, José. 2011. 'Feminists Translating: On Women, Theory and Practice', in Eleonra Federici (ed) *Translating Gender*, pp. 55–77. Bern: Peter Lang.

Shapiro, Arthur, Howard Margolis and Philip M. Anderson. December 1989–January 1990. 'The Vocabulary of Disability: Critical Reading and Handicapism', *The High School Journal*, 73(2): 86–91. www.jstor.org/stable/40364667 (accessed on 25 August 2016).

Shildrick, Margrit. 2012. 'Critical Disability Studies: Rethinking the Conventions for the Age of Postmodernity', in Nick Watson, Alan Roulstone and Carol Thomas (eds) *Routledge Handbook of Disability Studies*, pp. 30–41. London and New York: Routledge.

Spivak, Gayatri Chakravorty. 2005. 'Translating into English', in Sandra Bermann and Michael Wood (eds) *Nation, Language and Ethics of Translation*, pp. 93–110, Princeton and Oxford: Princeton University Press.

Walters, D. Gareth. 2002. 'From Linguistic Monument to Social Memory: Translation Strategies in Philip Pollack's Version of Espriu's "Primerahistòriad' Esther"', *The Modern Language Review*, 97(4): 863–876. www.jstor.org/stable/3738617 (accessed on 27 May 2016).

Watson, Nick, Alan Roulstone and Carol Thomas, eds. 2012. *Routledge Handbook of Disability Studies*. London and New York: Routledge.

Whitaker, Zai. 2015. *KannaPanna*. Chennai: Tulika.

3

GITOPADESHA ON WHEELCHAIRS AND CRUTCHES

An alternative aesthetic

Himani Kapoor

'Bhagavad Gita on Wheels' is a combination of dance, mimetic representations, drama and music from performers with hearing or limb impairments who use either the wheelchair or crutches to bring home a significant change in the aesthetics of disability representation. The chapter takes into account such counter-hegemonic representations of disability with the study of inter-semiotic translations and representations of disability narratives. In this context, the chapter tries to understand the representation of the Gitopadesha with respect to disability, community, social welfare and marginality. The attempt is to highlight efforts towards disability advocacy and cultural activism in India, consequently suggesting possibilities of an alternative aesthetics of disability representation.

As examples of such subversive readings of a disability text, after the Introduction, the second part of the paper demonstrates ways of re-reading the character of Sakuni as represented in Sarala Dasa's version of *Mahabharata* and a performance of puppet theatre based on traditional *Togalu Gombeyaata* created by Katkatha Puppet theatre. In the third part of the chapter, the performance 'Bhagavad Gita on Wheels' is analysed with respect to its semiotics and innovative usage of wheelchairs and crutches. The different sections of the chapter talk about ideas and issues related to translatability, interpretation and inter-semiotic translation in addition to disability representation in India and the possibilities of new ways of its representation.

Translation and activism

When we talk about translation, there is a tacit assumption that it will be the reproduction of the same text in a politically neutral space. Of late, such assumptions about translations and their supposed political neutrality are gradually losing ground. Mona Baker, in her paper, 'Translation as an Alternative Space for Political Action' (2013) argues that translation is in fact not a neutral or a 'liminal' space and that translators and interpreters in recent times have challenged the erstwhile political status quo and are breaking away from the tradition of being considered 'unengaged professionals'. Political activism could therefore be attempted through translation. In fact, translators 'themselves constitute a space of resistance, a means of reversing the symbolic order' (qtd. in Baker 25).

Although Baker talks about the contemporary times and about translators who are consciously making their political interventions apparent, we see a very similar attitude in the medieval Indian tellings and renderings of narratives. Medieval translators like Sarala Dasa and Jnaneshawar, in their own ways, have tried to politically engage with their times by way of translations.

The porous ground of Indian literature offers numerous examples of translations as tellings and renderings that not only offer different translated versions of the same text but also offer dramatically different interpretations of the same. The *Mahabharata* corpus itself would be a significant example in this regard. Different regional versions not only differ from each other in terms of the script but would also offer dramatically different tellings of the same episode.

In the introduction to the *BORI Mahabharata*, the earliest 'critical' edition[1] of the epic, collated by the Bhandarkar Oriental Research Institute, V.S. Sukthankar, one of the key editors, explains the probable reason behind the correlation between the script and the version. He says that the scribes being not conversant with any other language but that of their own particular province could copy only manuscripts written in their specific provincial scripts, exception being made only in favour of the Devnagari which was a sort of 'vulgar' script widely used and understood in India (Sukthankar 1933: LXIII). Scribes, therefore, while translating the Devnagari text, would interpret it afresh while putting it down into their own provincial scripts. Translation, interpretation and renewal thus go hand in hand for Indian literature as in the case of the *Mahabharata* corpus.

The different regional versions of the same text would often become a way of reinterpreting it for a different audience and re-orienting the text towards a different culture system. An important example in this regard would be Sarala Dasa's version of *Mahabharata*. This is discussed in the next section.

Inter-semiotic translation and translatability

As a practice, translation is concerned not only with two different languages but also two different value systems and different target audiences. Román Alvarez and M. Carmen-África Vidal in 'Translating: A Political Act' (1996) argue that since translation can never be completely neutral, as it automatically plays a part in the power relations of the cultures it brings together, the role of the translator is automatically subversive, and therefore, it is necessary to locate the subversive aspects of translations in the larger framework of social interaction.

Roman Jakobson (1959) in his tripartite classification of different kinds of translations as 'intra-lingual', 'interlingual' and 'inter-semiotic translation' gave a basic framework for translations to be defined and understood. It is his conception of inter-semiotic translation, that is the interpretation of verbal signs 'by means of signs of nonverbal sign systems' or 'transmutation' that is the most lucid and flexible category of translation as it calls for an alliance between translation studies and other disciplines like cinema and performance studies.

The concept of inter-semiotic translation is thus concerned with the semantic extension of linguistic translation to include different media and sign systems. In this regard, Theo Hermans in 'Norms and the Determination of Translation. A Theoretical Framework' (1996) demarcates the relevance of Jakobson's definition of inter-semiotic translation, which, although is not considered in the 'commonsense' understanding of translation, is nevertheless a valid subtype of translation itself. He says,

> Jakobson's extension of the term to intralingual and intersemiotic modes, accepted in academic circles as perfectly legitimate from a linguistic and semiotic point of view, acknowledges in its very designation of 'translation proper' for interlingual translation that as a social category this is what constitutes the entire concept of translation, to the exclusion of the other two forms. The formulation itself concedes that the extended meaning may claim validity in the academic community, but that it does not coincide with common usage.
>
> (Hermans 1996: 43)

Therefore, even though inter-semiotic translation does not coincide with the common usage of translation, it is nevertheless a way of exercising translation across different sign systems. Stage performances and cinematic adaptations automatically fall within the purview of this category, despite being autonomous and having their own internal coherence.

Herein lies another crucial aspect of this new translated/ transmuted/transposed[2] text: since, most of the time, the translated text is also an inter-temporal or cross-cultural product, it has to be 'domesticated',[3] leaving scope for further renewal. Stage performances of traditional literature like *Mahabharata* given their inter-temporal nature can therefore be deemed as such translations where there is ample opportunity for cultural and temporal appropriation, thus offering possibilities of renewal and redressal.

Translation, performance and disability representation

Manthra, the hunchback nursemaid from Kaikeyi's natal family, is often said to be the catalyst that sets in motion Rama's exile in the *Ramayana*. An often-omitted detail of the Manthra-Kaikeyi-Dashrath instigation episode is the bride-price agreement of Kaikeyi which promised the coronation of her future son as king. This argument, however, is never picked up by Manthra or even Kaikeyi herself (Sangari 1993: 873). Even though Manthra speaks in a language of material interests, and it is her own power over her husband that Kaikeyi wields, it is Manthra's evil instigation that is said to be the cause of disruption of the social order of the royal family. Her disability is often highlighted as her guiding characteristic.

> The hump is where Manthra's intellect, inclination, recollection, jurisprudence, wisdom, sagacity, statecraft, knowledge of fraud and delusion ('mati'

'smriti', 'budthi' 'rajniti' and knowledge of the 'maya') are stored, if Bharat is crowned Kaikeyi will ornament the hump with a gold necklace and anoint it with 'chandan'.

(1993: 875)

'Kaikeyi will also provide her with a retinue of dwarf and hunchback women servants!' (1993: 880). Thus, the hunchback on her body in a way stands for Manthra herself. It is clearly the most dominant aspect of her characterisation and perhaps at the root of her supposed instigation.

This bride-price agreement, however, is not a part of Tulsidasa's retelling of the *Ramayana*. In *Ramcharitmanas*, Manthra, mostly referred to as *kubari* (hunchback), *mand-mati* (dull-witted), *kujati* (lowborn), *paapini* (sinner), *sampini* (serpent) and so on, is purposely beguiled by goddess Sarasvati on the request of various *devatas* (lesser gods) so as to set in motion Rama's exile which will also ensure the killing of the *rakshasas* (demons) residing in the forests (Prasad 1990: 257). Despite this background which could evoke a certain understanding of her behaviour, Manthra is never entitled to any sympathy. When Shatrughna returns to Ayodhya and comes to know of his father's death and brother's exile, he kicks the "kubari" with a steady aim at the hump, which gets smashed and leaves her head split and teeth broken (1990: 352). Her backstory, however, given a cursory mention in the beginning of the episode is never dwelt on in the narrative. Her malevolence and deceit therefore seem unreasonable and mean, and it is as if her hump is its root cause.

While Manthra's disability may not impair her physical mobility, it does carry a stigma that makes her a figure of disapproval. In the beginning of the episode, Kaikeyi reprimands Manthra thus:

> *Kane khore kubare kucila kucali jani,*
> *tiya biseshi puni ceri kahi bharatamatu musukani.*
> The one-eyed, the lame and the hump-backed, are known [to] be perverse and wicked, especially if they are women and more especially when they are servants! So saying, Bharata's mother smiled.

(1990: 258)

This extremely prejudiced distinction about particular kinds of non-normative bodies, which gets further problematic with added gender and caste distinctions, highlights a glaring, multilayered social bias. Manthra's disability is therefore not only physical; there is distinct gender and caste baggage which comes alongside the physical struggle.

The backstory of Manthra has mostly been untold. Stage and televised representations of the *Ramayana*, borrowing a lot from *Ramcharitmanas*, do not offer variations to her portrayal. The bride-price agreement mentioned by Valmiki or the episode of Sarasvati's intervention mentioned by Tulsidasa does not find its way into stage and TV representations.

Another, perhaps even more crafty, figure in popular literature is the character of Sakuni, whose malicious plotting unfolds into the game of dice leading to the Kurukshetra war. Vyasa's *Mahabharata* portrays Sakuni as a vengeful, jealous, manipulative and malignant man without a clear justification for his hatred for the Pandavas or, for that matter, the rest Kuru clan which he knows is doomed to fall. Like Manthra, the motivation for his ways is left unclear or perhaps only hinted at. The most lasting and often highlighted feature of his personality, however, is his limp, which is automatically interpreted as the locus of his malice much like Manthra's hunchback.

In most of the renditions, while disability per se may not be overtly chastised, the disabled however are often subjects evoking anger or hatred, by being inherently malevolent and evil. An exception to such portrayals, however, is Saral Dasa's depiction of Sakuni. Sarala Dasa, the 15th-century Oriya poet known for his thought-provoking works, deviates in a number of ways from the more dominant versions of the *Mahabharata*. His portrayal of Sakuni is of victimhood, suffering and, then later, revenge.

In Sarala's version, Sakuni is intelligent, well read, good with a sword and smartest of all the sons of the Gandhara Clan. Having been imprisoned by Duryodhana with his ninety-nine brothers and father, Sakuni sees his entire family shrivel to death for the lack of food offered by the Kauravas for the prisoners. All his brothers and his father sacrifice themselves willingly to let one of them survive in order to get back at the injustice done to their clan by the Kuru kings. He then develops a set of dice with the bones of his dear ones and makes it the most potent weapon to manipulate the reality of his times (Mohanty 2005: 148). Such a portrayal thus corresponds to a different archetypal construction, taking the focus away from disability to a hero-villain figure that has a more rounded construction.

Interestingly, it isn't only Sarala Dasa who gives Sakuni a strong backstory. Similar narratives about Sakuni are found in many other, albeit oral and performative, traditions, *Togalu Gombeyaata* or the traditional leather puppetry of Karnataka being one of them. A contemporary puppet theatre company by the name of Katkatha Puppet Arts[4] that collaborates with traditional *Gombeyaata* artists has also, in the recent past, worked for creating a counter-narrative of Sakuni through its performances that are powerful, in their own way throwing askew all the assumptions associated with the character.

Katkatha's interpretation of the *Mahabharata* is done through the individual tales of some key characters that lead to the consequence of war. For traditional puppeteers, being among the lowest castes in the society, their narratives are thereby different from the mainstream narratives. Katkatha's depiction of Sakuni is remarkably counter-hegemonic. Here, Sakuni's father Subala, after having been imprisoned and choosing Sakuni as the survivor, entrusts him with the role of taking revenge and leaves a disabling injury on his right knee as a painful reminder of the sacrifice made for him. The director of the performance, Anurupa Roy, explains:

> Judgements have already been passed on certain characters. For instance, take Shakuni. It is only when you listen to his back story, you realise that he is not

that much of a villain. In fact, he is not very different from a Draupadi or a Bhima, who seek revenge for something that was done to them. Shakuni too was seeking revenge for something that was done to his family.

(Nathan 2016)

Counter to the hawk-like evil character of Sakuni only remembered for his sinister plot hatching and his disability, Katkatha's Sakuni (Figure 3.1) is a martyr figure who has a personal tragedy motivating his actions. The disability, on the other hand, is strategically designed to remind him of the vengeance and malice he should retain in order to take revenge from the violators of his family.

Translations, interpretations and representations can thus easily be counter to the normative assumptions associated with the source text. Stage performances could, in fact, go a step further in assuming the role of changing erstwhile hegemonic configurations into more meaningful and thought-provoking interpretations. By their very nature, performative arts survive generation after generation not only on the basis of the innovations made by the individual artists but also on the tremendous memory banks that the performances rely on. While they may be absorbing from already-existing traditions they nevertheless undercut the practice of reproducing readymade, standard interpretations of literary texts. As Roy puts it, having

300 versions of any narrative is not just about diversity – it is about protest, counter-protest, dissent, dialogue, linguistic heritage and anthropological clues

FIGURE 3.1 Shakuni from *Mahabharata* production by The Katkatha Puppet Arts Trust, New Delhi.

Photo by Adeeb Anwar, copyright of The Katkatha Puppet Arts Trust.

about cultural practices. The retellings of *Ramayana* and *Mahabharata* by the shadow puppeteers – who work with leather and were automatically relegated to the lowest rung of the caste ladder – explicitly question the upper castes.

(Shah 2016)

Performance thus, by virtue of extending the narrative space, uses language and translation as a means to reverse the symbolic, hegemonic order. In the following section we discuss another performance with respect to disability and translation.

'Bhagavad Gita on Wheels'

Conceptualised by a not-for-profit organisation focused on healing, training and rejuvenating the physically disabled, Ability Unlimited (hereafter AU) primarily engages in providing healing and therapy to children and adults with disabilities both physical and mental. The founder Syed Sallauddin Pasha,[5] a Bharatnatyam dancer and choreographer, calls this form of dance and theatre 'therapeutic theatre' for the disabled. Their performances are often characterised by spinning wheelchairs and swift movements of performers with limb or hearing impairments. On a basic level then, their performance can be considered a step towards disability cultural activism in India.

'Bhagavad Gita on Wheels' has about ten to fifteen actors/dancers, both male and female. The male actors here have disabled limbs and are either using crutches or wheelchairs. The female dancers have a hearing disability and are seen dancing along with the actors on wheelchairs. Selected *slokas* from the *Gita* are set to music that forms the background (which may be a live orchestra in many performances) to depict the scenario of events that take place on the Kurukshetra battlefield. Arjuna's wheelchair symbolises his *ratha* (chariot), and Krishna is on crutches. His crutches depict sometimes the *sudarshanchakra* or the war weaponry of bow and arrow or even sometimes extension to his arms to depict the height of his stature as Krishna. The fellow dancers, too, represent charioteers, their wheelchairs depicting *rathas*. Fast and frenzied movements by all the actors suggest different scenes from the *Mahabharata* battlefield.

The performance, through the admixture of disability, creates not only a new alternative aesthetics of disability but also a counter-aesthetic of ability. Moreover, the performance itself offers a discourse on normalcy in opposition to disability. This is discussed in the following sections.

Wheelchairs as 'chariots of war'[6]

Pasha devised his education programme after studying the sensory responses of people with special needs to movement and music. His initiative involves not only teaching the students in dance gestures or *mudra* from Bharatnatyam but also training them to use the wheelchair for swift movements and spins. One of the students, Gulshan Kumar,[7] the actor playing Krishna in the chosen performance, recalls how his teacher would teach them how to spin the wheelchair, sometimes tying his own feet together so as to get the demonstration right. Kumar is now a world-record holder for the maximum number of spins on the wheelchair, beating the earlier record by almost double the number of spins (Sawhney 2011).

The wheelchair therefore in the AU performances loses its connotations associated with a physical handicap. It not only gets an aesthetic purpose but also plays around with the normative assumptions about power dynamics and control. In fact, the wheelchair is used with a gymnast like swiftness where the performers are seen defying gravity with an acrobatic swiftness.

Therefore, its use and representation as a chariot in war dismantle the viewer's perception of a wheelchair as a remedial vehicle for constricted and slow movement. Here, on the other hand, the wheelchair becomes a metaphor of combat. A similar language of combat is often used to describe wheelchair sports as well. The 2005 American documentary film *Murderball* centres on athletes who play wheelchair rugby, leading up to the 2004 Paralympic Games in Athens. In the opening scenes, one of the Pit Crew members of the US team describes the making of the rugby wheelchairs as '[w]hat we do is we take these wheelchairs and turn them into a gladiator, a battling machine, a *Mad Max* wheelchair that can stand knocking the living daylights out of each other' (Shapiro, *Murderball*). Indeed, this description stands true for AU's unique deployment of the wheelchair on stage; Pasha suggests that in his shows, 'the wheelchair has a life of its own. We treat it like another member of the group' (Sai 2015; Figures 3.2 and 3.3).

The same thing holds true for the crutches as well. As Krishna, the crutches are his *sudarshanchakra*; as Vishnu, they are his bow and arrow, and as Parshuram, they are his axe. The crutches therefore are represented not only as symbols of empowerment but also as weapons of destruction. The climactic moment in the dance performance is when Krishna demonstrates his *Vishvarupa* (Figure 3.5). The crutches here become the signifiers of his extended limbs as he points to Arjuna demonstrating the expanse of his omnipotent divinity urging him to fight.

FIGURE 3.2 Wheelchairs being put to an innovative aesthetic use in 'Bharatnatyam on Wheels'.

Photo courtesy Syed Sallauddin Pasha.

FIGURE 3.3   A scene from 'Bharatnatyam on Wheels', wheelchairs hanging from the top.
Photo courtesy Syed Sallauddin Pasha.

Thus, all the dancers on stage not only ask series of questions on the stereotypical conception of passive disabled bodies; here, on the other hand, the muscularity of the wheelchair-bound actors is a prominent feature as well. Besides, the performance also seeks to break out from a conventional articulation of a dancing body. While semiotics of such a performance cannot in the least be overlooked, the text in consideration also plays a very significant part. This is looked into in the following parts of the chapter.

Form and content

In the Indian system of knowledge, there could be alternative ways of conceiving form and content relationship, especially with the theatre, music and dance, which may be in the form of scriptocentric, phonocentric and bodycentric cultural discourses. These pluralistic epistemologies in the form of tellings and renderings enable people of various categories to preserve and have rights over their cultural knowledge systems (Satyanath 2009: 55).

In the performance we see a mutual relationship between various forms of arts. While there is a recitation of the *Bhagavad Gita* in the background, the mimetic representations have a combination of dance wherein the actors represent the *Dashavatar* from the *Vishnu Purana*. The dancers are trained in Bharatnatyam *mudras*, and the instrumental music in the background is a complete orchestra with Indian, as well as Western, instruments.

Keeping the previous discussion in mind, the performance the 'Bhagavad Gita on Wheels' thus becomes an apt example to understand the aforesaid overlap of media, as well as narratives and imagery with each other, suggesting again that the meaning of the representations are assumed to be known to the audience. The conflation of the verses of the *Bhagavad Gita* with the iconography of the *Dashavatar* therefore doesn't surprise the audience. This means that two different narratives with temporally different origins have been conflated with Krishna/Vishnu as the only referral point.

Text and performance

While the *Bhagavad Gita* has been variously translated and represented, its interpretation varies with the contexts. Here, the verses that are selected for the recitation in the background also make a difference to the scope of the presentation. As mentioned earlier, the language of combat is a significant feature of the performance. The very first *shloka* itself establishes the dynamics of the Kurukshetra battlefield:

> *Dhritaraashtra Uvaacha:*
> *Dharmakshetre kurukshetre samavetaa yuyutsavah;*
> *Maamakaah paandavaashchaiva kimakurvata sanjaya.*
> (1.1)

'In the field of righteousness, the field of the Kurus, when my people and the sons of Pandu had gathered together eager for the battle, what did they do O Sanjaya?[8]' In the span of the next 5 minutes, Arjuna's dilemma (shloka 1.32) and Krishna's motivation to engage in the battle (shloka 2.38, 2.47) are enacted by the two key dancers after which Krishna goes on to recite,

> *yada yada hi dharmasya glanir bhavati bharata*
> *abhyutthanam adharmasya tadatmanam srjamy aham*
> (4.7)

'Whenever there is a decline in religiousness and the rise of unrighteousness O Bharata, then I descend forth myself'. Here, the dancers get together to represent the image of Vishnu, with Krishna/Vishnu at the centre and the fellow dancers representing the seven heads of the *Shesha naga* (Figure 3.4).

FIGURE 3.4   Representation of Vishnu in the centre and the seven heads of the *Shesha Naga* around him.

Photo courtesy Syed Sallauddin Pasha.

Unlike the other *shlokas* which use the language of combat, the climactic moment in the presentation take up the *shlokas* 10 and 11 of Chapter 11, Vishvarupa Darshanam:

> *aneka-vaktra-nayanam anekadbhuta-darsanam*
> *aneka-divyabharanam divyanekodyatayudham*
> (11.10)

> *divya-malyambara-dharam divya-gandhanulepanam*
> *sarvascarya-mayamdevam anantamvisvato-mukham*
> (11.11)

'Of many mouths and eyes, of many visions of marvel, of many divine marvels, of many divine uplifted weapons, wearing divine garments and raiments with divine perfumes and ointments, made up of all wonders, resplendent, boundless, with face turned everywhere'.

These interestingly present an antithesis to disability and conceptualisation of disabled bodies. The idea of an aesthetically pleasing 'whole-bodiedness' is undercut by a Krishna's all powerful sublime body with 'many mouths' and 'many eyes'. This is further problematised by Krishna's own use of crutches in both his hands and the many wheelchairs surrounding him (Figure 3.5).

This form with all his magnificence and limitlessness is here depicted with the iconographic representations of all ten incarnations of Vishnu: Matsya, Kurma, Varaha, Narasimha, Vamana, Rama, Krishna, Buddha and Kalki, few of which are shown in the Figures 3.6 and 3.7.

These representative images of the *Dashavatar* finally conflate with the *Vishvarupa* (Figure 3.5) which is the last and final representative image. This is denoted

FIGURE 3.5 Krishna's *Vishvarupa*.

Photo courtesy Syed Sallauddin Pasha.

FIGURE 3.6   Narasimha.

Photo courtesy Syed Sallauddin Pasha.

FIGURE 3.7   Ramavtar.

Photo courtesy Syed Sallauddin Pasha.

with Krishna in the centre, crutches held high in his arms in a gesture denoting his limitlessness. Arjuna is finally shown as going into the battlefield, taking his bow and arrow.

The use of crutches, the wheelchair and the subversive dance aesthetics put together an unparalleled depiction of disability arts, which not only is innovative but also deeply shakes audience perspective of the conventional roles assigned to them. The wheelchair therefore can be looked at simply as a vehicle of movement, irrespective of who it is being used by – the whole-bodied, the 'normal' or the 'disabled'. The 'normal' as a configuration itself can thus be questioned. One of the interviewers describes his meeting with the founder and dancers of AU, wherein he was offered a wheelchair to sit on, after sometime 'the initial discomfort and awkwardness evaporated' (Sai 2015)

Conclusion

Stage performances like cinema adaptations create opportunities to translate, renarrate and readdress traditional texts apart from offering new perspectives and counter-hegemonic interpretations of the given texts and narratives. The chapter tried to demonstrate that a new aesthetics of disability could be subsumed to counter the ableist representations of disability in popular narratives. Alternative models of cultural production, such as the examples demonstrated in the chapter, offer ways of looking afresh at the supposedly 'disabling' aspects in narratives and representations of the differently abled.

Concerning the spectacle of the performance by AU, the ongoing debate centres on the language of combat and the 'shock value' associated with performances like this. Amit Kama, in 'Supercrips versus the Pitiful Handicapped: Reception of Disabling Images by Disabled Audience Members', studies the stereotyping processes inherent in the media portrayals of disabled characters. He says that the popular media coverage mostly focuses on capturing 'glorified supercrip', who 'embodies the popular image of disability as "something" that one must successfully overcome, rather than learn to adjust to' (Kama 2004: 3). One might agree with Kama to some extent as the performance does capitalise on the shock value over the audiences. Of late, many of the AU performances have been aired by many reality television programmes, capturing simultaneously the audiences' (often celebrity) shocked reactions.

Yet one would also agree that such performances are also pioneering steps towards an innovative way of disability cultural activism in India. More important, they shake the ableist perceptions associated with classical Indian dance forms. The Natyashastra itself, as Pasha says prescribes an aesthetically pleasing, whole body which the AU Bharatnatyam performances undermine: 'The Natya Shastra dictates that a dancer's body has to be perfect. My dancers don't fit that category. Yet they do all the *adavus* (dance sequences) and *mudras* (hand gestures) as prescribed by the text perfectly' (Sai 2015).

Another significant aspect of the performance is that while disability cultural activism and disability arts are more familiar to the West, such performances are first of their kind in India, wherein generally speaking, disability apart from being a medical and social disadvantage is also a development issue. As Nilika Mehrotra (2012) very clearly points out, that the majority of the disabled in India have to negotiate not only with social discrimination but also with nearly inaccessible education and employment opportunities.[9] Sensitisation and awareness of the disability community is therefore a much-needed effort in the disability rights movement. Pasha calls their work as a *parivartansabha*, 'something which is aimed at changing the viewpoint of audience who enter the auditorium expecting a slow performance but leave the auditorium with a different picture of disability in their mind'. One of the performers, Ashiq Usman,[10] goes on to say that the AU performances are 'not merely for entertainment'; the higher goal which is intended through their dances is to bring a change in perceptions about disability so that people become aware, *jagruk*, about issues surrounding disability. Hailing from a Muslim background in Uttar Pradesh, Usman recounts that despite his community being against dancing and his family forbidding him to be a dancer with AU, he nevertheless made the choice to do so. Having left his home 15 years ago, he continues to live separately from his family, finding a new livelihood in dance.

AU as an organisation thus provides an identification to the disabled community itself. As disability activist Paddy Masefield suggests, 'disability culture gives disabled people a chance to collectively validate the shared specificities of their lives as disabled people, and to find ways of representing these lives faithfully' (qtd. in Conroy 2009: 10). The disability dance of AU can be thus seen as a political intervention on behalf of the disabled community to be a public community. The performance thereby creates not only a new alternative aesthetics of disability but also a counter-aesthetic of ability.

A reconceptualisation of aesthetics of disability and alternative methodologies of production and representation could thus be a possible move towards a change in the conventional outlook about 'disabled' bodies. Disability arts and theatre have the potential to shift the paradigms of reception and production, politics and aesthetics of articulation and representation.

Stage performances in the form of theatre or dance as demonstrated in the previously mentioned instances could make opportunities for creating new cultural encounters. By intervening in the process of narration and renarration, such performances not only re-create the original text but also construct alternative cultural realities. Whilst being autonomous works in their own right they nevertheless are inter-semiotic translations that seek to subvert the traditional interpretations of given texts. Since the act of translation is in itself not neutral as it invests in the power relations of the people, such subversive renditions become important grounds for initiating a dialogue towards positive changes.

Notes

1 V. S. Sukthankar in the Prolegomena of the first volume of the critical edition of the *Mahabharata* suggests that the need for having a critical edition of the epic was mostly felt by Western Orientalists and with some initial persuasion was also taken up by the Indian Sanskritists. He highlights the difficulty in conceiving the whole task, saying that it was impossible to conceive a text that would simultaneously satisfy both *aryavartya* and *dakshinatya* versions.

It also goes without saying that the entire project composed of collation of written narratives. Oral narratives which are equally rich and debatably even older were not dealt with in the project.

2 Dusi (2015) offers the term *transposition* to the intersemiotic translation of a text as 'the process of translation may be only partial, or may shift to a particular textual level when areas of untranslatability are encountered, that is to say, levels of texts which represent a challenge for the target language and may therefore also be a potential source of renewal' (Dusi 2015: 184).

3 Lawrence Venuti in *The Translator's Invisibility: A History of Translation* describes "Domestication" as 'where translation serves an appropriation of foreign cultures for agendas in the receiving situation, cultural, economic, political' (Venuti 1995: 14).

4 Founded in 1998, Katkatha Puppet Arts trust is a travelling puppet theatre company which has worked with various forms of indigenous puppet theatre. In the past, Katkatha has also travelled to conflict zones, villages and urban slums in order to connect with people from different walks of life. They have trained community health workers, village schoolteachers and youth leaders to use puppets to talk about taboo issues in India like reproductive health and sexuality, the stigma around HIV/AIDS, gender discrimination and violence, among other topics.

I thank Anurupa Roy, the founder of Katkatha and the director of the chosen perfor-mance, for all the vital information she provided about Katkatha and its performances.

5 I sincerely thank Syed Sallauddin Pasha for all the inputs he gave for the chapter. Pasha is the recipient of the national award for outstanding performances in the field of empow-erment of persons with disabilities. His work in the area of disability has won both national and international recognition.

6 Cynthia Barounis in "Cripping Heterosexuality, Queering Able-Bodiedness: *Murderball, Brokeback Mountain* and the Contested Masculine Body" describes an interviewee using this term for a wheelchair.

7 Kumar suffered from polio as an infant as a result of which he has an impaired leg. The son of a washer-man, Kumar became a student of Sallauddin Pasha in his teens who taught him dance.

8 Translations of the verses here are taken from S Radhakrishnan's translation, *The Bhaga-vadgita*, 1948.

9 Pasha also attests that a majority of his own performers come from a weak financial background; the lack of a medical facility is a constraint most have had to face.

10 I thank Ashiq Usman for all the inputs he gave for the chapter.

Bibliography

abilityunlimited. 2016. 'Bhagawad Gita on Wheels', *YouTube*, 7 February. www.youtube.com/watch?v=ghRLG8yA8Ng (accessed on 9 September 2017).

Alvarez, Román and M. Carmen-África Vidal. 1996. 'Translating: A Political Act', in Román Alvarez and M. Carmen-África Vidal (eds) *Translation, Power, Subversion*, pp. 1–9. Clevedon: Multilingual Matters.

Arlene. 2013. 'An Incredible Indian Story: I Have Polio, Watch Me Dance', *Firstpost*, 19 July. www.firstpost.com/living/an-incredible-indian-story-i-have-polio-watch-me-dance 969327.html (accessed on 9 September 2017).

Bajaj, Tanvi and Swasti Shrimali Vohra. 2013. *Performing Arts and Therapeutic Implications*. New Delhi: Routledge.

Baker, Mona. 2013. 'Translation as an Alternative Space for Political Action', *Social Movement Studies*, 12(1): 23–47.

Barounis, Cynthia. 2009. 'Cripping Heterosexuality, Queering Able-Bodiedness: Murderball, Brokeback Mountain and the Contested Masculine Body', *Journal of Visual Culture*, 8(1): 54–75.

Chakrabarty, Sreeparna. 2013. 'Disabled Grow up to Be Achievers, Thanks to "Ability Unlimited Foundation"', *Weekend Leader*, 7 June.

Conroy, Colette. 2009. 'Disability: Creative Tensions Between Drama, Theatre and Disability Arts', *Research in Drama Education: The Journal of Applied Theatre and Performance*, 14(1): 1–14.

Corker, Mairian and Tom Shakespeare. 2002. *Disability/Postmodernity: Embodying Disability Theory*. London: Continuum.

Davis, Lennard J. 1995. *Enforcing Normalcy: Disability, Deafness, and the Body*. London: Verso.

———. 1997. *The Disability Studies Reader*. New York, NY: Routledge.

Dusi, Nicola. 2015. 'Intersemiotic Translation: Theories, Problems, Analysis', *Semiotica*, 206: 181–205.

Hermans, Theo. 1996. 'Norms and the Determination of Translation: A Theoretical Framework', in Roman Alvarez and M. Carmen Africa Vidal (eds) *Translation, Power, Subversion*, pp. 25–51. Clevedon: Multilingual Matters.

Hockenberry, John. 1995. *Moving Violations: War Zones, Wheelchairs, and Declarations of Independence*. New York, NY: Hyperion.

Jakobson, Roman. 1959. 'On Linguistic Aspects of Translation', in Reuben A. Brower (ed) *On Translation*, pp. 231–239. Boston: Harvard University Press.

Kama, Amit. 2004. 'Supercrips Versus the Pitiful Handicapped: Reception of Disabling Images by Disabled Audience Members', *Communications*, 29(4): 447–466.

Khilani, Shresht. 2016. 'Katkatha Mahabharata'. https://shreshthkhilani.github.io/Kat kathaMahabharata/articles/about/ (accessed on 9 September 2017).

Lindemann, Kurt and James Cherney. 2008. 'Communicating in and Through "Murderball": Masculinity and Disability in Wheelchair Rugby', *Western Journal of Communication*, 72(2): 107–125.

Mallik, Basanta Kumar. 2011. 'Cultural and Social Radicalism in Medieval Orissa', *Economic and Political Weekly*, 46(17): 52–59.

Mehrotra, Nilika. 2012. 'Methodological Issues in Disability Research: An Introduction', *Indian Anthropologist*, 42(1): 1–10.

Melucci, Alberto. 2003. *Challenging Codes: Collective Action in the Information Age*. Cambridge: Cambridge University Press.

Mohanty, Prafulla Kumar. 2005. 'The "Mahabharata": A Reading in Political Structuring', *Indian Literature*, 49(1): 146–151.

Murderball. 2005. Dir. Henry Alex Rubin and Dana Adam Shapiro. MTV Films, Paramount Pictures, Film.

Nathan, Archna. 2016. 'They Are Awake Even While on Strings', *The Hindu* [Bengaluru], 16 August. https://www.thehindu.com/features/friday-review/They-are-awake-even while-on-strings/article14576168.ece (accessed on 19 May 2019).

Prasad, R. C., ed. 1990. *Tulasidasa's Shriramacharitamanasa: The Holy Lake of the Acts of Rama*. Delhi: Motilal Banarsidass Publishers.

Radhakrishnan, S., ed. 1974. *The Bhagavadgita*. Bombay: Blackie and Son.

Ramnath, Ambili. 2013. 'Wheelchairs on Wings', *The Hindu*, 23 January. Reiffenrath, Tanja. 2016. *Memoirs of Well-Being Rewriting Discourses of Illness and Disability*. Bielefeld: Transcript.

Sai, Veejay. 2015. 'Bharatanatyam on Wheels: A Classical Dancer Breaks New Ground', *Scroll.in*, 1 August. https://scroll.in/article/740499/bharatanatyam-on-wheels-a-classical dancer-breaks-new-ground (accessed on 9 September 2017).

Sangari, Kumkum. 1993. 'Consent, Agency and Rhetorics of Incitement', *Economic and Political Weekly*, 28(18): 867–882.

Satyanath, T. S. 2009. 'Tellings and Renderings in Medieval Karnataka', in Judy Wakabayashi and Rita Kothari (eds) *Decentering Translation Studies: India and Beyond*, pp. 43–56. Amsterdam: John Benjamins Publishing Co.

Sawhney, Gunjan. 2011. 'Spin It Right', *The Hindu*, 18 May. https://www.thehindu.com/ news/cities/Delhi/spin-it-right/article2029337.ece (accessed on 19 May 2019).

Shah, Tanvi. 2016. 'Dying Art Forms, Static Traditions and Religious Mumbo-Jumbo: Puppeteer Anurupa Roy on Our General Ignorance', *Junoontheatre.wordpress.com*. https:// junoontheatre.wordpress.com/2016/09/21/dying-art-forms-static-traditions-and religious-mumbo-jumbo-puppeteer-anurupa-roy-on-our-general-ignorance (accessed on 9 September 2017).

Stathi, Irini. 2015. 'Inter-semiotic Translation and Transfer Theory in Cinematic/Audiovisual Adaptations of Greek Drama', in Peter Pericles Trifonas (ed) *International Handbook of Semiotics*, pp. 321–338. Dordrecht: Springer.

Sukthankar, Vishnu S. 1933. 'Prolegomena', in Vishnu S. Sukhtankar (ed) *The Mahabharata*, Vol. I, pp. I–CX. Poona: Bhandarkar Oriental Research Institute.

Tollestrup, Benjamin Neal. 2009. 'Challenging Normalcy? Masculinity and Disability in Murderball', Unpublished MA dissertation, Queen's University Kingston, Canada.

Venkat, Lalitha. 2012. 'Dancers with Unlimited Abilities', *Narthaki.com*. www.narthaki.com/info/rev12/rev1173.html (accessed on 10 September 2017).

Venuti, Lawrence. 1995. *The Translator's Invisibility-a History of Translation*. Abingdon: Routledge.

4

DISABLING NORMALCY IN 'THAKARA'

A comparative reading of P. Padmarajan's short story and its film adaptation

Sanju Thomas

Introduction

Translation Studies and Disability Studies share a similar trajectory in many ways. While the concept of disability presupposes ability, the act of translation too primarily assumes the existence of an 'original'. Negotiating differences and finding a meaningful space of existence in relation to a 'superior other' have been ontological orientations in both disciplines. While Translation Studies confronts the hegemony of language and culture, Disability Studies primarily challenges the hierarchical categorisation based on difference and strives towards an equal inclusive world. Both disciplines have moved towards what can be considered an attempt to resist discrimination and homogenisation and exclusion of the margins, facilitating a more nuanced understanding of the world we inhabit. Both Translation Studies and Disability Studies have a very strong interdisciplinary nature and can present interesting perspectives to allied disciplines. In such a context, it is also worthwhile to ponder over how both these disciplines can interact and empower each other.

From the meaning of the very term *disability* to the different approaches to disability to the various kinds of disabilities and their physical, psychological and social impact, Disability Studies as an academic discipline has a lot to offer. Scholars like Tom Shakespeare have stressed the need to have ethnographic studies (Shakespeare 2014);one way to add to this interdisciplinary area is also through a study of literary representations of disability. Translation helps access these representations in other languages, which is essential for the understanding of the various approaches that exist in different cultures towards disability. Translation, as often mentioned, is not just a linguistic activity. It has been observed that

> there is always a context in which the translation takes place, always a history from which a text emerges and into which a text is transposed. Translation

involves so much more than the simple engagement of an individual with aprinted page and a bilingual dictionary.

(Lefevere and Bassnett 1990: 11)

Which text gets translated is as important a question as to how and when a text gets translated. The texts that do not get translated have their own tales of exclusion to narrate.

Malayalam literature has been vibrant and open to literature from other parts of the world. Even in contemporary times, Malayalam literature is probably one amongst the most translated literatures in India. Short fiction has always enjoyed a prime position as a genre in Malayalam literature and offers a wide variety of themes and craftsmanship that can undoubtedly be compared to the best in world literature. From its early beginnings in the late 19th century through its development to modern form in the 1930s to the experimental contemporary times, Malayalam short story has explored the changing hues and contexts of the immediate society and the world. Therefore, it is intriguing to discover that there are not many short stories that talk about disability and even fewer ones that are translated. While Malayalam filmmakers have dealt with physical and mental disability, from *Iruttinte Aatmavu* (1966) to *Su SuSudhi Vathmeekam* (2015), short story writers have not been too readily representing disability in their works. The short stories that represent disability have been made into films, and invariably, the movies have become more popular than the stories themselves. The story 'Thakara' (1978) is one such example. This chapter, through a close reading of the story, tries to locate the text within the disability discourse and to understand the categorisation and stigma associated mainly with intellectual disability. Moreover, the chapter also compares the short story to the film adaptation that interestingly seems to offer a different reading and explores how it informed my own understanding of the story as a translator.

Stereotyping disability

The story 'Thakara' is narrated by a young man who, when he was a school-going boy, used to be close to Thakara, an intellectually disabled person and an orphan. He and another senior friend, Chellappanasari, get Thakara initiated into sex through titillating stories and later encourage him into a love affair with Subhashini, the heartthrob of the village. However, Subhashini is the daughter of the local ruffian, Mathu Mooppan, who is the custodian of the one and only stud bull in the village. He used to thrash anyone who tried to be close to his daughter. Subhashini herself is no meek village maiden, but she seems to have a soft spot for Thakara. However, when Mathu Mooppan gets wind of the goings on, he assaults Thakara. He is rescued, and days later he comes back with a knife to stab Mathu Mooppan. He believes that Subhashini is now free to go with him, but she refuses his proposal and tells him not to see her again. Heartbroken, Thakara hangs himself.

Even though the story revolves around Thakara, he is perceived through the eyes of the narrator. He recalls that when he was an infant, he used to have nightmares about Thakara. The first emotion that the narrator feels towards Thakara is 'fear'. This is very much in keeping with what Bill Hughes has pointed out as 'a fear for the precariousness of one's own being and the vulnerabilities of our ephemeral flesh.' He elaborates:

> The misrecognition and disrespect – not to mention segregation and oppression – that disabled people suffer at the hands of their non-disabled counterparts is a form of violence bred from our fear of and anguish about our alienation from the human condition where being human is simultaneously a facet of self and other. The feeling of anguish with respect to others is indivisible from the feeling of disgust for oneself but in an ableist culture these feelings become separated. The body beautiful creates its eugenic opposite and proceeds to tyrannize the forms of physical and mental difference that are products of its own existential insecurity.
>
> (Hughes 2006: 69)

As the narrator grows, his idea of 'normalcy' and self are reinforced by his education and interaction with other children. Thakara is marked as one who is not like the rest of them, and so there is pity reserved for him. Pity is considered a hierarchical emotion that underlines inequality. What marks Thakara as completely different from others is his lack of discriminatory power. He does not understand more than what is stated. The narrator, too, is enthralled by Chellappanasari's erotic stories. All the stories were supposed to be Chellappanasari's experiences with different women in the village. While the narrator has the intellectual ability to discriminate between reality and fiction, Thakara does not have that competence. He also tends to trust people completely. He fails to understand that Chellappanasari does not intend to give his blue ear studs to him and that it is not proper for him to repeatedly make that demand. Thakara also cannot be trusted with anything valuable because he might just pass them on to anyone who would ask him with love. Since he does not understand the devious ways of an adult's world, Thakara is considered to be just an overgrown boy. He drools constantly which creates disgust in onlookers. Still, the narrator claims that Thakara was 'loved as a large doll' and that 'he too wanted only that' (Padmarajan 2010: 102). Interestingly, the society seems to be deciding the extent of Thakara's desires. Thakara's age is not mentioned, but he is surely infantilised by the society, which, according to Chrissie Rogers, is a way of 'disabling and dehumanising' (2016: 113). But by treating him as a doll, the villagers believe that they are being sympathetic towards him. Dolls are lifeless, harmless things that can be petted and cast away at will. Dolls are not expected to have a mind, to have feelings, to talk back, resist, and rebel. Since he is intellectually challenged, it is also taken for granted that he would not have emotions and desires of a 'normal' human being.

Thakara not being Thakara

It is this superiority that makes the narrator feel amused, then disgusted and later angry towards Thakara when he behaves in a way that is not expected of him. The very first instance of this unexpected behaviour is noticed when Thakara responds to erotic stories, making the narrator wonder if he might have some idea or he might want to have some idea about man–woman relationships. Chellappanasari sees Thakara as a 'guinea pig' (Padmarajan 2010:105); it is the curiosity about how he will respond to sex in contrast to 'normal' human beings that rules his actions. He believes that Thakara cannot have sexual intercourse since his muscles do not have the energy to be a 'real man'. He selects Subhashini for Thakara because she is one who does not get seduced by normal young men. Moreover, there is added drama in the form of Mathu Mooppan, her rowdy father. But the narrator and his friend are aghast when Subhashini responds to Thakara. Whatever was earlier thought of as disadvantages now become his privileges. Thakara slowly drifts away from his friends and tries to be a responsible lover to Subhashini. This is, again, not something that is expected of Thakara. It is utter jealousy and disgust at one's own self that prompt Chellappanasari to reveal about the affair to Mathu Mooppan. Thakara does not understand this subtle betrayal. He only understands that Mathu Mooppan is against his relationship with Subhashini and that Mathu Mooppan has to be killed for him to marry her.

Subhashini, too, does not expect Thakara to propose to her. Through professing his love for her and by displaying a staunch determination to marry her, Thakara proves that he is not just a doll. He can think, he has emotions and he can be consistent with these emotions. The ability to love is one of the greatest qualities of the human mind. But Thakara's love frightens Subhashini. Would it have made Thakara realise that he does not belong with the rest of the society? His suicide comes in the wake of his sense of betrayal and his sense of failure to fit into 'normal' society. He rejects life, thus rejecting the 'superior normal world' itself.

Thakara, the Malayalam name for the plant Cassia Tora, is a common weed that is seen everywhere in Kerala during the monsoons. It is a nuisance for regular cultivation of crops and is not considered to be of any use normally. It also does not require much nourishment and grows wild by itself. The lack of a proper name itself is an important trope in the story. It is symbolic of the lack of recognition disabled people suffer in society. His emotions are either too trivialised or magnified, ridiculed and trampled on. In fact, there is no discussion about who gave this name to him or how could a human being be called 'thakara'. There are direct references about his weed-like existence when the narrator says in the beginning that 'Thakara had sprouted in the market' (Padmarajan 2010: 102) by the time he was born. Later in the context of the drought that had hit the sesame fields of the village that now is filled with weeds, Chellappanasari comments ruefully that 'even nature is on the side of Thakara' (Padmarajan 210: 110). Thakara's existence is unwanted and even cumbersome for other, more 'useful' crops. Disability in this sense could be understood as a 'contagious disease' which might affect the 'normalcy' of society pulling it back from the race to perfection (Davis 2013: 19).

Language, technique and translation

The story setting in a central Kerala village, as is evident from the dialect, is narrated in simple Malayalam and in short sentences. Readers are told right in the beginning that Thakara had committed suicide. But the events that lead up to it, including the narrator's part, come as a surprise. Still, the story lacks sentimentality as it is told from the point of view of a 'friend' who nevertheless remains detached. Still, he is the first one to realise that Thakara is not being Thakara. He is also one who knew about Thakara's desire to commit suicide. So there is a kind of ambiguity about his relationship with Thakara that he himself seems to acknowledge. To begin with, there is a hierarchy among the three boys because of their caste positioning in society. The narrator is called Pilley, koche and so on since he is a high-caste Nair. Even when Chellappanasari is senior to him by two or three years, the narrator calls him by name as he is below him in the caste hierarchy. Thakara does not obviously have any such social markers, because he is outside the realm of this social grouping. Thakara does not seem to have any other identity and is 'defined by his impairment'. The story also does not mention what kind of intellectual disability Thakara has. He has been referred to as *budhiurakkatha,* which may be translated as 'mentally retarded'. The term *retarded* suits the perception of Thakara as a 'boy'. It is interesting that Thakara is only dressed like a boy, but he does not have a deformed or stunted body. He also refers to himself as Thakara, the way children many times do, that is again a way of infantilising him. But he talks in complete sentences and comprehensible Malayalam. He is also self-reliant and economically productive. So his extent of disability is not really disabling, even though he is qualified as a fool, stupid and idiot in conversation among friends. The narrator, in fact, embodies the insensitive attitude of the society: he still remembers Thakara, but even when he narrates the story years later, revealing his own role in the events that led to the catastrophe, he does not offer a re-evaluation of the situation. His death evokes fear and pity but not indignation in the narrator. The last line of the story reads as follows: 'We were able to only glance at the many footprints on the sand below and walk away terrified' (Padmarajan 2010: 120). The word *able* highlights, rather ironically, the failure of the ableist society in bringing justice to the ones who are disabled by their own insensitivity and exclusion.

Adaptation and Malayalam cinema

The story 'Thakara' was made into a successful movie in 1979 by Bharathan. Malayalam cinema has a long history of drawing inspiration from literature. In the 1950s and the 1960s, novels of Thakazhi, Kesavadev and M.T. Vasudevan Nair brought in their concerns of caste and class inequalities to the big screen. The 1970s saw a new wave in Malayalam cinema with the entry of trained film professionals from institutions like Film Finance Corporation, the Film and Television Institute of India and the National Film Archives. 'The new wave brought a new sensibility and self-consciousness to form and treatment. Apart from "what", "how" to tell also became crucial. If "commitment" and "social change" were the buzzwords of the earlier generation, the new word was "self expression"' (Venkiteswaran 2012). In the 1980s, with the rise of middle cinema, the focus shifted to the individual and the more complex interpersonal relations. P. Padmarajan and Bharathan belong to this era and played a major role in connecting the 'art' cinema with the mainstream popular cinema. Many of Padmarajan's stories have been adapted into movies by Bharathan and later by Padmarajan himself.

Recently there has been an attempt to draw adaptation studies away from translation studies, still, many scholars would agree that there are more points of convergence than differences. According to Roman Jakobson, translation may also involve 'transmutation or interpretation of verbal signs by means of signs of non-verbal sign systems' (1959: 261). Thus, a movie adaptation becomes an inter-semiotic translation. From Roland Barthes, who argued '[a]ny text is a new tissue of past citations' (1981: 39), to Julia Kristeva, who looks at a text as 'constructed of a mosaic of quotations; any text is the absorption and transformation of another' (1986: 66), many critics have argued that the word or text is not sacrosanct. This especially holds true in a multilayered complex process such as inter-semiotic translation. While every text is one that already existed, every reader is also a translator and an author. Dudley Andrew suggests that there are mechanical aspects of fiction generally elaborated in any film script such as the characters and their inter-relation; the geographical, sociological and cultural information providing the fiction's context; and the basic narrational aspects that determine the point of view of the narrator. However, he points out, that it is 'intangible aspects such as is fidelity to the spirit, to the original's tone, values, imagery, and rhythm' that would pose a serious challenge to the filmmaker (Krebs 2014: 26). How a director responds to these depends on how he reads and interprets and later translates it in a different medium. Does the movie retain the sensitivity of the text in problematising the concept of disability and society's engagement with it?

Changed point of view, changed focus

The film retains the title of the short story, which follows that the film had the intention of keeping the disability angle in mind. But there are certain changes that are made in the film, and one of the major changes is in the point of view. This alteration affects the structure and focus of the film. In the short story, all through the narrative the reader follows the adolescent narrator's perception and therefore becomes an accomplice in the tragedy that befalls Thakara. The first-person *I* becomes every reader and every other person in the society who does not show sensitivity towards the disabled. The author powerfully withholds any glimpse into Thakara's psyche because his focus is on society's view of him which is dubious. At one level, there is pity but only when he exhibits the characteristics of a disabled. This pity often turns to ridicule as it is evident from the way the friends laugh at him and exclude him from their conversation about him by talking in English right in front of him. But the film employs an omniscient point of view. The movie's changed point of view itself dilutes its focus on Thakara's character. There is no attempt to delve deeper into Thakara's mind in the film. There is nothing to suggest what Thakara thinks of his disability and the society's treatment of him. He is portrayed as a simple, pleasant young man in a dirty vest and *lungi*. The opening shots of the movie have Thakara chasing after trains, running after cotton strands and playing with toys made of palm leaves. Thus, it is established that he is child-like but that he is not completely naïve. He can see through Chellappanasari's tricks, he politely refuses when Pillai's mother offers him a cup of morning tea, he gulps down his share of coffee before serving Mathu Mooppan his cup. He is also aware of his misfortune as an orphan. When Subhashini tells him that he is better off than her, he tells her reflectively, 'Subhashini, you have no idea about Thakara's pain.' It is clear that he thinks of himself as an unfortunate orphan and not very much as a marginalised disabled. This is because society's exclusion is toned down to a great extent in the film. In fact, everyone seems to know him and treat him fondly, like a child.

In the film, Thakara largely works as Mathu Mooppan's assistant, and he eats at their place and is a constant companion of Subhashini. She is close to Thakara, and she is concerned about him often admonishing him with affection about trusting others too much. Subhashini seems to relate to him at the level of a sorrowful soul as mentioned in the instance cited earlier. The relationship between Mathu Mooppan and Subhashini is fleshed out in the film. Subhashini's character has a deep attachment to her father. She is as stubborn and spirited as Mathu Mooppan is, and he is unashamedly proud and possessive about her. This explains why she rejects Thakara after he stabs Mathu Mooppan.

Chellappanasari's character is portrayed as an adult in the movie. This is a significant departure from the short story. Chellappanasari has designs on Subhashini. He approaches her and is rebuffed. This becomes a motive for revenge in the film. In the short story, Chellappanasari being an adolescent lends a lot of credibility to the way it is narrated. It depicts Thakara's standing, or the lack of it, in his 'peer group' and highlights the sadistic pleasure of the boys in taunting Thakara and even leading him, even though not deliberately, to his tragic death. The horror of what they have done fills them when they understand that he has committed suicide. But in the film, it becomes the scheming villainy of one person, that too of an adult, and the other friend, who is a school-going adolescent becomes just an onlooker. This takes away a lot of subtlety from the storytelling.

Love story in focus

What gets explicitly displayed in the film is the sexual awakening of Thakara. This is a significant approach because, mostly, disabled people are considered to be asexual or impotent. Chellappanasari believes the same. The story says that both the friends educated Thakara in sex-related matters. They read out titillating stories to him and even demonstrated how to masturbate. In the film, all this is reduced to a few whisperings of Chellappanasari in Thakara's ears. It is only after this that Thakara starts to look at Subhashini differently. But he does not express anything in words. Rather, the camera resorts to the clichéd male gaze to depict the change in Thakara. Significantly, there is a daydreaming sequence of Thakara that features in a song where he fantasises mostly about her physical attractiveness. It is pointed out that people

with mild intellectual disability have normal sex drive while they might have difficulty in appropriately expressing their desires due to reduced cognitive functioning
and a lack of peer experience (Mc Cabe and Cummins1996: 14). Bharathan here
seems to be capturing the spontaneous, basic instincts of human beings which is a
preoccupation in most of his ventures. Subhashini is aware of his attraction to her
but does not stay away from him like she does with others. In fact, she tells Thakara
that another girl had expressed her desire to marry him, which makes Thakara bold
enough to reach out to her, and they end up making love. Subhashini seems to find
Thakara desirable, debunking all existing concepts about disability. When she hears
that there are rumours that Thakara is dead, she goes to Chellappanasari enquiring
after him. A song 'Mouname' lyrically highlights the silence that fills her life and
her despondency as she recalls their moments of love. In the film, the story also
becomes the sad dilemma of a woman caught between her lover and her father.
When Thakara meets Subhashini after he kills Mathu Mooppan, she tells him that
she cannot go with him because he killed her father. The relationship between
Thakara and Subhashini is completely rewritten in the film. In the story, the reader
understands that Subhashini was not really keen on Thakara and that she might
have been using him in understanding and experimenting with her own sexuality.
There is nothing that hints at love. But the film depicts Subhashini falling in love
with Thakara and becoming intimate with him. This would have remained a radical
move if the director had been consistent with his portrayal of Thakara till the end.
But sadly, Thakara's 'madness' is foregrounded in the last scenes of the movie.

Intellectual disability to madness

Thakara recalls how brutally he was beaten up, and he seems to be working it up in
his mind into a frenzy. The story says Thakara stabbed Mathu Mooppan just once.
But the film portrays him stabbing Mathu multiple times in great passion and as a
response to the challenge by Mathu Mooppan. It seems as if the onus of the tragedy
is on Thakara as he could not control his emotions. After Subhashini's refusal, he
suddenly turns towards the crowd with the knife in his hand, and as the crowd scat-
ters away, he races across the field to reach the railway line. Thakara hysterically runs
through the railway tracks and is hit by a train. Even the way he commits suicide
underlines his impulse and madness. In fact, it is not even clear whether it was an
accident or a deliberate act of giving up life.

The story, however, maintains a rather calm, detached and objective commentary even towards the end, echoing the society's attitude towards disabled people. In
fact, Thakara commits suicide because the rejection becomes absolutely complete
with the villagers, too, wanting to turn him over to the police. His sense of exclusion from society and his inability to remain even in the fringes now become totally
impossible. Thakara's visit to Subhashini's house after the stabbing is only reported
later in the story. The reader does not have access to the last moments of Thakara.
He runs away after Subhashini's rejection, and days later, he is found dead. One can
only try to imagine the extreme sense of loneliness he felt during those moments

when he decided to embrace death. Just like the narrator, one can only come away scared because one feels complicit. In the movie, one comes away with a feeling of tragic sense but not necessarily of guilt. The inter-semiotic translation rewrites the story, where Subhashini becomes the victim and Thakara more of a perpetrator of violence and ruin.

Film's appeal and the male gaze

The film received critical acclaim as well as popular approval as one which dared to talk about a bold theme. However, a Google search today would take one to a page on YouTube where, along with *Thakara*, feature scintillating films such as *Layanam* and *Kinnarathumpikal*. Undoubtedly, one of the main reasons for the success of the film was its objectification of the woman's body. Malayalam cinema, though largely considered to be progressive with regard to thought and sophisticated with regard to technique, has always been a male bastion. This is more than evident from the trajectory of the male-oriented movies that have been churned out from the early 1930s. The portrayal of women has been according to the patriarchal norms largely falling into the category of the self-sacrificing mother/sister/wife/lover or the sexually driven seductress who would be predictably punished for her waywardness. Needless to say, most of the movies objectify women for the male characters and for the audience. Laura Mulvey has commented on the scopophilia associated with films. In a gendered world, men are the ones who look and derive sexual pleasure while women are the ones being looked at. The male gaze works in the way male characters look at women characters, urging the audience to take part in a kind of a voyeurism heightened especially by the dim light in the theatre and the eye of the camera involved in the act of filmmaking (Mulvey 1985: 806). In the story, Subhashini is qualified as a 'good girl'. The village used to be thrilled by her seductive youthfulness. The word that is used in Malayalam is *kozhutha*, which literally translates as 'fleshy' or 'plump'. This is the only reference to her body in the story while in the film, the camera lingers on her body clad in a cleavage-revealing tight sari blouse and a lungi that reaches just below her knees. In fact, Subhashini is introduced in the movie while she takes a relaxing bath in the pond. There are many instances when one can distinguish the male gaze: Chellappanasari, the other friend and Thakara himself, at different times, derive sexual pleasure from Subhashini's naked legs and thighs. The changed point of view helps in these multiple male gazes. The posters of the movie figuring a drenched Thakara and Subhashini on the beach would very well substantiate the changed focus of the movie. Thus, it brings one back to the argument 'translation is not an innocent activity' (Lefevere and Bassnett 1990: 11). Linda Costanzo Cahir observes that

> [w]hile literature-based films are often, customarily and understandably, referred to as adaptations, the term 'to adapt' means to alter the structure or function of an entity so that it is better fitted to survive and to multiply in its new environment. To adapt is to move that same entity into a new

environment. In the process of adaptation, the same substantive entity which entered the process exits, even as it undergoes modification – sometimes radical mutation – in its efforts to accommodate itself to its new environment.

(Cahir 2006:14)

In the context of Thakara, it has to be noted that the movie came out immediately after the story. Therefore, temporally the context remains the same. However, Venuti describes that while adapting a text one can recognise formal interpretants and thematic interpretants. While the former deals with structural aspects, such as plot, characters and so on, the latter deals with core values and ideology of a text. Either of these might require a revision or a manipulation to suit the style of a director or the concept of the genre or the morality and ideology of the times (Venuti 2007: 33). One can conclude that the director believed that the audience of the film would not be the same as readers of the story. The story is addressed to a more discerning set of readers while the movie banks on the mass appeal of its visual images. Bharathan and Padmarajan, even while dealing with complex human emotions and relationships, employed techniques of the popular mainstream cinema followed.

P. Padmarajan has been a prolific writer and won his first state Sahitya Akademi award for his novel *Nakshathrangale Kaaval* in 1972. He worked with Bharathan as a scriptwriter before turning a filmmaker himself. Padmarajan's status as an iconic filmmaker seems to have eclipsed his standing as a short story writer and a novelist. Predictably, none of his works has been translated into English, though many of his short stories have been made into films. I had watched the movie before I read the story, and therefore, the story came as a surprise to me. I tried to find any hidden sign that would help me to understand with clarity Subhashini's level of engagement with Thakara. Since I had always remembered it as a love story, I was deeply disappointed at first to find out that the story was more about a lack of love or manipulative love, and the tragedy is solely of Thakara and not of Subhashini. The story offers a very nuanced understanding of the level of society's involvement in labelling someone as abled and disabled. The challenge I felt as a translator was not to let the movie determine my reading of the story. The movie need not be a true copy of the story and 'repetition without replication' (Hutcheon 2006: 7) is what an adaptation aims for, according to Linda Hutcheon. It could be that more focus on a disabled person who drools and runs around in knickers, especially since it is a visual medium, couldn't have been very appealing to the audience of the movie. Instead, a tragic love story with melodious music and ample eroticism is a definite recipe for success. Thus, Thakara's simple delights and extreme loneliness that peep through in the short story get overwritten in the movie by Subhashini's overt 'irrational' love. This love predictably wreaks havoc. Although in the story it is reported that Mathu Mooppan's wound is not serious, in the movie Thakara's rage is enough to kill him. This is very much in keeping with the popular concept of intellectually disabled people as 'abnormal' and 'demoniac.' The 'disability text' when translated into a movie falls into the trap the story has so cleverly avoided. This undeniably is a matter of choice. Translation becomes an ethical, ideological and a political act of resistance only when one stands against the co-optive forces of history and society. Maria Tymoczko elaborates:

> Translators must make choices: they cannot capture all aspects of a source text, and their choices establish a place of enunciation, as well as a context of affiliation. Because of anisomorphisms of language and asymmetries of culture, because meaning is both open and overdetermined, because texts make contradictory demands that cannot all be simultaneously satisfied (say, the demands of complex content and spare form), and because the information load associated with a source text is excessive, among other reasons, translators must set priorities for their translations. They must make choices about what to translate and what to silence. Translation is thus a metonymic process.
>
> (2006: 453)

As much as one would appreciate the creativity behind the retelling of the story in the film adaptation, one also understands that the film's primary intention was to cater to the audience by means of which the radical perception on disability of the story has been muted to a great extent.

Conclusion

The story is a commentary on the perception of society, which is disabling. While Thakara is exploited by many in the village, he is excluded from society. It is this exclusion that is personified in tangible terms by Subhashini. Through his death he proves that he is able to distinguish this exclusion; in other words, he displays a power of discretion that one would expect of a 'normal' person; based on that understanding, he acts. Thakara exhibits self-reflection and agency, two traits of a socially accepted 'normal' human being, but ironically this journey to 'normalcy' must also end in his death. Thus, the story raises powerful questions about the concept of accepted 'normalcy' which stigmatises those who deviate even a little from that notion and thereby, disables them and pushes them to the margins of society forever. In the film, however, this exclusion and exploitation are more or less missing. The film's interest seems to be more on interpersonal relationship, which is the hallmark of all Bharathan movies. However, this comes at the cost of the story's focus on disability. Even the bold move to present desirability in a disabled person is not explored in-depth. Rather, the attempt slips into a voyeuristic voyage bringing centrality to the woman's body. Thus, the film becomes what the story is not. The film seems like a warning to society while the story reads as a critique of the society. Precisely for this reason the story required to be translated. According to me, it is imperative that a translator understands and retains the primary focus of the author especially with regard to a hitherto marginalised subject such as disability. Translation here becomes an enabling act that retrieves the short story from the shadow of its popular adaptation.

References

Barthes, Roland. 1981. 'The Theory of the Text', in Robert Young (ed) *Untying the Text: A Post Structuralist Reader*, pp. 31–47. New York, NY: Routledge.

Bassnett, Susan and Andre Lefevere. 1990. *Translation, History and Culture*. New York, NY: Pinter.

Cahir, Linda Costanzo. 2006. *Literature into Film: Theory and Practical Approaches*. Jefferson, NC: McFarland and Co.

Davis, Lennard J. 2013. *The Disability Studies Reader*. New York, NY: Routledge.

Hughes, Bill. 2006. 'Fear, Pity and Disgust: Emotions and the Non-disabled Imaginary', in Nick Watson, Alan Roulstone and Carol Thomas (eds) *Routledge Handbook of Disability Studies*, pp. 67–77. New York, NY: Routledge.

Hutcheon, Linda. 2006. *A Theory of Adaptation*. New York, NY: Routledge.

Jakobson, Roman. 1959. 'On Linguistic Aspects of Translation', in R. Brower (ed) *On Translation*, pp. 232–239. Cambridge, MA: MIT Press.

Krebs, Katja. 2014. *Translation and Adaptation in Theatre and Film*. New York, NY: Routledge.

Kristeva, Julia. 1986. 'Word, Dialogue and Novel', in Toril Moi (ed) *The Kristeva Reader*, pp. 34–62. New York, NY: Columbia University Press.

Mc Cabe, Marita P. and Robert A. Cummins. 1996. 'The Sexual Knowledge, Experience, Feelings and Needs of People with Mild Intellectual Disability', *Education and Training in Mental Retardation and Developmental Disabilities*, 31(1): 13–21.

Mulvey, Laura. 1985. 'Visual Pleasure and Narrative Cinema', in Gerald Mast and Marshell Cohen (eds) *Film Theory and Criticism*, pp. 803–816. New York, NY: Oxford University Press.

Padmarajan, Padmanabhan. 2010. *Padmarajante Kathakal Sampoornam* [Complete Works of Padmarajan]. Kottayam: DC Books, pp. 101–120.

Rogers, Chrissie. 2016. *Intellectual Disability and Being Human: A Care Ethics Model*. New York, NY: Routledge, pp. 112–135.

Shakespeare, Tom. 2014. *Disability Rights and Wrongs Revisited*. New York, NY: Routledge.

Thakara. 1979. Dir. Bharathan. Jovial Pictures. DVD.

Tymoczko, Maria. 2006. 'Translation: Ethics, Ideology, Action', *The Massachusetts Review*, 47(3): 442–461.

Venkiteswaran, Chittur Subramanian. 2012. 'Local Narratives, National and Global Contexts', *indianseminar.com*. www.india-seminar.com/2012/637/637_c_s_venkiteswaran.htm (accessed on 19 September 2017).

Venuti, Lawrence. 2007. 'Adaptation, Translation, Critique', *Journal of Visual Culture*, 6(1): 25-43.

5

DISABILITY, TRANSLATION AND CURRICULUM

A case study of Rangeya Raghav's 'Goongey'

Shubhra Dubey

> [T]oday we are far from thinking that translating is a simple communicative act.
> —Venuti (2000: 468)

Lawrence Venuti, in his concluding chapter in *The Translation Studies Reader* titled 'Translation, Community and Utopia', contends that translation is more than a means of communication across two cultures. Informed by continental theories of phenomenology and poststructuralism, Venuti observes that translators never communicate in an 'untroubled fashion' (Venuti 2000: 468). Rather, they domesticate the foreign or the unfamiliar through the process of translation to enable community building processes to 'invent for the foreign text new readerships who are aware that their interest in the translation is shared by other readers, foreign and domestic – even when those interests are incommensurable' (*ibid.*: 482). Echoing Benedict Anderson, Venuti states that this function of translation – to negotiate through linguistic and cultural difference translation – fosters its own *imagined* community (482). Venuti suggests that an ethically and politically motivated translator enables a sharing of 'understanding with and of foreign cultures and to collaborate on projects founded on that understanding . . . to revise and develop domestic values and institutions' (469).

The potential of translation, as explored by Venuti, to enable cultural transformation follows from the recognition in the 1980s that translation is inflected by various factors which are socio-economic and cultural in nature. Andre Lefevere, in 'Mother Courage's Cucumbers: Text, System and Refraction in a Theory of Literature' (1982),[1] treats translation along with teaching, criticism, editing and historiography as forms of *rewriting* that aim to carry a work of literature from 'one system to another' and are determined by factors such as patronage, poetics and ideology (244). Introducing the term *refraction* – adapting a work of literature to a different audience, with the intention of influencing the way in which that audience reads the work – Lefevere states that refractions have been an integral part of history. Turning to a systems approach to literature, wherein literature is seen as embedded in a culture or environment and consists of 'texts, as well as people who write, refract, distribute, and read those texts' (235), Lefevere observes that historiography and anthologies are integral to the making and breaking of reputations of writers and works. While his essay explores the potential of translation for canon formation within the domain of the literary, this chapter narrows its focus to explore the role that translation can play in language and literature pedagogy in schools in India.

Modern classrooms in India have begun to distance themselves from punishment-oriented authoritarian teaching practices. Such classrooms are aimed at building vibrant learning communities where each student feels valued and respected. Recent modules for teaching by governmental and non-governmental organisations have focused on fostering the principles of plurality within the classroom to help students grow physically and mentally as well as emotionally. These modules echo a question posed by Clare Barker elsewhere: 'Instead of insisting on a common humanity and a healthy body as a default to difference, what about making *alterity* a position from which to develop an imagined community?' (Barker 2011: 189). This chapter focuses on language and literature curriculum of both Hindi and English to investigate if the present-day curriculum does indeed focus on plurality.

The National Council for Education, Research and Training (NCERT) is tasked with designing books for schools affiliated to Central Board of Secondary Education (CBSE) the national board of education in India. The main CBSE course book on Hindi literature for the students of class eleven *Antra* carries a short story titled 'Goongey' by Rangeya Raghav. 'Goongey' relies on an affective engagement with a disabled (a deaf-mute who has no name in the story) protagonist for maximum impact. This chapter discusses at length the ableist bias that has resulted in the story being taught as a text on disability even as the title and the plot suggest that the story uses the *metaphor* of disability to touch on more abstract social issues of marginalisation and oppression in society. The chapter discusses how the paratexts – the introduction as well as the question/answer sections reiterate the ableist frame of the story. After exploring the damaging impact of such refractions within Hindi curriculum, the chapter then explores how a target-oriented translation of the story into English can help disseminate a radical understanding of corporeal difference to help counter the benign, rather depoliticised nature of existing English curriculum.

This chapter is cognisant of the fact that neither translation nor disability is mentioned in the Core English curriculum for students of class eleven and twelve in CBSE curriculum. The discussion returns to paratexts, this time in the context of the translation of a text on disability into English. The chapter argues that language and literature curriculum and pedagogy, along with translation, are two important systems of knowledge that can be brought to bear on texts on disability, in order to re-orient classroom discussions towards difference and alterity. By taking the specific issue of the representation of disability in English-language and literature curriculum in schools, this chapter explores the potential of translation to approach difference within classrooms. Having explored the potential of pedagogy and translation as forms of refraction, the chapter comes back to Venuti's theory on the potential of translation as a community-building exercise. More specifically, how can a functionalist, audience-specific or target-based translation be used to disseminate a radical cultural understanding of disability within English language and literature classrooms? How can this approach be used to challenge the persistent view of disability as a medical and sociological problem in the public domain?

Struggling to create language: on translating 'Goongey'

The title 'Goongey', a plural form of the Hindi word *goonga* (meaning a person with speech impairment), opens with the protagonist – a speech- and hearing-impaired homeless young man being accosted by a group of villagers. They are a curious lot who want to know how the *goonga* sustains himself. Chameli, a charitable woman in the group takes pity on him and offers him a job as her house help. Even if his impairment prevents him from assisting, at least he will be of 'some entertainment for the kids' (National Council for Educational Research and Training 2006: 47), she thinks to herself.

During the course of translating the story, the first major challenge was to find a way to translate the title itself. It is not the *goonga* but 'goongey', that is a speechless mass of people, the title suggests, who are at the centre of the story. Chameli sees reflected in his speechlessness the 'imposed silence' of the oppressed and marginalised masses. More than disability, the title suggests, it is the social 'condition' of speechlessness that is the locus of the story; the former, at best, a rhetorical device. After a cursory mention of his deafness as a congenital issue that *results* in his inability to speak, the story goes on to ignore his deafness altogether.

Although in the introductory scene, *goonga* shows promising 'abilities' and an impressive potential to earn his own livelihood, the story traces his failure to keep up with the promise as he plays truant and often disappears from his master's house (we are never told where; Chameli's conjecture that he goes off to beg is never contested). As days pass by and Chameli's patience as an employer begins to run thin, as a mother she finds herself sympathising with *goonga*, an underprivileged and deprived young man. As frustration and anger simmer within Chameli's household, one day she punishes *goonga* for his involvement in a fight with her own son. Things finally come to a head when *goonga's* defiant and unbending behaviour compels her to turn him out of the house. We see *goonga* for one last time as he comes back bleeding and crying, physically assaulted for standing up to the local boys. As Goonga lies bleeding and crying at the foot of her doorstep, Chameli stands pondering the general helplessness of humankind in their quest for love and dignity in the face of oppression, as she hears 'eons of accumulated rage and lamentation echoed' in his cries. (*Antra*: 51, translation mine)

Rangeya Raghav wrote prolifically between 1944 and 1958. It was a time marked by huge international and national upheaval – the Second World war, Indian independence, partition, death of Gandhi and the Nehruvian project of nation building. The country was only just coming face-to-face with severe soci-opolitical and economic struggles. The tumult of the time appears in the tone of his stories that range across a variety of subjects. However, 'Goongey' departs from Raghav's other works in significant ways. Where most of his work borrows heavily from the linguistic registers of Rajasthan and mid–Western Uttar Pradesh, 'Goongey' adopts a standardised lexical register of Khari Boli. Raghav's ancestors migrated from Tamil Nadu to Rajasthan and then to Agra, where he completed his formal education, earning his PhD in Hindi literature from Agra University. His works depict an intimate knowledge of the cultural mores of these two regions of North India. In 'Goongey', however, there are no definite geographical or linguistic markers. The setting of the story is vague – a generic village in North India whose people use heavy, Sanskritised Hindi in everyday exchanges. The switch towards a mix of Sanskrit and Urdu registers prompts one to think that the regional has been sidelined to aim at the national, giving the impression that the social issue(s) being spoken of transcend the local. While the national language debate began simmering from the mid-1950s onwards, this trope is consistent with the concep-tualisation of the Khari Boli as a language that transcends the local or regional and speaks of the nation.

'Goongey' also experiments with narrative techniques and rapid shifts in per-spective. From a third-person reporting of conversation between *goonga* and con-gregation in the beginning of the story, the next paragraph goes:

> *Goonga* gestured at his mouth and answered – She ran away. Who? Then they understood. As an infant his 'mother', the one constantly in-the-veil aban-doned him, because his 'father' as in Big-Moustache, died. Since then he has been brought up by – who? This was not very clear, but from his actions it was clear that they beat him a lot. (translation mine)

The paragraph that follows this, shifts into a general commentary by the narrator:

> Pity tugged at their hearts. He tries hard to speak. But the effort results in nothing but a barrage of harsh, guttural croaks. A vomit of incoherent sounds, as if the earliest man was still at work, struggling to create language. (transla-tion mine)

The shifts are a bit more complex in the latter paragraphs:

> At home, *bua*[2] would thrash him, *phoopha* would thrash him; they had brought him up and felt they had an ownership over him. They wanted him to work in the market, earn a few pennies to give to them; in exchange they would throw his way *rotis* cooked from the dough of barley and gram. So *goonga* stopped going home. He stays here now and works for them. The kids tease him. But he does not get angry. Chameli's husband is a nice, gentle person. Poor thing will grow up okay enough. He knows that man's charity is a

reflection of his own muteness, haplessness. He wants to achieve so much, but is unable to. And so the days pass. (translation mine)

The reader is initially drawn into feeling sympathy and pity for him. However, as the story progresses, his muteness expands to incorporate the oppressed and marginalised masses, his 'speechlessness' an operating metaphor for failing to get heard. By the end of the story, not only has he been denied a singular identity and a name; his tragedy is also lost within a collective composed of those who

> have increased in number and have taken multiple forms all around us – they want to speak but are unable to. Their hearts can tell justice from injustice; yet, they cannot challenge iniquity and wrongdoing. They have voices but which lack meaning . . . lack coherence. Because they are incapable. (translation mine)

The field of 'inability' expands to incorporate a collective of hapless and helpless masses who

> fight their own disgust against the wrongs in their society, country, religion or person. And yet they get trapped in the fickle desires for material happiness – in search of affection and dignity! (translation mine)

The shift from the individual to the collective nation-state is complete. This association of 'helplessness, subnormalcy and dependency' of an underprivileged collective to a young and disabled protagonist is not unfamiliar to the readers of postcolonial fiction.

Some reflections on metaphorisation

Clare Barker in *Postcolonial Fiction and Disability* analyses the various uses of disabled child protagonists in postcolonial fiction. Tracing the presence of disability metaphors in Salman Rushdie's *Midnights' Children* (1981) and Ben Okri's *Famished Road* (1991) to the historical, cultural and fictional texts of imperialism, Barker remarks,

> Colonized identities were variously depicted in terms of physical degeneracy, psychological dysfunction, behavioural disorder and/or limited intellectual capacity, meaning that in the terms of imperialist ideology, 'the colony [was] not only a child, but an oafish child' . . . unable to advance, producing a model of arrested development.
>
> (2011: 8)

In this sense, the complex treatment of disability in works by Rushdie and Okri can be seen to be 'situated within and respond(ing) directly to the contexts of this powerful representational history' (13) and as the trope 'lends itself persuasively to narratives of nation-building and cultural transformation in post-colonial communities' (2).

Around the same time as Raghav in 1954, Dharamvir Bharati wrote a play titled *Andha Yug* (*The Blind Age*), whose plot concentrates itself on the last day of the battle of Mahabharat. The play was read as a nationalist allegory in the decade following the India–Pakistan partition carnage. Considered to be a watershed moment in the history of Indian theatre, the play relies on a blind clairvoyant protagonist to communicate the horror and tragedy of war. One may argue that the sympathetic representations by Bharati and Raghav anticipate the exceptionally gifted child protagonists of the 1980s and 1990s, in a way that their work can be seen to be situated between the hostile representations in colonial narratives and the new-age postcolonial writers of the Third World.

While Rushdie's *Midnights Children* revisits the post-independence era to explore nation building, Raghav's story is situated within and embodies the anxiety and forebodings of the time. Despite his claim to earn his livelihood, *goonga* fails to do so and is seen as living off charity. Raghav's protagonist is shown to be irrational, instinctual and incapable of self-reliance. But the revulsion of the colonial master has been replaced by one sympathetic of the people of the new nation.

Chameli and her family, as well as the inhabitants of the village, oscillate between pity, fear and disgust in their interaction with *goonga*, whose body remains a battle-ground for mobilisation of these emotions. Even at its most progressive, 'Goongey' invites a self-ironising gaze on itself. As *goonga* lies bleeding at her doorstep, Chameli stands still and contemplates the haplessness of humankind. This last moment appropriates the metaphor of 'speechlessness' to refer to ordinary persons as *mook-darshak*, or 'silent spectators' of someone else's tragedy.

Deconstructing these emotions in their economic, social and historical contexts within the West, Bill Hughes in 'Fear, Pity and Disgust' in the *Handbook of Disability Studies* (2012) explores the heirarchisation of certain bodies over others calling it 'body fascism' of an ableist culture. The impulse to other-ise is a reflection of one's will to project its own frailty and precariousness onto others who become 'anomalous, monstrous, defective, strange and alien' (69). Hughes's theorisation can be used to understand the emotional response of the *imagined* public within 'Goongey' as reflecting the ambiguous relationship of a rising class of people with modernity and modernisation in the nation-building process. As a new aspirational class emerged from the old order, the rhetoric of the sentimental continued to fascinate the paternalistic impulses of the new class of authors for whom the poor and the oppressed needed immediate tending to. Fifty years later, metaphors of disability and impairment continue to enjoy widespread popularity within the political discourse in India. Political commentators, satirists and journalists can often be caught talking about '*andha kanoon*' and '*behri sarkaar*'.

Given the continued use of metaphors of disability – which Barker tells us is specific to former colonies – within the contemporary popular discourse on national politics, it is important to discuss such metaphors in language and literature classrooms to help students to critically analyse and shun such usage of disability in public discourse. These discussions are especially relevant as 'Goongey' continues to be taught to students of secondary level for Hindi language acquisition.

Reflection: ableist ways of seeing

The previous section dealt with the problem of representation of disability in the story – the sentimental mood that metaphorises and homogenises the experience of impairment. The dominant emotions of pity, disgust, displaced anger and aggression make 'Goongey' a deeply problematic text to approach disability within the classroom. This section focuses on introduction and question/answer sections that surround Raghav's story in the CBSE course book. A discussion on paratexts is used to understand the current vocabulary of representation of disability in the CBSE/NCERT curriculum.

The introduction to 'Goongey' in chapter five of *Antra* posits it more as a text on disability than as one about social awareness. The introduction gives us the core 'meaning' or the 'essence' of Raghav's story:

> The writer has underlined the insensitivity lodged deep within society against the disabled. Besides, the writer has tried to say that they must be understood and treated as any normal person and we must behave with compassion towards them so that they do not remain alienated in society.

As is clear, the section makes a very problematic jump between disability and impairment as if they are the same; its appeal to treat the disabled as 'people like us', apathy or insensitivity against the disabled is likened to a kind of '*goonga-behrapan*'. There is no attempt in the introduction to create a distance from the text that allows a questioning gaze. This *could* have been done, for instance, by giving a list of 'points to think about' while reading the text, wherein the students should have been asked to think through the distinction between *viklaang* and *goongey-behre*.

The questions at the end of the story are equally devoid of criticality towards the story. Some of these questions are What does Chameli experience when she heard the harsh, guttural croaks of *goonga* for the first time? How does *goonga* show that he has self-respect? 'Man's charity is the reflection if his own helplessness': Explicate with reference to the current context. If Basanta had been a *goonga*, what according to you would have been Chameli's behaviour towards him? '*Goonga* wants rights, not sympathy' – give proof. What are the emotions you feel on reading the story 'Goongey'? The title of the story is 'Goongey' when there is only one '*goonga*' in it. What aspect of society does the author seek to point out through this? (52)

Similarly, the last section, titled *yogyatavistaar*, or 'ability enhancement', carries two activities: How can you contribute to the efforts being made in society for the betterment of the disabled? Based on the problems of the disabled are films such as *Sparsh*, *Koshish* and *Iqbal*. Watch and provide reviews. (53) It is worth noting that the last activity has no alternative. All students are expected to 'watch' movies.

As is clear, the paratexts at the beginning, as well as the end, of the story continue to focus on the emotional response of the students to the story. The 'other-ising' of the disabled subject continues where the questions carry an 'us–them' vocabulary. No question is aimed at interrogating the metaphor of 'muteness' itself. The question/answer section continues to operate within the ableist framework. It gives off the impression of faithfully trying to 'reflect' or render the meaning of the texts while offering almost no resistance to the ideology of the story. In the absence of critical tools, students are at the mercy of particular teacher's interpretation.

Critical refraction

The CBSE handbook to senior school curriculum mentions the following as the Objective of senior secondary curriculum design:

> A student enrolled at this level . . . enters from a general to specialised dis-
> cipline for the first time. In his (*sic*) last ten years of study, the student has
> been introduced to the various aspects of language. . . . He has reached a state
> where he can contemplate the cultural, social, political and economic aspects
> of the country, and can begin to understand his position as a responsible
> citizen of the country. Drawing from such a firm linguistic and ideological
> foundation, it is imperative to provide a comprehensive understanding of
> Hindi as a language to deliberate over these issues.
>
> (Curriculum 2016: 40, translation mine)

It is clear, that the packaging of 'Goongey' in *Antra* is a conscious attempt on part of the curriculum designers to include a text of social relevance. That disability has been made visible in a literature curriculum owes itself to years of struggle of disability activists and scholars. However, it is clear from the previous sections on paratexts that much is still to be done. The problem can be traced to curriculum design, wherein there is a blurring of distinction among creative-, appreciative- and issue-based approaches to literature.

In his essay 'Mother Courage's Cucumbers: Text, System and Refraction', André Lefevere studies three types of translations of Brecht to look at how 'translations', or what he calls more generally 'refractions', influence the social acceptance of Brecht. Lefevere rejects the category of truth or falsehood of representation of texts within society and, in fact, asks for a more pragmatic approach. He advocates for the acceptance of these so-called distortions or 'second hand opinions or ideas' (Lefevere 1982: 234) as simple facts of life, seeing as how these so-called misunderstandings or misconceptions (*refractions*) are means through which writers and works achieve prominence. He defines refractions as 'the adaptation of a work of literature to a different audience, with the intention of influencing the way in which that audience reads the work', pointing out that they have always been with us in literature through 'translation, criticism . . . commentary, histori-ography, teaching, collection of works in anthologies, production of plays' (235).

These refractions, he points out (be it a translation, criticism or historiography), perpetuate the canonization of certain works of literature, and school and college anthologies play an immensely important part in this essentially conservative movement within the literary system (238). The process of designing school curriculum is an exercise in determining what is worthy of reading, study and analysis. Added to this is the privileging of certain reading practices over others, determining the value of a text by privileging certain meaning over others. Previous discussion on paratextuality can be brought to bear on how the packaging of 'Goongey' as a text on disability can influence the way disability will be perceived in the classroom.

Studying 'Goongey' in translation: English in classrooms

The objective of an English language and literature curriculum of CBSE/NCERT for senior secondary is stated as

> [t]he course is intended to give students a high level of competence in English with an emphasis on the study of literary texts. The course will provide extensive exposure to a variety of rich texts of world literature as well as Indian writings in English, including classics, develop sensitivity to the creative and imaginative use of English and give them a taste for reading with delight and discernment. The course is pitched at a level which the students may find challenging yet interesting.
>
> (Senior Secondary Curriculum: 38)

The English textbooks have 'chosen' to not be weighed down by local or immediate concerns and to focus on the 'delight' in reading and thinking in the language. The emphasis on humour and delight is understandable for a country where a devastating majority of students have English for their second, third or even fourth language. While the curriculum tries to maintain a proportionate balance between global writings and Indian writings in English, CBSE textbooks for Core English do not contain any Indian writings translated into English. Instead, the board has a separate course on translation titled 'Creative Writing and Translation Studies' at the senior secondary level. Disability, too, finds no mention in the syllabus. This section looks to the translation of 'Goongey' as a case study to discuss modes and strategies of reading texts on disability. I propose to show that target-oriented translation can be employed for critical distancing for an in-depth engagement with disability to underscore ideological biases and prejudices of the author-figure regarding normality and deviation.

While translating the story for students of class eleven, retaining the title 'Goongey' from the original into English would serve more than one purpose. The first purpose would be to replicate in English the authorial choice of naming the story after the silent masses, not the protagonist. A second and related point is that there is no equivalent term for a group of silent/mute people. A third, and most important, point is to retain foreign words into the translation to enable a distancing of the reader from the text. Hindi speakers, in particular, would be familiar with the way 'Goonga' is often thrown like an abuse or an accusation on television and film screens, as well as in real life. Retaining the word in the English would serve to jar the reader. It is clear that texts meant to be included in a curriculum must be translated keeping the target audience – in this case the students of language and literature in school – in mind. The phonetic impact of the word *goonga* is such that it could not have been captured by *dumb* or *mute*; it has a ridiculous, pejorative and insulting sound to it like certain North Indian nicknames, such as *chhotu*. Footnotes must be provided flagging this cultural tendency to reduce people to their (in)capabilities and its political implications.

Second, translation can be used to teach paradigmatic aspects of language to students. For instance, the deliberate translation of *stabdh* as *dumbfounded* in the story is to flag the issue of the interchangeability of *dumb* and *mute* in the English language. Students in high school should be asked to research the reasons for the collapsing of the two terms. An exercise such as this may help students discover that

> [t]he Greek philosopher Aristotle (350 BC) is credited with being one of the first to associate 'deaf' with 'dumb': 'accordingly, of persons destitute from birth of either sense, the blind are more intelligent than the deaf and dumb.' Over the years the word 'dumb' when used in this context became synonymous with 'silent'. The American National Association of the Deaf point[s] out two reasons why deaf people consider this offensive. First, deaf and hard of hearing people are by no means silent since they use sign language and lip-reading to communicate. Second, the word 'dumb' is misleading since it automatically implies that all deaf people also have a learning difficulty. . . . The two words are associated with each other a couple of times in the Bible: 'And were beyond measure astonished, saying, He hath 'Mute' all things well: he maketh both the deaf to hear, and the dumb to speak' (Mark 7: 37).
>
> (Clark and Marsh 2002)

Alternatively, explanations such as these could be provided to the students in the annotation to the translation. Third, in order to teach students about the social construction of metaphors, questions should also focus on the overemphasis on muteness over deafness in the story when the protagonist is both. Could it be that this distortion serves a purpose in the story? Fundamental questions such as what is wrong in using words such as *deaf*, *dumb* or *retarded* as terms of abuse must be highlighted with in-text annotations. The issues flagged in the previous section on the problems of metaphorisation can be brought to students' notice in a succinct manner to draw attention to the ideological construction of metaphors of disability in the English language.

At points where the text privileges some emotions over others, students need to be made aware of the sociality of emotions. It is for curriculum designers to simplify the texts to suit their mental, emotional and social development, but the focus could be one of criticality. For instance, in the question/answer section, students should be asked to think through the distinctions of pity, sympathy and empathy and which of the three emotions is dominant in the story. How would the story proceed if the people in the story show empathy for the *goonga*? Would anything change? What does it say about the author's intentions in communicating the pathos of a disabled protagonist?

To date, English is taught in Indian classrooms as God's own language, a language that must not be played around with. Nissim Ezekeil's 'Goodbye Party for Ms. Pushpa T. S.' mocks a 'deviation' that is not interrogated in a way that it empowers students already burdened with the expectation of 'perfecting' the language. The need should be to draw attention to the idea of translation as a negotiation with difference. Seeing as there is no such thing as English but Englishes, the English curriculum needs to be revised. It needs to be politicised, and an issue-based curriculum could be a step in this direction. For a pedagogy of praxis, there needs first be a systematic engagement with politics. Disability texts written in Indian languages and translated into English could provide such an entry point.

Conclusion

This chapter highlights the issues that arise in including a story such as 'Goongey' as part of the curriculum. It points out the problematic way in which introduction and the question/answer section in CBSE books for Hindi add to the already-present ableist interpretations and 'other-ise' and isolate disabled students in the classroom. In the absence of any critical tools to deal with such a text, the danger of reifying ableist constructs multiplies manifold. Instead of focusing the discussion on 'disability' as 'difference' or a minority culture, the focus is regressively rhetorical and emotional in nature.

In a democratic set up the space of a classroom is meant for students to learn, care for and respect difference and plurality. Curriculum and pedagogy are designed to help build such learning communities over a period of twelve years. In order for each student to be valued and respected, the curriculum needs to focus on difference and alterity to build such leaning communities. By applying the concept of 'refraction', the chapter looks at the active process of canon formation that curriculum designs propagate. The chapter applies Lefevere's concept of 'critical refraction' to bring together the three fields of pedagogy, disability and translation studies in order to provide an effective contrapuntal solution to counter political challenges of exclusion and othering. This chapter looks to paratexts as effective pedagogic tools in translation studies as a political strategy to challenge ableism and homogeneity.

The stated objective of the CBSE curriculum of both Hindi and English languages is to advance a critical pedagogy in classrooms. Ideologically, Hindi textbooks by their own admission tend to focus on an issue-based engagement with literature in Hindi. English curriculum, on the other hand, is more inclined towards encouraging an appreciation of the language wherein Indian literature translated into English is conspicuous by its absence. In this chapter, a case has been made to redesign the course to include issues of immediate and social relevance in English core curriculum. This has been done via exploring possibilities of inclusion of literature translated from Indian languages as a means of classroom intervention in teaching English – a language with a far wider reach than any other in CBSE curriculum. Using Lefevere's conception of 'critical refraction', the chapter tries to show how translation can be used as an intervention to advance a critical and creative engagement with disability along with issues of 'difference' in languages as well as societies. The challenge should be to initiate students into engaging with issues at both the creative and the critical level while exploring translation as a mode of intervention. Effectively then, critical refraction as a theoretical framework will be applied at two levels, at the level of curriculum design as well as translation.

The potential for adopting a functionalist approach to translation for English studies has been highlighted. It must be pointed out, however, that the concerns raised in this chapter were based on just a few textbooks of CBSE/NCERT that are part of the current curriculum, therefore the concerns raised are contextual and thus limited in scope. But in a linguistically diverse country such as India, the engagement with issues of translation need to begin at the primary level and gradually evolve till senior secondary level. Through the case study of 'Goongey', this chapter has merely tried to highlight the potential of an issue-based engagement with translation to advance a critical pedagogy. The advancement of a critical pedagogy is possible when a more elaborate study of the representation of disability in school curriculum spanning across all education boards – state and national – is undertaken in order to focus on all fronts of schooling – curriculum, instruction and evaluation – when it comes to disability. The ultimate goal should be to bring together formal and informal forms of learning and teaching language and literature in an inclusive classroom to yield insights that this chapter with a unidirectional study of textbooks may not have done.

Notes

1 Republished in *The Translation Studies Reader* (2000) edited by Lawrence Venuti, 233–249.
2 *Bua* (Hindi) refers to father's sister; *phoopha*, to her husband.

References

National Council for Educational Research and Training. (2006) 2013. *Antra*. New Delhi: Published by Secretary, NCERT Print.
Barker, Clare. 2011. *Postcolonial Fiction and Disability: Exceptional Children, Metaphor and Materiality*. Basingstoke: Palgrave Macmillan. PDF.
Central Board of Secondary Education- i. 2013. *Senior Secondary Curriculum*. New Delhi: Published by CBSE. Retrieved from l-1_c-91_1347248668397

Central Board of Secondary Education-i. 2016. *Curriculum Hindi (Aichhik)*. New Delhi: CBSE. Retrieved from http://cbseacademic.nic.in/web_material/Curriculum19/Main-Senior Secondary/4_Hindi_302. PDF

Clark, Laurence, and Stephen Marsh. 2002. *Patriarchy in the UK: The Language of Disability*. Retrieved from http://www.leeds.ac.uk/disability-studies/archiveuk

Davis, Lennard J. 1995. *Enforcing Normalcy: Disability, Deafness and the Body*. New York, NY: Verso. PDF.

———., ed. 2013. *The Disability Studies Reader*. Abingdon: Routledge.

Lefevere, André. (1982) 2000. 'Mother Courage's Cucumbers: Text, System and Refraction in a Theory of Literature', in *The Translation Studies Reader*, Chap. 18. London: Routledge.

Venuti, Lawrence, ed. 2000. *The Translation Studies Reader*. London: Routledge. PDF.

6

TRANSLATION AS 'RE-PRESENTATION'

The disability spectrum in selected Urdu short stories

Deeba Zafir

> Disability is a life lived before a looking glass that is cracked and distorted by the vandalism of normality.
>
> – Hughes (2012: 68)

It is a truism of Disability Studies that disability is axiomatic to the human condition, even though it has been and continues to form the basis for discrimination across cultures. The permeability of constructs such as normality and disability clearly suggests that these are not polar opposites but as Christina Papadimitriou points out, 'fall along a continuum of . . . humanly possible ways of being' (Berger 2016: 14). In the Indian context, its intersection with other factors like caste, class, gender and religion makes disability a locus of multiple jeopardies. Socially invisibilised for its deemed aberrant and deviant aspects, disability is marginalised even in literary representation. The paucity of stories that are disability centric bespeaks an exclusion that has its counterpart in the public sphere. It is only through a close examination of stories through the prism of disability that the spectrum of disability-related issues is revealed. As a category of analysis, disability is an enabling critical tool that opens an entirely new approach to literature while simultaneously widening its horizon.

As an auxiliary argument, it can be said that translating a disability text thus enables the struggle for representation to be pitched into a wider cultural field. Through translation, the Indian experience of disability can draw from and contribute towards an enhanced understanding of the challenges that confront an increasingly exclusionist world. Translation then becomes a metaphor for representation itself and the translator's task that of an activist who strives to make the invisible visible and the voiceless heard.

Thus, as in the case of Dalit or women-centric texts, the translation of disability texts does not merely involve a linguistic transfer but can become the vehicle for consciousness raising and sensitisation in the campaign for a more inclusive world. Translation, therefore, does not just 're-present' the original text in another language but also opens space for a wider cultural and literary representation. This paper is divided into two parts, where, in the first section, I examine the representation of disability in the three Urdu short stories that I have translated and, in the second section, theorise my translation practice.

In the context of Urdu fiction, the well-known short story writer Saadat Hasan Manto comes immediately to mind for his masterful chronicling of the trauma of Partition. Among his gallery of mentally disturbed characters, Bishan Singh in 'Toba Tek Singh' stands out as a fine example of Manto's use of madness as a metaphor to underscore the senselessness of the so-called wise (Manto, in Hasan, 2008: 9–15). Bishan Singh's mad utterances and probing questions serve as a mode of truth telling that diffuses not just the distinction between madness and sanity but also, paradoxically, to reverse it. This fluidity of categories also forms the crux to understanding disability as a conceptual framework. Much like gender, it poses a challenge to normative criteria. Both disability and gender are constructs that involve a complex interplay of social, political and economic forces. Defined in terms of a 'lack' of attributes and capabilities, women are subjected to prescriptive norms that confer a limited role allocation and, as in the case of persons with disability, are seen as passive recipients, lacking agency. In an Urdu poem by Bilquis Zafirul Hassan, gender is portrayed as a disabling condition, where in the urban housewife, whose mobility is severely restricted by her dependency on other men, speaks of her existence as a 'Life in a Wheelchair':

> *Sitting in the wheelchair of my life*
> *I watch*
> *People come and go*
> *And wait*
> *For the one who would come*
> *And push my wheelchair*
> *Through the lanes and roads*
> *And help me see my own city*
> (Zafir 1997: 51)

However, in both cases, disability is used as a metaphor to stand for something other than itself. The three Urdu short stories that this paper examines, display the wide spectrum of disability in what Margrit Shildrick refers to 'as diverse forms of embodiment' (Shildrick 2012: 34).

'Ganjefa': the liminal zone

The first story titled 'Ganjefa' is by Naiyer Masud, a writer who enjoys a formidable reputation as a teller of elliptical tales. Known as the 'Kafka of Lucknow', Masud was known to have led a reclusive life, having been struck with paralysis a few years back. The story centres around an unnamed protagonist whose life takes a 'turn for the worse' (Zafir 2008: 72) when after the riots, he is accosted by many people on the roads, who enquire after his name and occupation. This interrogation makes him confront the fact that he has been 'living off' ('Ganjefa' 73) his mother, who is a *chikankari* worker. The context establishes him as a member of the minority Muslim community in Lucknow and as not belonging to the economic sphere. His indolence is set against an industrious mother, whose *chikan* embroidery is highly valued and who also trains other women into it as a means of their livelihood.

Even though the story is not ostensibly about disability, it is replete with references to death, disease and impairment, therefore linking all the three. The mother's ill health and failing eyesight foreshadow her death, which is preceded by the death of the father due to economic ruin many years ago and followed by the death of another character, Husna, due to jaundice. It is Husna's father, Laadley, who is the only visibly disabled character in the story. A seller of herbs and the Royal Tooth powder in his heyday, Laadley has fallen to bad times due to the wasting away of his legs, on account of which the narrator's mother refers to him as 'worse than a dead man' ('Ganjefa' 82).

The narrator recalls the fascination he held for Laadley as a child, when he would spread a sheet at the corner of the street in the Sunday bazaar to display his wares. His wooden box would contain bottles of all sizes with oils of herbs and his signature Royal Tooth powder. Laadley, we are told, used to be

> a well built man with a perfectly regular set of teeth . . . who could easily pull a crowd of buyers with his brand of English and would claim that he had studied 'abroad' and if he wished he could become the Deputy Collector that very day except for the fact that he found greater pleasure in making the Royal Tooth Powder.
>
> ('Ganjefa' 83)

This flashback to the narrator's childhood serves as a sharp contrast to Laadley's present incapacitated condition. Laadley's curious will, which Husna gets the narrator to read to her, is all about 'what is not her share' ('Ganjefa' 86) and is a tacit admission about the ineffectiveness of his magical cures for his own condition. Even though the narrator helps out Laadley to put away his things, he finds it painful to watch him move around and derives much relief from looking away. In both cases, the narrator's responses of pity and avoidance are typical of the reactions to persons with disability, and Laadley is shown to be conscious of them. Just as the narrator's father had 'lived off' Amma, so, too, has Laadley survived on Husna's earnings. After her death, it is significant that Laadley hands over his box of belongings to the narrator, whom he probably regards as a more befitting heir to his legacy and disappears into the unknown, conjectured by most people to be reduced to a state of beggary.

At the end of the story, even though the narrator is hired by the retail trader, Laala, for whom his mother had earlier worked, it is not specified what is it that he is required to do. Like Laadley's claim of having studied abroad, the narrator's father, too, had wanted him to study abroad, but for some unknown reason, he was reduced to a state of bankruptcy, with the burden of earning a living falling on the mother. The narrator's aimlessness and inability to work suggest a certain paralysis of will, which in his case comes to stand for a form of invisible disability. A victim of his father's thwarted ambitions and his mother's sheltering love, the narrator realises very early on, 'I was behaving exactly like a child, trying to walk with the help of his mother' ('Ganjefa' 76). The reference to his child-like status for the thirty-year-old narrator works as a shorthand to acknowledging his own torpidity. Compelled to seek work after his mother's death, the narrator approaches Laala, who declares to him that with the passing away of Amma, an entire tradition of embroidery has come to an end. Significantly, he uses the image of amputation to describe this loss: '"What can I say, son? It's like my hands have been cut . . . one won't get to see such work anymore" and bowed his head in its tribute for a long time' ('Ganjefa' 90–91).

The reference to *ganjefa*, the Persian game of cards, figures only in the title, the rules of which are enunciated in the epigraph to the story:

> The sun is the most important card in the game and the status of the moon is lower than the sun, but this is true only till the sun is radiant . . . in the night the powers of the Sun are passed on to the moon and the sun is relegated to the status of an ordinary minister.
>
> ('Ganjefa' 72)

The story closely parallels the fate of the narrator and Laadley, a so-called able-bodied man with that of a man whose legs have wasted away. Both have seen a time when their 'sun' was ascendant and with the passage of time have come to depend on the women in their lives for their sustenance. The women represent the 'moon' to whom the powers are passed on and who are, in turn, struck by age and disease. After their death, both men are reduced to an impoverished state, wherein one becomes the recipient of Laala's charity and the other to that of a beggar. The story exemplifies that ability does not exist in an absolute sense and that disability is inevitably a part of human existence in some measure or the other. The categorical clarity, as Margrit Shildrick suggests, between 'the status of disabled and able-bodied is at best provisional rather than marking a fixed identity' (Shildrick 2012: 34). Thus, the story not only is about the passage of time and the role of chance but also illustrates that disability is inescapably implicated in the two. It must, however, be remembered that the characters in the world of the story also happen to be those who exist on the fringes and therefore impairment serves to only further compound their fates.

'The one-armed man': acknowledging the 'other'

The next story, 'The One-Armed Man' by Anjum Usmani, is a prime example of the opportunistic use of disability, to what Mitchell and Snyder refer to as a 'narrative prosthesis', that serves as 'a metaphorical signifier of social and individual collapse' (2011: 47). This dystopic tale depends entirely on the trope of disability to carry its narrative burden and is a purported attack on Leftism. It conjures up a world gone awry when people of an unnamed *basti* discover that 'the tasks that they had been performing with their right hand were now being carried out by their left hand' (translation mine). The disabling of the right hand is referred to as a 'curse', invoking images of a doomsday scenario:

> Eventually, it dawned upon every one that this curse had befallen upon them collectively and it was something about which they had read in books and heard their elders speak of:
> There will be a day when evil people will carry a catalogue of their mis-deeds in their left hand and stand on one side, while the righteous will have the details of their good deeds in their right hand and stand on the other side. Then the sun will blaze over the heads of those evil people and their minds will simmer like a bubbling cauldron. People will stand so exposed to each other that parents will not recognise their offspring and their children too will turn away from them. (translation mine)

Initially, everyone in the *basti* conceals it from the other, but when it becomes clear to them that it is a collective fate, they begin to seek a cure for it. This surreal tale unfolds like a political allegory as the author deploys the stigmatisation of the left hand, perhaps a peculiarly Asian feature, to associate leftism with all things evil. Day by day as the situation worsens, people begin to die since they refuse to use the left hand for eating and drinking. It also portends an epistemological collapse: 'Even the pen seemed to move from right to the left. Alphabets lost their shape, words their meanings and sentences changed their intent' (translation mine). Read in this manner, the tale seems to associate disability with an apocalyptic curse, which, if it strikes one, then, from it there is no escape.

However, the ambivalent end to this tale makes a contrarian reading possible. Viewed from the enabling prism of disability, the tale can be unpacked to reveal a more affirmative meaning. The tale concludes with the arrival of a stranger, who appears from nowhere and his one arm is missing. It is significant that the text does not mention if it is the right or the left arm. As the people of the *basti* turn towards him,

> [t]he one-armed man cast a glance in the direction of the gathering and raised his lone arm over his head. The entire crowd looked at him thought-fully and dispersed quietly. The next morning the people of the basti found that all the children were using their left hand for all those tasks they earlier did with their right hand and none of their faces showed any trace of anguish. (translation mine)

From a disability perspective, the tale can be read as an exemplum of the human condition, wherein disability is the 'unacknowledged other' (Shildrick 2012: 35) of the so-called able self. Once the people of the *basti* are struck with it, their extreme anxiety and fear of disability provoke first denial of it, followed by a panic-driven desire for a cure. However, this invisible disability is made visible with the arrival of the one-armed man.

With the raising of the lone arm over his head, the stranger liberates the people of the *basti* not only from the norm but also restores them to a way of life in which disability is not seen as distinct from the norm. The people of the *basti* come to accept disability as evidence of a 'wider systemic predicament' (Mitchell and Snyder 2011: 51), and the liberatory gesture is a defiant rejection of the norm and its substitution with disability. Thus, in this story, as Mitchell and Snyder put forth in their argument, 'disability is a narrative device upon which the literary writer of "open ended" narrative depends for his disruptive punch' (*ibid.*, 49), but this also brings forth a conundrum that 'while stories rely upon the potency of disability as a symbolic figure, they rarely take up disability as an experience of social and political dimension' (*ibid.*, 48).

'Luminescence': desire and subversion

The last story, 'Luminescence' by Agha Sohail, addresses the previously mentioned problem. It does not use disability as a trope, rather speaks of it as a lived experience. It is a first-person account which reads like a monologue by an unnamed narrator, who has lost his sight. The story begins with the narrator's tactile memory of a woman's body which imbues him with a warmth and luminosity and, more significant, a desire to live. The woman we are told is mute. On the other hand, the narrator's world is dominated by sounds, but as he points out, 'they keep receding.' Not only is his exclusion from the rest of the household indicated, but so is his being at the receiving end of his sister-in-law's cruel and abusive behaviour.

It is significant that both the narrator and the woman were not disabled earlier. No reason is given for the narrator's loss of sight, but the woman, we are told, has been muted by her third husband, who placed a burning ember on her tongue in a fit of rage. Not only is she the victim of misogynistic violence, but she has also been passed on from her first husband's brother to the other after his death. These details relating to the woman's life are told to the narrator by his nephew, who, along with an old woman, are the only two people who care for him. The mute woman's name is not revealed and she is called 'Goongi' (literally 'the mute') by the narrator. Her story remains largely unrepresented, since, as Kevin Paterson points out, 'people with speech impairment find it difficult to reveal themselves as "social beings" and articulate bodies' (2012: 174). However, Goongi's actions seem to speak louder than her silence.

The story is unique insofar as it delves into the relatively unexplored realm of sexual desire of persons with disability. The nephew is the source of information about the outer world, and it is he who describes Goongi's beauty, as well as the uncouth appearance of all her three husbands, to the narrator. Interestingly, the nephew thinks that he has discerned a soft spot for the narrator in Goongi's glances towards him, but his knowledge is trumped by the narrator, who has already taken the reader into confidence: 'It makes me secretly happy that my nephew does not know that Goongi's fourth husband' (translation mine). The incomplete sentence invites the reader to fill in the blanks with the information the narrator has provided in an earlier statement: 'There remains nothing in the world for me but for the one who comes to me in the silence of the night and quietly enters my bloodstream like a current and fills me up with vitality to the core' (translation mine). The narrator repeats not once but thrice the feel of Goongi's body, which he describes lyrically as

> voluptuous, with skin as smooth as butter and hidden within the soft folds of her skin is a slow fire that arouses a new sense of intense warmth in every pore of my body. I feel as if a series of lamps have lit me up from within and illumined every part of my body.
>
> (translation mine)

The story ends with the narrator waiting for Goongi to turn up. The city has been lit up, perhaps on the occasion of Diwali, the festival of lights, but for the narrator it is Goongi who will 'dispel the darkness of his soul' and 'illumine' his life. While Goongi's rendezvous with the narrator can be interpreted as her subversion of the terrorising tactics of her third husband, the narrator's desire for her is his *raison d'etre*. The secret solidarity between the two, though understated, signals what Shildrick calls 'a productive positivity' (2012: 39).

Conclusion

The spectrum of disability that the three stories display can hardly be seen as exhaustive and in fact point to an important lacuna – that of self-representation. As the epigraph to this paper suggests, the mirror cracked by the vandalism of normality is bound to reflect back only distorted images and therefore it is imperative to be able to tell one's own story rather than have it told by others. However, the right to self-representation for a marginalised community is not easily won and involves activism that must emerge from the reading, writing and translating of disability centric works. As the lines from a poem by the famous Urdu poet Faiz suggest,

> *My sorrow is a melody without sound*
> *My identity a speck without trace*
> *When a voice for my pain is found*
> *I will find my name and trace.*
> (my translation)

In the hands of a sensitive writer like Naiyer Masud, the representation of disability is seamlessly woven into the narrative and if the reader is not sensitised enough, she may miss the import altogether. The critical perspective of disability opens the layered narrative in such a manner that the story does not remain the same when viewed through this analytic prism. The uncanny in Masud loses some of its inexplicability when the enabling critical tool of disability is applied to it. As someone who had translated 'Ganjefa' long time back and was quite reconciled to its seeming opacity, the revisiting of the story from a disability lens yielded up an entirely new meaning. Masud's story explores the liminal zone where ability and disability meet, in what can be termed as a salutary reminder to the reader that '[d]isability plays a trans-historical and ontological role as a shadow that reminds the human community of its frailty' (Hughes 2012: 73). On the other hand, Anjum Usmani's tale seems to progress along a typical trajectory of how disability is conventionally viewed and represented. The author, in a telephonic conversation, had confessed that disability was the last thing on his mind when he wrote the story, and yet, as my reading suggests, it is possible to bring the disability perspective to it as a disruptive exercise. Although the tone of the story remains satirical throughout in order to show leftism as a disabling ideology, read against the grain, this meaning can be turned on its head, as the ambivalent end to the story warrants.

Sohail Agha's story is more about what remains untold and is therefore replete with possibilities. Its title was somewhat difficult to translate as 'Roshni' in Urdu literally means 'light'. Yet 'luminescence' seemed a better choice as it evokes the sense of something that radiates from within rather than the more mechanical association of switching on the light, which, to person without sight, would, in any case, have no meaning.

The translation of these three stories did not pose the kind of challenge that, for instance, a Dalit text does. Dalit texts usually draw on specific regional contexts and have a significant component of dialect and folk idiom, even when they do emerge from urban loci. Thus, they pose an entirely different set of challenges to the translator. Unlike the romanticised perception of Urdu as a quaint and mystified language, these three stories clearly have an urbane register and lent themselves easily to a translation into English.

However, it is my contention that a disability text battles perception through language and often speaks from the cracks within it. This is most obvious in the case of Manto's Bishan Singh, whose gibberish remains untranslated in most English versions. The breakdown of language mirrors the incapacity for representation, that moment of disablement that defies representation. Thus, the translator of a disability text can perform any of the following roles, as in my case, act as a collaborator with the author in portraying disability sensitively, in the manner that Naiyer Masud does. Alternatively, she can offer a resistant interpretation to a text antagonistic to disability like Usmani's or uncover the silences within a text to provide a subversive reading as in the case of Sohail Agha's story. As Lori Chamberlain puts forth in her theorisation of a feminist theory of translation, women translators must, 'Speak through and against translation' (1988: 471) by subverting hegemonic forms of expression. The presence or absence of women in the three stories that we have discussed has a crucial role to play in the making of meaning in the story and the translator must provide a critical introduction to the story or footnotes to unpack its layers. In the case of a disability text, by bringing that lens to bear on it, it is possible to tease out a particular reading since the translator is, first and foremost, a reader of the text.

Thus, the issue of access, so central to the disability narrative, can be facilitated through translation to reach those domains that have hitherto been immune to it. Both disability and translation have the power to unsettle hierarchies, blur binaries and break silences as my reading of the three stories has demonstrated. Even though both disability and translation are conventionally perceived as suffering from a 'loss', they are, in fact, modes of enablement that renegotiate the boundaries between disability and normativity, the source and translated text. This 'in-betweenness' has been theorised by many postcolonial critics such as Harish Trivedi, who, in his references to both Homi Bhabha and Sherry Simon, suggests a new space that the translation of an Indian text, especially into English opens up, wherein inter-cultural transfer may be negotiated on more equal terms (Bassnet and Trivedi 1999: 6).

The translating of an Indian disability text into English then involves a double gesture: not only does the content push at the limits of what we consider 'normality', but the very act of its translation into English also unskews the power differential between the target and source language. As Homi Bhabha puts it,

> [w]e should remember that it is the 'inter'-the cutting edge of translation and renegotiation-that carries the burden of culture. . . . And by exploring this Third Space, we may elude the politics of polarity and emerge as the others of ourselves.
>
> (Bassnet and Trivedi 1999: 8)

The added dimension of perspectivism that a different language register brings into English through the translation of an Indian disability text, as this chapter suggests, then enables us to confront the 'other' of ourselves in more senses than one.

Acknowledgements

I wish to express my grateful thanks to Dr. Someshwar Sati, Dr. Khalid Alvi and Naghma Zafir for their invaluable help in providing critical material as well as insights into the stories.

References

Bassnet, Susanand and Harish Trivedi, eds. 1999. *Post-colonial Translation*. London: Routledge.

Berger, Ronald J. 2016. 'Introducing Disability Studies', *Lyn Rienner*. www.reinner.com (accessed on 17 August 2016).

Chamberlain, Lori. 1988. 'Gender and the Metaphorics of Translation', *Signs*, 13(3), Spring: 454–472. The University of Chicago Press. www.jstor.org (accessed on 25 May 2014).

Hassan, Bilquis Z. 1997. 'Life in a Wheelchair', Trans. Naghma Zafir, *Urdu Alive: Association for Cultural Fraternity*, Summer Issue (3): 51.

Hughes, Bill. 2012. 'Fear, Pity and Disgust: Emotions and the Non-Disabled Imaginary', in Nick Watson, Alan Roulstone and Carol Thomas (eds), *Routledge Handbook of Disability Studies*, pp. 67–77. New York, NY: Routledge.

Manto, Saadat Hasan. 2008. *Bitter Fruit: The Very Best of Saadat Hasan Manto*. Trans. and ed. Khalid Hasan. New Delhi: Penguin.

Masud, Naiyer. 2008. 'Ganjefa: The Game of Cards', Trans. Deeba Zafir, *Indian Literature, Sahitya Akademi's Bi-Monthly Journal*, November/December 248 (Vol. LII) (6): 72–97.

Mitchell, David T. and Sharon L. Snyder. 2011. *Narrative Prosthesis: Disability and Dependencies of Discourse*. Ann Arbor, MI: University of Michigan Press.

Paterson, Kevin. 2012. 'It's About Time! Understanding the Experience of Speech Impairment', in Nick Watson, Alan Roulstone and Carol Thomas (eds), *Routledge Handbook of Disability Studies*, pp. 165–177. New York, NY: Routledge.

Shildrick, Margrit. 2012. 'Critical Disability Studies: Rethinking the Conventions for the Age of Postmodernity', in Nick Watson, Alan Roulstone and Carol Thomas (eds) *Routledge Handbook of Disability Studies*, pp. 30–41. New York, NY: Routledge.

7

TRANSLATING DESIRES OF THE *UNDESIRED*

Re-reading Tagore's *different* women in 'Subha' and 'Drishtidaan'

Somrita Ganguly

> There is a time-honoured tradition of using texts for revolutionary purposes.
> – Tymoczko (2000: 40)

There is nothing called objective translation. Translators are humans and human beings have their own agenda and prejudice, and this subjective position of the translator colours the translation. No translation takes place in a vacuum. This chapter looks at the role that translation plays and can play in disability studies. It reflects my experience of having translated two short stories by Rabindranath Tagore (1861–1941), centred on the theme of disability and acceptance, from Bangla to English: 'Subha' (1892) and 'Drishtidaan' (1898).

The chapter has been divided into four major sections: explaining why I chose to translate the aforementioned stories, despite the existence of preceding translations, I go on to briefly discuss certain linguistic choices that I have made in my translations, aesthetically and politically motivated. These choices give rise to the questions of political correctness and permissibility when representing marginalised voices. The chapter then comments on the idea of desire in a disabled individual, with particular reference to the protagonists of the aforementioned texts while theoretically reading the politics of exclusion and ableism that make a disabled person *undesirable* in the eyes of a hegemonic, normative, socially functional and physically able society. In conclusion, the chapter posits certain questions regarding the need to build a theory of translation for disability studies.

Choosing Tagore, 'Subha' and 'Drishtidaan'

'Subha' is the heart-wrenching story of a young girl who could not speak. Pointing out the irony in her name, Subhashini – the one whose speech is sweet – Tagore's story narrates the problems of a person who has a heightened sense of imagination, a keen sensibility and deep desires but who cannot articulate them in a language that her society can fathom. In 'Drishtidaan' Tagore charts the journey of Kumu, a young girl married to a medical student, who suffers from a disease that afflicts her vision. Her husband, in his zeal to treat his wife based on the knowledge that he was acquiring in his medical college, does her more harm than good. Kumu loses her vision completely. However, in all her benevolence, she forgives him. Her repentant husband swears never to marry again and raises her to the pedestal of a goddess. Kumu gradually learns to not depend on him and finds her way around by relying on her other senses. Their marriage suffers. Lies, guilt and unstated complaints create a chasm between the couple that is almost unbridgeable. Kumu's journey is one that involves frustration (*why me?*), helplessness (*how will I survive?*), acknowledgement (*this is indeed happening to me and it is irreversible*), depression and the courage to start afresh.

One can trace a change in Tagore's narrative style from 'Subha' to 'Drishtidaan'. In the former we hear the voice of the third-person narrator, the voice of the author whom we are prone to trust. Six years later, when Tagore writes 'Drishtidaan', it is no longer from a removed, objective perspective. The able-bodied, male authorial voice is sacrificed, and Kumu recounts her story in first person. However, we cannot, as scholars, entirely eschew the fact that both stories are, after all, conceptions and creations of a physically able author. That gives rise to the question of genres and canonicity. How do we qualify something as disability literature? Should all texts by disabled writers find space in this genre? Should texts on the theme of disability – even by non-disabled writers – be seen as disability literature? Should we consider how the author's own dis/ableism has been presented in the text? If the author's subject position is not available for scrutiny in the narrative, should we read the story for the story's sake, or should our reading be coloured by biographical information on the writer? Personally, I am of the opinion that any work that deals with the theme of disability, irrespective of the *ability* of the writer, should be seen as disability literature. The canon should be defined by the motifs, themes and ideas explored in the work by the writer rather than considerations on the writer's physical functionality.

I chose to translate Tagore because Tagore is less of an individual and more of an experience that has enthralled the Indian imagination for decades now. Tagore's works are replete with metaphors that are a dissector's delight. Both 'Subha' and 'Drishtidaan' have been translated before. I have closely read two translations each of these two works: 'Subha', translated by Shormishtha Panja, included in the Fakrul Alam and Radha Chakravarty edited *The Essential Tagore* (2011), published by Harvard University Press in the United States and Visva-Bharati University in India; 'Subha' by an unacknowledged translator, included in the anthology *Mashi and Other Stories* (1918) published in New York by The Macmillan Company; Yasmin Faruque's translation of 'Drishtidaan' ('Second Sight') in the anthology *Tribute to Tagore* (2012) published by Trafford in the United States; and Arunava Sinha's translation of 'Drishtidaan' ('The Gift of Vision') which was undertaken as part of a symposium on Tagore – 'The Nation and its Poet' – held in July 2011.

I decided to translate these stories despite the existence of preceding translations for the following reasons:

a. I was not aware of 'Subha' and 'Drishtidaan' having been translated as part of any disability project earlier, and I was eager to explore the possibilities that can be thrown open by such an undertaking. As a translator, and as a scholar, I found that this work has been especially challenging given the lack of a comprehensive category of Indian disability literature in our academia. Characters with major physical disabilities have found a place in Indian literature since its inception – for instance, the blind king, Dhritarashtra, or the villainous uncle with a hunched back, Shakuni, in *The Mahabharata*. There are courses designed for Indian scholars at the undergraduate and/or graduate levels on Indian Writings in English or Women's Writings or Postcolonial Literatures, for example. The absence of a structured course or canon on disability literature is conspicuous. There are certain choices that I make in my translations that are experiential and politically motivated. Translation can be a form of social activism, and it is certainly an academic act, conscious of knowledge production and its dissemination.

b. When we translate Tagore we do so keeping in mind the Nobel laureate's 'inclusive genius' (Mehrotra 2011: XXXI). In his texts, there is just enough space for each reader to accommodate him- or herself, and therefore, every translation becomes an act of re-interpretation. It is often held that subsequent translations are done to better the existing one. However, a retranslation can very well complement the previous one instead of competing with it. My translations interact with the preceding ones. However, through my translations, I have tried to highlight an aspect of these stories which Tagore had possibly implied, but not mentioned explicitly, and which, to my mind, might have been undermined in previous translations: desires in the disabled and the issue of the rights of a disabled woman to be represented as 'a productive social subject *and* a reproductive sexual being and her right to represent others' (Millet-Gallant 2013: 398).

c. There is dignity, poise and balance in Tagore's portrayal of his women, Subha and Kumu. They are not stereotypes. Tagore's heroines are doubly marginalised: as women in nineteenth-century Bengal and as disabled individuals. Disability often becomes a site of cultural and social oppression. Disability is less of a clinically recognised medical condition and more of a sociocultural construction – a product of the hegemony of what we consider *normalcy*. Tagore is not guilty of representing his disabled characters as 'sentimentalized heroes or freakish spectacles' (Millet-Gallant 2013: 403). They have human needs. They have human flaws. They have human talents. They are of flesh and blood, immediately believable. Kumu is not the goddess that her husband idolises. Subha is not the freak that her husband rejects.

Desire and Disability

The title of this chapter hinges on three critical words – *translation, desire* and *undesired*. What makes a disabled person *undesired*? In his seminal essay, 'Fear, Pity and Disgust: Emotions and the Non-Disabled Imaginary', Bill Hughes argues that a non-disabled person's attitude towards a disabled subject is a consequence of the person's perspective which governs his emotions: emotions that range from fear to pity to disgust, emotions that are considered *normal* because they are shared and widespread. There is a traceable pattern to this kind of prejudice. The result, as Snyder and Mitchell point out, is 'the creation of a lethal social atmosphere' (2006: 30). While Tagore does not include disgust as a direct emotional attitude towards his subjects, he certainly shows fear and pity as common responses to Subha and Kumu. Subha was companionless. She found solace in the friendship of two cows – Sarbashi and Panguli – who understood her wordless expressions better than any human could. Tagore points out the reason behind other girls in the little hamlet of Chandipur avoiding Subha:

> They who from birth have had no other speech than the trembling of their lips learn a language of the eyes, endless in expression, deep as the sea, clear as the heavens, wherein play dawn and sunset, light and shadow. The dumb have a lonely grandeur like Nature's own. Wherefore the other children almost dreaded Subha and never played with her.
>
> (1918: 146–147)

Tagore delves into child psychology to find an explanation behind the able-bodied children staying away from Subha. The answer is fear. Subha is different. That instils in others a sense of awe.

In 'Drishtidaan', Kumu's friend Labanya asked her how she could forgive the husband who was responsible for her fate. Kumu benignly explained to her neighbour the need for understanding and adjustments for a happy family to work. Labanya is the prototype of the woman who is unwilling to make such compromises. She therefore shook her head in exasperation at Kumu's philosophy and left Kumu to her own devices. Kumu, because of her infinite love for her husband, because of the helplessness of her situation, and because of her need for peace, forgave her husband. Avinash saw in this act a sign of godliness and began to worship her. When their relationship was in ruins and Avinash was going out to bring home a second wife, he confessed to Kumu that he was scared of her:

> I'll tell you the truth. I'm afraid of you. Your blindness has shrouded you in an endless veil which I cannot draw or push aside to enter. You are my goddess, nay, more terrible than she; I cannot carry on mundane chores with you.
>
> (Tagore 2012: 49)

Tagore probes into the mind of a guilt-ridden husband to see what removes him gradually from the wife whom he had once sworn to serve. The answer is fear. Kumu is different. That instils in him a sense of awe. Hughes explains:

> The misrepresentation and disrespect – not to mention segregation and oppression – the disabled people suffer at the hands of their non-disabled

counterparts is a form of violence bred from our fear of and anguish about our alienation from the human condition where being human is simultaneously a facet of self and other.

(2012: 69)

The fear, as Hughes succinctly explains, is a consequence of our identification with the disabled person as essentially human, yet witnessing in this individual, aspects that are markers of obvious difference. Our inability to negotiate with the arbitrary, lucid definition of what it means to be human results in the creation of a chasm: between the Self and the Other, where, to borrow from Said's work, the Other is more of an idea, a reflection of what the Self imagines the Self is not (1978: 6–7). What the able-bodied society considers *ability* is arguably a temporary situation, with the threat of accidents, diseases or simply old age looming large over this notion of completeness and stability.

Tagore tells us that Kumu was once visited by her husband's aunt. The aunt wanted her nephew, Avinash, to remarry and possibly had her niece, Hemangini, in mind as a potential bride. Hemangini was summoned to the household. She was unaware of these adult machinations, and when she realised that Kumu had lost her vision, she wondered if their aunt had decided to visit the poor girl out of pity. She joked with Kumu that if their aunt had indeed come out of pity, she was not likely to budge from their house in a long time. Tagore, through Hemangini, makes fun of this kind of pity, this attitude which warrants that the 'less fortunate must be cast in the role of the subaltern' (Hughes 2012: 71). Tagore's story works wonderfully for me because he recognises that pity is a 'hierarchizing emotion in which superiority is at work in those who feel it and inferiority the projected status of those who are its targets' (Hughes 2012: 71). Tagore's narrator and protagonist is not in need of pity, she is in need of companionship, camaraderie. Hughes, referring to Nietzsche's critique of Christianity, points out how the German philosopher did not see pity as the 'highest-virtue' (2012: 71) but as an emotion that has a 'depressive effect' (2012: 71). He quotes Nietzsche's rejection of this Christian value: 'Nothing in our unhealthy modernity is more unhealthy than Christian pity' (Nietzsche 1968: 119). Tagore, too, recognises this gangrenous emotion – pity – as something that multiplies misery instead of alleviating discomfort. Consequent to such emotional responses (of pity, fear and disgust), the disabled subject becomes undesirable, and there is 'rabid segregation' (Snyder and Mitchell 2006: XI) in society.

Is the *undesired* capable of, and allowed to by the 'hegemony of the dominant group' (Sengupta 1996: 159) – in this case, the able-bodied – to have desires? An ableist space, which tilts in favour of the male gender and covets the white skin, does its worse to push anybody that doesn't fit this 'reified worldview' (Gentzler and Tymoczko 2002: XVI) to the periphery. A disabled woman is not supposed to have desires since such desires can provoke the 'fear that the disabled body will reproduce another "damaged" child' (Millet-Gallant 2013: 401), given that somewhere in the human psyche – the social *animal's* psyche – the role of sex is still perceived as limited to procreation and not recreation. The body of such a woman, thereby, becomes 'a site of social regulation' (Snyder and Mitchell 2006: 32).

The Translator's Choices and Political Correctness

Through my translations, I have attempted to foreground the desires in Subha and Kumu. Tymoczko says, 'translators must make choices, selecting aspects or parts of a text to transpose or emphasize' (2000: 24). These choices make translations of the same text different, and there cannot be any one kosher translated version of a text. The passage that I find most moving in 'Subha' is the one where she imagines herself to be the princess of a fairytale setting with her Prince Charming completing the picture. Pratap, a village loafer, passionate only about fishing, would spend hours by the stream that ran through their hamlet. Subha would sit under a tree nearby and give him silent company:

> And I think that, sitting and gazing a long while, she desired ardently to bring some great help to Pratap, to be of real aid, to prove by any means that she was not a useless burden to the world. But there was nothing to do. Then she turned to the Creator in prayer for some rare power, that by an astonishing miracle she might startle Pratap into exclaiming: "My! I never dreamt our Su could have done this!"
>
> Only think! If Subha had been a water nymph, she might have risen slowly from the river, bringing the gem of a snake's crown to the landing-place. Then Pratap, leaving his paltry fishing, might dive into the lower world, and see there, on a golden bed in a palace of silver, whom else but dumb little Su, Banikantha's child! Yes, our Su, the only daughter of the king of that shining city of jewels!
>
> (Tagore 1918: 150–151)

In my translation, I have deliberately used the word *mermaid* where *water-nymph* has been used in the given passage.[1] The story of the lovelorn mermaid is familiar to the English reading audience. A young Subha, with her fertile sense of imagination, fired probably by local fairy tales that she must have grown up on, is no different from an able-bodied girl of her age: in her search for love, as in her obvious difference from the norm, she becomes akin to the mermaid and her quest for romance. Pratap's (pre)occupation with water makes it easy for me to draw a link between him and the mythical merman. Subha's desire is unreciprocated. Her parents arrange to get her married off to a stranger (her tears of protest are misunderstood by her mother as well as the groom, who later rejects her in favour of a bride who can talk). When Pratap hears of Subha's parents having found for her, at long last, a suitable boy, he congratulates her and callously goes back to his fishing: 'As a stricken doe looks in the hunter's face, asking in silent agony: "What have I done you?" so Subha looked at Pratap. That day she sat no longer beneath her tree' (Tagore 1918: 153).

Subha's silence is both literal and metaphorical. How often in nineteenth-century Bengal had a girl been able to convey her confused love to a boy of her choice? How often was she able to refuse the plans that her parents proposed? How often was she been able to fight the blatant torture at the hands of her husband? How often had she not withered away, the victim of an ableist, patriarchal society? Subha silently lives her fate. She draws comparisons between Nature and herself – and in her psyche Nature is a symbol of female fecundity, the Prime Mother. Repeated instances in the story highlight Subha's feminine, maternal instincts too: the way she tends to her cows, the way she caresses her pet cat to sleep, even the way in which she brings Pratap his *paan* daily. Tagore counters the typical desire to represent the disabled as asexual, as beings without desires, by representing Subha as an adolescent with adolescent dreams. Tagore writes:

> All the world seemed to think that, because she did not speak, therefore she did not feel.
>
> (1918: 145)

Tagore's contention is clear: our inability to perceive or comprehend something does not negate the existence of that thing. Subha is inaudible to the world, but that is less because of her inability to speak and more because of our inability to hear. Therefore, as humans, we cannot be 'designating what disabled people want' (Snyder and Mitchell 2006: 6), and as artists, we cannot bind them through the tyranny of our representation. Tagore's practical observation, along with his sensitivity, informs my translation as well. The two words in the English language that describe a person who cannot speak are *mute* and *dumb*.[2] The word *dumb* in the English language has also, however, come to be used derogatorily to describe someone who is slow to learn or understand, who lacks intellectual acuity. In my translation I have deliberately made a certain linguistic choice: I have used the word *dumb* in only two places – once to describe the animals that Subha was friends with and with whom she is compared and then in the situation where the world looks at Subha as an object, as a cow that can be bought and sold or bartered with. In that my translation significantly differs from the preceding ones[3] where *mute* and *dumb* have been used interchangeably. I want to take responsibility for my choice of language. Kumu says in 'Drishtidaan', 'words can hurt' (Tagore 2012: 41). Words are not simple. They bear implications which as translators we need to be accountable for.

This leads us to the all-important questions of ethics: What kind of idiom can we use when representing disability? What kind of idiom is permissible when translating a text on disability? The issue of permission is rather complex and necessarily calls for an analysis of power structures. Who is the permitting body? Who is seeking permission? Who are we addressing? And, who are we offending? Helena Halmari in her essay 'Political Correctness, Euphemism and Language Change: The Case of "People First"' argues that while reformation in language is expected to bring about an attitudinal shift in people, it is not a foolproof method of addressing the problem of discrimination that disabled people face because language itself is arbitrary: words gather significance with changing times and politics (2011: 828–829). While *dumb* is today largely regarded as a derogatory word and *mute* is understood as permissible, it is quite likely that the latter word, too, will be rejected in future in favour of the more politically correct phrase 'people with hearing and/or speech impairment'. As Halmari puts it, 'unless all variation among humans – physical and intellectual variation included – gets somehow eliminated language will always find ways to refer to this variation' (2011: 839). There can be no such thing as perfect terminology. As writers, as translators therefore we need to aspire to fix attitudes instead of trying to fix language alone. Rita Kothari astutely highlights in her essay on translating Dalit literature that the translator's task is 'not simply aesthetic, cultural and political, but one that involves an attitude of praxis' as well (2007: 47). My Subha, therefore, is not dumb, only mute, and as a translator of a text on disability my attempt is to push for a worldview where disability is 'a simple physical characteristic rather than an ominous mark of otherness' (Kleege 2013: 455[4]).

Kumu's physical deficiency takes her husband away from her. Avinash needs an everyday woman for a wife. He says:

> I want a woman whom I can scold, fight with, love, and make jewelery for.
>
> (Tagore 2012: 49)

Avinash not only wants somebody to love but, more specifically, somebody to make love to as well.[5] My translation does not sanitise his longings. When plans of his second marriage do not materialise and he returns to his wife a chastised, reformed and humbled man, Kumu forgives him a second time, simultaneously reminding him that she is human:

> No, not a goddess, I am your wife; and only a mortal woman at that.
>
> (Tagore 2012: 51)

Earlier, too, Kumu had begged Avinash to see her humane side:

> Cut my chest open and look! I am just a woman, at heart no more than the child-bride you first married. I want to trust, to depend and to worship; don't humiliate yourself to make me larger than life and hurt me more than I can bear.
>
> (Tagore 2012: 49)

Avinash had not looked. For him, with Kumu's loss of vision there was a loss of the woman whom he had wedded. Kumu saw this coming:

> I understood that my blindness had served to distance us, so much so that perhaps my husband would never understand me again.
>
> (Tagore 2012: 43)

The yawning gap between Kumu and Avinash had been filled momentarily in the story by Hemangini. Hemangini was the cousin that Avinash wanted to marry and bring home as his second wife. For Kumu, Hemangini stood for the 'soft fragrance and beautiful music of friendship . . . the radiant glow and crisp freshness of real affection' (Tagore 2012: 48). Between the homosocial and the homosexual lies the liminal zone of the homoerotic. Where do the limits of a homosocial bond end, and when does a relationship become homoerotic? When Hemangini first visits their house, Kumu is immediately drawn to the simple, sweet laugh of the innocent village belle. She tells us:

> Taking Hema's hand I led her to our bedroom; I touched her all over to see her. She probably had a pretty face, and was no less than fourteen or fifteen.
>
> (Tagore 2012: 45)

In my translation, I deliberately use the word *caressed* instead of *touched* to direct my readers in a particular way. How does Kumu guess Hemangini's age by touching her? Presumably by running her hands over the girl's anatomical features to get an idea of her build and her growth. Hemangini's response is noteworthy:

> What on earth are you doing? Do you want to exorcise me? . . . Am I a bean or an eggplant in your garden that you have to feel me to find out how big I've grown?
>
> (Tagore 2012: 45)

What kind of space did Iras and Charmian occupy in Cleopatra's life?[6] Did Olivia love Orsino (or even Sebastian – the lookalike that she was forced to marry to adhere to the conventions of an Elizabethan comedy) as much as she loved Viola dressed as Cesario[7]? Can Orsino ever be as drawn to Viola as he was to his Man-Friday Cesario?[8] Can one really be blind to the dynamics between Binodini and Ashalata?[9] Hemangini asks Kumu, soon after they meet, 'What do you say, dear? You are not that close to me, I believe' (Tagore 2012: 45). Kumu does not have answers to Hemangini's searching questions; she simply draws the girl close to her bosom and solidifies their ties. Hemangini immediately takes the next step. When their aunt tries to separate them by frivolously asking the young girl to take a shower, Hemangini tells Kumu, '[C]ome, my sister, let's go bathe together' (Tagore 2012: 46). The bathing area, the kitchen, the backyard – the places that women in the average Bengali household in the nineteenth century were relegated to – became spaces for female bonding. Hemangini unceremoniously rejects Avinash by throwing away the pearl ring that he had bought her and by marrying Kumu's elder brother. In that she is not doing Kumu a favour; there is no patronising here, only solidarity and fraternity. Did Tagore imagine Kumu and Hemangini as Sapphic heroines? Did he wish to represent their relationship as secretly homoerotic? If not, then as Benjamin points out in 'The Task of the Translator', 'the original undergoes a change' (1923: n.p.) necessarily and even 'words with fixed meanings undergo a maturing process' (1923: n.p.) in the act of translation. A translation gives a new lease of life the original; it is a kind of rebirth. Translation is personal and partial. This rereading, this opening up of spaces, this active intervention of the translator that leads to new interrogations and challenges becomes the translator's contribution to the original, thereby making the process of translation akin to 'reinventing' (Doniger 2011: XX).

Translating Literature on Disability

To conclude my chapter, I shall posit certain questions that translators of texts centred on disability could ask themselves. In this, I follow the model that Sujit Mukherjee had proposed (2004: 39–41) when he identified the need for an Indian theory of translation:

a   Who is fit to translate a text on disability? (Someone who is an expert in the language pair? Someone who is an expert on disability studies? Someone who is differently abled?)

b   Why do we translate a text on disability? (Are we following somebody's instructions?[10] Do we have a political agendum?[11] Are we doing it for the love of the text?)

c   Which texts should we select? (The answer to this is dependent on the answer to the previous question.[12])

d   Who are we translating this text on disability for? (The non-disabled reader? The disabled reader who is not familiar with the language of the original text? Or are we not thinking of a specific target audience and attempting to do a meaningful translation that might benefit anybody who chooses to read it?)

e   Should there be a particular idiom to represent marginalities, specifically disability?

The translation of a text on disability could be critical to 'the growing social recognition and analysis of disabled people's situation[s]' (Snyder and Mitchell 2006: 4) and a conscious, political act 'to reclaim disability as something more than tragedy, dysfunction and misfortune' (Snyder and Mitchell 2006: 4). Through my translation of 'Subha' and 'Drishtidaan' I have attempted to make theory meet praxis. My translations have the ideological purpose of making a language in which I read, write, think and dream, a language that has spoken for me, speak for the disabled woman and her desires.

Notes

1 The original Bengali phrase used by Tagore is *juvol-kumari*.

2 The Bengali word that describes such a person is *boba*, and Tagore has used that word in his story several times.

3 As in Shormishtha Panja's translation, for instance.

4 Kleege here refers to Deborah Kendrick's image of the future of blindness in Kendrick's story '20/20 with a Twist' (1987) which was anthologised in *With Wings: An Anthology*

of Literature by and About Women with Disabilities, edited by Marsha Saxton and Florence Howe, New York, NY: Feminist Press at the City University of New York.

5 Tagore originally used the phrase *sohaag koribo*. *Sohaag* in Bengali means 'love' – though not necessarily sexual, definitely physical.

6 In Shakespeare's *Antony and Cleopatra*.

7 Is it a mere coincidence that the letters of Olivia's name rearranged read: I –Viola?

8 In Shakespeare's *Twelfth Night*.

9 In Tagore's *Chokher Bali*.

10 We cannot undermine the 'role and power of the editors in enabling the publication of such texts' (Kothari 2007: 39) and creating some disturbance in the area of disability studies. Publication of this kind of literature can help widen the scope of disability studies beyond 'sheltered workshops' (Snyder and Mitchell 2006: 3).

11 It is often argued that translators undertake the work they do 'because they believe the text they produce will benefit humanity or impact positively upon the receptor culture in ways that are broadly ideological' (Tymoczko 2000: 26). Translation could be effective in the following political ways: (a) it could be 'a tool of empowerment' (Kothari 2007: 49) for the disabled who can carry their narratives forward to a larger readership; (b) translation could play a role in 'the formation of cultural construction' (Tymoczko 2000: 24) and make us take a hard, second look at our preconceived notions of disability and functionality (not only physical functionality by social functionality too); (c) translation could become that site 'where questions of representation and history converge as we attempt to account for the practices of subjectification' (Niranjana 1989: 109) and try to break the hegemony of the norm – the norm which is not necessarily the ideal.

12 Tymoczko goes to the extent of suggesting that texts should be chosen with 'political goals in view, and, if need be, there must be a willingness to manipulate the texts in translation so as to adapt and subordinate the texts to political aims and agendas' (2000: 50–51).

References

Benjamin, Walter. 1923. 'The Translator's Task'. Trans. Steven Randall. www.google.co.in/url?sa=t&rct=j&q=&esrc=s&source=web&cd=1&cad=rja&uact=8&ved=0ahUKEwiHpq7V9ZrWAhVBp48KHeRvD7cQFggnMAA&url=http%3A%2F%2Fwww.enl.auth.gr%2Fstaff%2Fapostolou%2Fthe_Translator%2527s_Task.pdf&usg=AFQjCNFv4WfEpn8_5wDq46MfVFpz7RdiqQ (accessed on 22 October 2013).

Doniger, Wendy. 2011. 'Preface', in *Songs of Kabir*. India: Hachette Book Publishing India Pvt. Ltd.

Gentzler, Edwin and Maria Tymoczko. 2002. 'Introduction', *Translation and Power*. Boston and Amherst: University of Massachusetts Press.

Halmari, Helena. 2011. 'Political Correctness, Euphemism, and Language Change: The Case of "People First"', *Journal of Pragmatics*, 43: 828–840.

Hughes, Bill. 2012. 'Fear, Pity and Disgust: Emotions and the Non-disabled Imaginary', in Nick Watson, Alan Roulstone and Carol Thomas (eds) *Routledge Handbook of Disability Studies*. London: Routledge.

Kleege, Georgina. 2013. 'Blindness and Visual Culture: An Eyewitness Account', in Lennard J. Davis (ed) *The Disability Studies Reader*. New York, NY: Routledge.

Kothari, Rita. 2007. 'The Translation of Dalit Literature into English', in Jeremy Munday (ed) *Translation as Intervention*. London: Continuum International Publishing Group.

Mehrotra, Arvind Krishna. 2011. *Songs of Kabir*. India: Hachette Book Publishing India Pvt. Ltd.

Millet-Gallant, Ann. 2013. 'Sculpting Body Ideals: "Alison Lapper Pregnant" and the Public Display of Disability', in Lennard J. Davis (ed) *The Disability Studies Reader*. New York, NY: Routledge.

Mukherjee, Sujit. 2004. 'The Craft Not Sullen Art of Translation', in Meenakshi Mukherjee (ed) *Translation as Recovery*. Delhi: Pencraft International.

Nietzsche, Friedrich. 1968. *The Twilight of the Idols and the Anti-Christ*. Trans. Reginald John Hollingdale. Harmondsworth: Penguin.

Niranjana, Tejaswini. 1989. 'Representation, History and the Case of Translation', *Journal of Arts and Ideas*, 17–18: 109–115. Delhi: Tulika Print Communication Services.

Said, Edward. 1978. 'Introduction', in *Orientalism*. New York, NY: Pantheon.

Sengupta, Mahashweta. 1996. 'Translation as Manipulation: The Power of Images and Images of Power', in Anuradha Dingwaney and Carol Maier (eds) *Between Languages and Cultures: Translation and Cross-Cultural Texts*. Delhi: Oxford University Press.

Snyder, Sharon L. and David T. Mitchell. 2006. *Cultural Locations of Disability*. Chicago, IL: University of Chicago Press.

Tagore, Rabindranath. 2012. 'Second Sight', in Yasmin Faruque (trans), *Tribute to Tagore*. Manchester: Trafford.

———. 1918. 'Subha', in *Mashi and Other Stories*. New York, NY: Macmillan Company.

Tymoczko, Maria. 2000. 'Translation and Political Engagement: Activism, Social Change and the Role of Translation in Geopolitical Shifts', *The Translator*, 6(1): 23–47. Manchester: St. Jerome Publishing.

8

'BLIND' FATE AND THE DISABLED GENIUS

Postcoloniality and 'translation' in Saurabh Kumar Chaliha's 'Beethoven'

Rajashree Bargohain

Saurabh Kumar Chaliha[1] was the pen name of Surendra Nath Medhi (1930–2011), a renowned short story writer in the Asamiya[2] language. With more than a dozen published short story collections to his credit, Chaliha was honoured with the Sahitya Akademi Award in 1974 for his anthology *Ghulam* (*Slave*). His short story 'Beethoven' (1974) is based on the struggles of the eponymous musical genius against his hearing disabilities. The narrative unfolds with a frame story: two musician friends are found reflecting on the essence of Beethoven's music. They muse over the underlying philosophy about human life that the music seems to convey. One friend, the first-person narrator, proposes that it is the musical expression of the general human condition. The friends, then, try to visualise a young Beethoven who has arrived from Bonn in the streets of eighteenth-century Vienna. They follow the young Beethoven of their imagination through the exciting days of his early success and then through the agonising days of his gradually decreasing auditory power. The friends infer that the disability and resultant suffering undergone by Beethoven is not pointless; it had a superior purpose: the creation of music that is infused with the pathos and pain, the joys and desires and a protest against the unfairness and imperfections of human life. The narrator, in fact, expresses gratitude for the fact that medical science in that age was not advanced enough to cure the musician of his disability; although he feels for Beethoven's personal sufferings, he is grateful for the priceless music that it helped produce.

Many postcolonial scholars have drawn attention to the numerous and crucial intersections between postcolonial writing and the practice of translation (Bassnett and Trivedi 2002; Tymoczko 2002; Tymoczko 2014). However, there is a lack of engagement in current theoretical discourses with the cultural interactions between postcolonial societies and the Western world manifested in texts produced in languages of non-Western origin. This chapter proposes that all postcolonial texts, especially those written in indigenous languages, are complex repositories of multiple layers of translation and 'transcreation'. Through an analysis of 'Beethoven', the chapter also seeks to examine the power hierarchies inscribed in acts of translation from Indian languages into major world languages like English, which also happen to be the languages of former colonisers. The chapter also situates Chaliha's short story within the broader context of the evolution of attitudes towards disability in postcolonial Assam and its literary representations. It has been facilitated by a comparative understanding of the representation of disability in Assamese folk literature and an investigation of the continuities and changes in these attitudes in modern postcolonial Assamese texts.

Translation and 'Beethoven'

Another short story by Saurabh Kumar Chaliha, 'Ghulam', from which his collection derives its title, narrates the story of a man from Assam undergoing a diploma course in the basic usage of the German language in Germany. The first-person narrator of this story finds a clever way of securing his diploma with minimal effort. He is required to write an essay about his hometown in German, based on the quality of which, he will be rewarded with his much-needed diploma. In order to make his task simple, the narrator copies out an essay titled 'Snow in our City' from an old German–English handbook. All he does is replace the German city in the essay with his hometown, Guwahati. The story describes how the essay that he hands over to his German instructor ends up sounding rather absurd and farcical; instead of a monsoon-ravaged Guwahati, with its poor amenities and lack of infrastructure, and a lower middle-class family to which he belongs, the Guwahati of his essay becomes a merry German town in the snowy season.

The story 'Ghulam' is relevant here as a comment on the complex web within which the postcolonial world and the postcolonial writer is caught. In a similar context, Maria Tymoczko compares the works of postcolonial writers to a house of mirrors (Tymoczko 2002: 19). Although Tymoczko does not elaborate on the analogy, the metaphor can be used to visualise the peculiar situation of the modern writer who writes in a regional Indian language, especially in the writing of stories like 'Ghulam' and 'Beethoven',[3] for he or she gets tangled in a similarly intricate process of translations and cultural transference. In a vein similar to Tymoczko's, citing Salman Rushdie's observation that all postcolonial migrant writers like him are 'translated men', G.J.V. Prasad underlines the fact that all texts created by Indian English writers are, in fact, 'translated' and that their very act of writing is one of translation (2002: 41). Prasad's observation can be extended to include not just Indian English writings but texts written in other Indian languages as well, although the process gets reversed in the case of the latter; while the Indian English writer's task is to present a non-Western world in the English language, the latter is faced with the challenges of communicating in a non-Western language the manifestly hybrid world of the postcolonial person. Most postcolonial scholars have focused their attention on the presentation of the non-Western world in Western cultural and literary texts or the negotiations with the Western world embodied in works written in the languages of the colonisers. However, scholarly thinking on translation studies has mostly been found to overlook the engagements of postcolonial societies with the Western world manifested in works written in languages of non-Western origin. Doris Jedamski has drawn attention to this rather surprising lack of scholarly attention paid to postcolonial literary works written in languages other than the languages of the colonisers (Jedamski 2009: IX–XVII). It is in this context that the short story 'Ghulam' becomes an inadvertent but telling comment on the layers of translation or cultural transference that the postcolonial Indian writer writing in a regional language has to undertake and undergo. It would not be an exaggeration to assert here that at one level, a modern Asamiya literary text, like a modern text in any of the other Indian languages, is always already a work of 'translation'. This section of the chapter seeks to therefore unearth the ways in which 'translation' presents itself as a crucial component in the writing of the story 'Beethoven'.

The story 'Beethoven' revolves around an autobiographical episode in the life of the Western musical composer. Thus, the writer of this story has had the task of presenting in the Asamiya language and idiom, a tale that is set in a Western city (Vienna) with an alien culture. Chaliha has thus translated a Viennese landscape, language, culture and way of being into Asamiya and without the use of footnotes too. The writer's task has been doubly complicated as he has had to convey to an Assamese reader not only a story set in an alien culture but also that from a different era, for although the frame story involves events occurring in contemporary Assam, the events of the core story are set in the distant past. Thus, Chaliha has translated or rather 'transferred' a Viennese cultural setting both spatially as well as temporally. Maria Tymoczko has also highlighted the fact that the task of literary translation and that of postcolonial writing share a central concern with the translation and transmission of elements from one culture to another (Tymoczko 2002: 22). In other words, translation and postcolonial writing are similar exercises. The translator of a postcolonial text thus naturally finds herself in an extremely tangled situation. In a way, then, the story 'Beethoven' already contains layers of translation and 'transcreation'. A translation of Chaliha's 'Beethoven' into English at this point would just be a continuation of the process already initiated by the writer.[4]

The complicated position of the translator of this short story becomes especially evident while engaging with a portion of the story which employs a substantial amount of scientific jargon in providing physiological explanations of the condition of Beethoven's ears. Translating this part does not prove to be a particularly difficult task, as the equivalent terminology for the technical terms is quite readily available in English, the *lingua franca* of scientific communication in today's world. But it is also important to remember that this simplicity of the task owes to the fact that the scientific terminology and description employed in the story has its origin in the Western medical tradition; the Asamiya terms are mostly translations from their English originals, which in turn have been derived from eclectic cultural and linguistic sources. The ironies involved in the task of the postcolonial writer-translator are illustrated by the fact that certain terms (such as *cochlea* and *cochlear osteosclerosis*) have been left untranslated by Chaliha and simply been transcribed into Asamiya characters, for they do not have equivalent terms in the Asamiya language. Evidently, it is the writer of this story, rather than his later translator, who has been faced by challenges of untranslatability and linguistic anisomorphism.

Throughout its history, the Assam valley has been a busy conduit of human migrations as well as cultural and trade-related interactions between various peoples. A composite Assamese identity that first took shape due to the political and cultural unification of the entire Brahmaputra Valley during the reign of the Ahom kingdom (1228–1826 CE) was characterised by the fusion of a multiplicity of cultural traditions. This composite character of the Assamese identity reached further consolidation during the colonial and post-independence periods and the modern Asamiya language bears marks of this inherent hybridity of modern Assamese culture. Linguists have even identified the presence of words of Persian and Arabic origin in medieval Asamiya texts like *Buranjis*[5] and Vaishnavite writings (Goswami 2003: 112). The conspicuous presence of loan words, phrases and expressions of Western origin in the modern Asamiya vocabulary is a testament to the lasting effects of the exposure of the region to Western cultures mainly through colonial association. Postcolonial contact of the people of Assam with the Western world not only led to enormous impacts on the culture and language of the valley, but it also exposed the Asamiya literature of the period to a wide range of influences from Western artistic movements and literary styles. The emergence and growth of modern literary forms such as the short story and the novel are evidence of the literary influences of the West on literature in Indian languages, including Asamiya. Assamese historians have pointed out colonial contact as a kind of life-giving touch to the decadent Assamese culture and literature of the late medieval age (Neog 2013: 226; Phukan 2005: 0.07). Assamese writers of the post-independence period have especially been deeply influenced by the dominant literary movements in their contemporary world.[6] The manifestly hybrid character of its language, literature and culture is indicative of the intensity of the cultural osmosis that has taken place in postcolonial Assam through its interactions with the Western world. This hybridity plays a crucial role in facilitating the writing of a story like 'Beethoven', where the presentation in the Asamiya language of events set in a Western culture has been a mostly seamless process. Moreover, it leads to relatively few complications in the process of translating it into English. While translating an Asamiya text set in a traditional Assamese background would have met with difficulties of conveying cultural peculiarities in the English language, the largely modern setting of the frame story and the evolved nature of the language in 'Beethoven' simplifies the task of the translator. Thus, the translation of the story poses relatively very few challenges in terms of cultural translation.

However, postcolonial scholars have drawn attention to the asymmetrical power relations between peoples, races and languages embedded in acts of translation, especially in the context of postcolonial cultures (Niranjana 1995;Tymoczko 2014). Tejaswini Niranjana has illustrated how translation was employed by the coloniser to represent the colonised subject and his world through a colonialist lens and thereby push the colonialist agenda (Niranjana 1995: 2). However, the end of colonialism did not mean the end of translation activities or a dramatic shift in the power hierarchy between languages and language communities. I seek to situate this translation of 'Beethoven' as a postcolonial Asamiya text into English, the language of the former coloniser, in the context of the continuing validity of the hegemonic influence of languages introduced through colonialism in the postcolony. Although English is no longer considered to be the reserve of native speakers alone, it is impossible to undermine the fact that the growth of English language speakers across the globe and its continuing relevance in the postcolonial world are largely colonial legacies. The need or desire to translate a text from a minority Indian language into English today owes mostly to the hegemonic power of English as a major world language. Although spoken by a tiny minority of the Indian population, the powerful position of English in this country, as in postcolonial societies elsewhere, is closely related to its coveted status as the language of power, privilege and upward mobility. In the intensely multilingual set up of India, the role of English as a useful link language cannot be denied. Yet, the continuing position of English at the very top of the language hierarchy in postcolonial India has generated much anxiety and has been at the heart of debates regarding the threat it poses to the visibility of bhasha literature in the country.

In the context of this unequal power distribution between languages underlying translation activities, Susan Basnett contends that 'the only way for translation to become valid is for it to take place from the dominant into the less powerful language . . . [which, then] becomes a political statement that asserts the rising status of the formerly marginalized tongue' (Bassnett 2007: 20). By employing the representation of a Western culture and setting in the Asamiya language, Chaliha's story has effected a reversal in the direction of the translation process. Yet such a reversal cannot do away with the skewed power equation between a colonising culture and the post-colony. The choice of the title in Chaliha's story 'Ghulam' foregrounds the continuing hold of neocolonial forces over the postcolonial world. Although the Western material has been handled in 'Beethoven' with an air of casual confidence, the unequal power relations between the two cultures that it seeks to bridge manifest themselves in the narrative at many subtle levels. The very need to narrate the story of a Western musical icon in an Asamiya short story underscores the lasting impact of the colonial hegemony that the satire in 'Ghulam' is directed at. The ease with which a Viennese cultural setting has fit into the setting of the frame story is because the latter belongs to an evidently upper-class elite setting; the narrator's friends not only have access to Western classical music but display considerable skills of appreciation of the music, which would be unusual among ordinary Assamese masses. The story, in fact, provides very little description of the setting in the frame narrative, which has saved the writer from the dilemma of handling incongruities arising from bringing together two completely disparate cultures. The ineluctable power dynamics between the two cultures represented in the story manifests itself in these textual absences.

Yet, the hegemonic control of Western powers over the postcolonial world has never been left uncontested. By reversing the process of cultural translation, 'Beethoven' acts as an instance of returning the Western gaze. 'Ghulam' not only offers a parody of the domination of Western imperialist powers over the world of the postcolonial person, but in a playful manner, it also goes on to show the ingenious ways in which the postcolonial subject negotiates with and works around the powers that seek to control him. In 'Beethoven', although a Western musical figure has been used as an example of human triumph over the trials of life and nature, it would be too simple to assume that the story espouses an unproblematic, naive admiration for the Western world. Chaliha's stories are known for their complex narrative techniques and it is the intricate tale-within-a-tale structure of 'Beethoven' which indeed poses a fair amount of challenge during its translation. His stories seldom employ an omniscient narrator. The narrative in 'Beethoven' follows a conversational style and contains a fair amount of incomplete sentences and free-floating phrases conveying the narrator's half thoughts and impressions, which almost amount to interior monologues at times. Transitions between the frame narrative and the core tale often assume a fluid character, creating much ambiguity for the reader/translator. This complex narrative structure of 'Beethoven' can be read as a disguise for the deep-seated postcolonial anxieties generated by imperialist legacies of cultural and racial hierarchies and oppression. The narrative unreliability produced by the first-person narrative structure affords the story with an emotional and rational distance that serves to veil the complex love–hate relationship of the postcolonial writer/person with his or her powerful Western oppressors. However, at one point in the story, the narrator takes the liberty of mildly mocking typical German names: 'do not worry (the physician says), do not worry, Herr Kapellmeister (or Herr Hofforganist, or something of that kind)' (Chaliha 2012: 92, translation mine). This superfluous bit of information added inside parentheses in the story, which sounds like an afterthought, is an instance where the anxiety underlying the narrative breaks through to the surface.

Disability and 'Beethoven'

A translation of the short story 'Beethoven' also calls for an engagement with the treatment of disability in the text and in literature in general. The short story needs to be situated within the broader context of attitudes towards disability as reflected in its cultural representations, especially its literary representations, in Assam. The available literature on the area reveals an intricate history behind the development and consolidation of the concept of 'disability' in modern societies. Most European scholars acknowledge that the concepts of the 'normal' and 'disabled' have varied and evolved through the course of history. The transfer and absorption of modern Western value systems and world views introduced through colonial and postcolonial contact have been crucial in shaping postcolonial cultures around the world. As 'translated' spaces, the postcolonial experience has also influenced the complex process through which disability has come to be conceptualised and represented in postcolonial cultures around the world, including modern Assamese culture and literature. The treatment of disability in the story 'Beethoven' must be understood by placing it in the context of this evolution of attitudes towards disability in Assamese society and literature. The postcolonial experience has not been uniform across the world. This chapter is an attempt to understand the particular history through which the cultural representation of disability and disabled bodies in Assam has taken shape through close readings of several Asamiya texts employing disability and disabled figures. In order to trace this history, the following sections of the chapter take a detour and first examine the representation of disability in Assamese folk literature and then investigate the continuities and gradual changes that have taken place in literary representations of disability in modern Assamese texts under postcolonial influences. The presentation of disability in the short story 'Beethoven' is then studied in the light of this modern, postcolonial literary and cultural context.

Disability in traditional Assamese culture

While postcolonial scholars have illustrated that concepts of what constitutes as 'normal' or 'disabled' are culturally contingent and not universal (Barker 2011; Ingstad and Whyte 1995; Quayson 2007), most European scholars fail to take account of these horizontal variations that may exist across cultures at a given point of time. However, it must also be remembered at this point that most of the cultural distinctions have become or are in the process of becoming obliterated in the postcolonial world, mainly due to the incursion of modernity. If the colonial subject fixed to his or her native site and the migrant postcolonial are 'translated persons' (Bassnett and Trivedi 2002: 12), most indigenous cultures across the globe are also in the process of getting 'lost in translation'. In fact, the loss of indigenous cultures, traditions and value systems in the postcolonial period is a cause of much anxiety among cultures across North-East India (Chasie 2005; Thong 2012; Zama 2006). Most of the cultures in postcolonial societies in their current form are in a state of dilution, with elements imbibed from modern cultures that they have come into contact with since colonialism. This is true in the case of attitudes towards and representation of disability as well. The following two sections of this chapter try to understand the evolution of modern attitudes towards disability in postcolonial Assamese texts and undertake an analysis of Beethoven in this context.

Growing out of a region that has been riddled with battles, diseases, insurgency and economic backwardness at various stages of its history, Assamese culture and literature abound with images of disabled, deformed and diseased bodies. Without trying to be exhaustive, this paper will make a quick survey of a few Assamese folk narratives that employ cultural representations of disabled figures. Ann Schmiesing points out the presence of frequent portrayals of disability, deformity and disease in the *Grimms' Fairy Tales*. Although her work lays its focus on the fairytales collected by the Grimm brothers alone, she has pointed out that the portrayal of deformed or disabled subjects is found to appear frequently in fairytales all around the world (Schmiesing 2014: 2). The collection of Assamese folktales *Burhi*

Air Sadhu (*Grandma's Tales*) by Lakshminath Bezborooah is peopled with several characters that possess disabilities and deformities. Thus, Chutibai, one of the central characters in the tale 'Tikhar aru Chutibai', is an orphaned girl with stunted growth; the story 'Kukurikona' describes the misadventures of a man suffering from nyctalopia (Bezborooah 2013). As a significant departure from modern fictional narratives, folk tales usually do not include elaborate descriptions of the scene or setting; they merely furnish the bare details that are most essential to the plot. None of these folktales display a propensity to attach a sentimental value to the disabled condition of its characters; the matter-of-fact nature of the storytelling does not allow for such sentimentalising. This feature in the folktales is noteworthy here, for as a later section will show, a close analysis of modern Assamese narratives reveals a marked attitudinal shift in this regard as far as their treatment of disabled characters is concerned.

Mitchell and Snyder have explained how disability and deformity act as metaphorical devices in literature. They have termed this appropriation of disability in literary narratives as 'narrative prosthesis' and claim that 'all narratives operate out of a desire to compensate for a limitation or to reign in excess' (Mitchell and Snyder 2000: 53). According to Schmiesing, in fairytales, the proposed theory of narrative prosthesis manifests in the form of what Vladimir Propp and Alan Dundes have pointed out as a basic pattern 'that moves from disequilibrium to equilibrium, from enchantment to disenchantment, and from disability to ability and bodily perfection' (Schmiesing 2014: 2). The tale 'Kona Aru Kuja' from Bezborooah's *Koka Deuta Aru Nati Lora*, which recounts the adventures of a blind man and a hunchbacked person, concludes with a scuffle between the two in which they miraculously end up being 'healed' of their respective disabilities. 'Nimati Koina' ('The Silent/Mute Damsel'), another folktale from the same collection, has a tale-within-a-tale structure. It narrates the story of a clever prince who, at the end of a series of adventures, finds a 'mute' princess, whom he must 'cure' of her disability. The prince does not produce a miraculous cure for her muteness but tricks the king into believing that he has cured her and 'wins' the princess for a bride as a reward, along with a fat dowry (Bezborooah 2013). Reaching a 'cure' for the disability of the character(s) in each of these tales, in fact, becomes the vehicle which brings about the resolution in the plot. Although both these folktales thus manifest instances of 'narrative prosthesis', the use of disability as the MacGuffin around which the action of the narrative is structured assumes yet more complex metaphoric proportions in modern narratives. I shall illustrate this point by analysing a modern rendition of the folktale about the mute princess in the following section.

Disability in modern Assamese literature and Chaliha's 'Beethoven'

The arrival of the British colonisers in Assam in the early part of the nineteenth century brought about great changes in the society and subsequently in the literature of Assam. Efforts by the American Baptist Missionaries led to the setting up of the first printing press in Sibsagar (1836) and the subsequent standardisation of the Asamiya language, which paved the path for the arrival of the modern era in the history of Asamiya literature in the late nineteenth century.[7] Colonial modernity, introduced through Western education led to gradual changes in the attitudes, customs, culture and lifestyles of the Assamese people. This section examines the changes and continuities in the treatment of disability in Asamiya literature produced in the postcolonial period.

With the spread of modern value systems and ways of living, the conceptualisation of and attitudes towards disability in the Assamese society also underwent significant departures from its pre-modern past. Societal changes that brought about shifts in the way disability was constituted and treated in modern Assamese society were accompanied by a different, more complex way of presenting disability in modern Asamiya literary texts as well. The fairytale 'Nimati Koina' in Bezborooah's book contains a series of adventures in the life of a prince and the part concerning the mute princess is a brief tale that appears only at the end. This tale from Bezborooah's book was adapted for the musical play 'Nimati Koina' (1936) by Jyotiprasad Agarwalla (1903–1951), a doyen of modern Asamiya literature as well as modern Assamese music (Jyotiprasad 2007). However, in his dramatic rendition, Agarwalla retained only the last episode of the tale which narrates the story of the mute princess. The bare narrative style of the earlier folktale now received an intricate treatment in the hands of the modern writer. While the folktale has a rather ambiguous ending, in Agarwalla's version of the story, the mute princess is 'cured' of her disability as she breaks into song at the end of the play. Besides, in this modern rendition of the folktale, Agarwalla has used the figure of the mute princess to embody an elaborate metaphor of Art-as-goddess, and the narrative is intended to stand for the victory of relentless spiritual striving and perseverance (*sādhanā*) in the effort to please the goddess of Art. The focus in Agarwalla's text has thus shifted from a simple narration of the basic story to its appropriation in metaphoric proportions for conveying an underlying philosophical message. Mitchell and Snyder have termed such metaphorical use of disability the 'materiality of metaphor' (Mitchell and Snyder 2000: 48). This explicit metaphorical appropriation of the comparatively simple folktale by Agarwalla is indicative of the complexities that emerged in Asamiya literary narratives as well as in their conceptions and representations of disability in the postcolonial period. As the analysis of the Assamese folktales has shown, they did not display the propensity to sentimentalise and dramatise the depiction of disabled figures. But the arrival of colonial modernity and the spread of Western education led to the emergence of a modern consciousness, and as Agarwalla's play demonstrates, descriptions of disability in postcolonial Asamiya texts were now no longer value-free.

Chaliha's 'Beethoven', too, makes use of biographical information about the great musician to construct a narrative that conveys a philosophical reflection on human life. The chief purpose of the story is not to narrate the already-well-known story about Beethoven's disability; rather, the tangibility of his disability becomes a vehicle that bestows concreteness on the abstract philosophy that the story seeks to convey. Chaliha's treatment of the disability of the character revolves, if not so much, around finding or not finding a 'cure' than on justifying or finding a rationale for the 'misfortune'. The characters in the frame story, who are found reflecting on Beethoven's disability and his music, try to find an explanation for Beethoven's sufferings. The narrative is thus structured around the hero/heroic quest motif which is occupied with overcoming a barrier and achieving glory. The postcolonial shift becomes clear when we see that unlike the pre-modern Assamese writings which treated disability in an unsentimental matter-of-fact manner, in Chaliha's story, the disabled body becomes a dramatised value-laden entity.

The conception of disability varies across cultures, and it is impossible to arrive at a single accurate definition of disability. Yet, current scholarship on disability agrees on the view that disability is largely a social construct. The condition of disability arises not so much out of a physical or mental 'disorder', as much as it is created by the social constraints and disadvantages imposed upon a non-normative body by an ableist social order. Disability in its particular social and cultural context is brought into existence through the non-disabled gaze. Bill Hughes has identified fear, pity and disgust as the 'building blocks of the emotional infrastructure of ablism'(2012: 68). The story 'Beethoven' supplies elaborate descriptions of the conditions of Beethoven's life both before and after the loss of his auditory powers. The initial picture of his life is one of vibrancy, prosperity and supreme success. However, this picture of his life before he loses his hearing ability contrasts starkly with that of his life as a disabled person, which is marked by loneliness, despair and defeat. While the earlier picture is one of health and tidiness, the latter is ruled by images of squalor and slovenliness.

Both passages describing Beethoven's circumstances before and after the onset of his hearing condition begin in a similar manner, which serves to deepen the contrast between the two stages. By highlighting the contrast between the two pictures the story has managed to intensify the poignancy of Beethoven's situation. It is important to note here that the story does not claim historical truth or concrete biographical facts from Beethoven's life as the basis of any of its descriptions. They have been presented as conjectures based on the two friends' imagination of what Beethoven's situation may have been like. What is significant here is that their imagination is based on normalist expectations regarding the image of a disabled person; Beethoven's disability here becomes a construct of their imagination. While the historical Beethoven may or may not have experienced the situations imagined by the friends, their construction of a mental image of Beethoven as a disabled person is couched in a language of pity and disgust. Bill Hughes has also explained how pity, fear and disgust figure as the ruling emotions in the modern conception of disability. Social exclusion and disadvantages as the 'tragic' but essential component of the condition of disability are the very foundation on which disability is sought to be configured in modern, post-industrial societies. Thus, the focus in 'Beethoven' lies on the troubles and sharp decline in Beethoven's social and professional circumstances, as imagined by the narrators, for they are assumed to be a natural corollary to the disabled condition.

'Constructing' Beethoven's disability in the story in a poignant manner by providing a vivid and evocative description of the 'tragedy' in his life is also vital from a narratorial point of view, for more the intensity of his hardships and misery, the greater the value of his struggles and eventual achievement. Moreover, it serves to heighten the drama in the story, which, in turn, reinforces its philosophical argument. As a modern postcolonial text, 'Beethoven', then, has come a long way from the simple bare descriptions of disability found in pre-modern Assamese texts. In 'Beethoven', as in most other modern Assamese texts, disability has become a romanticised narratorial trope and, in the words of Mitchell and Snyder, 'the master trope of human disqualification' (2000: 3).

If the postcolonial text is a work of translation and if the writer of 'Beethoven' qualifies as a translator, Chaliha can be said to have produced a fairly faithful and objective translation of the Western material in his story. Yet, this does not necessarily imply an unsophisticated acceptance of the Western worldview in Chaliha's text or in postcolonial cultures in general. A close reading of the text reveals a tacit critical undercurrent in the short story. Chaliha's stories are conspicuous for his strong grip on the narrative structure and the short story 'Beethoven' makes a very clever use of repetitions. The narrative in 'Beethoven' is the stringing together of two alternate contrasting scenes from Beethoven's life which play out in the narrator's imagination. As pointed out earlier, the narrative has juxtaposed the alternate scenarios from Beethoven's life by making them look almost identical by only altering a few basic elements in their descriptions. Both the scenes begin with the phrase 'Let us imagine then'. Chaliha could have easily told Beethoven's story using a simple omniscient narrative structure, yet the emphasis on the role of 'imagining' a distant alien cultural scene is significant here. It acts as a comment on the author's nervous awareness of the derived nature of the information contained in the story. As a postcolonial narrative, 'Beethoven' only has second-hand access to the incidents that it seeks to describe. By constructing the narrative around two friends who have to take recourse to their imagination to enter a world which is 'distant' in all senses of the word, the author has foregrounded his awareness of the political, cultural and economic gap between the Western world and the post-colony.

Most critics of Ludwig van Beethoven, the composer, have interpreted several compositions from his middle period as the artistic expression of 'disability overcome', believed to have been based on his personal experiences with his disability. This approach is founded on several indications from Beethoven's own journal entries. In fact, the beginning decade of the nineteenth century was marked by several musical compositions based on this theme of overcoming disability through personal heroism. These artistic compositions reflected the general proliferation of concepts of the 'normal' and 'abnormal' in Europe of this period (Straus 2011). Chaliha's story is based on these popular interpretations of Beethoven's musical work. But the story is not an uncritical espousal of these received ideas, which can be illustrated through an examination of the concluding part of the story. The first scene from Beethoven's life described in the story ends with the lines, 'Our hearts cry out for him, but we cannot lose this music' (Chaliha 2012: 91, translation mine). This line is repeated at the end of the second alternate scene as well, and it serves as the concluding line of the story; only this time, it has been constructed in the form of a question: 'our hearts weep for him, but could we lose this music?' (Chaliha 2012: 93). Concluding the story with a question not only serves to leave the narrative open-ended; it also creates a space for its reader to reflect and engage with the received wisdom underlying the popular narrative surrounding Beethoven's life and disability.

Conclusion

Saurabh Kumar Chaliha's choice of a German musical composer as the subject of a short story in Asamiya is not a random indulgence. As the frame story makes it clear, he finds universal relevance in the story of the musical icon. The 'universal' value of the figure of Beethoven manifests itself in two basic assumptions on which the story is based. First, what makes Beethoven, a person from a distant culture, relevant to the two Asamiya-speaking friends in the frame story and to the Assamese reader is the 'universal' character and appeal of his music. Although Beethoven belonged to a distant time and cultural zone, the two friends can appreciate his creations because of the 'universal' language of music. However, this first assumption loses sight of the fact that classical music is after all highly elitist and hardly 'universal' in character. The second assumption on which the story is founded is the projection of the figure of Beethoven, the person, as a symbol of the universal man. The friends view Beethoven's story as a model of human life in general: it is composed of momentary joys and great sorrows and hardships, and the greatness of life lies in making it all purposeful, in relentlessly moving forward and achieving glory. However, an intrinsic irony in this heroic quest motif of the story stands to be overlooked: the person who has been projected as the 'universal man' is not a 'common' man but a 'special' disabled person.

A sensitive consideration of the short story reveals many other similar ironies. Quayson talks about a prevalent attitude among the Greeks, Egyptians and others in antiquity, in which disability was perceived as a reflection of the proximity between the divine or metaphysical world and the human life world (2007: 8–9). In the short story by Chaliha as well, the characters attribute Beethoven's disability to what would be called in Asamiya as *Kona Bidhata*, which literally translates as 'Blind Fate'. It is quite fascinating to note that the supposedly all-powerful fate, in most cultures of the world including that of the Assamese, is imagined as a disabled entity. Moreover, Chaliha's story revolves around the vicissitudes in the life of a musical genius. A genius is identified by his or her possession of a skill or gift not available to the ordinary man. In other words, the genius possesses something in excess while a disabled person is characterised by a lack. The visualisation of Beethoven as a 'disabled genius' in the story, then, qualifies as an oxymoron.

Translation is an undeniable presence at the heart of all postcolonial societies and their literary texts, yet the element of translation in 'Beethoven' has a more explicit presence for it narrates the story of a Western musical figure. The arrival of colonialism brought about tremendous changes in the culture and literature of Assam. Simultaneously, the conception and literary representation of disability also underwent complex transformations in postcolonial Assam. Chaliha's 'Beethoven', like Assamese folk literature makes substantial use of disability and disabled persons as tropes, yet a careful examination of these works reveals what Mitchell and Snyder have already pointed out about literary works in general: they fail to take up disability as an experience of social or political dimensions (Mitchell and Snyder 2000: 48).

Notes

1 The author will be henceforth referred to by his pen name.
2 The term *Asamiya* is used here to refer to the language spoken by the people of Assam as well as the literary tradition in the language. The term *Assamese* here generally means 'relating to Assam'.
3 Saurabh Kumar Chaliha had obtained his master's degree from the University of London and then spent nearly a decade teaching in various institutions in England and Germany. Although a writer does not always need to travel physically to know or write about a distant culture, Chaliha's close acquaintance with European cultures may have been a significant influence on his writerly imagination. A large number of his stories are partially or fully set in European locations; many stories set in Assam, too, make references to and include descriptions of events and customs in European countries. Many of his stories are also set in or make references to non-European cultures outside Assam. In fact, the practice of describing other cultures in their Asamiya writings is commonly found among most Assamese writers of the postcolonial period. A noted example is Indira Goswami, who wrote exclusively in the Asamiya language, but many of her novels, as well as many of her short stories, are entirely set in locations outside Assam and employ characters and stories that have no apparent connection to Assam.
4 Saurabh Kumar Chaliha has also translated the novels *The Strange Case of Dr Jekyll and Mr Hyde* and *Around the World in Eighty Days* into Asamiya.
5 Medieval Assamese chronicles.
6 Critics of the works of Saurabh Kumar Chaliha have found them constantly display significant influence of the styles and philosophies of Impressionism, Cubism, Stream-of-Consciousness, Existentialism and Surrealism. Readers of Chaliha's stories are confronted with a staggering range of references as diverse as Kandinsky's geometric designs on the wall of a house, Picasso's 'Harlequin's Family', references to Cézanne, Mozart, Salieri, Beethoven, Dvořák, Benny Goodman, Dixieland Jazz, barcarole, Rabindra Sangeet, Ravi Shankar and even Mohammad Rafi and Mukesh (Dev Goswami 2015: 328).
7 The modern era in the history of Asamiya literature was actually inaugurated with the publication of a translated text, for the first Asamiya book to appear in print was the *Dharmapustak* (1913), a translation of the Bible into Asamiya.

References

Agarwalla, Jyotiprasad. 2007. *Jyotiprasad Rachanavali*, 7th ed. (Complete Works of Jyotiprasad). Ed. Hiren Gohain. Guwahati: Publication Board Assam.
Barker, Clare. 2011. *Postcolonial Fiction and Disability: Exceptional Children, Metaphor and Materiality*. Basingstoke and New York: Palgrave Macmillan.
Bassnett, Susan. 2007. 'Culture and Translation', in Piotr Kuhiwczak and Karin Littau (eds) *A Companion to Translation Studies*, pp. 13–23. Clevedon: Multilingual Matters.

Bassnett, Susan and Harish Trivedi, eds. 2002. *Post-colonial Translation: Theory and Practice*. London and New York: Routledge.

Bezborooah, Lakshminath. 2013. *Sadhukatha Aru Sajkatha: Bezborooahr Hatot Dhori Jnan Aru Kalpanar Rajyaloi* (Fairytales and Words of Wisdom: Holding Bezborooah's Hands into the Kingdom of Knowledge and Imagination). Eds. Homen Borgohain and Arindam Borkotoky. Guwahati: Students' Stores.

Chaliha, Saurabh Kumar. 2012. *Ghulam*, 6th ed. (Slave). Guwahati: Lawyers' Publication.

Chasie, Charles. 2005. 'Nagaland in Transition', *India International Centre Quarterly*, Special issue of Where the Sun Rises When Shadows Fall: The North-east, 32 (2/3): 253–264.

Dev Goswami, Ranjit Kumar. 2015. *Prabandha 1973−2015* (Essays 1973−2015). Guwahati: Lawyers' Publication.

Goswami, P. 2003. 'Loan Words in North-eastern India', in Mrinal Miri (ed) *Linguistic Situation in North-East India*, pp. 111–116. New Delhi: Concept.

Hughes, Bill. 2012. 'Fear, Pity and Disgust: Emotions and the Non-disabled Imaginary', in Nick Watson, Alan Roulstone and Carol Thomas (eds) *Routledge Handbook of Disability Studies*, pp. 67–77. London and New York: Routledge.

Ingstad, Benedicte and Susan Reynolds Whyte, eds. 1995. *Disability and Culture*. Berkeley, CA: University of California Press.

Jedamski, Doris. 2009. *Chewing over the West: Occidental Narratives in Non-Western Readings*. Amsterdam and New York: Rodopi.

Mitchell, David T. and Sharon L. Snyder. 2000. *Narrative Prosthesis: Disability and the Dependencies of Discourse*. Ann Arbor, MI: University of Michigan Press.

Neog, Maheswar. 2013. *Asamiya Sahityar Rooprekha*, 13th ed. (Outline of Asamiya Literature). Guwahati: Chandra Prakashan.

Niranjana, Tejaswini. 1995. *Siting Translation: History, Post-Structuralism and the Colonial Context*. Hyderabad: Orient Longman.

Phukan, Nilamani. 2005. *Kuri Satikar Asamiya Kabita,* 3rd ed. (Assamese Poetry of the Twentieth Century). Guwahati: Publication Board Assam.

Prasad, Gaurishanker Venkateshwara. 2002. 'Writing Translation: The Strange Case of the Indian English Novel', in Susan Bassnett and Harish Trivedi (eds) *Post-colonial Translation: Theory and Practice*, pp. 41−57. London and New York: Routledge.

Quayson, Ato. 2007. *Aesthetic Nervousness: Disability and the Crisis of Representation*. New York, NY: Columbia University Press.

Schmiesing, Ann. 2014. *Disability, Deformity and Disease in the Grimm's Fairytales*. Detroit, MI: Wayne State University Press.

Straus, Joseph N. 2011. 'Musical Narratives of Disability Overcome: Beethoven', in Joseph N. Straus (ed) *Extraordinary Measures: Disability in Music*, pp. 45−62. Oxford: Oxford University Press.

Thong, Tezenlo. 2012. '"To Raise the Savage to a Higher Level": The Westernization of Nagas and Their Culture', *Modern Asian Studies*, 46: 893−918.

Tymoczko, Maria. 2002. 'Post-colonial Writing and Literary Translation', in Susan Bassnett and Harish Trivedi (eds) *Post-colonial Translation: Theory and Practice*, pp. 19−40. London and New York: Routledge.

———. 2014. *Translation in a Postcolonial Context: Early Irish Literature in English Translation*. London and New York: Routledge.

Zama, Margaret Ch. 2006. 'Globalization and the Mizo Story', *Indian Folklife* Special Issue of Globalization and the Tribes of the Northeast, 22: 10−11.

9

FIGHTING AGAINST MULTIPLE BODIES!

Translating 'Nāri o Nāgini' and 'Tamoshā' by Tarashankar Bandyopadhyay and 'Bonjhi Gunjomālā' by Jagadish Gupta

Subhadeep Ray

The intersection between the task of the translator and that of the disability scholar/ activist seems to rest on their common thrust on the signs of difference in investigating different ability statuses in culture and society, and addressing a wide range of receptors from varied backdrops to unveil and subvert the codes of 'normalcy'. By examining the multiple forces underlying what is canonised as the 'origin', the 'source', the 'provincial' or the 'traditional' the process of rereading involved in the translation process can supply new tools to the disability studies in appreciating our cultural heterogeneity. In this connection, the texts in the so-called regional languages often exhibit a continual exchange between the local and the transnational and draw upon their complex composition with an inherent inclination towards discarding what is normalised as 'uniform' in an exposition of multiple forces of cultural diversity within one's own community. They could affect both translation project and disability studies in meaningful ways by unsettling any effort of considering either the 'source' or the 'target' text as undifferentiated cultural units, and offering new insights into the sociocultural constructions of corporeality as 'fit' or 'unfit', 'normal' or 'challenged'.

In this light, Bengali modernist fiction of the first half of the 20th century with its multicultural affiliations and a specifically cosmopolitan sensibility continuously 'translates' contemporary experiments in art, philosophy, politics and science, as well as a globally oriented historical consciousness, into explorations of sociocultural contingencies and uncanny sensibilities of a prolonged colonised subjectivity of the native land. The precise social capacity of the sign system developed by the new writing in Bengali that had come to the forefront during the inter-wars period or a little earlier and was continued to be practised across the divide between the Raj and the Republic persuasively foregrounds what may be termed as 'a new politics of in-betweenness' (Bassnett and Trivedi 1999: 6), which is of particular relevance to both translation and disability studies. Already informed by the cutting edge of sociocultural contacts of the late colonial period, which results into a complicated sense of 'source', Bengali 'modernist' texts offer a series of new challenges to the project of translating them into any 'target'.

Such textual dynamic necessitates remodelling of relations between the vernacular and English by undermining the reified totality of the language of Empire with a more complex consciousness of the world evolving in a period of radical changes. To quote Kris Manjapra,

> Bengali intellectual life, framed within a centre-periphery imperial axis in the 1870s was resolutely reframed within a multipolar international constellation by the 1920s. This change was reflected by the new conversations in which young Bengali became entangled in the years after the war.
>
> (2011: 327)

This internationalism – an exposure to the 'unbearable' and 'unmanageable' in experiences of radical movements and violent exercise of power around the world – equips Bengali novels and short stories to trace the uncharted areas of human physiognomy and dispel essentialist notions of 'organic community' by decoding the emergent socio-ideological crisis under the contradictory pressures of capitalist search for money and an oppressive feudal order.[1]

The present chapter attempts to locate the ideological and technical motives and challenges involved in translating three representative modernist disability texts in Bengali: 'Nāri O Nāgini', or 'Woman and Snake-wife', and 'Tamoshā', or 'Darkness', by Tarashankar Bandyopadhyay (1898–1971) and 'Bonjhi Gunjomala', or 'Niece Gunjomala', by Jagadish Gupta (1886–1957).[2] Each of these texts raise the issues of contacts, conflicts, exclusions, negotiations and assimilations among different bodies, marked as 'able' or 'disable', as part of the complex rise of the modernist aesthetics of motion and dissonance in Bengali literature.

A continuous discursive shift could be followed in the course of Bengali literature during the final century of the colonial rule, incorporating the foreign influences according to its varying needs. And these shifts play crucial roles in the reassessment of the body in modernist writing, offering significant 'source' texts for disability studies in the postcolonial context. The colonisers' particular anxiety over the insidious elements in Bengali literary practices, violating the norms of 'normalcy' and 'progress', and the institutionalised reservations imposed upon them were simultaneously internalised by the English educated elitist intellectuals of the second half of the 19th century. Thus, bare corporeality and crude violence, once central themes in pre-colonial literature, were encoded within the model of 'nineteenth century positivist sociology and utilitarian political economy' (Chatterjee 1986: 61) by the Bengal Renaissance. Countering this essentialising tendency of colonial knowledge and its derivative discourses, the modernist works of the 1920s, and after, revived unclear and 'irrational' utterances, nightmares and illusive dreams and mannerisms of all sorts, representing a body, both challenging and rooted deep in the country soil.

Resultant cultural conversations, therefore, are seen to investigate the codes and conducts of 'normalcy' in a worn-out colonial social and discursive structure from the perspectives of marginalised or repressed, including that of the physically 'deviant' in a language that is equally devoid of sentimentalism. This also questions the conventionalisation of corporeal attractiveness of 'motherland' as well as the figure of the 'sanctified native' in the nationalist discourse. Paradoxically, such a project of Bengali modernism adapts many of the techniques of representation and philosophical revaluations that mark a paradigmatic shift in the West from Enlightenment art and philosophy. Such a project undercuts basic features of liberal humanism and gives expression to the anger, confusion and despair of socially marginalised people. Susan Bassnett and Harish Trivedi observe that the postcolonial theorists need to focus on 'the role played by translation in facilitating colonisation' (1999: 5). However, an equally powerful role translation could play in the diffusion of strategies from foreign sources that questioned the dominating implications of the imperial mission and the mobilisation of people's feelings and utterances across inter- and intra-cultural boundaries.[3] In this context, post-Tagore Bengali writing explores the hidden radicalism of the fact that 'the colonised, the migrant, the exile – all speak from a context that cannot be defined clearly and unproblematically as the home or source' (Kothari 2009: 119). This also sets the ideological motif behind translating their works, in which suggesting an intricate relation between context and usage contributes centrally to any activist reading as that of disability studies.

These texts exhibit how '[b]eing cosmopolitan can . . . [also] be a wiliness to recognise and accept the forms of difference' one sees in 'own local communities' (Kalliney 2016: 61) and, on the other, unearth the liberating energy from those very forms. Thus, leading modernist author Manik Bandyopadhyay (1908–1956) recognises in a literary review that even there is revolutionary truth in sexual perversion (Bandyopadhyay 2015: 25). The task of the artist is then to enquire into the very human condition in which perversion becomes a sort of freedom. The anthropocentrism of Bengali modernist narrative, in this sense, is preoccupied with disability as one of the most affecting corporeal incarnations of the marginal experience. A series of tales like Manik Bandyopadhyay's 'Pragaitihasik' ('Primitive'), Tarashankar Bandyopadhyay's 'Boba Kanna' ('Dumb Weeping') and 'Shapmochon' ('Redemption') and Balaichand Mukhopadhyay's (1899–1979) 'Chaya o Bastab' ('Shadow and Reality') and 'Boba' ('The Dumb') examine how the category of disability is shaped by and shaping the vectors of class, nationality, caste, religion, gender and sexuality. They show the long and consistent association between disability and forms of multidimensional social deprivations and discriminations. The narrative examination of the margin in these works obviously engages the translator's capacity of residing on the boundaries between different consciousnesses inside and across a sociocultural constitution.

Three case studies, mentioned earlier, therefore, represent a strategic 'in-betweenness' of interfacing consciousnesses and sign systems that lay bare, on one hand, the repressive social disablism, and, on the other, dangerously unsettling borderlines where 'comprehensible' and 'incomprehensible', 'able' and 'disabled' mutually dislocate each other. They also connect disability and subalternity. To set a translation strategy for each of them employing English as a tool of transcultural communication with the activist's cause may begin with the basic conviction, as recorded by Antonio Sousa Ribeiro's most pithy appreciation of Bakhtin's relevance to translation:

> the concepts of culture and of the border imply each other. . . . On the other hand, to reflect upon the inner heterogeneity of cultures implies conceiving of translation as having to do with not just intercultural, but also intracultural relationships.
>
> (2004: 189)

In order to address the potential of Tarashankar and Jagadish's narratives in explicitly encountering supposedly alien perspectives towards life and also pointing towards its own internal cultural heterogeneity, the present project proposes to re-appropriate a term that Walter Benjamin uses to point out the closeness between the source text and the process of translation, that is, 'translatability' as 'inner-translatability' (1996: 254). The narrative portrayal of disability in the concerned stories underscores strong empathy towards signs of difference and of supposedly ungainly and misshapen, which form a substantial part of the interactions between living individuals and often refuse to be completely appropriated by the institutionalised purism. The 'inner-translatability', or the potential of being in-translation, re-orients literary modernity and redefines regional culture in terms of 'its ability to defy identification with the dominant idea of national culture as *the* culture' (Thomsen 2008: 65). As the interrelation between narrative representation of disability and its translation across culture is to be established in 'Woman and Snake-wife', 'Darkness' and 'Niece Gunjomala' on the basis of critical interpretations of circumstantialities of the author, the text, the translator and the reader, it needs to consider the 'extraordinarily differentiated' nature of cultural signifiers (Said 1994: XXIX) in the narrative process. These signifiers signify the interaction between the 'comprehensible' and the 'incomprehensible' as mutually transforming each other within a broadly defined framework.

'Difference', in case of a translator, 'is not necessarily a loss of the 'original'. Difference, in translation, is to be read as a gain' (Mehrez 2007: 110). Thus, texts having an inherent tendency towards a different life, discarding what is normalised as 'uniform', could affect translation attempts in meaningful ways. This also directly associates the question of political engagements in the most complex way, for even when the narrative of a text like 'Tamoshā' maintains a cautious silence regarding the expressions of feeling of its central character, a blind boy, leaving him solitary/rootless amidst a crowd of people, it simultaneously implies that, to apply Gayatri Chakravorty Spivak's citation of Derrida's *Politics of Friendship*, he is 'solitary . . . but . . . all[ied] . . . in silence' with some distant body 'within the necessity of keeping silent together' (2003: 30). This textuality sets the motif of translating solitariness into a responsible search for togetherness to help disability studies in decoding unequal relations within a social order. On the contrary, in 'Woman and Snake-wife' or 'Niece Gunjomala' the dangerous potential explored in the body with the stigma of disabled is let loose only to be circumscribed by authoritarian policies of indifference, separation and suppression. The representation of disability similarly relates to specific linguistic codes according to interactions of active individuals within a way of life, involving a whole set of control over the 'target' subjects, whose points of departures, however, continually create disruptions in and new associations beyond the signifying practice of social order. In connection to the dialectics of individual and society, the narratives concerned moreover employ multiple genres and speech acts suggestive of intra- and intercultural dialogues which engage several ideological forces.

To set a methodology for the present project, therefore, approaching the previously mentioned notion of difference involves translating each register in relation to its historical engagements and every dramatic movement from a stance of dialogic interactions among fighting physicality. Through this dynamic encounter between the source and the target text, our concept of regionalism is also translated into the mutual dependency of people at both the intra- and intercultural levels. In reflecting on his proposal of an enclosed system of knowledge in *Orientalism*, Edward Said, in *Culture and Imperialism*, develops a flexible model of discursive study through 'contrapuntal' reading that would uncover 'intertwined and overlapping histories' (1994: 18) in metropolitan texts produced by the colonising culture. However, such reading is equally viable in the current project of developing a metastatement through translation on the representation of disability in the late colonial Bengali source texts on the subaltern life. Concerned texts, too, create a site where numerous socio-economic, cultural, bio-political, technological and psychological forces collide with each other to produce interwoven histories of the production of social subjects and suppressed subjectivities. Contrapuntal reading is, in this sense, interwoven with what in the present essay is tried to be established as the 'inner-translatability' of the source text, to be carried over to the target text.

In the light of this textual multifunctionality, a text requires to be approached by receiving it as what is termed as 'macro-structure', 'through which the language user can take a 'stance' on an issue or a set of issues. In language use of this kind, the 'function' or 'value' of an utterance is negotiated and taken for granted' (Hatim 2009: 47). To extend Hatim, several such 'stances' could then evolve from an ideologically encoded context, each having a definite history of cultural/ linguistic construction. For instance, the narrative of 'Woman and Snake-wife' opens by introducing the central character in the following manner:

> Lame Sheikh or *Khora* Sheikh was separating bricks from a burnt-block at the brick-kiln. . . . Nobody knows *Khora*'s actual name; even *Khora* himself could not remember it. Since his left leg was broken in some distant childhood, he has come to be identified by the name, '*Khora*'.
>
> (my translation)

The Bengali register *Khora*, that is, in English 'lame', is a specific language 'stance' that discloses the nature of social discipline absorbing a long history of humiliation of physically impaired people. It is applied so comprehensively and casually to a person with a crippled leg that he or she no longer even needs a proper noun to individuate him or her. There are widespread narratives in folk literature about some 'lame cobbler' or any such working-class (wo)man, represented as a distinct type with a set of attributes and socially defined roles. The 'Khora Sheikh' is likewise restricted to a circular way of life, involving a set of shifting occupations – of a snake charmer, a daily paid labourer and a beggar – much of which being on the verge of extinction due to new economic pressures. Tarashankar's modernism seems to represent a disconcerting convergence between this interplay of a general indifference accompanied in social reception by an elaborate discursive strategy signifying a series of 'undesirable' qualities, holding the individual responsible for his or her 'sorry' state of being, and a quest for differently ordained 'ability' on part of that individual subverting institutionalised definitions. 'Khora Sheikh', originally a member of the working class, thus continues to be featured as having a ghastly appearance, excluding him from the codes of 'healthy' living:

> Not only is his leg broken, but sinful exploits of his youth caused some vile disease, which has flattened Lame's nose. Only an ugly hole can be seen there. Further, he had suffered from small-pox; and, with marks of pox on his skin, ugly Lame has become horrifying to look at.
>
> (my translation)

In this connection, in the proposed target text, *lame* is chosen for *Khora* primarily because of the rudeness associated with the usage of this English register. Almost for the same reason, the register *blind*, instead of *sightless*, is chosen in the next tale, at the risk of creating cultural shock. The strategy adopted for the present translation process, therefore, exerts primacy to intra-cultural relationships before allowing it to assume an intercultural form.

The same Lame, significantly, claims his individuality with an uncanny taste for Natural beauty, particularly evident in his attachment towards snakes:

> Within a short distance, on the field, probably the same young snake, facing the eastern sky, had been playing with her swaying hood. The bloody-rays of the rising sun had made it thick red. In the midst of this red glow, the black wheel on its finely tinged hood had bloomed with an unmatched splendour. The spectacle was as soothing as that of the colour-scales of the wings of a butterfly. Lame was spellbound. He whispered to himself, *Bah!* – Beautiful!
>
> (my translation)

Margrit Shildrick contends that

> disabled people continue to be the targets of widespread discrimination, oppression and alienation, not so much for their differences (both visible and hidden), but because their performitivity of embodied selfhood lays bare the

psychosocial imaginary that sustains modernist understandings of what it is to be properly human.

(2012: 31)

Shildrick's critique of the modernist interest in the exceptional and differently embodied features of the disabled body grounds it in the strategic deployment of power by the normative majority to overcome the anxiety towards a social minority. However, the project of poststructuralist/ postmodernist understanding of disability as 'simply a part of a multiplicity of possibilities' by linking it to the multiplicity of 'human morphology' (Shildrik 2012: 34) requires to be complemented by the modernist examination of the role of sociocultural (im)mobility. Any posthumanist distinction between impairment and disability cannot afford to overlook the want of medical and other amenities for a great number of people, mainly subalterns, to be victimised to permanent impairment in frequently occurring accidents and, therefore, socially ordained irresponsibility in physically 'disabling' its subjects. The generation of multiple risks due to widespread social discrimination in rural communities under the colonial state is a fact that mid-20th-century texts throw light on. To return to the use of the synecdoche, *Khora*, for a complete man, further relates to the social strategy of alienation, or inner-distancing, in which a fragment signifies a complex individuality and this certainly operates along lines between diverse intersectional categories like class, caste, occupation, age and gender. And the translation project, accordingly, is motivated to follow the bodily acts of Lame in response to multiple segregations. Thus, it is perhaps to counter the anxiety encoded in the alienating objective reality – modernist anti-hero seeks liberation in sexuality as a highly productive corporeal realisation of subjectivity, or a miraculous energiser of bodily parts to an unknown level of capability. Tarashankar's 'Woman and Snake-wife' posits an extreme case of such attempt to overcome 'disabilism':

> Next, he comes out with a snake round his neck – that very snake. The reptile has grown up a little in the meantime. But it now lacks its previous spirit. It has been sliding along Lame's necklines and on to his shoulders, raising its face a little, very coyly without any expression of fury. Jebeda warns: Look. Don't do that. However shy it may be, one can't just trust that species.
>
> Lame remarks, again with a smile: One can't trust their fang – the venomous tooth. Otherwise, they, too, have passions. It does not have the tooth with venom, but it has other teeth, intact. But, you see, it never bites me. Jebeda, you tell, how lovingly my *bibi* is moving in the manner of a good girl! Having said this, Lame presses the lips of the snake, and gives her a warm kiss.
>
> (my translation)

In the entire narrative, the individual body is perceived as a process rather than a totality, and it is continually under influence of alien elements – an important clue for the translation project which has always to readjust its position to the foreign.

And this process demands to disrupt normative and textual control. Against the spirit of challenge in Sheikh's 'romance', the social power could only be restored through powerful normalising capacity of the patriarchal form of tragedy: the snake, carelessly left 'unshaved' for long, bites Jebeda, as the latter tries to hit the former – an end to the feminine rivalry over a male body – and this completely destroys Lame's life and career. Mainly to address the implication of Jebeda and the snake being two contenders for Lame, as also suggested by the register *bibi*, the present target text chooses as its title 'Woman and Snake-wife' rather than 'Woman and She-snake'. Now, as Octavio Paz suggests, 'language itself, in its very essence, is already a translation – first from the nonverbal world, and then, because each sign and each phrase is a translation of another sign, another phrase' (1992: 154). In this sense, Lame typifies a cultural product in which social relationship, as the conjugal one, is shown to be 'retranslated' into a pre-social passion.

Another challenging aspect of Sheikh's character is that he is a performing artist, that is, a snake charmer and a singer. His lyric being a folk variation on the myth of Radha and Krishna involves layers of creative reproduction and multi-layered translation amongst different lingua franca:

> I am not sure, O, this could happen
> Kesto would leave Gokul, flying to Mathura, so often
> O, I could never know –

The position of artist as an internal bohemian residing on the margin of the community and being exposed to external cultural effects, is a modernist prototype, which is explored in detail by Tarashankar in the character of a partly orphan blind beggar, Pankhi, in 'Tamoshā'. Pankhi's travelogue begins in a railway station on a branch line and amongst a cross-sectional community involving varied occupations, classes and migrant performers – the narrative interestingly employs a set of railway terminology, with their peculiar amalgamation of English origin and Bengali usage. Although treated with special care by and enjoying a special bond with the community around him, Pankhi, with his extraordinary sensitiveness, setting the tone of the narrative, both directs towards the immediacy of sounds and smells around and crosses their limits:

> He is swinging with full concentration on two sides, holding an instrument of single string in his hand, and smiling sometimes. His lips are moving. It could be understood that he is murmuring some words. Sometimes he is turning restless, and trying to listen [to] something. Sometimes, he is taking [a] deep breath to smell something.
>
> (my translation)

Pankhi's music, however, creates the opportunity for coming in terms with people on a voyage – a collage of multiple speech acts across overlapping social stratifications. His crucial interaction is with a lady singer of a *Khemta* – a traditional musical orchestra that moves through places. The narrative revolves around the exchange of songs between Pankhi and this girl, whom the former begins to adore:

> Pankhi remains silent for a few seconds, and says: I've already crossed my limit. Should I sing in front of you?
>
> 'Why not? You sing so well. How nice is your voice.'
>
> 'Did you like it?' There is again a big smile on Pankhi's face in his usual way . . . 'Would you sing me a song . . .?' Pankhi leaves his sentence incomplete, and starts to scratch his head with a wide silent grin on his face.
>
> The girl laughs: 'Want to listen to me singing?'
> Pankhi touches the end of toes of the girl. He rubs the ground with his hands to touch the girl's feet. He says: 'Tell me, where it would be possible for me to touch your feet. How could I have a chance to listen to you? But . . .' Pankhi again remains quiet, and turns his face upwards and says: 'I'm also a human being. I, too, have my desires.'
>
> (my translation)

This is significant to note how the preceding dialogue allows Pankhi to express his autonomous consciousness and feeling. Pankhi also enthusiastically introduces flora and fauna of the locality, posing particular problems for finding their English equivalents in the target text. Critics like David T. Mitchell and Sharon L. Snyder throw light on '*discursive dependency* upon disability' by which 'literature [has] made use of disabled characters', but disability studies can also find cases of active participation of the differently abled character in the productive dialogue in a number of texts, which sees them beyond what the above critics call 'the pervasive nature of disabled images' (2000: 51). As the train departs carrying the troupe, Pankhi starts to follow them only to lose connection in the junction station of Burdwan. While Pankhi's career totters under socio-economic forces, his song, 'I'm lost – if I were your bracelet, / Not gold, mirror-glasses / I could happily die without any regret / To live a life of success / Blessed to enfold your arm' (my translation) finds a flight when that girl later records it for gramophone – a technical device to convert human voice into something more potent for reaching out to a larger community that Pankhi has not even thought of. In its complex journey the song always remains to be a sort of 'translation' from one form of cultural communication to another. The proposed target text tries to literally translate Bengali registers and follow the rhythm as close as possible. The narrative progresses to focus on the fragmentation of life by the spatiotemporal forces and cruelties of the materialistic demands. The boy finally reaches the girl in a distant place of pilgrimage when both of them are unable to identify each other. He is so happy in receiving a coin of fifty paisa from her! Modernity and liberation, and social discrimination and disability, are in conflicting relationships in the tale to offer a forceful discursive study of self-interrogating and ever-generative characteristic of cultural collectivity in its contest against socially alienating bodies. Maria Tymoczko proposes to be 'concerned with translation as a sort of speech act' (2000: 26), but these speech acts, while engaging the neglected and insulted, need to be understood in terms of a dialectics between their limiting and transgressing attributes. In this light, target texts may be more attentive to thought and action of Lame and Pankhi, rearranging those places in source texts, which, in overemphasising specific peculiarities of their action, tend to ignore their way of reacting to the world's odds.

This also leads to reconsider Walter Benjamin's powerful reflection on the task of the translator in terms of the '[a]ll purposeful manifestations of life, including their very purposiveness, [which] in the final analysis have their end not in life but in the expression of its nature, in the representation of its significance' (1996: 255). If the task of the translator is directed towards intention in art, in collective and/or individual efforts, this involves foregrounding the relatively underrated author, who could unearth the repressed intentions of his or her time to form a more problematic structure of feeling than that could be accommodated within normative expectations and values. Translation as recovery is particularly applicable to Jagadish Gupta, writing from outside the metropolis although closely informed of the developments there. Although one of the inaugurators of Bengali modernism, Jagadish's shocking tales and novels, characterised by a narrative struggle with raw materials to disclose some poignant, mostly bitter, truths about the most atypical areas of life, and written when Rabindranath and Saratchandra were still looming large, remain mostly forgotten.

Jagadish's 'Niece Gunjomala' is a study of a middle-aged working-class lower-caste woman character, who would like to 'bite and tear other people' (my translation) and whose impaired left arm and diseased body, along with other forms of ineffectiveness, dehumanise her to exploit another able-bodied young girl, under her care, and her final defeat by the spirit of life. Jagadish frankly uses Bengali slang in a deliberate disclosure of psycho-physiological fragmentation under the cruel forces of deterministic social bio-politics that record women's bodies either as tools of reproduction or commodities to be sold to male lust. Jagadish's narrative draws heavily on the typical registers of the womenfolk of rural Bengal, having a component of interiority that loses much of its effects while being transmitted in a different linguistic practice. In the process of this English translation of the raw energy of Maheswari's abuses and her affected sentimentalism that derive from a class- and caste-ridden rural India the role and 'status of English' itself from 'a language of the elite, of a modern and caste-free urban population of India' is redefined (Kothari 2007: 46). The narrative, with a distinct dialogic structure, continuously works on the borderline. Maheswari Harini recklessly tries to manoeuvre a strategy of her survival in a patriarchal and profiteering society only to turn herself into an agent of the same before discovering the futility of all her efforts:

> Looking at the fresh look of her niece after [a] bath, and fully dressed in that parrot coloured sari, Maheswari comments, 'take that low wooden seat and sit quietly on the balcony, lest cats and dogs don't enter the house – you're such a blind girl!'

Gunjomala laughingly replies: 'Aunty, you're telling me blind! Look at my eyes.' She raises her full and sleepy but naughty eyes towards Maheswari's face . . .

Maheswari's satisfaction is that of one who has acquired the capital for a new enterprise, one has been engaged in!

Your eyes are really stunning. . . . There's nobody around us who is not going to be caught at your sight!'

Listening to Maheswari's so soothing words, one could easily understand that they actually mean to reflect uttering of her target customers.

(my translation)

The regressive nature of the narrative leads translation to trace back what is cruelly and too true to acknowledge about the human condition and, therefore, defamiliarises Bengali society with the evocation of 'unfair' and 'ugly'. When Gunjomala finally manages to escape with her husband, '[c]ursing the world, herself and Gunjo, Maheswari cries aloud like a mad woman' (my translation).

Translations of the preceding texts in English for a larger audience not only serve to redefine the representation of disability in regional writings, but the multiplicities involved in these texts are meant also to cut across regionalism itself in being responsive to the ethical claims of different sections of mankind upon one another. This is particularly important in redefining our postcolonial condition. Our literature is an important reminder that the independence of this subcontinent is based on the vision of a shared future, continuously fighting with and against multiple bodies. Translating disability across cultures is certainly an important weapon in this long historical struggle.

Notes

1 A series of political changes in both home and the world since the first colonial decision to partition Bengal – one of the most sociopolitically resourceful provinces of the British Empire – in 1905 that generated a powerful wave of anti-partition movement, engaging artists and intellectuals as vanguards, contextualises the new transnational consciousness of the inter-wars Bengali modernism. The radicalism of the 1905 Bengal itself coincided with the early revolutionary attempts in Russia. And, towards the end of the first decade of the new century, the outbreak of the Great War, followed in quick succession by the Bolshevik Revolution, the Spanish Civil War, women's rights movements and Nationalist and anti-Fascist struggle of Asia, Africa and East Europe unshackled human consciousness in an unprecedented manner and helped a counter-discourse to the colonial hegemony evolve.

2 The Bengali text of 'Nāri O Nāgini' (pub. 1934), followed here, is taken from the first volume of *Tarashankar Galpa Guccha* (368–72) and that of 'Tamoshā' (pub. 1945) is taken from the second volume of *Tarashankar Galpa Guccha* (582–92), both being edited by Jagadish Bhattacharya, published from Kolkata by Sahitya Samsad in 1975. The source text of 'Bonjhi Gunjomala' (pub. 1937) is from *Jagadish Guptar Galpa* (167–79), edited by Subir Raychaudhuri and published from Kolkata by Dey's Publishing in 1991.

3 To refer to a single relatively lesser known case, *The Independent*, a newspaper published by the Nehru family, published a series of articles on the constitution of Soviet Russia in the 1920, and on October 2, 1920, it published the full text of Lenin's address to the Ninth

Congress of RCP (B) in English translation, as it was found useful for anti-colonial struggle at the home. Translation in English at the cause of social activism of any form may be enlightened by such historical evidences.

References

Bandyopadhyay, Manik. 2015. *Samagra Prabandha Ebong* (Complete Essays Etc.). Eds. Subhomay Mandal and Sukanta Gangopadhyay. Calcutta: Deep Publishers.

Bassnett, Susan and Harish Trivedi. 1999. 'Introduction: Of Colonies, Cannibals and Vernaculars', in Susan Bassnett and Harish Trivedi (eds) *Post-colonial Translation: Theory and Practice*, pp. 1–18. London and New York: Routledge.

Benjamin, Walter. 1996. 'The Task of the Translator', in Marcus Bullock and Michael W. Jennings (eds) *Selected Writings: 1913–26*, pp. 253–263. Cambridge, MA and London, England: Belknap Press of Harvard University Press. http://users.clas.ufl.edu/burt/deconstructionandnewmediatheory/walterbenjamintasktranslator.pdf (accessed on 31 August 2016).

Chatterjee, Partha. 1986. *Nationalist Thought and the Colonial World: A Derivative Discourse?* London: Zed Press.

Hatim, Basil. 2009. 'Translating Text in Context', in Jeremy Munday (ed) *The Routledge Companion to Translation Studies*, pp. 36–53. London and New York: Routledge.

Kalliney, Peter. 2016. *Modernism in a Global Context*. London, Oxford, New York, New Delhi and Sidney: Bloomsbury.

Kothari, Rita. 2007. 'The Translation of Dalit Literature into English', in Jeremy Munday (ed) *Translation as Intervention*, pp. 38–53. London: Continuum.

———. 2009. 'Being-in-translation: Sufism in Sindh', in Judy Wakabayashi and Rita Kothari (eds) *Decentering Translation Studies: India and Beyond*, pp. 119–131. Amsterdam: John Benjamins Publishing Company. Pro Quest ebrary. http://site.ebrary.com/lib/inflibnet/reader.action?docID=10355452&ppg (accessed on 1 October 2016).

Manjapra, Kris. 2011. 'Abstract of "From Imperial to International Horizons: A Hermeneutic Study of Bengali Modernism"', *Modern Intellectual History*, 8(2): 327–359. http://journals.cambridge.org/action/display/Abstract?fromPage=online&aid=8338321 (accessed on 8 June 2016).

Mehrez, Samia. 2007. 'Translating Gender', *Journal of Middle East Women's Studies*, 3(1):106–127. JSTOR. www.jstor.org/stable/10.2979/mew.2007.3.1.106 (accessed on 11 August 2016).

Mitchell, David T. and Sharon L. Snyder. 2000. *Narrative Prosthesis: Disability and the Dependencies of Discourse*. Ann Arbor, MI: University of Michigan Press.

Pazz, Octavio. 1992. 'Translations of Literature and Letters', in Irene del Corral (trans), Rainer Schuttle and John Biguenet (eds) *Theories of Translation from Dryden to Derrida*, pp. 152–163. Chicago, IL: University of Chicago Press.

Ribeiro, Antonio Sousa. 2004. 'Translation as a Metaphor for Our Times: Postcolonialism, Borders and Identities', *Portuguese Studies*, 20(1): 186–194. JSTOR. www.jstor.org/stable/41105227 (accessed on 12 August 2016).

Said, Edward W. 1994. *Culture and Imperialism*. London: Vintage.

Shildrik, Margrit. 2012. 'Critical Disability Studies: Rethinking the Conventions for the Age of Postmodernity', in Nick Watson, Alan Roulstone and Carol Thomas (eds) *Routledge Handbook of Disability*, pp. 30–41. London and New York: Routledge.

Spivak, Gayatri Chakravorty. 2003. *Death of a Discipline*. Calcutta and New Delhi: Seagull Books.

Thomsen, Mads Rosendahl. 2008. *Mapping World Literature: International Canonization and Transnational Literatures (1)*. London: Continuum. Pro Quest ebrary. http://site.ebrary.com/lib/inflibnet/detail.action?docID=10362038&p00=contemporary+world+literature(accessed on 7 September 2016).

Tymoczko, Maria. 2000. 'Translation and Political Engagement: Activism, Social Change and the Role of Translation in Geopolitical Shifts', *The Translator*, 6(1): 23–47.

10

NEGOTIATING DISABILITY IN/AND TRANSLATION

A reading of two Tamil short stories

B. Mangalam

Negotiating disability in life or literature has its share of challenges and manoeuvres that require considerable soul-searching and a commitment to engage with the lived experience of others. One such engagement that requires almost immediate attention is the issue of visibility/invisibility of the disabled in literature and our everyday life. How often and where do we meet the disabled in our quotidian life? How often do we look the other way when the disabled cross our paths? What is our expectation as readers when we take up a novel or short story that explores the lives of the disabled?

And how many such characters or narrators do we come across in our readings of literary works? Is there a conscious erasure of their visibility in both the domains? Or do we render them invisible by turning away from them? Another possibility pertains to the operation of an opaque gaze in our dealings and readings concerning the disabled/disability. Is this a conscious gaze, or is it a socially acquired and approved one?

Furthermore, when we do locate disabled persons in our everyday life or in literary writings, do we perceive them as an assertive or as a passive presence? Do we notice the props/gadgets used by them to enhance the socialising of their presence as intrusive or as obstructing our easier access in our own efforts at socialising? Do we allow them an assertive voice in the public domain or do we expect them to locate themselves in as passive a manner as possible? Is there condescension in our allowing of their voice to be heard amidst our chatter or debates?

Another significant aspect of our engagement with the disabled pertains to issues of their representation and self-articulation in literary as well as in social domain. How are the disabled represented in literature? Is there a qualitative difference to their representation when it is done by themselves? Does the difference lie in modes of perception or in the awareness or a lack of it in terms of experiential reality? Finally, when a literary work about the disabled gets translated, what are the likely reverberations in the context of the questions raised earlier? Does the translator, in this instance, act as an interventionist? Is the translator a mediator of unfamiliar experience to readers largely unaware of the challenges encountered by the disabled in our society?

Mirroring the "Other"

This chapter argues that the metaphor of negotiation is an apt image to capture the process of translation of a literary text on/by the disabled. The exercise of the translator can, thus, be perceived as a negotiation that operates at the level of linguistic, cultural, ideological and most significantly, of human interest as primary contours. This chapter looks at the act of translation as a mirroring of the "Other". While the otherness of language or culture is widely recognised in the domain of translation, the otherness of the subject experience or of the experience of the protagonist who is differently abled in mainstream society and therefore less accessible to the translator's imaginative or lived experience is hardly accounted for or conceded. The otherness of gender or caste is challenging too, but these categories are too familiar and embedded in the translator's social consciousness and being. The otherness of disability runs the risk of being overlooked or underplayed, scuttled or not engaged within one's social interaction. Such a possibility does not operate in the context of caste or gender. Disengagement with the disabled is a choice that is socially permitted by means of treating the subject as a medical condition or as a decree of fate beyond human praxis.

The translator, thus, has to negotiate a social construct that works as a blocking mechanism, overcome his or her inherent lack of familiarity with the agency of a disabled person to explore and disseminate the experience, voice, struggles and accomplishments of the disabled in the material world. The translator's awareness of the agency of the disabled narratorial text finds its way into the translated text. It paves the way for the agency of the translator, in turn, to negotiate new areas of experience in a matrix of assertion, affirmation, subversion and resistance. The translator, in turn, disseminates the process of evolving an agency of self-articulation of hitherto silenced, muted, unrepresented voices in the academic and social domains. In this context, the negotiation through translation emerges as an enabling, empowering reading of the "Self" and "Other".

My earlier experience of translating poems, short stories or essays from Tamil Dalit writings led me towards exploring literary texts on/by the disabled in my mother tongue. The project revealed some astonishing facts. I could neither recall nor find even a couple of short stories on the subject of disability. After scurrying through libraries and enquiring from friends, when I drew a blank, it brought to the fore the underlying neglect towards the issues concerning the disabled in our society. I reworked a Dalit short story about a young Dalit girl rendered disabled and ostracised on that count which I had translated a few years earlier as a Dalit text. When I looked at the same text as a text about the disabled, I had to negotiate its translation in a markedly different manner. This was an eye-opener in terms of reckoning with the intersectionality of identities and social categorisation. This chapter discusses two short stories from Tamil on the disabled in a context of overlapping identities and the reality of social exclusion as they operate in our society. The project allowed me to explore writings on this subject in Tamil from the Sangam era to folk arts and contemporary writings. The representation of disability, invariably, stands fraught with gaps, silences, mythmaking and two-dimensional representation in classical literature. Contemporary Tamil literature highlights disability in a social, historical context that merits legal reforms and social support systems.

Disability in classical literature and folk arts

Disability as a subject has found representation in Tamil literature both in the classical and popular genres. A performative mode formed an essential principle in both categories. The epic, *Manimekalai*, showed the protagonist feeding the hungry and the disabled who partook of food from the magic bowl conferred on her, miraculously, as a reward for her virtuous life. We are told that the blind, the deaf, the crippled, the orphans, the idiots and all those who were hungry followed Manimekalai on the streets. In *Cilappatikaram*, Kannagi, following the wrenching off of her breast to burn down the city of Madurai for its denial of justice to her husband, gets quickly elevated as a divinity endowed with miraculous powers. A physical disabling of a woman's body is thus subsumed into an enabling narrative that seeks to valorise chastity, justice and good governance.

Kannagi's loss of a breast/her self-mutilation is not represented as a physical loss or an emotional trauma of a woman. The social or psychological disabling of such a woman is never explored in the narrative. Instead, she is valorised as a goddess of chastity who could grant boons to powerful kings.

The mythifying of the body identity scuttles the possibility of examining such an identity as that of a disabled person. The enumerative catalogue of the disabled in *Manimekalai* or the silence over Kannagi's physical and psychological trauma as a woman in *Cilappatikaram* indicates a disregard for the subject of disability as such. Furthermore, the references to the disabled in the epic *Manimekalai* appear to be perfunctory. The clubbing of different categories or degrees of disability reflects a casual disregard for the persons. Their presence is invoked only to enhance the prestige of the virtuous protagonist Manimekalai, who could feed the hungry and provide succour to them.

A popular tradition of dance theatre during the 17th and 18th centuries in Tamil Nadu was *Nondi Natakam*. Performed widely at Murugan temples as a mode of devout offering, *Nondi Natakam* held out salvation to a disabled hero through suffering and repentance of one's former way of life. The lead actor was a thief in love with a prostitute. He would perform with one of his legs folded and tied up. He would thus pass off as a lame/cripple which can be translated as "Nondi". This one-legged performance termed *Nondi Natakam* was a popular form of entertainment of its times. The hero's tale of love steeped in bawdy innuendoes was entertaining, but its structure was emphatically that of a morality play. The performance was a prayer and a plea for forgiveness, an act of devotion towards the Lord. Disability was represented as a punishment for his immoral/criminal conduct while repentance was rewarded through divine intervention. The disability discourse in both the classical and popular narratives in Tamil, one can infer, is riddled with notions of charity, compassion, punishment and valorisation.

Notions of pity and piety governed the representation and treatment of disability as a subject, image or mode of performative subjectivity. A reading of Tamil short stories and novels published in the last two decades shows certain interesting points of departure as well as a continuity of the older literary tropes pertaining to disability. Disability, by and large, can be negotiated under three major frameworks or categories: congenital, acquired, and social. However, a more significant aspect lies in deciphering the perspective or the voice of the narrator in disability narratives. This, in turn, falls under two broad categories: (a) narratives on disability by the non-disabled and (b) self-articulation by the disabled.

The two different modes of narration ensue in a discourse of pity or of statements: of report or of experiential accounts, respectively. The two categories of narratives do not intersect in terms of their respective trajectory or sensibility. The narratives of self-articulation by the disabled are marked by interrogation of social attitudes towards the disabled and documenting quotidian challenges and struggles of the disabled community. Narratives on the disabled by the non-disabled writers focus on the need for reform, compassion, a directive for change of perspective/ heart of the abled in the story and amongst the readers.

Disability narratives and translation

The act of negotiating disability narratives (of either of the stated categories) as a reader encompasses the process of translation as a strategy of reading. Translations involve an act of mirroring the "Other", accommodating the "Other", grappling and negotiating the embedded cultural, linguistic or semantic otherness amongst the source and target texts/languages. An analogous strategy, when deployed in disability studies, would prove enabling to decode the articulation of the disabled or a representation of the disabled. A parallel between the process of negotiating a text by/on the disabled and the process of translation of any literary text exists. My awareness of this has been a major gain in my experience of translating the two short stories under consideration. The translator, I realised, becomes a mediator not only between source and target language readers at multiple levels (cultural, linguistic, semantic) but also moves beyond to bridge the gaps of unfamiliarity of the non-disabled reader and the experiential reality of the disabled narrator/character. This process is a self-reflexive process for it gets initiated at the consciousness of the translator to begin with. Translation, therefore, is an enabling enterprise that opens a dialogue between the disabled and the non-disabled in society.

As a translator, I became aware of my acquired, internalised presumptions and biases towards the disabled. In everyday life, one could get away with minimal physical contact with the disabled. A self-conscious physical distancing or avoiding interaction with the disabled around our space is possible by a simple, inhuman act of pretending to snooze while travelling in public transport or keeping one's eyes shut in a meditative pose. At the workplace, one could pretend to act busy working on a laptop or accessing one's smartphone. These strategies are commonly resorted to in order to avoid the challenge of reaching out to the disabled. A disabled unfriendly society, invariably, looks the other way rather than overcome the lacunae in the system including conduct/attitude/perspective related ones.

One's engagement as a translator of narratives of/on the disabled demands a more rigorous regimen. One cannot but engage with the challenges headlong. The primary reason for this lies in the linguistic matrix that binds translation practice and discourse on/by the disabled. It is through language that negotiations are carried forward to carve either enabling or limiting readings on a translated text. Hence, getting sensitised on the biases, assumptions pertaining to the disabled that get absorbed at the linguistic level (reflecting cultural stereotyping) emerges as the first major challenge faced by the translator. The choice of labels used in the context of various categories of disability, gender-specific constraints of the disabled, representing issues of sexuality and relationship concerns without compromising the dignity of the disabled persons prove equally challenging to the translator as much as to the narrator. A conscious strategy to weed out inhumane references that might have inadvertently crept into the original text would be a positive intervention by the translator and not an instance of violation of fidelity.

A translator is not always an enabling interventionist. She could partake of the hegemonic social discourse on the condition of disability. Hence, a conscious engagement to function as a critical outsider is imperative. Translations of texts on the disabled have to evolve a critical and not a cathartic engagement with the subject at hand. The translator's gaze has to be located in a critical and self-reflexive matrix. Would there be a critical difference in the quality of translation if disability narratives are translated by a disabled person? Is it ethical to raise this sensitive differentiation? Perhaps pushing every form of literary transaction into a narrow pigeonhole is not desirable. Nonetheless, the subject position of the translator has to be borne in mind while analysing or comparing translations of texts on a specific theme. This aspect, of course, merits a wider discussion. However, I find myself inadequate in delving into this more elaborately at this juncture.

The two stories that I have translated offer two different pointers on disability studies. One of them is self-representation of a disabled person who foregrounds his or her struggles and accomplishments in a world that lacks the ability to imagine his or her needs and fears, his or her aspiration to mingle with the mainstream even while rejecting the status quo. The other story is a heartwarming, empathetic narrative of a person rendered disabled by social discrimination and caste restraints. A protest against the given social order, a resistance and the ultimate triumph of the individual mark the graph that is common to both the stories. Questions of agency of the disabled subject, self-representation, resistance to prevailing stereotypes pertaining to disability, a forceful critique and demand for reform by the disabled subject either through acts of subversion, resistance or unmasking of biases amongst the abled concerning the disabled in matters pertaining to identity, sexuality and choices form the major core concerns in the two stories discussed/translated here.

Bama's "Ottha" in translation

Bama, the well-known Dalit feminist writer in Tamil, narrates the tale of a young girl, rendered disabled by a discriminatory social structure. Her short story, "Ottha", was published in Tamil in 2002. It is the tale of a Dalit girl, Illamalli, who is forced to defecate in the open, like scores of other girls from her community. She is attacked by a pig at one such defecating session. The flesh and tissue of one of her breasts are gorged out by the burly pig. She is left with a deep scar and grows up to be Ottha – signifying the status of the single/singular position. She grows up stuck with an unfair sobriquet Ottha. Unlike the valorisation of Kannagi in the Tamil epic, Ottha, the one with a single breast, gets teased and harassed by one and all. The awe and admiration which breast cancer survivors receive at their brave straddling at public spaces, following their mastectomy, evade Ottha. She remains a laughing stock amongst her peers. She remains single as no man wishes to marry her. The biases and discrimination faced by Ottha (it's indiscernible at which point the narrative shifts from referring the girl Illamalli as Ottha, the nickname that the villagers bestow on her) are on account of her physical deformity. It cannot be construed as indicative of caste discrimination per se as even members of her own community harass her and call her "Ottha".

As she grew older, the pain hit Illamalli harder. When she attained puberty, people whispered to each other, "That singleton has blossomed." People sniggered behind her, labelled her "Singleton". Slowly, she began to be addressed openly as Single. "Hey Single, hey Ottha!". Her name Illamalli was erased out of everyone's memory. Her name became Ottha/Single. When someone called her by this name, she would become furious. She would curse and swear. But people only heckled her even more. They teased her constantly, called out deliberately – "Hey you Single! Single!" (translation mine).[1]

Although Ottha has a "single" dream of getting married and nursing a baby at her breast, she understands that it shall never be realised. Bama makes a strong juxtaposing of Single's socially disabling situation and her physical disability. One causes the other. The resulting disability ensues in further marginalisation of the Dalit woman.

While translating this story, the key challenge lay in capturing the linguistic otherness of the spoken vocabulary of Dalit women, resonating with a rural, non-standardised, idiomatic diction into English. The multiple resonances of the title thrust upon the protagonist Illamalli – Ottha – posed a challenge. It converged on the fact of her physical disability – a woman with a single breast, her marital status as a single woman, her mode of livelihood in terms of selling milk of a single milch cow and many such layered implications of this term in the Tamil language.

> What if I have a single breast? Don't I have desires? But perhaps . . . I would be left single until my last day
>
> OR
>
> Single bought a milch cow and took care of herself by selling its milk. Every day she would fetch grass and feed the cow. That cow was her sole companion. People did not spare her cow either. They called it, "Single's cow, Single cow". Single put up with everything and carried on.

(Translation mine)

Single woman, Single breast, Single cow, Single's cow, Singled out, Singular . . . the play on words is not, after all, wordplay. It is a scathing social critique and a constant reminder of her disability. The story concludes dramatically with Illamalli's vindication. The Naicker landlord molests her in the fields, grabs her single breast and makes insulting remarks on her disability. Single resists his sexual advances, raises the sickle in her hand and attacks the upper-caste landlord. She aims at his hand but misses her mark and hits his eye. The Naicker loses one of his eyes and is rendered Ottha Kannan – the single-eyed fellow.

> The news of how she rendered the Naicker landlord single-eyed spread like wildfire in the entire village. From that day no one called her Single anymore.

The disabled Dalit woman's resistance enables her to recover her identity, her name (Illamalli), her dignity and admiration from the villagers. This is how molesters should be dealt with, Loorthu Patti points out, and it is endorsed by the villagers in one voice.

Bama's narrative on the disabled stands synchronised with the self-articulation of the disabled. The victimhood of Ottha, her self-pity, the constant teasing and bullying stand subverted through an act of resistance that results in an emancipatory gesture. Illamalli's use of the sickle evokes an association of her class position as a small-time self-sustaining worker. The violence of the assault depicted is rooted in the gender-caste matrix that places Single at a greater disadvantage and social vulnerability. Disability in Bama's story is, thus, both a fact and an image of a disabling, discriminatory social structure. Single's resistance results in an emotionally satisfying, neat ending that incorporates poetic justice and endorsement by the community. The interplay of physical and social disability, on the one hand, and the affirmation of the self and the community on the other highlight that the disabling social structure needs to be challenged to facilitate empowerment/rehabilitation of the disabled self. At the end of the story, Ottha still remains single-breasted. However, the village community's perception of her disability is radically altered. It is this change in attitude that empowers Ottha – Single – to re-emerge as Illamalli.

Bama's story depicts the rigours of overlapping of identities in a given situation. Ottha's disability is a result of marginalisation faced by her as a Dalit and a girl born in a poor household in rural India. Her parents are farmhands and cannot provide medical attention that her condition required. A lack of basic civic amenities combined with enforced open defecation enjoined on her community and the rearing of pigs by upper-caste men who allow them to roam around without supervision not only precipitate the accident resulting in Illamalli's loss of a breast but also foreground how disability/disabled are located in a sociocultural context, riddled with caste, identity politics fraught with economic deprivation. The story brings to the fore how issues pertaining to disability/the disabled need to be located, examined, negotiated and sought to be resolved without losing track of the overlapping, intersecting categories of discrimination. The translator's intervention stands embedded in this complex labyrinth. The translation of this story, therefore, has to show up a layered representation of the disabled. The dynamics of a caste dialect, social exclusion aggravated by a physical disability, the emotional trauma of a young woman constantly teased by one and all for her singular condition demanded a restrained but reflexive intervention. The story's narrator was an educated, empowered Dalit woman while the protagonist occupied the other end of the social spectrum. In my earlier translation of this story, I had focused on the caste identity much more and traced her situation to oppression on account of her caste and gender. I had translated the title "Ottha" as *singular*, foregrounding her singular/exceptional circumstances. Nearly a decade later, with an orientation on issues concerning disability, I chose to modify the title to *single* to highlight her physical and marital status that cause her most intense agony. Thus, the focus of the translation can offer a corrective to perceptions on disability.

This story whether read as a Dalit text or as a disability narrative stands embedded in a stark agrarian, patriarchal social context. The intersection of categories renders Ottha's condition quite poignant. While translating the story for the project on short stories on disability, I could never lose track of it as a Dalit narrative as well. For that matter the quotient of gender never gets erased either in the narrative. For instance, how do we locate this terse observation: "Seven or eight years rolled by. Illamalli's left breast swelled up steadily. But on her right side, only the scar remained" (translation mine). Illamalli's disability is intimately linked to her gender, precipitated by her caste and delimited by her class. Bama's "Ottha" makes a vivid example of overlapping identities that argue for locating disability beyond the physical dimension.

Self-articulation of the disabled: challenges in translation

The second story, "Maadippadigal", written by Abilash Chandran, translated as "Steps and Stairs", depicts the perspective and experience of the disabled person in his own assertive, interrogative, subversive voice and acts. Disabled due to polio, the narrator-protagonist fights his way to gain a space in society that recognises "climbing up" as the only legitimate image – in the public and private domain.

Confronted by steps and stairs at every turn, the narrator sulks, protests, yearns but ceaselessly negotiates ways and means to overcome the obstacles – more real than metaphorical.

The story captures moments and moods from the quotidian life of a disabled person. Trapped and cornered by stairs – at school, college, government offices – the narrator makes a series of choices (including the choice of rejecting the choices imposed on him by his family or institutional infrastructure). Thereby, the narrator asserts his agency. He revels in making decisions for himself, to take control over his life.

> I put a full stop to my schooling after fifth standard. They tried their best to coerce me . . . I flatly refused . . . No. I won't go. Kill me if you wish, but I won't go back to school ever.[2]
>
> (translation mine)

The narrator makes a series of choices and decisions pertaining to his lifestyle, his career, his choices of friends and his modes of mobility in the public domain. As a child, he refuses to be turned into an object that is gazed at. He refuses to be carried to school on his father's shoulders and prefers to study on his own at home. His friends visit him at home and they chat and exchange ideas. He turns his bed at his own home into a centre of learning. At college, he would rather crawl up the stairs on his hands than be kept out of classrooms. Once he becomes a writer who delivers public lectures, he relies on a wheelchair to optimise his mobility. Finally, he employs an assistant to negotiate his ways through the numerous steps and staircases that dot our public spaces. Mobility becomes an important mode of self-assertion and an affirmation of his dignity. The story employs powerful images of self-affirmation which, in turn, render disability a visible presence in public spaces.

In this process, the narrator learns to subvert the obstacles, face them, carve alternative strategies to combat the ever-present stairs and steps in his life. The perception and perspective of an orthopedically disabled person are conveyed most graphically as well as lyrically in the story:

> It's not just an elevated floor. The world outside is full of steps. Steps that obstruct my wheelchair, prohibit it to cross them, go beyond them. What is the utility of these steps, honestly speaking? People who cross them might feel pretty brave about it. But for persons like me, they exist only to keep us out of a world that exults in buses, cars, offices, homes, auditoriums – before I seek to enter, the steps proclaim loudly that I am not wanted there.

A friendly chat or a wave of the hand from a classmate energises him even if his daily grind remains unchanged. Abilash's story throws up complex issues in the most disarming, matter-of-fact tone and tenor. The narrator's memorable meeting with one of his women classmates, Lata, on the opening day of his college and later after a gap of 22 years, when he is a popular writer and speaker are talked about with winsome casualness and ardour of feelings. Spotting her after two decades of college, he describes her thus:

> I saw her walking with a grace that is accessible only to those who wake up each morning, aware of how precious and sweet life is.

Issues of relationships with the opposite sex, friendships that affirm the sheer weight of an individual's notion of dignity and self-esteem are more esteemed and pre-ferred, the narrative points out. The narrator contrasts his warm admiration for Lata, her reciprocal warm friendliness and easy acceptance of his physical condition as a healthy "given", on the one hand, with the unhesitant outpourings of their innermost emotions shared with him (a male) by the girls of his age group during his adolescence, on the other. He prefers Lata's non-invasive acceptance of his per-sonality in an inclusive way as more humane and reassuring than the candid chatter of the young women in his town:

> Girls of our town conversed with me without inhibition. They poured forth their private sorrows and yearnings to me as if they spoke before a mirror.

The disabled male narrator does not want to be viewed or treated as a non-sexual being. His interactions with the opposite sex merit being negotiated on an equal footing, as between two adult, thinking individuals. Devoid of dramatic twists or events, inconclusive and open-ended, Abilash's story is a challenge to the transla-tor in terms of the sheer weight of unfamiliar, unexplored terrains of the lived experience of a brilliant mind compromised by disabling social givens and his own physical constraints. The narrator becomes a writer and popular speaker at public meets and discussion groups. But he is petrified by stairs and insists on being carried physically up/down the stairs while being seated on a wheelchair. He gets into a sweat, panics, screams, pleads with his escorts not to drop him down the stairs. His fears assume a surreal dimension and convey to the reader the deep trauma and insecurities experienced by the disabled in a society that is callous and unfriendly. The need for public spaces and educational institutions to be inclusive and mindful of the needs of the disabled is powerfully brought out in this story. The story, thus, emerges as a vocal plea for the rights of the disabled, an insight into the challenges they are forced to negotiate in their everyday lives not on account of their physical condition but due to the flawed mindset of society and its statesmen.

Reception to the plight of the disabled, a matter of fact acceptance of their con-strained mobility and an appreciation of their subversive coping mechanism form an important aspect of Abilash Chandran's short story. The narrator's friendship with Lata is a subtle brief for the rights and attitudinal change required in our soci-ety in the context of disability. On his first day at college, the disabled protagonist almost decides to turn away from the building and put an end to his aspiration for his higher studies. But Lata's response, friendly and "normal", sustains his inner grit and resilience:

> We entered the building together. But soon we reached the stairs. The steps made my heart sink. What do I do now? Shall I put on my gloves and crawl up the stairs? In her presence? Would she look at me with pitying eyes? How could I bear to see that? I should have turned back from the entrance gates, I mused to myself. Shall I tell her someone is waiting for me at the gate? She proceeded to climb the stairs with a cool greeting, "Come on, let's start". I didn't know for a moment how to react. Alright, I thought to myself. I put on my gloves and began to sit, crawl, sit, crawl, step by step. She kept chatting. About her family, school days, favourite song, last movie seen . . . the conversation steered smoothly. Every now and then she enquired about me, my interest, my likes. I peered into her eyes hard. It was such a relief to notice no change in her eyes – towards me. That is how I climbed my first staircase.

Climbing or rather crawling up a staircase is a painful experience. The disabled protagonist exults after one such session solely on account of his realisation that he is being treated as a fellow human being, at par with his other classmates, by a woman acquaintance studying at the same institution as himself. The converging of gender and peer-group anxieties and the success of surmounting them on the strength of humane reception to questions surrounding disability are deftly represented in the story.

The lived experience of a disabled person is unfamiliar terrain for a majority of readers. It is often imagined or sentimentalised in literary discourse by the non-disabled writers. Self-articulation by the disabled in the literary domain acts as a critical corrective. It functions as a powerful subversive tool that seeks to augment realistic modes of perception of ground realities concerning disability in the Indian social context. Abhilash's rendition of the experience of the orthopedically challenged is a good instance of challenging complacency and sensitising the reader towards issues of disability:

> The smell of floors, its cold touch mingling with the sweat of one's hands, leaving smudgy stains with its momentary shine that captures a glimpse of one's reflection, the strong odour of one's palms fused with a peculiar scent of the floor – has anyone experienced it? Merging with the floor, rather turning into floor oneself was getting to be disagreeable. The ever present dust, footprints, shoe marks, filth, foul smell, uneven floors, worrying over holes and gaps left me bitter and resentful.

The story, "Steps and Stairs", posits a young, dynamic, intelligent person with a wry sense of humour whose interventions in the literary and cultural domains are insightful, imaginative pertinent critiques of our polity. The story argues for an inclusive assimilation of the disabled as persons in the personal and as citizens in the political (and the intersecting/converging) spaces. This explores an important concern pertaining to the sexual as an integral aspect in the lives of the disabled. But, invariably, this is not reckoned with in our society. The narrator's affirmation of his sexual preferences as integral to his personality is as vocal as his resistance to being treated as a "thing", as a being devoid of sexual consciousness or needs. This is brought out in hard-hitting images laced with black humour:

> While I was waiting, some folks rested on my arm rest. Huge buttocks, almost touching my nose. These middle-aged women in nylon saris, don't they feel shy at caressing a man's nose with their buttocks? Perhaps they think of me as yet another commodity?

Then again:

> My eyes were transfixed on the wide, zig-zag steps on my left. From the ramp, those wide steps looked like a woman's expansive waist.

The narrator finds the steps a perennial challenge, not easy to overcome. His association of a woman's expansive waist in the context of a staircase lays bare the taboos imposed upon his consciousness that force him to imagine the opposite sex as inaccessible. He resents politicians, dressed in spotless white veshties, mounting the stairs with aplomb and creating a noisy ruckus. This group's blocking of the stairs blocks out his view of Lata on the other side of the staircase. He reacts angrily and wonders: 'Why are politicians invariably so fat? . . . They blocked the steps just as a bulldozer would make the street invisible'. When he loses track of Lata's face, the narrator's anger pours forth images that suggest how bitter, exasperated and caustic he could get:

> The white veshtied brigade's buttocks filled up the steps as quickly as a herd of piglets marching ahead.

The wheelchair-bound person resorts to black humour to get even with the mobile-footed. The story's conclusion is a non-event. Lata and the protagonist do not meet again. He wishes to have a glimpse of her, but the crowded staircase does not permit such a possibility. He is carried down the steps in his wheelchair. The non-closure at the end of the story indicates the continued struggles and challenges which the disabled face in our society, notwithstanding their moments of fulfilment, success and accomplishments.

The issue of overlapping identities operates in this story as well, although in a muted manner. The self-articulation of a disabled, educated, middle-class, male, public figure raised a different set of challenges to the translator. The register of the protagonist was standardised, an urban, educated, middle-class speaker who posed no specific linguistic challenges to the translator. The recurring resentment or tongue-in-cheek comments by the protagonist on matters of sexuality and the treatment of his disabled body by women in public places had to be captured with a candid forthrightness. It made me aware of a female gaze (of the translator) scrutinising the intimate, private monologue of a male, disabled narrator/speaker and ponder the inherent friction in terms of gender and disability quotients in this instance. The subject position of the translator and the political choices/stances of a translator assume a layered subnarrative in translation studies. This aspect remains crucial and pertinent in the context of the translation of disability narratives as well.

An enabling negotiation

Understanding one's "Other", accommodating the "Other's" perception and position on matters pertaining to the personal and the political emerged as my chief challenges (albeit stimulating) in negotiating disability in literary discourse as much as in translating the same into another language. The various stages and strategies employed in the process of literary translation were found enabling in negotiating disability and the voice of the disabled. Language of disability discourse is embedded in the agency of the disabled body/enabled voice that carves out its own representation and reception in the literary and social domains. A translator emerges as a listener and a carrier of such a voice that she seeks to record in an enabling, empowering language that guarantees visibility, power and attention in the academic and cultural domains. Translating from Tamil to English in the context of disability studies in India politicises translation activity, challenges academic neutrality and enables a wider engagement with questions relating to disability at multiple fronts.

Mirroring, mediating and defamiliarising a text emerged as crucial interventions followed in my translation practice. Such interventions prove enabling and empowering in accessing disability as a subject and as a subject position. Without subsuming the voice of the disabled, to be able to reach out to readers the aspirations, struggles, joys, privations and, most significant, their rights – is a fulfilling negotiation, indeed!

Notes

1 All references to this story in English are to my translation, undertaken for the purposes of this chapter.
2 All references to this story in English are to my translation, undertaken for the purposes of this chapter.

Bibliography

Bama. 2002. 'Oodaru', *Ottha*, May; 2003, 'Vitiyal', *Oru Thathavum Oru Thathavum Oru Yerumaiyum*, December.
Maadippadigal. 2013. December. Chennai: Tamil Femina.

11

READING INTERRUPTED

Translating disability in 'Subha'

Ananya Ghoshal

> Bodies speak, without necessarily talking, because they become coded with and as signs. They speak social codes. They become intertextuated, narrativized . . . in them-laws, norms and ideals become incarnated . . . if bodies are traversed and infuriated by knowledges, meanings and power, they can also, under certain circumstances, become site of struggle and resistance, actively inscribing them on social practices.
>
> – Grosz (1995: 35)

Introduction

In recent years, the human body has been fundamentally rethought by both science and philosophy. The body is no longer a natural object but a cultural representation, constructed through various media, especially language. Societies produce ideals of the perfect body in order to define their identities, and yet, time and again, the body's boundaries turn out to be fluid, uncertain and pose significant questions and concerns by challenging how a culture perceives itself. Physical disability is one such concern. In the short story 'Subha', understanding the social structures of control and exclusion surrounding the figure of a disabled mute girl, Rabindranath Tagore wants us to confront our anxieties surrounding stereotypical beliefs and move towards a more creative understanding of disability. Although written over a hundred years ago, 'Subha' is invested with a contemporaneity that a new genera-tion of readers in English can appreciate. Tagore's keen insight into disability can also tell us much on the possibilities of reconceptualising disability studies. The chapter contextualises this discussion with the social circumstances surrounding the disabled in contemporary India. The historical context is also touched upon, through examples from early Indian texts (such as the *Vedas*, the *Upaniṣads*, and the *Sāṁkhya Kārikās*) which have been influential in shaping the cultural fabric of India. The objective is to trace a wide range of multiple viewpoints and attitudes on disability and physiognomic differences in historical texts. In conclusion, approaches for more detailed studies have been suggested, and discussions around possible alternatives have been marked out.

Disability-impairment and able-bodiedness: a sociocultural conundrum

It is not an exaggeration to claim that Disability is as old as humankind as its archaeological origins can be traced to the Neanderthal era. It is therefore rather surprising that academic interest in disability has been rather muted. Amongst the select groups of scholars who do study it, the overarching view is that disability is a medical and psychological problem than social concern.

The scholarly attitude towards disability is rooted in a specific philosophical context of European Enlightenment thought. Enlightenment thinkers celebrated the 'European', 'whole', 'rational' individual as the norm. Anyone departing from this norm was considered either irrelevant or abnormal. Consequently, common responses to disability have been patronising, abusive and derogatory. Terms such as *invalid, cripple, spastic* and *defective* continue to persist in the common language parlance on disability. Even newer terms such as *handicapable, differently abled, physically challenged* or *special* are unreasonably euphemistic and problematic. Their usage also indicates the presence of a wider context – the problem of language.

At the heart of the problems on linguistic usage surrounding disability is a sociocultural conundrum concerning the meaning and interpretation of a related term – *impairment*. Strictly speaking, impairment refers to an actual physical loss or reduction of functioning in an individual, for example loss of vision, hearing, movement, speech and ability to learn. Disability, on the other hand, refers to how an individual with impairment is *dis*abled by society, through barriers to access, discrimination and exclusion. Thus, disability refers to the social context in which impairments affect an individual's everyday life. The differences between disability and impairment, however, are frequently misunderstood. Take, for instance, the definition adopted by the World Health Organization (WHO):

> Disabilities is an umbrella term, covering impairments, activity limitations, and participation restrictions. Impairment is a problem in body function or structure; an activity limitation is a difficulty encountered by an individual in executing a task or action; while a participation restriction is a problem experienced by an individual in involvement in life situations.[1]

I argue that definitions (such as the WHO's) are incomplete because they present the body in exclusively organic terms. Consequently, all discussions on impairment are epistemically restricted to an examination of the body's physicality.

In practice, the human body carries not only an organic but also a powerful symbolic import, and the deprivations of the senses cannot be reduced only to physical or bodily concerns. The senses that constitute the organic body also create distinct worlds of communication and symbolic information (such as musical, visual, spatial, etc.), that cultures, communities, and individuals share and partake in. However, each sense is vulnerable to harm and 'reductions' of the body entail denials of the shareable world. *Dis*abled bodies are often denied a fuller role in this shareable world, and consequently, suffer isolation and repression. One might genetically inherit the effects of impairment or be exposed to them later in life. But every 'body' reaches the limit of losing the sense(s), and we are all but 'temporarily able-bodied' or 'currently able-bodied'. In the long run, old age, disease or accidents inevitably lead to the 'able-bodied' turning to the 'disabled culture' for advice and direction. Therefore, although intimately woven into the social fabric, the questions are, why is impairment often treated as a personal, isolated predicament and responsibility of individuals? Is 'disabled culture' a reality? And how do communities perceive and participate in this culture?

Disability in literature: dis*ability* in 'Subha'

'Subha' was first published in the magazine *Sadhana* in its Magh 1299 issue (January–February 1893). Stories written during this period (1891–1895) were largely influenced by Tagore's sojourn as a landowner to the village countryside of his family estates spread over Nadia, Pabna and Rajshahi Districts, as well as parts of Orissa, where he experienced everyday rural life and wrote poignant stories about this context.

The story is about a mute child, Subhashini (ironically meaning 'sweetly speaking'). She is the third daughter in her family and is largely ignored by her kin and community alike because of her impairment. Her friends are two cows, goats, a kitten and an idle young boy, Pratap. Subha's parents, weighed down by the contemporary social obligation of getting their daughter married, arrange a match with an older man in Calcutta. The narrative poses a drastic juxtaposition of the supple intuitive life of a mute girl who readily communicates with nature and domestic animals in rural Chandipur with a gritty urban household in Calcutta. Subha is duly married, but her husband soon realises that she is mute and marries another woman who can speak. Worse still, Subha is blamed for her disability by the community at large. Tagore devotes considerable space to the impact of this tragic event on Subha herself:

> Within a week everyone knew that the bride was mute. However, they did not realize that it was not her fault, for she had deceived no one. Her eyes had said it all, but no one understood her. She looked everywhere but found no language; could not find the faces familiar to her since birth, of those who had recognized the words of a mute girl. In the ever silent heart of the young girl an endless, unvoiced wailing resounded which only the Supreme Being could hear.[2]

Subha is 'unable' to offer this narrative through verbal cues, and hence, the author narrates 'her' story, and I translate 'his' reading. How authentic is the entire practice? Did I speak 'his' tongue or 'hers'? The use of disability as a trigger for narrative is evident in stories ranging from the blind Oedipus in *Oedipus Rex* and Shakuni in *Mahābhārata* to the scarred, physically impaired slaves in Tony Morrison's *Beloved*. Disability also sparks the imagination and, in the words of Michael Bérubé, "demands a story" (Bérubé 2016: 43). Disabled people are often expected to describe and even explain their bodies that are not expected from those perceived as normal. For many, the 'scar,' the 'limp,' the 'missing limb' call for a story. It is precisely this very unknowability and the demand for an explanatory narrative that consolidate one's need to speak about them.

While literary representations of disability provide creative opportunities for close reading, they can also initiate a re-imagining and rewriting of our literary and cultural history in fighting oppressive ideas of normality and categorised appearances of disability. These perspectives, in destabilising established theoretical paradigms, can transform old understandings about structure, genre, and narrative forms and introduce provocative approaches in analysing literary works. This is crucial because literary representations of disability help open discussions about some of the most pressing issues of our time – empathy, minority status, caregiving, and social responsibility.

Translating 'Subha', a dis*ability* text: challenges, opportunities, and new paradigms

On 16 September 1901, Jatindra M. Bagchi produced the first modern translation of 'Subha' in *New India: A Weekly Record* and *Review of Modern Thought & Life*. Bagchi's translation was the first of many. While the 20th century has validated the enduring legacy of 'Subha' as an outstanding and popular story, the repeated efforts at translating it reveal the manifold challenges it presents to the modern scholar. Firstly, helping it move out of the confines of fidelity, authenticity and the like are key concerns. While translating, I often found myself transcreating a 19th-century tale for a modern-day audience and in the process, often untranslating the original. Untranslatability is a core principle that constitutes the heart of translation studies discourse and much has been written on the 'futile' attempts at recovering the continual nuances, subtleties, and intricacies while translating from one language into another. The term is often linked with a contemporary criticism concerning a translator for letting down the author by adding his or her own words, and hence his or her thought, to a text in a language which the readers mostly have no direct access to. I would, however, suggest that more than the *process*, it is the *manner* in which translators modify original texts through the choices they make (e.g. choosing *which* texts to translate, choosing *how* to translate, choosing *for whom* to translate, etc.) that define the discourse of untranslatability. Often, the choices made by me while translating the story seemed indicative of choices that could easily be made by other translators as well. As contemporary societies around the world are beginning to define themselves at a particular point in time in learning about disability perspectives and at times for which the translations of disability texts are being produced, certain individual choices are actively sought out to seek greater reach and encouragement for disability awareness. For example, I have made conscious digressions in the translation to tell the story from the perspective of Subha herself. The following translated passage marks an attempt to reduce the command/intrusion of the narratorial voice to a minimum, otherwise dominant in the Bengali version (which uses the third-person 'a silent girl' too often instead of Subha's first name):

> Subha was growing up, and slowly beginning to find herself. It was as if, a new indefinable sense of consciousness would sweep through her, like a tide from an unknown sea on some full-moon night. She was looking at herself; thinking about herself, asking herself questions and yet was not able to understand. On certain full-moon nights, she would slowly open the door of her bedroom and peep out timidly to find nature to the brim, like her lonely self, waking up over the quiescent world. In her youthful enigma, ecstasy and melancholy and the supreme reaches of enormous aloneness or even surpassing them; nature was overflowing with great stillness; yet could not utter a single word. At the periphery of this hushed, bewildered world of nature there stood Subha with similar yearning.[3]

The passages which describe Subha's communication with the natural world are profoundly poetic and written in a distinctive style that invariably loses much of its authenticity in linguistic translation. In the process of re-rendering them, I have found myself going beyond the apparent binary of 'domestication' and 'foreignisation' as potent strategies because, in the text, both are often taking place at the same time. If in many translations, the Bengali language was meant to conform to the codes of the English language, there were enough instances of the host culture self-reflexively abridging/commenting on the text, and thus bringing the meaning closer to the source context. For example, in this particular passage, culture-specific Bengali names/terms used for everyday objects, animals, plants, and natural phenomena, like *bakharir bera, aatchala, goalghor, dhenkishala, khaurer-stuup*, and *tentuul-tola*, could be translated using the closest English equivalents, but as the following passage illustrates, small digressions were called for to help the reader visualise the fringe spaces Subha occupies in her home, family, and society:

> Banikantha's house would look upon the river. His outhouse with its roof in eight parts, the bamboo lath fences, cattle shed, husking pedal, straws lying in heaps, foot of the tamarind tree and the backyard garden of mangos, jackfruits and bananas could all be noticed by the boatmen passing. I am not sure however if amidst these overt signs of domestic affluence anyone noticed the mute girl who, stealing away pockets of time would come and sit by the river amidst all hustle and bustle.[4]

A nuanced challenge in translating a text like 'Subha' also lies in the translator's basic commitment to see it as 'complete,' without the temptation of interpreting the life of the protagonist as a primary source of cultural meaning or metaphor. Many non-disabled writers' understanding of disability still operates in the form of what Mitchell and Snyder call 'narrative prosthesis' (2000: 47)[5] that uses disability as a rhetorical tool to convey messages unrelated to real disability discourse. According to them, any literary device through which the particular disability of a character is manipulated to evoke certain feelings mostly ends up creating a sense of unease and draws more of the prejudice that exists towards disabled people. Hence, such devices needed to be avoided while translating 'Subha'.

Michel Foucault's concept of 'disciplinary normalisation'[6] has also long propelled feminist disability studies to contest against reinforcing techniques of normalising subject bodies that deviate from the 'standard' – including any attempts to 'correct' the deviant bodies and their place in the society. This, too, must be foregrounded in attempts of translation work. It is because, in narrating the tales of protagonists with impairments, 'Subha' challenges our supposed assumptions on centredness, completeness, and enabled-ness. Such disabled/disability texts not only point towards all that is unstable with our bodies, selves, and languages but also urge us *not to* comply with conventional norms regarding how we read or interpret such texts. In deviating from normative expectations and telling the lives of atypical protagonists, texts like 'Subha' fight binary conceptions of gender/genre and national/ linguistic identities.

The exercise of translating 'Subha' thus required that as a translator, I remained open to questioning dominant and normative modes of textual interpretation(s) both in approach and in praxis. For example, there are many 'loose' strands in the story that seem to require some securing (especially in translation), and Tagore's narratorial voice is keen to work out the creases for the readers in English. However, I tried avoiding that as much I could since words and meanings are always insecure and can never be pinned firmly on the page, even more so when the protagonist speaks the tongue of nature. Much like disabled bodies unfairly disqualified by an able culture, texts and translations on disability, too, are sometimes disqualified for their perceived 'flaws.' However, the disability narrative in 'Subha' triumphs in its unique strength and aesthetic merit. What Tagore tries to see through linguistic signs is a new and radical representation of disability. In Subha's case, Tagore opines that, as opposed to the mouth or the tongue, it is her *eyes* that express her thoughts:

> Our expression in language requires efforts, somewhat like the process of translation – that is not always adequate and may turn imprecise due to a lack of skill. . . . Those who possess no other tongue than the trembling of their lips since birth carry in their eyes a speech that is eternal in expression and unfathomable and translucent as the heavens, wherein play dawn and sunset, light and shadow.[7]

Subha, dis*ability* and the discourse of gender

Gender and disability are both complex categories that operate and play out within the family as well as the social realm. The emergent field of feminist disability studies has demonstrated that disability, like gender, is a system of representation that marks bodies with acquired identities.

In 2001, the census of India included disability for the first time following a sustained campaign by the Indian disability movement. The 2011 census found more than two Crore disabled people of which women with disabilities constituted 44.1 per cent. More important, in this census, perhaps for the first time, disability was understood to be primarily a social phenomenon. Almost all informants spoke of being vulnerable to exploitation and abuse, especially disabled women, and of being socially marginalised and underestimated, being seen as useless and treated as objects. It was well understood that the degree of social exclusion that a disabled individual faces varies enormously according to her status as an individual, as well as the type and severity of the impairment and, in particular, her gender.[8]

While the status and representation of women in Bengali literature have traditionally been self-conscious, over the previous century, it has seen a complex process at work in the attempt to essentialise and homogenise the gender. The works of many Bengali authors have reflected on the role of traditional gender ideology in propagating a socially conservative ideal of the 'respectable woman' (*bhadramahila*) centred on privacy, marriage, and domesticity. In Tagore's story, the life of the disabled is governed by gender ideologies that are internalised, accepted, and negotiated by the way her life is carved. It tells us about the ways in which disabled women may or may not engage with and participate in the family and social life within their communities. It also brings to focus the social meanings attributed to the 'normal' female body which by default constructs it's 'other' – the disabled female body – as 'deviant,' 'inferior' and 'incapable' of full participation. For Subha's mother, she is a deformity upon herself, and Subha's muteness, having a lonely grandeur like nature's own, makes other children dreadful:

> Her mother, in particular, saw her as a blemish. For a mother, a daughter is a more intimate part of herself than a son ever is, and for this reason, any lack in her daughter seemed like a profound cause of personal shame. Banikantha,[9] Subha's father perhaps loved her a little more than his other daughters; but her mother, seeing her as a disgrace upon her womb, was always displeased with her. . . . The solitude of the mute possesses a grandeur; much like nature. This, the common children did not understand. Instead, they feared her and would not play. She was without words and friends, as lonesome as the noontide.[10]

Projected with the very qualities that the 'able' world rejects, fears, or disowns in itself, Subha is invalidated, marginalised and perceived as less or more than human. Tagore's views on disability from over a hundred years ago possess a striking contemporaneity. As recently as 1989, Ludmilla Jordonova expressed very similar views:

> The idea of otherness is complicated, but certain themes are common: the treatment of others as more like an object, something to be managed and possessed and as dangerous, wild, and threatening. At the same time, the other becomes an entity whose very separateness inspires curiosity, invites inquiring knowledge. The Other is to be veiled and unveiled.
>
> (Jordonova 1989: 109)[11]

Tagore's ideas of social progress had developed through changing historical contexts, and gender always formed a crucial constitutive category. Heterogeneity forms the core of his literary output. However, instead of totalising universalism, he yearns for an alternative vision of humanism that accommodates variations without overlooking commonalities. The position of women has a key role in his *oeuvre*, and 'Subha' must be read with this context in mind. Tagore's exploration of Subha's femininity takes the shape of an elaborate palimpsest in which she imagines herself as a mysterious princess endowed with primordial and mystic powers, a woman who cannot be ignored. This stands starkly juxtaposed with the socially conditioned, constrictive, and inferior roles that she is forced to surrender to. Subha's primary identity is her strong individualism rather than her 'disability'. She carefully rejects her disability as having anything to do with how she sees *herself* in her mind's eye:

> Subha ardently desired to be of some help to Pratap. . . . She prayed to God to grant her some supernatural powers – as if to create a miracle by mystic incantations, that Pratap would marvel at: 'I never knew our Subhi[12] had such powers!' Imagine if Subha had been a water-nymph, she might have risen slowly from the river, bringing a serpent's head-jewel with her. Pratap leaving his meagre fishing would then dive deep into the underworld with the jewel, and arriving there, who should he see on a golden bed in a silver palace, but our Banikantha's mute daughter, Su? Yes, our Su, the lone princess of that bejeweled silent city in the outer reaches of the netherworld. Could this never happen? Could this really be impossible?[13]

In Tagore's vision of the water-nymph, her body becomes a powerful and vital signifier for gendered subjectivity.

The daily life of Subha, in its communication with nature and the animals, also establishes a different kind of symbolic participation in our shareable world and challenges cultural ideologies that construct disabled female bodies as incapable, marginalised and dependent. Tagore emphasises the atmospherics by which Subha communicates with the world around her:

> Nature often seemed to be making up for her lack of words while speaking *for* her. The murmur of the brook, the noise of the village folk, the boatmen

singing, the birds chirping and the rustle of the trees would intermingle, turning into one vast oceanic wave like timbre that would beat upon her rest-less soul. Nature's myriad buzzing sounds were the mute girl's voice; her long shaded dark eyes expressed the language of an entire universe; from the trees, where the crickets ceaselessly chirped, to the indescribable stars, the incessant signs and gestures, and music, weeping and sighing. And at mid-day, when the boatmen and fishermen had left for lunch and the householders took naps; when the birds remained quiet, and the ferry-boats were idle; when the great busy world took a hasty respite from work and showed its remote, forlorn face – beneath the vast endless sky a mute nature and a mute girl would sit face to face – one under the streaming sunlight, and the other in the narrow shade of a tree.[14]

In *Space, Place and Gender Relations* (1993), Linda McDowell suggested that a woman's body challenges conventional ideas of boundaries, especially the assumed boundaries between the body and the object world or between the self and the other:

> Women's experiences of, for example, menstruation, childbirth and lactation, all represent challenges to bodily boundaries. The feminine construction of self is an existence centred within a complex relational nexus, compared to the masculine construction of self as separate, distinct and unconnected.
>
> (1993: 306)

While this argument posits the 'insecure' bodily boundaries of women (leaking, seeping) in juxtaposition with the bodies of 'rational' men 'in control'; a similar trope could also be used for ability/disability aesthetics, as Subha's tears give away more than her words ever could. There are multiple instances in the story in which Subha bursts into tears: when she knows from Pratap that her marriage has been arranged and she seeks to 'reason' with her father or when she goes to the cattle shed to bid good-bye to her childhood friends before leaving for Kolkata. She fed the cows, Sarbbashi and Panguli, with her hands; clasped their necks; and looked longingly into their faces – tears running from both her eyes. When her mother dressed her up for the bridegroom, tears ran down her eyes and her mother, instead of empathising, scolded her in the fear that her eyes would grow swollen. But the tears would not heed her reproach. These instances from the text hint that such bodies might not be trusted in the public spaces. While body studies aim at exam-ining new ways of developing frameworks for capturing the means through which each human 'embodied' subject is formed, focusing on a politics of fluidity does act as a strong hinge in disability discourse as well. Thus, the 'translation' of 'Subha' occurs across both social and bodily boundaries, and Tagore's imagery is fitting in mutually conveying them.

'Subha' does, however, follow the usual disability tropes, like notions of *karma* or action and *dukkha* or suffering as retribution for past sins. We are told that Subha had understood since early childhood that her birth is nothing short of a curse of God and would withdraw herself: 'It is best if people forget me' she would think, thus hinting at her impairment as a lonely burden to bear. Conversely, Tagore tries to understand Subha's disability not only as differences that exist in her appearance, behaviour, and daily functioning but, rather, what the 'able' human world makes of those differences. The societal assumptions that disabled people are incapable of mutuality and fail to fit in able-body standards are often critiqued as her empathic, symbiotic relations with animals are beautifully articulated:

> It was not that Subha did not have a couple of cherished friends. In the cattle-shed were two cows, Sarbbashi and Panguli. . . . When she fondled them or scolded or cajoled, they understood her better than her fellow human beings. . . . The young girl would visit them regularly, three times a day, and at many odd hours as well. Whenever she was made to hear unkind words in the house, she would come to her mute friends who as though in some blind inference could fathom the anguish from her melancholic, long-suffering stare. Coming close to her, they would rub their horns slowly, softly against her arms; and in a wordless, perplexed manner, would try to comfort her.[15]

The story of Subha thus clearly shows that she is well adjusted to the world around her. The 'problem' is not her muteness but the adverse reactions to her disability by the able-bodied people around her- her husband, her contemporaries and her mother. The story's perspective on disability is not unique to Tagore. Rather, as I will argue in the next section, such views were also expressed in Early Indian systems of thought.

Disability in the Indian literary/cultural landscape: notes from the past

The *Rig Veda*[16] is the oldest extant text in India. Written between 1300 and 1000 BC, *Rig Veda* is a text of socio-religious practices, wars, rituals, and cultural memory. It also contains evidence of early Indian ideas of disability. Along with references and scattered glimpses of peoples with physical and visual disabilities, the text also mythologises the concept of healing by insisting that disabilities such as lameness or blindness could only be cured by semi-divine beings who were themselves disabled. In this way, it argues that disability is not a question of making the human body whole, but rather, it is about an informed perspective on what being disabled entails. *Rig Veda's* references to disability are not unique to *Vedic* literature but can also be found in *Yajur Veda* (800–1000 BC).

Apart from the *Vedas*, the *Upaniṣadic*[17] corpus (500–800 BC) also discusses disability at length. For instance, the philosophical implications of blindness and loss of hearing are important arguments in *Bṛhadāraṇyakopaniṣad* (6.1.7–14), *Chāndogyopaniṣad* (5.1.6–15), *Chāndogyopaniṣad* (8.10.1), *Kaṭhopaniṣad* (1.2.2–6), *Muṇḍaka Upaniṣad* (1.2.8); and *Maitrāyaṇīya Upaniṣad* (7.9). However, the *Upaniṣads'* emphasis on the philosophy of blindness and hearing does not extend to a general philosophy of disability. This concern is, however, a core aspect of *Sāṁkhya*.[18]

Sāṁkhya is a philosophical system whose intellectual genealogy can be traced to the *Chāndogyopaniṣad* but came into its own as a distinct philosophy only in the 5th century CE when Īśvara Kṛṣṇa produced the definitive contribution to this system of thought – *Sāṁkhya Kārikā*. At its core, *Sāṁkhya Kārikā* is a bold, new interpretation of the nature of reality. What concerns us here is a specific part of the *Kārikā* (No. 21 to be precise) which examines the idea of incompleteness and disability.

> PuruṣasyadarśanārthaṁkaivalyārthaṁtathāPradhānasya |
> Paṅvandhavadubhayorapisanyogastatkṛtaḥsargaḥ | |
> (Kṛṣṇa: 63)

Kārikā No. 21 is concerned with the concept of evolution. It presents an intriguing argument that for the creation and evolution of the world (*Jagat*) the role of the incomplete or disabled is crucial. A parable is presented to illustrate this point further. In this *Karika*, *Prakṛti*[19] is compared to *blind* (*andha*) while *Puruṣa*[20] is compared to *lame* (*pangu*). Individually, it is tough for each to traverse a path alone, but when combined, their endeavour brings an effective result, that is the fruitful transformation of the world or *Jagat*. It is significant to note that the absence of sight and mobility are neither represented as infirmities nor contrasted with able-bodied normatives with sight and limbs intact. Furthermore, the emphasis on disability is not incidental as *Kārikā* No. 49 later identifies twenty-eight forms of physical and mental disability. The *Kārikā* explains that human beings are naturally prone to the loss of functions and characteristics of the senses that form the living body and thereby does not attribute to them the unique condition of being marked or different from their 'normal' counterparts:

> Ekādaśendriyavadhā, sahabuddhivadhairaśaktirupadishṭā |
> saptadaśadhābuddhir, viparyayāstushṭisiddhīnām | |
> (Kṛṣṇa: 100)

I argue that these texts recalibrate the discussion on the social fabric of disability in responding to singular bodies (like Subha's for instance) and, moreover, examine how these singularities help us rethink the concept of the body. In sharp contrast to Enlightenment modes of thought, as well as contemporary views on impairment and disability, the *Kārikā*s present a view that human bodies are fundamentally incomplete and the 'whole' individual cannot be treated as the norm.

Looking forward: disability and the otherness of the world

It can be inferred that the intolerance of communities towards bodies marked with singularity might have stemmed from an unconscious fear of death and oblivion which can be traced back to every culture. The Greeks saw disability as 'ungodlike' when Hephaestus was banished from Olympus and confined to the underworld because of his lameness. The Romans were keen on infanticide as a way of getting rid of bodies in ill health. In the Middle Ages, weak bodies were taken as evidence for the workings of Satan, and in the late 19th century, the 'Surplus Population Theory' stated that when economic survival is precarious, weak bodies must be disposed of. Yet, our contemporary times can write a different story. One must realise that deprivations of the sense cannot be reduced only to physical or bodily concerns but must also be addressed as at once physical as it is deeply absorbed in the symbolic. Reductions of the body entail denials of the shareable world, and without these receptions, bodies suffer isolation and repression. In Tagore's story, the little girl's profound connection with nature puts her in intimate contact with this shareable world, but the limited world of the humans seems unable to accommodate her 'differences'. Thus, in responding to bodies marked with difference, it is imperative to examine how these singularities help rethink the concept of the human body in its relation to the symbolic world. At this juncture of a global disability movement, we must also persistently discern if through the available discourses in homogenising the modes of access to the world we are simply providing a 'common language'. When the problems of impairment and deprivations of the body are addressed from the vantage of the unimpaired (as if the impaired must be made in the image of the unimpaired), no wonder the most commended support will seem to be the provision of 'assistive' or prosthetic technologies. However, in providing them to the impaired bodies or looking for immediately visible fixes like building a 'special' school while leaving the social perception towards the disabled as unchanged; are we ignoring the need of how the all-inclusive social system should try to grow more complete and non-disabling? While not refusing these 'tangible' approaches and achievements here, I do hope to suggest that to unravel the workings of the world that we share; a philosophical engagement with systems of thought such as *Sāṃkhya* enables a more nuanced understanding of disability. Such approaches might enable us to be in the world differently and understand the difference between the bodies and the difference they make to the world. However, until now, our persistent desire for the 'ideal' bodies bluntly points towards the fact that our understanding of 'disability' is indeed hopelessly meagre.

Notes

1 World Health Organization, "Disabilities", www.who.int/topics/disabilities/en/, accessed on 17 June 2017.
2 Rabindranath Tagore, *Subha* in *Galpaguchha*, Calcutta: Visva-Bharati, pp. 146–147. Translation mine. Henceforth, all passages from 'Subha' quoted in this chapter are translated by me unless stated otherwise.
3 Rabindranath Tagore, *Subha* in *Galpaguchha*, Calcutta: Visva-Bharati, p. 145.
4 Rabindranath Tagore, *Subha* in *Galpaguchha*, Calcutta: Visva-Bharati, p. 143.
5 David T. Mitchell and Sharon L. Snyder, *Narrative Prosthesis: Disability and the Dependencies of Discourse*, Ann Arbor, MI: University of Michigan Press.
6 In *Security, Territory, Population: Lectures at the Collège de France 1977–1978*, trans. Graham Burchell, New York, NY: Palgrave Macmillan (First published as Securité, Territoire, Population, 2004).

7   Rabindranath Tagore, *Subha* in *Galpaguchha*, Calcutta:Visva-Bharati, p. 142.
8   Nandita Saikia, et al., 2016, 'Disability Divides in India: Evidence from the 2011 Census', *PLoS One*, 11(8): e0159809.
9   The name means 'in whose voice Bani or Devi Saraswati (the Goddess of speech, learning, and music) dwell in.'
10 Rabindranath Tagore, *Subha* in *Galpaguchha*, Calcutta:Visva-Bharati, p. 142.
11 Ludmilla Jordonova, *Sexual Visions: Images of Gender in Science and Medicine Between the Eighteenth and Twentieth Centuries*, New York, NY: Harvester Wheatsheaf.
12 An affectionate adaptation of the name 'Subha.'
13 Rabindranath Tagore, *Subha* in *Galpaguchha*, Calcutta:Visva-Bharati, pp. 144–145.
14 Rabindranath Tagore, *Subha* in *Galpaguchha*, Calcutta:Visva-Bharati, p. 143.
15 Rabindranath Tagore, *Subha* in *Galpaguchha*, Calcutta:Visva-Bharati, pp. 143–144.
16 The *Rig Veda*, a compound of *rik*, 'praise'; *verse*; and Veda *knowledge*, is an ancient Indian collection of Sanskrit hymns and counted among the four Hindu canonical texts (*Shruti*).
17 The *Upaniṣads* form the Hindu scriptures which primarily discuss philosophy, meditation, and the nature of the Supreme Being and are considered as mystic or spiritual contemplations of the *Veda*s, their putative end, and essence, also known as the *Vedānta*. The *Upaniṣads* were composed over several centuries, and the oldest – *Bṛhadāraṇyakopaniṣad* and *Chāndogyopaniṣad* – have been dated to around the 8th century BCE.
18 *Sankhya*, also known as *Sāṁkhya*, is one of the six schools of classical Indian philosophy which is regarded as the oldest of the philosophical systems in India. I first learned about the relation between Sāṁkhya school and the disability discourse during a lecture delivered by Dr. D.Venkat Rao, Professor of English at EFL University in 2008.
19 *Prakṛti*, in the *Sāṁkhya* system refers to material nature in its germinal state which is eternal and beyond perception. It is the unmanifest (*avyaktam*), the sum of the universal energy, without cause but acting as the cause and source of all effects. Attributed with the *guṇa*-s, it is 'the ultimate basis of the empirical universe.' When *Prakṛti* (female) comes into contact with the Spirit, *Puruṣa* (male), it begins a process of evolution that leads through several stages to the creation of the existing material world.
20 In the *Sāṁkhya* philosophy, *Puruṣa* is metaphorically considered to be masculine but is devoid of the *guṇa*-s and therefore inactive and characterised as the conscious subject and pure consciousness. It is eternal, all pervasive, and self-sustaining.

Bibliography

Ayrault, Evelyn West. 2001. *Beyond a Physical Disability: The Person Within: A Practical Guide.* New York, NY: Continuum.
Banerji, Debashish, eds. 2015. *Rabindranath Tagore in the 21st Century: Theoretical Renewals* (Sophia Studies in Cross-cultural Philosophy of Traditions and Cultures). New Delhi: Springer India.
Barnes, Colin and Geoffrey Mercer. 2013. *Exploring Disability: A Sociological Introduction.* Cambridge: Polity Press.
Bérubé, Michael. 2016. *The Secret Life of Stories: From Don Quixote to Harry Potter, How Understanding Intellectual Disability Transforms the Way We Read.* New York, NY: New York University Press.
Gambier, Yves and Luc Van Doorslaer. 2016. *Border Crossings: Translation Studies and Other Disciplines.* Amsterdam: J. Benjamins.
Ghai, Anita. 2015. *Rethinking Disability in India.* New Delhi: Routledge India.
Ghosh, Nandini. 2016. *Impaired Bodies, Gendered Lives.* New Delhi: Primus Books.
Griffith, Ralph T. H. 1973. *The Hymns of the Rigveda.* Delhi: Motilal Banarsidass.
Grosz, Elizabeth. 1995. *Space, Time, and Perversion: Essays on the Politics of Bodies.* New York, NY: Routledge.
Hall, Alice. 2016. *Literature and Disability.* London: Routledge, Taylor and Francis Group.

Hall, Kim Q. 2003. 'Feminism, Disability, and Embodiment', *NWSA Journal*, 15(1), Spring.

Hume, Robert Ernest and George C. O. Haas. 1995. *The Thirteen Principal Upanishads: Translated from the Sanskrit*. Delhi: Oxford University Press.

Jordanova, Ludmilla J. 1989. *Sexual Visions: Images of Gender in Science and Medicine Between the Eighteenth and Twentieth Centuries*. New York, NY: Harvester Wheatsheaf.

Kṛṣṇa, Īśvara. 2006. *Sāṃkhya Kārikā*. Trans. Swami Virupakshananda. Mylapore, Chennai: Sri Ramakrishna Math.

Larson, Gerald James. 1998. *Classical Sāṃkhya: An Interpretation of Its History and Meaning*. London: Motilal Banarasidass.

Longhurst, Robyn. 2001. *Bodies: Exploring Fluid Boundaries*. London: Routledge.

McDowell, Linda. 1993. 'Space, Place and Gender Relations: Part II: Identity, Difference, Feminist Geometries and Geographies', *Progress in Human Geography*, 17(3): 305–318.

Miles, M. 2007. 'Disability and Deafness, in the Context of Religion, Spirituality, Belief, and Morality', *Middle Eastern, South Asian and East Asian Histories and Cultures: Annotated Bibliography*. www.independentliving.org/docs7/miles200707.html (accessed on 12 May 2017).

Mitchell, David T. and Sharon L. Snyder. 2000. *Narrative Prosthesis: Disability and the Dependencies of Discourse*. Ann Arbor, MI: University of Michigan Press.

Siebers, Tobin. 2008. *Disability Theory*. Ann Arbor, MI: University of Michigan Press.

Tagore, Rabindranath. 1957. *Galpaguchha*. Calcutta: Visva-Bharati.

Turner, Ralph Lilley. 1965. *A Comparative Dictionary of the Indo-Aryan Languages*. London: Oxford University Press.

Vlahos, Olivia. 1979. *Body, the Ultimate Symbol*. New York, NY: J.B. Lippincott Company.

12

'LOHINI SAGAI'

Translating disability, literature and culture

Shilpa Das

Ishwar Petlikar's short story 'Lohini Sagai,' for which he is most renowned, has been published consistently in school textbooks in Gujarat ever since it was written in 1951, and it was in school that I read it first. The story is a moving account of the relationship between Mangu, a young girl with mental retardation and speech impairment and her mother, Amratkaki, and the latter's extraordinary love for her daughter. Mangu is dependent on her mother for all her daily activities, including toileting. Amratkaki hopes and prays for a 'cure for Mangu's condition' and dreams of her subsequent marriage. She tries all manners of traditional healing systems to cure Mangu. The villagers and Amratkaki's other children insist that Mangu should be moved to a 'hospital' for 'mad' people in a nearby town for her own good. Amratkaki resists this move for a long time but eventually gives way to everyone's counsel and demands and leaves Mangu in the hospital. However, acute anxiety about Mangu's well-being in the hospital tears at her heart. The story ends with Amratkaki being so consumed with grief and guilt at 'abandoning' her helpless daughter that she loses her own sanity.

The first half of the paper discusses the raison d'être for the selection of this story in terms of disability theory. Since this chapter is located at the intersection of disability, gender, and feminism, I draw on the classic questions of the definition, experience, stratification, marginalisation, oppression and politics of disability and the feminine experience of disability. The second half discusses the specific challenges I faced in the act of translation with its attendant challenges and rewards.

I begin by articulating the many ways in which the host text in Gujarati aligns itself with the charity, morality and medical approaches to disability and reveals itself as a text of disablement and foregrounds some core issues of disability discourse. The charity model refers to the attitude that people are morally responsible for their own disability. It says that disability is caused by a moral lapse and brings shame to the individual and to the family. It equates disability with 'flawed minds and bodies', 'suffering', 'terrible bodily conditions', 'abnormality', 'social deviance', 'being a burden on society', 'a stigma' and 'the outward manifestation of inner evil'. Historically, depicting disability as divine reprisal or the product of one's sins was often seen, and in many cultures, including our own, this practice has continued till today. The invalidating view permeates language, media representations and cultural beliefs and is rooted in the idea that disabled people are unhappy and crave to be normal (French and Swain 2004: 3). Such an approach ensures care but encourages dependency among the disabled. Here, decisions regarding the nature, amount and recipient of charity are the prerogative of the donor. This is also known as the Charity model or Personal Tragedy model of disability. It depicts disabled people as unfortunate individuals who should be pitied (Oliver 1990: 14) and who are unproductive members of society (Wendell 1989: 109).

The onus of the disability, in this case, lies in Mangu's body, particularly her mind, and the authorial voice consistently evokes the *problem* of disability in the narrative. Disability is understood to be a deviation from the norm of 'able-bodied.' Being a man with disability then is a rung below the norm of the non-disabled woman who is below the non-disabled man, and so, disabled women are at the fourth level down. Physical impairments themselves are hierarchically structured: some categories considered weaker and less acceptable than others. For example, people and especially women with mental retardation and/or mental illness come at the bottom of the hierarchy of impairments, below those with physical and learning disabilities, because they are constructed as deviant and dangerous. Thus, disabled women form a heterogeneous group and, as a group, experience many different forms of injustice that interact in complex ways with other systems of oppression. Mangu is a girl with mental retardation who hails from a village in Gujarat, factors that immediately downgrade her.

Mangu is born into a traditional Indian household where daughters are considered temporary inhabitants of their natal households and are quickly sent away to their marital households. In a culture that lays a premium on a male child, a son, to carry on the family lineage, the birth of a daughter often rings in disappointment or anxiety, and she is often deemed a 'burden' (Hans 2003: 19), a curse (Ghai 2009: 416) or 'a permanent liability' (Bhambani 2003: 83). This notion of women as burdens is entrenched in the cultural belief that 'any economic investment in girls, such as an education, accrues to the husband, not to the natal family, as opposed to boys, whose education is seen as feeding back into the earnings and status of the family' (Kalyanpur 2008: 58). In the context of this cultural legacy of patrilineage and 'strong son-preference' among most communities in India, they say in Gujarat, *Tadharotla machhokripalvayijashe*, literally meaning 'a girl child can survive even on stale *rotis*'. Furthermore, popular culture is replete with maxims such as *dikri ne gay doretyanjaye*, that is 'a daughter and a cow go where they are directed', or *dikri to parki thapan kahevay*, that is 'a daughter is another person's property', disenfranchising women and divesting them of any decision making. On the other hand, *naritunarayani* venerates the principle of *shakti* in women. Such contradictions continue to beset the sociocultural fabric of the state.

Within patriarchal communities, the male head of the family (usually the father) takes decisions on important matters pertaining to the children such as education, health care, freedom of movement and employment while the mother is the traditional caregiver for all children, including the disabled girl child. 'Lohini Sagai' starts by illustrating such caregiving:

> When people advised Amratkaki to admit Mangu to a mental hospital her eyes welled up with tears and she told everyone the same thing, "If as a mother I cannot be a caregiver to her, how can I expect the people in the hospital to look after her with love and affection? Putting her in the hospital would be similar to deserting one's infirm or disabled cattle in a *panjrapol* or animal shelter. When Amratkaki's angst became common knowledge, no one broached the topic again. When people saw for themselves how she brought up, cared for and indulged her daughter – with speech impairment and mental retardation from the time of her birth – they praised her saying only Amratkaki can raise a mad daughter. Had Mangu been born in another home, she would probably have starved to death a long time ago and if per chance she had lived, she would never have been so stout they said.
>
> (my translation)

Sociological studies in India reveal that, at the onset of disability, often parents are consumed with a gamut of emotions ranging from denial, guilt, blame, helplessness, self-mortification, shock, depression and even shame (Rangaswamy 1995: 22). In a culture that views disability as a tragedy, parents' first reaction to the onset of disability in a girl child is 'she'd have been better dead than disabled for life' (Ghai 2003: 58). In the story, the 'better dead than disabled' approach to disability of the family and other villagers is clearly visible. The following passage best exemplifies how the disability-as-disaster narrative is perpetuated:

> Other people in the village could never say the kind of things her daughter said when Amratkaki compared the hospital to an animal shelter. But nonetheless they thought, 'Perhaps the hospital is like an animal shelter but if Mangu dies there, it will be blessed relief for both the family and her.' Amratkaki too felt that Mangu's death would bring in much relief, but only if it were brought about by a natural cause. She could not bear the thought of deliberately pushing her daughter to her death through neglect.
>
> (my translation)

Sometimes, their families are so sensitive to or ashamed of the disabled daughters and apathetic to their sentiments that they make no attempt to facilitate their integration with their social environment. The disabled girl 'ceases to exist as a person and is excluded from being recognised as a woman in the fullest sense because she does not fit in with the model of women defined by society and dear to the collective imagination' (Dignani 2003: 132). Mangu's siblings feel her presence disrupts the solidity of their family life. Amratkaki's daughters-in-law resent how she 'clutches her mad diamond close to her bosom'. On the other hand, parents of young disabled girls may be excessively overprotective, assuming that their daughters by virtue of being both female and disabled are doubly vulnerable. Their overriding anxiety is '[a]s long as we are there, it's fine; but who will look after her when we die?' Amratkaki feels the same apprehension:

> Mangu was growing up while she herself was growing old. It was clear that her daughters-in-law would not step into her own caregiving role. So far, neither of them had asked Amratkaki to move in with her. Times were such that in every household, sons were under their wives thumbs. So, she really had no expectations of her sons. Given that situation, whether Mangu recovered by god's grace or not, if she were to get adjusted to life in the hospital, then she would be able to die in peace with the assurance that her daughter was being looked after well if only by strangers. With that thought, Amratkaki shed copious tears. Her heart cried out in pain.
>
> (my translation)

The well-functioning female body is considered the primary locus of womanhood across all cultures, and the female disabled body is seen as deviance from the norm. As a response to patriarchal culture's ascription of traditional (read passive) roles to women, and in the system of arranged marriages in India, our able-bodied or ableist culture looks on disabled women as not quite 'women' – as imperfect or even deviant. Culturally legitimised representations depict them as inadequate and expendable and therefore unfit to fulfil the traditional roles of Indian women – of wife, homemaker and mother. In a culture where a great premium is laid on health and physical vigour and where the mythical belief of the body being controllable is idealised, the implications for those like Mangu who exercise no control over their bodies can only be imagined. Disabled women and their families often find themselves accepting the cultural dictum that marriage and motherhood, which are seen to bestow a sense of purpose and identity to a woman's life, are not fated for them. Consider the way Amratkaki agonises over Mangu's marriage prospects:

> An astrologer predicted that Mangu's stars would improve in the upcoming month of *Magshar* and she would recover fully. From then on, Amratkaki waited devotedly for Magshar to arrive. Mangu would turn fifteen that month. Amratkaki had married off her other daughter, Kamu, at the same age and so her mind of its own volition drifted towards thoughts of Mangu's marriage. 'Had Mangu been normal she would have been betrothed too by now. If she is going to be cured in the month of Magshar, her looks are such that any prospective bridegroom will immediately consent to marry her.' Her thoughts would drift towards planning Mangu's wedding as though Mangu were cured. 'At the time of Kamu's wedding, my

sons were not so well off. Today, they are both very prosperous, and spend money lavishly, then why should I restrain myself from having a grand wedding for Mangu?

(my translation)

The story perfectly exemplifies how we live in a world of norms. The text constantly brings up this opposition of *gandi* (mad) and *dahi* (good) playing them off against each other. But, this binary of *dahi* and *gandi* is also a hierarchy in which one term is accorded privileged status, and like in all binaries, *dahi* is conceived as anterior, essential or central and privileged over *gandi*, which is seen as a complication or deviance of the first and, hence, marginalised. Mangu is a *gandichhokri*, a 'mad girl'. Amratkaki's sole endeavour in life is to make Mangu, *dahi*, or 'normal'. *Dahi* (*dikri*) is repeated again and again in the text as a refrain to emphasise social expectations and to underscore what Mangu is not. 'Soon, Amratkaki's hope-filled month of Magshar arrived. There was no change in Mangu (*dahi na thayee*).' Even at the mental hospital, the elderly matron tells Amratkaki, 'Soon, your daughter too will become normal like Kusum.' It must be noted that she says *dahi thayee jashe*, or 'she will become a good girl', and not *saji thayee jashe*, which means 'she will be cured' in Gujarati. As Lennard. J. Davis says, '[t]he problem with disability is not so much the disability or the person with disability, but rather the way that normalcy is constructed to create the "problem" of the disabled person' (Davis 2006: 3). In defining disability, we always juxtapose it with concepts of normality, which exist within a society (Garland-Thomson 1997: 7). It is for this reason that I chose to translate <u>dahi</u> as 'normal'.

The oppression of disabled women is constituted in their entry in the public world where they are subject to either pity or hostility. The body becomes an important marker of identity for disabled persons, including women (Foucault 1980: 30). In *Discipline and Punish*, Foucault talks about how the bodies of both women and people with impairments are subjected to 'disciplining' all the time through social practices that shape and regulate them (Foucault 1977: 185). This is mainly done through the politics of medicalisation (surgeries for the congenitally disabled and institutionalised care among others). The medicalisation of the physically impaired bodies is often employed for the benefit of the politics of appearance or of control. Foucault says that the medical examination

transforms the economy of visibility into the exercise of power. In discipline, it is the subjects who have to be seen. . . . It is the fact of being constantly seen, of being able always to be seen, that maintains the disciplined individual in his subjection.

(1977: 187)

Mangu, who is completely ignorant about personal hygiene, who is almost completely unregulated, must therefore be sent to institutionalised care for her own enhancement and well-being, people rationalise.

This is directly in correlation with the Medical model of disability, which supplanted the more religious and traditional approaches. Constructed and sustained primarily by the medical fraternity, it led to the social control of disabled people. The focus here is still on the disability, not on the disabled person or the experience of disability. It considers impairment and disability as synonymous and treats disability as an affliction of the person's body, mind or senses, 'a deviation from a norm or a pathological condition' (Oliver 1990: 14), something less than human. Disability is again perceived as a 'personal tragedy' – a disaster or 'a tragic happening' that occurs to unfortunate and isolated individuals on a random basis which 'the disabled person needs to come to terms with' (Oliver 1996: 131). The key words in the lexicon of this literature include *suffering* and *coping*. It construes disability as an 'abomination of the body' (Goffman 1963: 4) or a problem and states that the body should be cured, surgically corrected, 'ameliorated' and 'controlled' (Titchkosky 2000: 200), managed or 'normalised' (French and Swain 2004: 2) according to medical and aesthetic standards in order to become 'whole' again. Such a representation of disability does not treat disability as a complex life experience, and the social production of knowledge also endorses the view (Titchkosky 2000: 203). In fact, the medical model stigmatises disabled persons by positing impairment as the ontological essence of disability. This means that they are marked apart as a distinct social group on the grounds of their supposed bodily difference and subordinated. The model is therefore seen as oppressive of the minds and bodies of people with disabilities as it conceptualises them as 'dependent' (Oliver 1993: 50) and 'being acted upon'. In doing so, it represents them as lacking the capacity to transform their lives without the help of professionals such as doctors and continues to propagate 'able-bodied normalcy' through its ideas, values and interests, further promoting segregation and perpetuating stereotypes. The normative culture in Mangu's village bears a neurosis with respect to disability as it 'differs' from the societal norm. This difference highlights a body to feel ashamed about. Able-bodied society's refusal to view the disabled body in any other form constitutes a social and cultural apartheid. Such a social indifference denies Mangu a voice or a space, deprives her of her social presence and any semblance of identity. She is made a 'case'; the individual 'who has to be trained or corrected, classified, normalised, excluded' (Foucault 1977: 191).

The categories of both women and disabled persons involve a reduction to some aspect of their physical presence; while women are subjected to the gaze, disabled persons are to the stare. While the male gaze makes the normative female a sexual spectacle, the stare reduces the impaired body to a grotesque object and is the definitive gesture that constructs disability as an oppressive social relationship (Garland-Thomson 1997: 26). In the story, the listeners stare at Mangu sitting on the ground 'in clothes wet from answering nature's call and scraping at the wet mud with her fingers'. Later, at the hospital, Amratkaki herself stares at the other inmates. In the case of both disabled men and women, a visible physical deformity is often taken as evidence of other limitations. Both are dehumanised, express a disempowering notion of human beings as having unworthy and immutable biological destinies outside of a social, cultural and historical context; both are objectified as *things* to be controlled, as lacking the power or choice to alter their lives and as parts of the vast 'Other'. Disturbingly, both categories acquire the garb of *natural* truths; both occupy a certain rung in the social ladder of hierarchy, and both indicate societal situations of inequality. The story expresses all these facets of the disabled existence and makes Mangu's disability 'hyper-visible'.

Another signature theme of feminist disability studies is at the centre of the story – the relation between disabled women and their female caregivers. The idea of caregiving dominates the narrative with great detail, given of all acts that constitute the ideal of motherhood. In fact, Petlikar is celebrated for his 'heart-rending' account of this caregiving by the mother. This is seen, for instance, in the host language (HL) expression, *Amratkaki nu samagra matrutva Mangu par abhishek hatu* which lends some kind of sanctity to the bond between mother and daughter, and its affective quality partially comes out in the receiving-language expression 'Amratkaki poured all her motherly love on Mangu'. The caregiving account poses a problematic for disability discourse; even as it upholds the ideal mother, it disempowers the disabled girl with mental retardation who has to be controlled, and is the perpetual outcast in the narrative. Throughout, the narrative the constant infantilisation of Mangu and caregiving of Amratkaki are in congruence with each other. It extends to the extent that in the end, 'Amratkaki joined the ranks of Mangu'. What will become of Mangu now? She may well have lost her biggest ally. Mangu is always already condemned; a passive object with little or no agency or selfhood. She is twice silenced: both in the host text where she is an outsider figure anyway and in terms of the discursive boundaries of disability discourse. Now, her and her mother's identities have merged into one. Will Amratkaki be admitted into the hospital as well?

The selection of this story for this workshop on my part itself provokes certain questions. Who is selecting the text and doing the translation? Since the translator filters the source text through herself during the hermeneutic process of the translation, the translator's subjectivity, world view and attitude are all significant factors impacting the process and the outcome. Thus, the vulnerability of the source text to me as the translator cannot be underestimated, and the outcome itself is always already *rupantara*, or a changed form, and *vivartam*, or an altered condition. My role as translator could also be related to that of a narrator suggesting the powerful potential of the translator's agency as one who 'tells' and hence frames the material 'told'. I never lost sight of its importance as a form of storytelling and of my 'visibility' in that sense. Added to this is the point of deciding what to emphasise and what to silence, what to foreground and what to put in the background. In this context, the other term for translation in India, *anuvada*, or 'speaking after' or 'following', has the scope for retelling an existing text as an integral part of the process.

The answer to the question asked earlier, that is who is the translator, in the context of this chapter is a multilingual, bicultural, disabled woman, professional and mother. Why the host text has been chosen and whose experience is being translated have already been discussed earlier. It is, in itself, a political act in that it brings up issues related to disability, an area of study that I have been engaged in for the past decade or more through writing and research. Add to this the fact that this is a perspective from the 'inside' being a translator with a disability who views the text and interprets it through the focal point of feminist disability studies, bringing all aspects of the narrative to a fixed convergence. This particular instance of translation must be looked at as embedded in a wider set of social and inter-textual practices, given that it posits disability-as-translation and translating disability in a dialectical relationship with each other. Even as it seeks to render a text that is linguistically and socially embedded in the source culture within the target culture, how disability is constructed and narrated through translation itself become useful points of departure.

We also need to consider here the host language of the host text and the author himself. Who is the author of the text? Petlikar is a non-disabled journalist, school-teacher and novelist, a prolific social chronicler and a reformist in terms of his writing, but he hails from an upper caste of Gujarat, the Patels. The particular register of the Gujarati language he deploys and in which characters speak is that spoken by higher castes in rural areas of central Gujarat with a greater influence of the kind spoken in Kheda, Nadiad and the commercially powerful Ahmedabad District. Amratkaki speaks the kind of Gujarati spoken by old women in Ahmedabad. The sentence with which the story ends, *Amratkaki Manguni natma vatlaigaya*, rich in connotative meaning, is its supreme example.

Translation has often been spoken of as a twice-lived existence. To understand the meaning of a lexical unit in one language and interpret it in another, to internalise the cultural significance of a language and to adopt it to another to convey in this other, as well as to release one text in the framework of another demands two layers, two cultures and at least two levels of interpretation making for a living cross-cultural dialogue across temporal and spatial geographies. At the outset, many questions arose. How would the English translation be bound to the reference point? How would I decide the quality and quantum of changes? When one translates discourse from one culture to another, one extends discourse across cultures. How would I determine the exact nature of this exchange? Most important, considering that 'Lohini Sagai' was written at least sixty years ago, how would I ensure that the accretion of another layer, that the translation, in some way subsumed the perspectives and approaches of contemporary disability discourse?

In attempting to translate the story from Gujarati to English, my allegiance has, for the most part, lain with the host culture with its attendant specificity and the host text. I have tried to do away with the oppositional framing of literal versus interpretive and done what I felt the narrative demanded. Translation of prose fiction entails cultural encounters and lexical challenges, but the objective at all times was to not forget the reference point, attend closely to the design and language of the source text and carry as much of the original across to the readers as possible in all its detail.

But this presupposes a degree of symmetry between languages, which makes the postulated equivalence possible. And between English and Gujarati, we do not really have the symmetry because they each belong to a different branch of the Indo-European family. There is, in addition, the question of the unequal power relationship that holds reasonable currency every time modern Indian literature gets translated into English. It continues to be the language of power seventy years after we freed ourselves from our colonial masters. It is indispensable as a link language nationally and internationally; its hegemony as a *lingua franca* has both a national and a global reach, especially in the production of Indian and world cultures. It is the proverbial alchemic stone enshrined in all institutes of higher learning, as a means of getting into lucrative professions, a tool for upward social mobility and the inevitable elitism. Translations from one modern Indian language to another are more fluid and evince greater equity. Translations into English assure immediate wider readership nationally and have the possibility of a readership internationally as well. Thus, we consider who composes the target readership.

I have strived to retain the original flavour of the story – in terms of both its cultural ambience and its linguistic flavour – and to allow for the translation to perpetuate cultural memory in the source language, Gujarati. However, both the host language and the receiver language have developed in different historical, social and cultural geographies half the globe apart. The syntax of modern Gujarati, including the register of Central Gujarat that Petlikar uses, is naturally at odds with English. This has necessitated a reflection on the essential qualities of both languages, what they represent, how they do so and to what degree. Paul de Man talks about the act of translation as transforming the poetic into the prosaic. Since one must concentrate on the hermeneutic aspects of the text, one loses out on the beauty of its poetry (de Man 1986: 82). This is evident in the source language (SL) expression, *Amratkaki nu samagramatrutva Manguupar Abhishekhatu* which lends sanctity to the bond between mother and daughter and whose affective quality is marred substantially in the target language (TL) expression, 'Amratkaki poured all her motherly love on Mangu.' To achieve some sense of style and natural writing one has to constantly turn the concentrated and figurative speech of the Gujarati into a looser, more diluted English form. The translated text could often not maintain the economy of words of the host text because of Gujarati's own syntax, which accommodates adjectives more easily. Furthermore, the host text is replete with expressions, both words and phrases that brim with a range of emotions. In fact, the emotional communicability of 'Lohini Sagai' is so strong that you feel that most of the time all you need to do is repeat in another language what is being said as in the passage here:

> Mangu, looking at this new world wide-eyed, suddenly leaped to Amratkaki's side. Amratkaki lovingly put her hand on Mangu's head and was about to use her daily endearment '*beta*' when her voice cracked and the word turned into a long death wail. The lamentation rang through the entire hospital. Tears flowed and flowed down the son's cheeks like a stream. Even the doctors, matron and attendants, who were used to witnessing such scenes, had heavy hearts that day. It was as if the walls also trembled for the very first time with the agony of a mad loved one.
>
> (my translation)

The guiding principle has been that while the main feature of Indian languages is hyperbole, that of the English language is understatement. For instance, in the sentence in the translation 'Finally, with a long sigh of resignation and supporting her knees with her hands, Amratkaki stood up', the import of *kadvo ghuntdo haiyama samavi* is not fully present, but it is a hyperbole, literally meaning 'with a bitter gulp in her heart.' So 'with a long sigh of resignation' seems appropriate in the target language to express that Amratkaki finally reconciles to the fact that the time to take Mangu to the mental hospital has arrived.

Translating the title of the story, 'Lohini Sagai' into English itself proved to be a huge problem. I have retained the phrase as the title of the story because it proclaims the theme of the story, is virtually untranslatable and is replete with a rich cultural resonance in *sagai*, for which *blood ties*, *ties of blood* or *bonds of love* are poor options. Perhaps, 'the true test of motherhood' is a closer expression in terms of meaning but is neither as evocative as nor as powerful as the Gujarati term. It is this *lohini sagai* that leads Amratkaki to join ranks with Mangu. In the end, I let it go as is.

With all its tremendous power and syncretic ability, the English language is still not fully capable of coping with the subtlety and hidden dimensions that are found in the Gujarati language. Some transpositions are simply not possible. It is not possible always to translate all connotations of the host text vocabulary, complete with associative shades of meaning as in the case of the term *panjrapol. Animal shelter* does no justice to convey the sense of abandonment, sickness, disease, and death that form the thick sociocultural tissue of the term. Without this understanding it may not be possible to fully comprehend Amratkaki's apprehension about admitting Mangu to a hospital for those with mental retardation. Furthermore, Dagut's remarks about the problem of translating metaphor are interesting in this context: 'Since a metaphor in the SL is, by definition, a new piece of performance, a semantic novelty, it can clearly have no existing "equivalence" in the TL: what is unique can have no counterpart' (Dagut 1976: 24). Here the translator's bilingual competence is of help to her only in the negative sense of telling her that any 'equivalence' in this case cannot be 'found' but will have to be 'created.' The crucial question arising thus is whether a metaphor can be translated as such or whether it can only be 'reproduced' in some way. The term *granthi* in the sentence, *Amratkakinia granthijaher thai gaya pachhi koi emneevi vat kartunahin* can mean both a 'tumour' and 'views'; *angst* seemed to communicate better the existentialist crisis that resonates with the term and foregrounds disability as something that is expendable and something evoking disgust. It is through such fissures and crevices that the translation betrays the classic Derridean *aporia*, a term used in deconstruction theory to indicate a kind of impasse or insoluble conflict between rhetoric and thought. *Aporia* indicates the lacuna between what a text means to say but what it nonetheless ends up to mean. And it is here that one half of the tension of the text lies, the other half being what it seeks to say about disability but is constrained to mean something else.

It appeared to me that the translation had to be an interpretation of the host text through a focus on the reverberatory qualities and textures of the disabilism in the narrative. On one hand, the receiver text or translation necessitated being read as a new writing since the readers of the translated text were not always going to be informed about or familiar with disability discourse or the disabilism inherent in the source culture, language and literature. On the other hand, the host text has a deep-seated history, and its elements were to be appropriated and presented to the receiving culture and readership with proper negotiation. This was an exercise fraught with some slipperiness because it entailed a passage through my own subjectivity as a disabled translator mentioned earlier.

Translation implies making political decisions with choice of words regardless of the host text. Thus, translation is seen as a text type in its own right, as an integral part of the receiving culture and not merely as a reproduction of another text. This is particularly the case in translating the discourse of disability from one language to another, which definitely muddies the view of what disability language itself necessitates. There is clearly in my translation the centrality of disability activism and resistance to disabling and ableist aspects of the source language and its semantics. The objective was to set in clear relief the oppressive and coercive aspects of the received etymological, linguistic, semantic, semiotic and ideological discursive universe of the host language and host text and thereby engage in a creative resistance. To throw up the translator as an agent of social change, so to say. The translation must be as true to the translator as to the source text. Translating in this context has been a strategy of questioning the hegemony of ableist culture and language and the oppression of the phenomenon of disability itself. The host text, if one were to translate literally, says that Mangu was *mook* (mute) and *gandi* (mad) right from her birth. It is not clear what Mangu's exact disability is, but a closer look at the text suggests it to be mental retardation combined with or leading to speech impairment. The very first instantiation of this in the text by the third person authorial voice led me to unequivocally choose these terms to describe Mangu's mental condition. However, I dropped it in all subsequent references where other people in the village refer to Mangu and used the term *mad* (*gandi*) in all its startling starkness. At first, the term seemed to me to be at odds with my work in disability studies. I intended to 'dis' the disability but soon realised that I must retain the term if I wished to bring about a rupture in the text from which meaning could escape. I needed to amplify cultural representations of disability instead of filtering them out, make of these a telling indictment of the non-disabled world, of the non-*ganda* world. Using *mental retardation* in subsequent references would have been problematic because the reader of the receiving text would miss out on the indignation and oppression of the host text's representation.

Interestingly, Amratkaki uses the word *abudhh* for Mangu when they are leaving for the mental hospital. She has just spent an anguished night wracked with anxiety for Mangu's well-being:

> Amratkaki could not sleep at all the night before Mangu was to go to the hospital. In the morning, she felt it would be better if she did not accompany Mangu. She would not be able to bear it when the authorities at the hospital separated her from her daughter. At the same time she could not rest content without seeing for herself what kind of facilities the hospital would offer her daughter. She had to go. And yet, when she stepped out of her home with Mangu, she felt as if the weight of the whole world was pressing in on her. Tears coursed down her face. She could not take her eyes off Mangu's face. Amratkaki's heart sank. She thought even cattle protest when a new master

tries taking them away. Mangu had not even sensed she was being taken away from her home to a new place. With that thought Amratkaki collapsed at the threshold of her home. Her heart cried out, 'An *abuddhh*girl has no one in the world. Her own mother can desert her!

(my translation)

Here, it was difficult to choose between 'one who has mental retardation' 'one with mental disability' 'one who does not have control over her senses', 'is not in her right senses' or even 'mad.' At first, I chose *mentally retarded* to be politically correct, to redefine or re-vision the disability identity by using the terms and terminology acceptable to disability discourse. Next I chose *mad* like an overwhelming label, in order to retain all its ableist connotations of helplessness, dependency, mental imbalance, a lack of control over one's senses and more. It is for the same reason that I retained disability metaphors used in the host text such as Amratkaki '*mutely listened*' to the villagers' string of advice. Then, I realised that it is Mangu's mother who is using the term and that she would never be able to call her daughter mad never mind if she calls the other inmates of the hospital *gandi*. So, perhaps the right choice, after all, would be a euphemistic one, 'a girl who is not in her right senses'. Eventually, I decided to retain the word *abudhh* with its attendant cultural and emotional signifieds. This is similar to the way I earlier translated the term *dahi* not as the literal 'good' but as 'normal' in my translation. Doing so is an attempt at what K. Satchidanandan calls 'reframing the boundaries of the sayable and changing the terms of affiliation' (Satchidanandan 2001: 6) This brings us back to the point of the ideological position of the translator colouring the translation.

As receiver text producer and host text interpreter, we translators do play with language to give the text a certain slope, embed it in our discourses and our thought, in language and, thus, in all symbolic systems. In that sense, translation not only remains at the level of mere linguistic transposition or literary creation but also becomes a cultural contestation, a political position, an ideological struggle and an ethical assertion. Tymoczko states, 'Within social systems, translation functions as an invisible means of cultural grounding and cultural appropriation, serving to construct identities and affiliations' (2006: 446) This raises questions of representation, dominance and power. Translation is also a form of meta-text or a text about a text. Although a translation's ideology is determined by the content of the host text, that is only a starting point, for the act of interpretation of the host text and its content and the representation of the host text with its resonances are political acts with an attendant ideology eliding all normative investigation. In this case, I feel translation through its interpretive exegesis precedes knowledge of disability and does not merely reflect such knowledge. This stakes out its political and ideological territories.

References

Bhambani, Meenu. 2003. 'Societal Responses to Women with Disabilities in India', in Asha Hans and Annie Patri (eds) *Women, Disability and Identity*, pp. 76–88. New Delhi, Thousand Oaks and London: Sage Publications.
Dagut, Menacham B. 1976. 'Can Metaphor Be Translated?' *Babel*, XXII(1): 21–33.

Davis, Lennard J. 2006. 'Constructing Normalcy: The Bell Curve, the Novel, and the Invention of the Disabled Body in the Nineteenth Century', in Lennard J. Davis (ed) *The Disability Studies Reader*, pp. 3–16. New York and London: Routledge.

Dignani, Vanda. 2003. 'Women, Affectivity, Handicaps', in Asha Hans and Annie Patri (eds) *Women, Disability and Identity*, pp. 129–136. New Delhi, Thousand Oaks and London: Sage Publications.

Foucault, Michel. 1977. *Discipline and Punish: The Birth of the Prison*. New York, NY: Vintage Books.

———. 1980. '"Body/Power" and "Truth and Power"', in Colin Gordon (ed) *Michel Foucault: Power/Knowledge*. Birmingham: Harvester.

French, Sally and John Swain. 2004. 'Whose Tragedy? Towards a Personal Non-Tragedy View of Disability', in John Swain, Vic Finkelstein, Sally French, Colin Barnes and Carol Thomas (eds) *Disabling Barriers and Enabling Environments*, 2nd ed., pp. 34–40. London, California and New Delhi: Sage Publications. http://disability-studies.leeds.ac.uk/files/library/swain-affirmative-chapter.doc (accessed on 14 April 2013).

Garland-Thomson, Rosemarie. 1997. *Extraordinary Bodies: Figuring Physical Disability in American Culture and Literature*. New York, NY: Columbia University Press.

Ghai, Anita. 2003. *(Dis)Embodied Form: Issues of Disabled Women*. New Delhi: Shakti Books.

———. 2009. 'Disabled Women: An Excluded Agenda of Indian Feminism', in Renu Addlakha et al. (eds) *Disability and Society: A Reader*, pp. 411-432. New Delhi: Orient Blackswan.

Goffman, Erving. 1963. *Stigma: Notes on the Management of a Spoiled Identity*. Upper Saddle River, NJ: Prentice-Hall Inc.

Hans, Asha and Annie Patri, eds. 2003. *Women, Disability and Identity*. New Delhi, Thousand Oaks and London: Sage Publications.

Kalyanpur, Maya. 2008. 'The Paradox of Majority Underrepresentation in Special Education in India: Constructions of Difference in a Developing Country', *The Journal of Special Education*, 42(1): 55-64. http://www.sed.sagepub.com/content/42/1/55 (accessed on 7 September 2010).

Oliver, Mike. 1990. *The Politics of Disablement*. Hampshire and London: Macmillan Education Ltd.

———. 1993. 'Disability and Dependency: A Creation of Industrial Societies?' in John Swain et al. (eds) *Disabling Barriers-Enabling Environments*, pp. 49-60. London: Sage Publications.

———. 1996. *Understanding Disability: From Theory to Practice*. Hampshire and London: Macmillan Press Ltd.

Paul, de Man. 1986. 'Conclusions: Walter Benjamin's "The Task of the Translator"', in *The Resistance to Theory*, pp. 73-105. Minneapolis, MN: University of Minnesota Press.

Rangaswamy, K. 1995. 'Parental Attitude Towards Mentally Retarded Children', *Indian Journal of Clinical Psychology*, 22: 20-23.

Satchidanandan, Koyamparambath. 2001. 'Reflections: Rethinking Translation', *Indian Literature*, 45(1): 5-8.

Titchkosky, Tanya. 2000. 'Disability Studies: The Old and the New', *Canadian Journal of Sociology*, 25(2): 197-224.

Tymoczko, Maria. 2006. 'Translation: Ethics, Ideology, Action', *The Massachusett's Review*, 47(3): 442-461.

Wendell, Susan. 1989. 'Toward a Feminist Theory of Disability', *Hypatia*, 4(2): 104-124. http://www.jstor.org/stable/3809809 (accessed on 12 March 2010).

13

GENDERING DISABILITY IN DHARAMVIR BHARTI'S 'GULKI BANNO'

'The Hunchback Bride'

Mukul Chaturvedi

> The task of the translator is to facilitate this love between the original and its shadow, a love that permits fraying, holds the agency of the translator and the demands of her imagined or actual audience at bay.
>
> – Spivak (2000: 398)

This chapter examines how the representation of disability in Dharamvir Bharti's 'Gulki Banno' mirrors religious, social and cultural attitudes of Indian society towards disability, in general, and towards disabled women, in particular. The chapter addresses the challenges of translating Dharamvir Bharti's 'Gulki Banno' and argues that translating disability calls for an attitude of praxis. Using feminist translation theories, the chapter argues that feminist translation strategies can highlight the gendered agency of the disabled protagonist and construct her as an active social subject. The chapter also explores the gendered dimension of disability and maps how the female experience of disability is fraught with anxieties related to the body and the customary roles it is supposed to fulfil.

Introduction

Published in the collection *Saans Ki Kalam Se* in 1969, Bharti's 'Gulki Banno' is the poignant story of a young woman, Gulki, who has developed a disability due to a physical injury inflicted by her husband. Twenty-five-year-old Gulki develops a severe hunchback when she is pushed down the stairs by her husband for giving birth to a stillborn child. Forced to live a life of penury, ridicule and rejection, Gulki finds a neighbourhood which is willing to accommodate her but treats her like a grotesque figure who inspires awe and fear. While the text delineates Gulki's character, what stands out in the story is the portrait of a community. The vibrant community which appears cohesive is highly stratified and the disabled are treated as outcasts. Gulki is subjected to compassion and kindness, but she cannot live a life of dignity and self-respect as she is perceived as incapable of looking after herself and perhaps does not deserve to as she is considered subhuman. Using a comic-ironic mode, the text shows how Gulki's effort to live her life independently as a vegetable seller is endlessly thwarted by the community, and she is forced to go back to her abusive husband as a domestic help to raise his child with another woman.

Disability is central to 'Gulki Banno' as the text begins with the arrival of Gulki and the disturbance her presence causes in the neighbourhood. The narrative is structured around Gulki's trials and tribulations, and finally, she is made to go back to her husband's house with the hope for redemption. The emotions of 'fear, pity and disgust' (Hughes 2012: 72) which inform the non-disabled imaginary, are evident in the reaction of the community towards Gulki as her presence unsettles the young and old alike. The children call her a thief, allege that she's stacked money on her back, and perceive her as deceitful. The text makes it amply clear that it is the fear, myths and fantasies associated with disability that are more handicapping than the actual fact of having an impairment. Gulki's arrival sets of a series of reaction, mostly hostile, amongst the community, and despite all odds weighed against her she is perceived as a threat. There is a perverse delight in making fun of Gulki and the children find her as their sole amusement. For example, the children raise slogans every time they go around Gulki's shop:

> 'In our land, we are the boss
> Gulki's shop we'll boycott'[1]

Impoverished Gulki's disability makes her an outcast figure within the community. No one buys vegetables from her, and she faces a near social boycott. Such is the fear of disease and disability within the community that the two poor and orphan children, Mirwa and Matki, who suffer from leprosy, are Gulki's natural allies, and she bonds with them. Unable to accommodate Gulki's unsettling presence, she is finally ousted from the community.

Disability and mythology

Interestingly, 'Gulki Banno' shows that the attitude towards disability is rooted in religious beliefs when Gulki is compared to Kubja, a young hunchback maidservant of King Kamsa in Mathura, in the Bhagwat Purana. Gulki is convinced by the women of the community that because of the way Lord Krishna saved Kubja and cured her hunchback because of her love and bhakti of the divine, she might also be redeemed and cured of her disability if she goes back to her abusive husband: 'Isn't there a God up there? Don't you know when the Almighty Krishna kicked the hunchback Kubja, her hump disappeared, and she became normal! A husband is like a God after all!'

The story of Kubja also appears in the Brahma Vaivarta Purana, where she is born as Surpanakha, who had lusted after Rama, and was consequently disfigured as a mark of punishment. She is redeemed in her next birth as Kubja when Krishna cures her (Pauwels 2008: 336). Gulki's suffering is also compared to the virtuous suffering of Sita during her exile, a temporary phase of banishment, and then she is united with her husband. The patriarchal social universe of the text rationalises Gulki's suffering in religious terms and sees it as an instance of bad karma. Gulki blames herself for her miserable condition:

> I know I wronged my husband; that's the reason God punished me and took my child away. When He forgives, he will bless me with another child. Am sure he will. I will pray to God for the well-being of your brother-in law, Mewa. You see, I am the one who has a problem. Once we have a child, that other woman in his life will not rule over him anymore.

Indian mythological literature highlights the association of disability with moral depravity and deceit and foregrounds the religious view that it is a punishment for bad karma, either in this birth or the previous birth. In Hindu mythology, disability could be a punitive or a derivative punishment. Sage Ashtavakra, mentioned in the Mahabharata, was born with eight deformities as he was cursed by his father Kahoda for showing off his scholarly arrogance as a foetus. Ajamukhi became a goat-faced woman because of her sins as the lustful beauty Chitralekha in her previous birth. Disability is also a derivative punishment, as in the case of Dhritrashtra, who was born blind because his mother Ambika closed her eyes as she was repulsed by the look of sage Vyasa during intercourse (Pal 2013: 116). Hindi cinema is replete with punitive, restorative and redemptive images of disability and, to a large extent, have fed the popular imagination and shape our responses to disability (*ibid.*, 112).

Femininity and disability

In 'Gulki Banno' the unintentional disabling punishment meted out to Gulki by her husband shows that violence is entangled with femininity, disability and the female body. Also, the rejection of a physically disabled woman is accepted as a suitable response, and ultimately physical violence against a female body becomes an appropriate teaching tool. For example, Gulki's husband does not regret his action, rejects her and later uses it as a teaching tool. Rather, Gulki blames herself for his action and thinks that she will be forgiven once she gives birth to a child. Both femininity and disability are inextricably caught in patriarchal culture ever since Aristotle's equation of women with disabled men (Garland-Thomson 1997: 279). This association of deviance and monstrosity with disabled women excludes them from the relative privileges of normative femininity. Gulki's disability appears to cancel her femininity, removing her from the sphere of womanhood and feminine beauty. For example, when Gulki, dressed in her bridal attire, is going back with

her husband who had abandoned her after she lost the child, she is described as
grotesque:

> The children looked on curiously. Mewa asked, 'Say, Gulki, are you really
> going back with your husband? Say, Gulki?'
> The hunchback Gulki, slightly embarrassed, smiled shyly and said, 'Keep
> quiet, you! Stop teasing me now!'
> The shy smile and faint blush which gives a lovely warm glow to a young
> comely girl's face looked so pathetic on Gulki. Her dry black lips pursed and
> corners of her bleary eyes crinkled as she smiled. With her furrowed face,
> dull and dreary look Gulki appeared almost grotesque. In a most unseemly
> manner, she drew the pallu of her sari over her head and tried to cover her
> crooked body so that she could hide her hump.

In this passage, the male gaze of the narrator casts hunchback Gulki as a grotesque
figure whose shyness and coy behaviour appear out of the ordinary and weird. This
is an awkward moment in the narrative as all through the text Gulki's wretched
plight as a poor, abandoned, hunchback woman is the focus, and nowhere is her
ungainly appearance referred to in such uncharitable a manner. Gulki's femininity
did not matter as until now she was perceived only as a disabled figure. In the large
part of the narrative, Gulki is an object of revulsion, amusement and scorn and
nowhere is her association with the grotesque more pronounced as in the previously mentioned passage. The point of view shifts in the narrative to draw attention
to the incongruity of Gulki's appearance as a bride. The apparent misogyny mirrors the sense of discomfort on seeing Gulki dressed as a bride, and it is the bridal
demeanour that appears grotesque to the narrator.

Emily Russell notes that the 'literary grotesque serves as a special case of language
in which the grotesque form constantly and explicitly thrusts the excessive body
into the realm of the symbolic' (2011: 62). Disabled bodies are thus excluded from
the normative assumptions of the able-bodied and are constituted outside of it. Thus,
disability prompts images that seek to contain it as grotesque and pathetic. According
to Russell, the literary grotesque is both real and symbolic, and the embodied tension
between the two becomes an animating contradiction (*ibid.*, 62). This tension between
the real and the symbolic is evident in the construction of Gulki's bridal image as grotesque. In the non-disabled imaginary of the narrator, the hunchback Gulki sits uneas-
ily as a bride, and in describing her appearance as grotesque, the narrator excludes
her from the normative assumptions of femininity and she is cast as an abject figure.
This ableist patriarchal gaze shows that the female experience of disability is closely
linked to the cultural oppression of the body, and since our culture idolises the body,
especially the female body, the problem of disability has an important social dimension
insofar as the relationship between the disabled individual and his or her environment
is concerned. More than the physical disability, it is the cultural stereotypes regarding
the female body and the roles that it is supposed to fulfil which determines the effect
of disability on a woman's daily life.

Rosemarie Garland-Thomson observes that while it is quite legitimate to decry sexual objectification of women within feminist discourses, she argues that 'what disabled women often encounter is what Harlan Hahn calls "asexual objectification", the assumption that sexuality is inappropriate in disabled people' (1997: 285). Disabled women are removed from the realm of womanhood and feminine beauty. 'This creates what Adrienne Asch and Michelle Fine and term as "rolelessness", a kind of social invisibility and cancellation of femininity, which sometimes prompts disabled women to claim an essential femininity which the culture denies them' (*ibid*.: 285). Thus, the asexual objectification of women with disabilities complicates the feminist critique of normative sexual objectification. The larger impact is that disabled women are perceived as unfeminine and asexual and they are less likely than non-disabled women or disabled men to fulfil roles customarily reserved for women. According to Asch and Fine, disabled women are 'exempted from the "male" productive role and "female" nurturing one, and having the glory of neither, they are arguably doubly oppressed – or, perhaps, "freer" to be nontraditional' (1997: 241). Thus, the normative assumptions of gender roles vary greatly and women like Gulki are not expected to have the aspiration of setting up a home and raise a family. But Gulki's womanhood and femininity find expression within the institutional framework of marriage, and like Kubja, she hopes for redemption by putting herself in the service of her abusive husband. She aspires for traditional roles like nurturance, caring and motherhood, which are widely perceived as being central to women's lives and their self-concept in a patriarchal society and which are not available to disabled women like her. Thus, while the narrator reflects on the incongruity of her bridal appearance, Gulki revels in her role and feels that going back to her husband might mark a new beginning in her life. She feels that perhaps her devotion to duty, which means looking after her husband, might fetch rewards for her like the birth of a child. More significantly, it reaffirms her femininity to her own self and counters the asexual objectification of her body by the community.

Translation challenges

While any cross-cultural translation involves loss of meaning, translating a disability-centric text also entails an added responsibility of making lexical and semantic choices which do not impose ableist assumptions about the body. The anxiety while translating a disability-centric narrative is whether there should be a particular idiom for translating disability narrative so that the translation is able to sensitise the reader towards the experience of disability. Rita Kothari's (2007) observation in the context of translation of Dalit literature is useful here. According to Kothari, while translating Dalit literature the responsibility is not only cultural, political and aesthetic but also involves an attitude of praxis. One possible way to achieve praxis in translating a disability narrative is to highlight the agency of the disabled protagonist and how she negotiates the adverse social circumstances. The translation could be interventionist if it is able to draw attention to the voice of the disabled and is not appropriative in nature. Translation as Gayatri Spivak reminds us 'is the most intimate act of reading' (2000: 313), and if we were to stretch the analogy further, translating disability calls for an intimate act of listening to the voice of the disabled in the text which can become counter-discursive to the stigmatisation that often accompanies constructions of disabled subjectivities.

Translating 'Gulki Banno' has been a challenging experience because the text depicts a layered response to disability and does not indulge in easy sentimentalism. The unique timbre of Bharti's voice, its scathing irony, mockery and humour create a social universe where the female disabled protagonist despite being contained towards the end of the narrative remains an unsettling presence. The story is rich in colloquial speech, proverbs, culture-specific words and rituals that are deeply rooted in the patriarchal cultural and social universe of the Hindi – Awadhi belt. The text employs several registers of Hindi – the educated and literate Hindi of the narrator, khariboli used by some characters and the Awadhi dialect of the less educated and illiterate characters. While it is impossible to convey the different registers of Bharti's Hindi and the subtle shifts in the speech and conversations that mark the social distance between the different characters, I have attempted to translate in a way that the idiomatic expression is retained in the target language and the reader can relate to the cultural nuances and humour. For example, after all the humiliation Gulki faces, and she is tricked into selling her house, she is given a customary farewell by the women of the community. The narrative comments on various rituals that mark Gulki's final departure from the neighbourhood are in an ironic voice, pouring sarcasm over cherished cultural and social practices of a patriarchal universe which contains Gulki's agency by casting her off in a socially sanctioned manner:

> Nirmal's mother asked Bua if any special rituals were required as the girl was going away to her in-laws house. Bua made a face and said, 'What do you mean? She isn't one of us, not even from our caste or community. Arre, just fill some water in a small tumbler and drop a few coins in it. Bless her with that when she leaves. This will save her from the evil eye. By the way, give the coins as alms to the poor.'

The tone and behaviour of the women change once they realise that Gulki is leaving for good:

> Say Nirmal's mother, is this how you send a daughter to her in-law's house? Go and get some roli for putting a tikka on the son in-law's forehead and don't forget sindoor for Gulki! Get down from the tonga, son!

The farewell ritual masks complete apathy and disregard for Gulki's well-being and exposes the hypocrisy and double standards of the society towards disability. In the context of the story, these patriarchal rituals are satirised, but it is difficult to convey the same resonance of the rituals in the target language. I have tried to use feminist translation strategies like 'supplementing' (von Flotow 1991: 7) in my translation because the purpose of the ritual would be lost to the reader who is not familiar with these culture-specific practices. I have added the phrase 'save her from the evil eye' because the purpose of the ritual in the previously mentioned passage is to mark a safe journey and protect the woman. In the source language, the term *evil eye* is not mentioned, but I have added it to explicate the meaning of the ritual and to heighten the irony of Gulki's situation who is duped into selling her house by the very same women who are now trying to bless her.

One significant difference when we translate a disability-centric text from one Indian language, in my case Hindi, is that it is not gender neutral like English. For instance, the term the *kubri* is a signifier – a gender-specific term embodying a disability and a specific body type. The English equivalent, *hunchback*, does not convey such a connotation. There are many instances in the text when Gulki is not called by her name but only 'kubri'. This word is used pejoratively and functions as an abusive term. Another difficult word with a whole lot of cultural connotation is *banno*, which I have translated as 'bride' for lack of any suitable equivalent. *Banno* is a North Indian Hindi belt term for a would-be bride, and it has inspired a whole lot of pre-bridal rituals and customary songs. Interestingly, Gulki is not a '*banno*' in the classical sense of the term as she is already married and has been abandoned by her husband. The title of the story 'Gulki Banno' is unusual because a proper name is rarely ever added to the epithet *banno*. For someone who does not know the meaning of the term can easily mistake it to be the second name of Gulki. Interestingly, the text hinges on this term, and it has been added in a satirical vein to heighten the incongruity of Gulki as '*banno*'. Gulki is finally cast away from her community in the socially sanctioned role of '*banno*' to her rightful place, her husband's home. Thus, I have retained the original title 'Gulki Banno' but have added the phrase 'The Hunchback Bride' to make visible both the latent and embodied potential of the title. The titles of the two earlier translations of Gulki Banno (Jagmohan 2003; Vanashree 2016) do not draw attention to Gulki's disability. While Jagmohan retains the original, 'Gulki Banno', Vanashree's title, 'Gulki, the Bride', misses out on the narrative irony inherent in the term *hunchback bride*.

The previously mentioned translations of 'Gulki Banno' are quite literal and somehow oblivious of Gulki's gendered experience of disability. For instance, there is this moment in the text when Gulki's husband comes to the neighbourhood to take her back with him. Gulki is embarrassed and does not want to be noticed when she is enquiring after her husband.

> Looking here and there, the humpback whispered to Mewa, 'Tell me what do you feel about Jijaji?' (Vanashree 2016: 18).
> Mewa sat close to Gulki and when she was sure that no one was looking at her, she whispered 'How do you like your brother-in-law, Mewa?
> (my translation)

The source language text uses *kubri* (hunchback) for Gulki, in this passage and in many other places. While it is perfectly justifiable to stick to the original, as in Vanashree's translation, substituting *Gulki* for *hunchback* here gives her more humanity and agency. Both Vanashree's and Jagmohan's translation retain quite a few words and phrases in Hindi. However, a keyword like *chabutra* is translated as 'platform' in both the translations. The translations do not attempt to highlight Gulki's humanity or agency, despite her obvious objectification as an asexual, disabled woman by other characters in the text. Interestingly, the text itself satirises the double standards and hypocrisy of the neighbourhood through irony and sarcasm and shows Gulki fighting the odds with great vigour. I feel that the translation should endeavour to capture Gulki's humanity and indefatigable spirit as embodied in the text.

The text locates the gendered experience of disability in a lower-middle-class neighbourhood, Atarsuia mohalla, in Allahabad, Uttar Pradesh, where Bharti spent his early years in a deeply stratified society ridden with caste, class and religious prejudices. Almost the entire action of the story takes place on a '*chabutra*', which I have retained in the original. By retaining some of these words, my endeavour has been to 'transcreate'(Lal, 1972) the overall feeling of the text and its social milieu. A *chabutra* is typically an open, raised platform in front of the house and in the context of the story has steps leading to it. By locating the entire action of the story on a *chabutra*, the text shows how a disability narrative is played out in the public domain and eventually acquires the quality of a theatrical spectacle, especially the fond farewell of Gulki replete with customary rituals. My translation also retains in original certain culture-specific terms like *roli*, *katha*, *sindoor* and *paan*, since it is difficult to convey the full weight of these terms in annotations. I have also retained the kinship terms like *bahu* and *bhaiya* in the original and relied on the reader's effort at contextual understanding. While translating the names of local fruits and vegetables I have retained the original name but have added self-explanatory terms like '*bilboti* berries' and '*nimkauri* fruits' so as not to over assimilate the text and yet make it accessible to the English language reader. Some strategies used to factor in the dialect are to introduce interjections like *ei*, *ai* and *arre* which bring in an element of colloquial speech instead of words like *hey*, *ah* and *oh*. For example, 'Ai Bua, why are you clearing this drain? Clear the other one, please!'

The translation tries to give an idiomatic flavour and use nonstandard registers wherever necessary: 'Say Gulki, are you really going back with your husband? Say, Gulki?'

Translation and agency

In her celebrated essay on the politics of translation, Gayatri Spivak's states that 'the task of the feminist translator is to consider language as clue to workings of gendered agency' (2000: 397). Spivak's injunction holds true for texts like 'Gulki Banno' which despite all strategies of containment demonstrate the disruptive power of Gulki's speech and how she negotiates the complexity of the everyday, gendered experience of disability. The translation makes a conscious effort to highlight Gulki's agency and how she resists strategies of appropriation. For example, there is an instance in the narrative when children devise a game of role play to humiliate Gulki. In the course of the song, the children ask several questions and the child playing Gulki's role gives fitting replies:

> Hunchback, hunchback, what did you lose?
> A needle, I did lose
> What will you do with a needle?
> Stitch myself a bag, with the needle
> What will you do with a bag?
> Will fetch firewood in my bag
> What will you do with firewood?
> Will cook my food using firewood
> What will of do with food you cook?
> Feed myself, of course! You crooks
> How about kicks, instead of food?

In the second last line when the children ask, 'What will you do with food you cook?' an exasperated Gulki answers, 'Feed myself, of course!' After several attempts at translating the passage, I decided to add 'You crooks', not just as a rhyming tool but to also highlight Gulki's anger and her keen awareness that the purpose of role-play is just to ridicule her. In keeping with the feminist translation practice, the larger goal of my translation is to make the 'feminine visible in language' and make the 'language speak for women' (Lotbiniere-Harwood 2008:69). 'Gulki Banno' marks many such moments when the feminine agency is made visible in the narrative and my translation endeavour has been to highlight the same. For example, there are instances in the text when the intrusive, demeaning and non-disabled gaze of the narrator reduces Gulki to a comic grotesque figure and excludes her from normative roles and assumptions of womanhood. However, Gulki springs a surprise for the readers by doing a complete turnaround towards the end of the narrative. The dramatic twist in the story occurs when Gulki falls at the feet of her husband who had abused and rejected her:

> As Gulki stepped forward, everyone was stunned. The man's face turned pale with fear as she climbed the steps of the chabutara.
> Gulki paused a little, looked at Satti and then all of a sudden fell at that man's feet. Crying bitterly, she said 'O my dear, why did you leave me all alone? I have no one in this world! Who will perform my last rites when I die?'

The performative aspect of Gulki's surrender is a classic moment in the text as the completely disenfranchised and disabled Gulki chooses to align herself with prescribed norms of femininity rather than reject them. Knowing well that she has been forced to make this choice, Gulki still wants to restore her status as a married woman, a feminine sexual being which had been denied to her all along during her stay in the community. By restoring the relative privileges of normative femininity,

Gulki's negotiates an identity crisis which marks and excludes her from within the larger social class of women:

> Gulki noticed that her husband was talking to Bua. Quickly, she covered her head with her pallu and turned her face away. 'O, my God, he's looking so weak. No one seems to be caring for him anymore. Listen, Mewa Bhaiya, just go and give this *paan* to your brother-in law. By the way, swear that you'll not tell him who sent this *paan!*' As she spoke, she again had that coy look on her face which made her look grotesque.

Gulki's coy gestures, her sexual overtures and her performance of a bridal role place her on par with normal, able-bodied woman temporarily. She harbours hopes of conjugal bliss and motherhood, and while she succumbs to the patriarchal ideology as espoused by the other women characters in the story, it offers her liberation from her categorisation as an asexual disabled woman on the margins of society.

The uniqueness of 'Gulki Banno' as a disability narrative is that it does not lapse into any sentimentalism or idealisation of the disabled protagonist. The text shows Gulki's feisty spirit despite the abjectness of her everyday existence. Moving beyond the metaphors of inadequacy and betrayal, my translation attempts to approximate the indefatigable spirit embodied by Gulki. The effort has been to be alert and faithful to the 'rhetoricity of the original' (Spivak 2000: 398) and re-create the disabled female protagonist as an active subject. The disruptive power of Gulki's speech has a performative quality, and she resists strategies of containment:

> 'Dare you do that!' retorted Gulki. Till date no one had ever heard Gulki speak in that tone. 'So what if I haven't paid those ten rupees as rent? Try and recall all that you have done! You sold off that door lying in my house to Basantu! You got another door pulled out and burnt! So what if I am poor and an orphan, you can't treat me like this!

Gulki's anger and her spirited defence in the preceding passage reveal that despite all the humiliation and objectification she goes through during her brief stay in the neighbourhood, she fights the odds with great strength and challenges the normative assumptions of a disabled woman on the margins of society. My translation attempts to retain the comic-ironic mode which highlights the prejudices and hypocrisy of society in dealing with disability. While Gulki's presence is unsettling and she is duped into selling her house and finally ousted from the community, it is her humanity and impish charm which stay in the minds of the readers.

Conclusion

Despite all challenges, translating 'Gulki Banno' which portrays an everyday experience of disability has been an enriching experience. The text highlights how disability like gender is a discursive construction and is enunciated at multiple sites.

The interface between gender, disability and translation which are plagued by the metaphor of inadequacy and loss have much to gain from each other. Translation in the postcolonial context is not about loss as much it is about significant gains in terms of addressing questions of representation, power and historicity. Tejaswini Niranjana has noted that the process of translation provides an opportunity to address the asymmetry and inequality of relations between races, languages and people. (1992: 1) Interestingly, translating a disability-centric text also confronts us with questions of power and asymmetry in the representation of disability. 'Gulki Banno' amply demonstrates that while translating a text centred on the female experience of disability, we have to contend not just with the physical aspect of disability but also with preconceived cultural notions of womanhood and the female body. The question of representation, thus, has an added dimension when it comes to the translation of the gendered experience of disability. Thomas G. Couser, in the context of life-writing, sounds a note of caution as he delineates fundamental fears that underlie the representation of 'vulnerable subjects'. By pointing out that representation in the mimetic sense could be fundamentally at odds with representation in the political sense, Couser warns that in our desire to speak for someone we may end up misspeaking her (2004: 33). This ethical dilemma is at the heart of or representation of vulnerable, subaltern and, in the present context, disabled subjectivities. In the context of the short stories dealing with disability, we find ourselves in a double bind – while we feel it is necessary and productive to introduce disability as an identity category along with gender, class and caste, we are also discomfited by the cultural and political function that these 'non-normative' bodies fulfil in these texts. As we grapple with this dilemma and feel that feminist translation practice may somehow offer a political corrective, I am of the opinion that a deconstructive reading of disability in the Indian context discloses ideological underpinnings about structures that underlie our inherently patriarchal culture ridden with caste, class and gender prejudices.

Note

1 All quoted material in the text are the author's own translation.

References

Asch, Adrienne and Michelle Fine. 1997. 'Nurturance, Sexuality and Women with Disabilities: The Example of Women and Literature', in Lennard J. Davis (ed) *The Disability Reader*, pp. 241–259. New York and London: Routledge.

Couser, Thomas G. 2004. *Vulnerable Subjects: Ethics in Life Writing*. Ithaca, NY: Cornell University Press.

Flotow, Luise von. 1991. 'Feminist Translation: Contexts, Practices and Theories', *TTR: traduction, terminologie, rédaction*, 4(2): 69–84. http://id.erudit.org/iderudit/037094ar (accessed on 13 December 2016).

Garland-Thomson, Rosemarie. 1997. 'Feminist Theory, the Body and the Disabled Figure', in Lennard J. Davis (ed) *The Disability Reader*, pp. 279–288. New York and London: Routledge.

Hughes, Bill. 2012. 'Fear, Pity and Disgust: Emotions and the Non-Disabled Imaginary', in Nick Watson, Alan Roulstone, and Carol Thomas (eds) *Routledge Handbook of Disability Studies*, pp. 67–78. New York: Routledge.

Jagmohan, Sarla. 2003. 'Gulki Banno', in Rajendra Awasthi (ed) *Selected Hindi Short Stories: An Anthology*, pp. 71–88. Delhi: Diamond Pocket Books.

Kothari, Rita. 2007. 'The Translation of Dalit Literature into English', in Jeremy Munday (ed) *Translation as Intervention*, pp. 41–49. London and New York: Continuum.

Lal, Purushottama. 1972. *Transcreation: Two Essays*. Calcutta: Writers Workshop.

Lotbiniere-Harwood, Suzanne de. 2008. 'Writing in No Man's Land: Questions of Gender and Translation'. *Ilha do Desterro*, 28: 63–73. http/periodicos.ufsc.br/index.php/desterro/article/viewFile/8751/10654 (accessed on 15 October 2016).

Niranjana, Tejaswini. 1992. *Siting Translation: History, Post-Structuralism, and the Colonial Context*. Berkeley and Los Angeles: University of California Press.

Pal, Joyojeet. 2013. 'Physical Disability and Indian Cinema', in Marja Evelyn Mogk and Jefferson (eds) *Different Bodies: Essays on Disability in Film and Television*, pp. 109–130. North Carolina and London: Mac Farland and Company, Inc. Publishers.

Pauwels, Heidi R. M. 2008. *The Goddess as Role Model*. London: Oxford University Press.

Russell, Emily. 2011. *Reading Embodied Citizenship: Disability, Narrative, and the Body Politic*. New Brunswick, NJ: Rutgers University Press.

Spivak, Gayatri, 2000. 'The Politics of Translation', in Lawrence Venuti (ed) *The Translation Studies Reader*, pp. 397–416. London and New York: Routledge.

Tripathi, Vanashree. 2016. 'Gulki, the Bride: A Translation of Dharamvir Bharti's "Gulki Banno"', *Indian Literature, Sahitya Akademi's Bi-monthly Journal*, March/April 2016, 292. www.academia.edu/27902930/_Gulki_the_Bride_A_Translation_of_Dharamvir_Bharatis_Gulki_Banno_

14

THE POLITICS OF TRANSLATION

Disability, language and the in-between

Ritwick Bhattacharjee

Introduction

Martin Heidegger in his essay 'The Way to Language' presents the idea that the very phenomenon of Language, articulated through speech and/or writing, is intricately tied to the fabric of existence through experience. To say that something is, in any language, for example, concretises the existence and the experience of that subject because it both reveals and makes apparent that subject's ontical, ontological and contingent immediacy in relation to the object or the target of that subject. Language, by exclaiming that 'It' is or 'I' am, becomes that transcendental entity which subsumes the fundamental self of the subject. In other words, it is not humans who include Language within their experiential and existential reality but the latter that takes into its fold and becomes a tool for the revealing of the fundamental aspects of the former. Furthermore, owing to the phenomenological essentiality of what Heidegger calls a 'rift-design' (Heidegger 2012: 285), Language carves out Truth: Truth which reveals that which is from its hidden stature or hides that which is not. It 'speaks by pointing, reaching out to every region of presencing, letting what is presented in each case appear in such regions or vanish from them' (Heidegger 2012: 295).

The implication of such an understanding is threefold. First, Language becomes a fundamental entity responsible for presenting and re-presenting a subject's Truth to itself. Second, insofar as the existence of an individual is a personal and experiential concern, the Truths that Language reveals for a person are Truths that are appropriable for that particular person or subject only. In effect, each human, so placed within Language and Truth, owns and propriates a niche of Language and Truth[1] for itself separate from the propriated Language and Truth of other persons. This separation, further, leads into the third implication which addresses the interactions that an individual has with another individual and, subsequently, society as a whole.

If each individual, post the propriation and appropriation of Truths for itself, finds these Truths novel, distinct and appropriable only to their existence through experience, the need to successfully interact with society leads them to form categories in which the Truths so revealed can be divided between the similar against the dissimilar. Such a binary division, in turn, allows each individual to remain within the comfort of at least the similar Truths that Language revealed for them from their existence and experience without paying heed to the others. This concern is a deeply political one as it creates, what Carl Schmitt calls the fundamental element of a political society: the division of the 'friend and the enemy'[2](2007: 26). Contemporaneous to this political aspect, such a division is also problematic for it creates qualifications. The opposition between the similar and the dissimilar here is also a simultaneous division between the known and the unknown, which, in turn, incurs a quantitative resonance of and to that which is the majority and the minority. Furthermore, by the virtue of being so, the subjects who find themselves in the majority always tend to situate their Truths and experiences as 'normal' and 'natural' simply because these Truths seem to be more than any others. This situation inevitably leads to the oppression of all those existences which find themselves in the minority and as 'not normal'. Divisions based on caste, class, gender, race and ability are all resultants of such positions of the 'normal' and its other. What follows is a systematic and institutional marginalisation of this group that is relegated as the 'minority'.

Where, then, lies the potential for a radical disruption to the takeover of one division by another which, owing to the primal nature of Language, are quite fundamental themselves? The current paper believes and intends to show that the answer to this question lies in the phenomenon and act of translation since such an act, working from within and through Language, contains the propriated Truths within their respective divisions. In other words, translation is seen here as a device that does not allow the suppression of one field of Truths by another even when the two such spaces are in interaction with each other. Focusing primarily on the division between the non-disabled subject and the disabled one, the current paper intends to investigate how the act itself of translating stories concerning the phenomenon of disability from one language system to another relays a potential for the simultaneous existence of the existential divisions that define them and their Truths as apart from one another and not allow the 'normal' non-disabled subjectivity to take over the 'deviant' one. Towards this objective, the chapter uses the English translation of two Hindi short stories –SaileshMatiyani's 'Hara Hua' into 'The Loser' and Sunil Kaushik's 'Andhere Ka Sailab' into ' The Flood of Darkness' –and uses Jacques Derrida's comprehension of the relevant translation to show where and how the aforementioned radical possibility lies, revealing translation as a possible political act.

Locating the translated

Before moving towards a conceptualisation of translation within the paradigms of the political; or at least presenting how it stands to become a radical act within the political, there is a pressing need to address two basic questions. The first concerns the nature of translation itself. Put differently, what does it mean to translate? The origin of the word 'translate' can be traced back to the Latin word *translatus*, which itself is a combination of two different words: *trans* and *oblatus*. The first, usually acting as a prefix, means 'across' or 'beyond' while the second denotes the process of 'bearing' or 'carrying'. Put together then, *translatus*, in its transitive form, refers to 'bearing or carrying across'. With the advent of medieval English, this idea of carrying across associates itself with the concept of language and indicates, as the Webster dictionary shows, a transfer of one set of symbols of a particular language into those of another. This transference, however, is not a simple 'carry across' of the lexical elements of the language since, as shown earlier, Language is not an isolated entity but always bound with existence and experience. What is carried across and transferred into another language instead is an entire being; a body of existence bound with and within the contours of language. To translate therefore means to transfer over entire structures of being, of history, of culture, of society, and of politics from one system into another.

This traversal, however, does not relegate the removal or the death of the original body. Jacques Derrida, in his essay 'What is a "Relevant" Translation?', presenting this quite unique characteristic of translation, notes that

> [translation], licks [the idiomatic singularity of the word] as a flame or an amorous tongue might:approaching as closely as possible while refusing at the last moment to threaten or to reduce, to consume or to consummate, leaving the other body intact but not without causing the other to appear.
>
> (2001: 175)

While translation, in other words, becomes a catalytic act towards the creation of a new body, it does so without disrupting, dissipating or discarding another. There is a supplementation of the form of one body into and as another and not a change or metamorphosis which, in turn, leads into the existence of a system or a body that is essentially a combination of two different bodies. What this further means is that this new body necessarily co-opts the two previously variegated systems from and to which translation transfers. Since there is an underlying sense of carrying across, the language (and the entire structure of being associated with that language) which is being translated is not put into a vacuum but placed inside of the structure(s) and system(s) of the language into which it is being translated. Translation, in such a scheme of things, requires botha space of initiation and a space for reception. For the new body to exist and particularly exist within the system of the target language there is a requirement for both the maintenance of the 'singularity' of the structures of the source language and a transformation of its form as dictated by the space into which it is moving to. If that were not the case, the threat of the annihilation of one body for the other would remain and the sense of a transfer or a carryover-into inherent in the act of translation wouldn't exist. This supplementary duality, in turn then, allows for the original body to exist in a hitherto alien system as the new body.

During the act of translation then, the source language, in order to maintain the entire baggage that it carries with it has to, necessarily, appropriate the baggage of the target language as well. In essence, it is this complicated nature of the translated that allows for, what Derrida calls, the creation without consumption.

The translation of 'Hara Hua' into 'The Loser' exemplifies this compound position of the translated. The short story narrates the tale of a wrestler, Gendamal, who, never having faced defeat by any other wrestler, finds himself unable to exact revenge on a frail cobbler. Notionally divided into two halves, the first and the major part of the narrative relates how Gendamalwrecks havoc to both the body and the social standing of any who challenges him either in combat or questions his strength. One day Gendamal is challenged to a fight by Dukharan, a frail-framed cobbler, because the former had kissed the latter's widowed daughter in front of everyone. Being quite literally five times Dukharan's size and almost similarly advantaged in strength, Gendamal is believed to be the obvious winner of the fight by the villagers. But he doesn't win. In fact, Gendamal is not even able to march up to Dukharan's hut and answer his call to arms. He keeps on procrastinating without ever knowing the cause for such procrastination. The much-desired altercation and spectacle of Dukharan's defeat, and even death, never happen. It is only in the second half, at the very end of the story that the narrative reveals that Gendamal fails to stand up to Dukharan because of a similar situation that he had to go through during the India–Pakistan partition. During the barbaric chaos that ensued after the partition of the country, an unruly mob had barged into Gendamal's hut and had raped and murdered his daughter in front of him as he lay stumped, unable to do anything but watch. Dukharan's stand against the wrong done to his daughter, in a sense, reminds Gendamal of the failure to protect his, and it is this remembrance that stops him and holds him back from fighting the cobbler.

The representation of the dual nature of the translated body works at two levels within the scheme of Matiyani's story. The first is at the level of structure. The original Hindi story is written in the third person and from the point of view of an omniscient narrator. This narrative method presents a disjunction when the two parts of the story are taken into account against each other. The first half of story spends all its space into the description of how Gendamal is ruthless and indefatigable, how his current predicament – of not being able to fight Dukharan – conflicts with his public and private persona and how the wrestler cannot pinpoint the reason for this inability. Then, suddenly, the second half of the story creeps up on the reader to relate Gendamal's history and locates the reason for his present quandary within that history. This suddenness of the second half highlights a discernible absence in Gendamal's memory as it adds a layer to the re-presentation of the subjectivity of the wrestler that had been absent till then. The first half of the narrative neither shows Gendamal remembering a major event of his own past nor relays any affect that it may have had on him. Even when the wrestler's failure to answer Dukharan's challenge is considered, it is done so as a malfunction and always measured against his present social standing. When seen from inside the shadow of the revelation of Gendamal's trauma, the initial part of the story seems empty: there is a traumatic presence that masks itself as an absence, never surfacing onto the body of the story. It is this absence, this gap in Gendamal's memory that is ultimately revealed by the second half of the narrative. The memory of his trauma is always there, even if as an absence. In fact, this absence becomes central to his subjectivity as it not only highlights his trauma but also shows the control that trauma has over him. In such a scheme of things, Gendamal's failure to stand up to Dukharan's challenge, even if to defend his reputation, becomes an exposition of the control that this absence has over him. This void, furthermore, becomes an important element within the structure of the story as it, firstly, represents the problematic position of a subject vis-à-vis the subject's construction of its own self when faced with trauma and the memory of that trauma and, secondly, brings out the historicalbaggage of the India–Pakistan partition that Hindi as a Language carries with itself.[3]

The major challenge faced when translating this story into English was the maintenance of both the delineation of the presence of this absence as an absence and the controlling power it has on the wrestler. While the presentation of this absence within the contours of the Hindi language and owing to its connection with the trauma of the partition works as it is in Matiyani's story, the English translation requires a different approach towards the same as it does not carry with it the historicalbaggage of this violence. In fact, it is possible to argue, by the virtue of being associated with the British, English bears the sociopolitical weight of that element which is responsible for the partition in the first place. In such a scheme of things, the translation of the story not only has to bring out the absence and the affect it has on the wrestler but also has to not seem alien or a parody while doing so. What helps here then is an appropriation and an application of similar baggage that English carries with itself: that of the modernist concept of the broken self resulting from the violence and the trauma of the two World Wars. The translation of 'Hara Hua' into 'The Loser' then, to bring out the aforementioned absence and the trauma associated with it, tells the story from the perspective of the wrestler who, having already remembered his past, knows that he cannot face Dukharan. He has realised that there has been a deliberate division of his self caused by the absence while, at the same time, establishing it. There are two viewpoints in the translation then: the 'I' which brings forward and makes clear the absence and a 'He' that shows the effects of it, both points being that of the wrestler.[4] The story hence opens as follows:

> You see, I truly believe that when you wear a mask for too long, you forget the face behind it. The thing is we all wear masks. Different forms, shapes, sizes and all that, but masks nonetheless: some wear it to hide from the world; others, like myself, to hide from ourselves. . . . [We] unleash upon this fucked up world another face, another being, another fucked up monster covering the shame of our true faces and selves; as long as that abyss of a reflection you look into, doesn't look back at you. Me, I created and wore this thing known as GendamalPahalwan-feared by all, across villages, unclaimed and undefeated

in the ring. Gendamal never just defeated his challengers but shred them apart with his bare hands; their dead bodies vanishing in thin air.

(my translation)

The second is at the level of the story itself. At the end of the narrative, Gendamal decides to not fight Dukharan at all and just move away from everything that the 'he' of Gendamal represents, and it is in this movement away that the wrestler finds his ultimate victory. This position of the wrestler, however, is not the same as the one of the person who 'not only destroy[s] his challengers but shred[s] them apart with his bare hands'. By the end of the narrative, this subject has been, in a sense, translated into the 'I' subject which is aware of the past. There are, as shown earlier, two halves of the same self: one which is within the trauma of the past and one which relishes an ultimate win. The final body of the 'I' is then a translation of the latter into the former; the third self which is created without the destruction of any of the other. Gendamal still wins, but this win is not through the death of the cobbler but within an understanding of the self that exists within the presence of the trauma and a comprehension of its absence as well. There is a translation here, a 'carry over into', not between languages but experiences and through experiences, Truths. The existence within the compulsive need to win is not destroyed but amended and maintained by its translation into the existence within the traumatic memory. What comes off at the end is a body that stands as a whole in relation to both these experiential existences. At the end then, the narrative relates that

> having lost once, I do not want to lose again. To do what is necessary: that is all that matters. I look at Dukharan once again, understanding that it is a father that I am standing against. Like me. Dukharan is doing what I couldn't. To do what is necessary. I bend down and pick up my torn dhoti, tie it around my waist and before the crowd catches up, I start moving towards the pond at the end of the world.
>
> (my translation)

Dis-abling language

The translation of 'Hara Hua' into 'The Loser' in this way, exemplifies, both in form and content, the supplementary duality of the translated body. While the former shows how the appropriation and application of the historical, social and political baggage of the English language maintains and keeps intact the prime concerns of the story carried by the Hindi language with it, the second shows how the translation of experiences also work by the adoption of the traits of that into which it is being translated. This then effectively leads into the second concern that the present section intends to address: that of the question of disability particularly in relation with Language and translation. Put differently, why does disability become an important phenomenon to understand the radical position that translation can occupy? The answer to this question lies, once again, in Language because the phenomenon, after the construction of the majority and the minority vis-à-vis the revealed Truths, always accentuates and acquiesces with the majority. A consideration of disability as an existential reality shows this paradigmatic characteristic of Language since, especially for the construction of a metaphor, it always acquires only those bodies which are non-disabled. George Lakoff and Mark Johnson, presenting this feature of metaphors in *Metaphors We Live By*, note that the process of the acquisition of a body (and the experiences of that body) by a metaphor takes into consideration only that body which has had the 'natural kinds of experience' such as 'moving, manipulating objects [and] eating' (Lakoff and Johnson 1980: 117). This body becomes a 'prototype' (Lakoff and Johnson 1980: 132) and the sole Self in which all experiences, whether abled or disabled, are subsumed. In other words, it is only the body which functions in accordance to social, cultural and political expectations and dictums that has a chance to be incorporated within the structure of metaphor and Language because they are 'natural'. The disabled body, understood as fundamentally dysfunctional, is, for all intents and purposes, ignored in favour of the 'Language' of the abled one. The metaphorical correlation of sight with clarity and comprehension ('I see' being associated with 'I understand') is one of the many examples of this phenomenon. Even if one considers the opposite of this correlation – of blindness and opacity – the experience of the disability is always seen through the experience of ability. Blindness, in a sense, is opacity because and only because vision is clarity.

If this were not the case, Lakoff and Johnson believe, inconsistencies would crop up inside the structure of a metaphor as the experience which explicates a concept will be incompatible with it (Lackoff and Johnson 1980: 10). In other words, since metaphors create 'our ordinary conceptual system, in terms of which we both think and act' (Lackoff and Johnson 1980: 3), the experiences that metaphors use *have* to be the 'ordinary' and the 'natural' ones as well. The disabled experience, being a minority, will be but a deviancy with which the 'ordinary conceptual system' will not be able to associate itself, giving rise to the aforementioned inconsistency. Blindness, in this sense, can never amount to comprehension because it is an 'unnatural' lack: something that is not*experienced* universally and hence cannot be a marker for transparency or, for that matter, anything else. What this results in, however, is the force fitting of the experiences and the lived reality of the 'deviant' body into those of the 'normal' one. By correlating an abstraction (something that becomes a governing paradigm for all our 'thoughts' and 'actions') directly with an experience to make clear and physically manifest that abstraction, metaphors posit the chosen experience as the only one that can be equated to that abstract. There is no space for any deviancy. In the correlation between seeing and knowing, for example, the experience of 'seeing' presents the impossibility of the experience of not seeing. Insofar as the metaphor is concerned, theblind have to mandatorily 'see' to 'know'. The very existence of this metaphor reveals the notion that there is not a single person who has not experienced seeing. Effectively then, the body that does not see is forced into a submission to the one that sees because only this latter body holds ground.

Such acquirements not only betray the social devaluation of disabled people but also feed into the processes of normalisation that inevitably oppresses them in the first place. On one hand, since Language creates Truths through an engagement with experiential existence, disability metaphors (such as 'seeing is knowing') reveal the takeover of those Truths and experiences which come to be quantitatively less than others. In essence, this takeover becomes a symptom of the way the disabled subject is seen by the majority that is, at least ostensibly and within a particular temporal frame, non-disabled. On the other hand, these metaphors, as Amy Vidali notes, elide 'the embodied lives of disabled people . . . for objectively emphasizing deficiencies . . . [and] "hide an individual's humanity"'(2010: 35). Language then not only forces the experience of a majority on a disabled individual but, by doing so, also highlights the lack of that experience. This, in turn, creates disability as an absence; a void that *has* to be corrected by being necessarily and fundamentally subsumed within the Language of ability. The deviant body then always becomes the negative articulating nothing but absences. In relation to seeing as knowing, for example, blindness becomes a representation of not-knowing and opacity. This, as David Mitchell notes, has a 'cumulative impact on cultural attitudes toward disabled people' because they equate disability primarily with 'things gone awry with bodily and social orders' (2002: 24). In other words, since the disabled body is fabricated to be a signifier of things that have gone wrong, they can never have the power to represent a presence for everyone (or, for that matter, anyone). By so 'exclud[ing] disabled bodies and experiences' (Vidali 2010: 37), these metaphors effectively feed into the process of the creation of the 'normal': that to which everyone can relate. There, then, *has* to be the experience of 'seeing', and the existence of that experience is so normal and natural that it is undebatable.

Notwithstanding the problematisation of the presentation of disability as a lack by Disability Studies scholars,[5] these metaphors (and through them Language itself), in this way, ignores and suppresses the experiences and lived realities of the disabled community ultimately condoning them as second-class citizens. The very consideration of disability as an experience and existence, in a sense then, allows this problem of an essential able-ist Language to be drawn out into the open. In fact, as shown earlier, this problem holds within it one of the primary reasons for the development of the category of the 'normal' body that *functions* against the 'abnormal' one that *does not*. Lakoff and Johnson for example, in their endeavour to understand how the body figures in a metaphor, neither challenge the second-tier position that the disabled experience is relegated to nor seek to include the disabled subjectivity within the construction of metaphors. In fact, as Vidali notes, they are not only inscribed within the discourse of the 'able' body as the natural and normal body but also further that process of naturalisation (2010: 36). Having said that, one cannot ignore the fact that such dis-abling metaphors do exist and that they inevitably lead to the marginalisation and subjugation of the disabled subject as these metaphors by ignoring the reality of the disabled experiences, always shade them as a negative. The inclusion of the phenomenon of disability, therefore, reveals an inherent problem of Language in how it acquires bodies and experiences. This also proves the notion that the current chapter begins with: of Language appropriating Truths and creating categories of the known and the unknown, ultimately marginalising the quantitative minority into the domains of the unknown simply because they are the minority. In other words, the known experiences of the able body are made into a transcendental entity so much so that they are forced on the disabled subject even though, for them, these experiences are unknown. In the process, the known experiences of the disabled body are all but destroyed. The attainment of only socially and politically able bodies by metaphors marks the preponderance of the terrain in which only these bodies reside, forcing the 'deviants' to either negativity and always the unknown or into an appropriation of the known Truths of the abled. How does one then get away from such demeaning and subjugating appropriations? The current chapter believes that the answer to this quandary lies in translation.

Politicising translation

What the last section effectively shows is that the root cause for the coercion of the disabled experience does not lie so much in the division between the terrains of the known and the unknown but in the homogenising tendency of Language that seeks to posit one known space over all others. In order to counter this form of oppression, at least within the rubric of Language and experiential existence, there is a need to reestablish all the known terrains in and as individual spaces themselves. Put differently, both, the known experiences of the able body and that of disabled one, have to be maintained separately so that one does not take over the other. The problem isn't in the categorisation of the known experiences of the able body against that of the disabled one. Such categorisations are in fact necessary for they bring about the political concern associated with each community and between them. They make clear the 'friend and enemy' division that Carl Schmitt finds at the base of any political society. Any disturbance to this categorisation would ultimately result back into the appropriation of the one over the other. In that case, the unknown experiences of one community will be forced down the throat of the other, to be taken up as a known experience without actually being so. Translation then does not deconstruct these divisions but, as already shown, maintains both the bodies of known experiences by creating a third space in which the two can interact with each other without the danger of being annihilated. For a better explication of this phenomenon, it is perhaps best here to present an interrogation of Kaushik's short story 'The Flood of Darkness' as it effectively shows how translation becomes a political entity by maintaining the individual terrains of known experiences.

On the face of it, the short story narrates how a six-and-a-half-year-old boy Saurabh loses his eyesight due to an accident and has to go through a surgical procedure in order to get it back. More important than Saurabh's story, however, is the way it is told. Narrated by the young boy's father, the story is rife with anxieties that he, as a parent of a blind child, has. These apprehensions, further, are not just related to Saurabh's surgery or its outcome. While it is not possible for the father to be altogether indifferent to his son's operation, what concerns the narrator more is his failure to understand what his son actually experiences. From the beginning of the narration itself, the father grapples with the unknown terrain of his son's experience. He keeps on repeating that he doesn't know what his son feels and experiences. Interestingly, while he tries to understand his son's position, the narrator never forces what he knows of blindness on to his son. Of course, being a father, the narrator tries to protect Saurabh from hurting himself, but he never oppresses his son by forcing him to live according to the known terrains of his non-disabled self. This position of the narrator becomes clear at the beginning when he wakes up from a dream he has had.[6] The dream, the narrator says,

> started out with placing me in a garden. It was green. Trees all around. Birds flying. Children Playing. I was walking down a yellow path when I started feeling very hot. I felt I could do with a bath. Suddenly I saw a lake in front of me. The water was clear and blue as they come. I removed my clothes and dove in. The moment I hit the surface of the lake, the water turned into black sludge. Surprised and wondering what to do I start throwing my arms about for someone to come and save me. But the more I squirm, the deeper I go. The water slowly turning into tar; sucking me in like a hungry giant. In a moment nothing remains of the blue and the green and the red and the yellow. It's just a deep dark hell of black all around and I am left swimming in the dense void of my life, going nowhere; stuck in an unimaginable flood of darkness.
>
> (my translation)

What this dream shows is that the narrator already has prefigured notions of blindness. He sees it as a black tar that sucks him in, 'an unimaginable flood' that washes him out, rendering him helpless. Effectively then, the dream relates to the father's a priori knowledge of blindness. But he never forces this knowledge of helplessness onto his son. After the dream ends, he says, 'Is that how my son feels? Fishing around in the darkness hoping for something to grab onto. I don't know' (my translation). By the very act of not knowing if his son feels as he does, he allows the experience of his son's blindness to have a position of its own. In a sense then, the narrator *translates*, or at least seeks to do so, his son's experience into his. Since, as shown in the second section, translation keeps intact both the bodies it works with, the narrator's attempt at translating his son's experience allows him to know that he does not know. There is no appropriation of one over the other here. Herein lays the political potential of translation as well. It does not destroy the two bodies it is working with but allows both of them to exist simultaneously while in interaction with each.

To know and to not know then becomes a crucial phenomenon in itself, especially when considering their relationship with the disabled experience. But why call the father's admission of not knowing a translation? The answer can be found in the structure of the act that is translation. Derrida, intending to define what a relevant translation is, says that it is

> whatever feels right, whatever seems pertinent, apropos, welcome, appropriate, opportune, justified, well-suited or adjusted, coming right at the moment when you expect it-or corresponding as is necessary to the object to which

the so-called relevant action relates: the relevant discourse, the relevant prop-osition, the relevant decision, the relevant translation. A relevant translation would therefore be, quite simply, a "good" translation, a translation that does what one expects of it, in short, a version that performs its mission, honors its debt and does its job or its duty while inscribing in the receiving language the most relevant equivalent for an original.

(2001: 177)

What is 'relevant', 'appropriate', 'opportune' and 'justified' in the case of the disa-bled experience is, as already shown, its very acceptance rather and an appro-priation. The father's position of not knowing in 'The Flood of Darkness' is a translated position because it becomes a third space (of the translated) in which the 'most relevant equivalent' of the original is inscribed onto the receiving body: that of not knowing, for the father can never know what his son experiences. Furthermore, interestingly enough, this translated position also, in a way, changes the metaphor of seeing as knowing. Even though the father 'sees' his son's blind-ness, at least in terms of his comprehension of the phenomenon, he does not 'know'. To see, here, does not mandate a contemporaneous and coterminous 'knowing'. The space of the clarity of an understanding is left for Saurabh to fill through his blindness. Translation, then, neither destroys the two bodies it is acting between nor allows a dissonance to creep up between the two bodies. It maintains the individual experiences while allowing them to come into contact with each other. No wonder then, the narrator of the story never dissuades his son from doing the activities that an able-bodied six-year-old would do. Roughly halfway into the story, for example, the narrator relates how Saurabh wants to play cards:

> The other day, Saurabh comes to me and starts pestering me that he wants to play cards. He has seen me play with my friends; throwing cards on the table. Hah. For him that is what playing cards entail. Throwing cards on the table. How could I tell him that it is not possible for a kid to play cards when he cannot see? I bought him a pack anyway. Night before last he bought them to me, started shuffling them to the best of his knowledge and ability, threw some cards towards me, some towards himself, and then picked up his cards made a fan and hid behind it. I could see that the num-bers on his cards were towards me. One by one he threw all the cards on the table and said 'Papa I have won'. I also agreed 'Yes son. You have won.' Then he started the process all over again. 'Papa this time, you have won'. I just say 'yes'.

> (my translation)

While the narrator believes that 'it is not possible for a kid to play cards when he cannot see', he does not force Saurabh into submitting to not playing. He buys his son a pack anyway and plays with him, however absurd that act may be. This happens because the narrator neither knows what (and how) his son experiences nor forces him to cower down to the knowledge that he has.

This is not to say that Kaushik's story is a shining beacon of political correctness and presents something entirely politically radical. It is filled with problems that are of major concern for any who intend to study it as a representation of disability. For one, the story is steeped in the medical discourse as it presents Saurabh's blindness as a lack that requires an operation to 'cure' him and tries to incite pity on the realisation that his blindness cannot be cured. For another, it never gives any voice to Saurabh. His blindness never figures in anything that he does. Neither is he allowed to say what he feels. For all the talk of creating a translated third position that allows the experiences of the disabled subject to remain intact, the young boy is never really imparted an experience outside of what his father relates. Having said that, it is not possible to neglect the fact that the narrator's constant anxiety of never knowing what his son feels opens a space for the experiences of his blind son to exert and express themselves, even if that space is kept empty. What the story does is show how translation can become a method that can negate the appropriation of known experiences of the disabled subjects by giving them a space of their own even as they interact with the known spaces of the able body. Translation becomes important because it allows the two political categories to remain intact and allows them to interact without destroying each other. This is where the political potential of translation lies as well: in maintaining heterogeneous identities as themselves rather than allowing the majority to take over and subjugate the minority.

Notes

1 By this Truth being revealed by language.
2 While defining the political, Schmitt finds that the fundamental political category (Schmitt 2007: 25) that informs political action and motivation can be traced down to is the division between the 'friend and the enemy' (Schmitt 2007: 26). This is neither a communitarian enmity, not a metaphorical nor a psychological one. He says that '[t]he friend and enemy concepts are to be understood in their concrete and existential sense . . . not mixed and weakened by economic, moral [or] . . . private emotional tendencies' (Schmitt 2007: 27–28). The enemy, in that sense, is not someone (or a group) who merely competes or is a private rival. It is something much more basic and fundamental that characterises existence itself.
3 Especially considering that Gendamal's position within the absence can be read as a microcosm of a nation that has gone through a violent division and chooses to forget that violence till the time it is jolted back out.
4 A writing style which bases on English Modernist conceptualisation of a self which is not a whole in itself, something which modernist writers like James Joyce in *Finnegan's Wake* and T.S. Eliot in *The Waste Land* use.
5 Disability Studies scholars have pointed out that the construction of disability as a lack is primarily due to medical discourses. But disability is not a medical problem surrounded by eugenics. It is a social phenomenon and has to be understood as such. See Lennard J. Davis's *The Disability Studies Reader* for more.
6 This dream sequence has been, in fact, added in the English translation of 'Andhere Ka Sailab' into 'The Flood of Darkness'. It effectively brings to light the anxiety that the narrator has (in the original Hindi version) regarding his son and becomes a sort of preamble to his nervousness that pervades throughout the narrative.

References

Davis, Lennard J., ed. 2013. *The Disability Studies Reader*. New York and London: Routledge.

Derrida, Jacques. 2001. 'What Is a "Relevant" Translation', Lawrence Venuti (trans), *Critical Enquiry*, 27(2): 174–200. www.jstor.org/stable/1344247 (accessed on 22 March 2009).

Eliot, Thomas Sterns. 1922. 'The Waste Land', in Helen Vendler (Intro), *The Waste Land and Other Poems: Including The Love Song of J. Alfred Prufock*, pp. 32–59. New York, NY: Signet Classic.

Heidegger, Martin. 2012. 'The Way to Language', in David Farrell Krell (ed) *Heidegger: Basic Writings*, pp. 279–306. India: Routledge.

Joyce, James. 1939. *Finnegan's Wake*. Hertfordshire: Wordsworth Classics.

Kaushik, Sunil. 2010. 'Andhere Ka Sailab', in Giriraj Sharan (ed) *Viklang Jiwan Ki Kahaniya*. New Delhi: Prakash Publication.

Lakoff, George and Mark Johnson. 1980. *Metaphors We Live By*. Chicago, IL and London: University of Chicago Press.

Matiyani, Sailesh. 2010. 'Hara Hua', in Giriraj Sharan (ed) *Viklang Jiwan Ki Kahaniya*, pp. 122–131. New Delhi: Prakash Publication.

Mitchell, David. 2002. 'Narrative Prosthesis and the Materiality of Metaphor', in Sharon Snyder, Brenda Brueggemann and Rosemarie Garland-Thomson (eds) *Disability Studies: Enabling the Humanities*, pp. 15–30. New York, NY: MLA.

Schmitt, Carl. 2007. *The Concept of the Political: 1932*. Trans. George Schwab. Chicago, IL: University of Chicago Press.

Vidali, Amy. 2010. 'Seeing What We Know: Disability and Theories of Metaphor', *Journal of Literary and Cultural Disability Studies*, 4(1): 33–54.

15

'VIKLANG'

Performing language and cripping modernity through translation

Shefalee Jain

> [T]he problem of the representation of disability is not the search for a more 'positive' story of disability, as it has been often formulated in disability studies, *but rather a thoroughgoing challenge to the undergirding authorization to interpret that disability invites.*
>
> – Mitchell and Snyder (2011: 59)

The preceding quotation captures precisely the reason for my choice of the story 'Viklang' for translation. While language has a performative potential that facilitates the proliferation and play of meaning, it can as easily be reduced to being a mere representational tool. In 'Viklang' language plays an interesting role that is a precarious swerving between these two positions. While at first reading, the story seems to offer a very narrow and unidimensional representation of poverty and failure through the metaphor of disability, a more careful reading reveals that the authorial voice subtly unsettles this disturbing 'truth'. It is this subtle swing of interpretative possibilities that compelled me to attempt to translate and critically examine 'Viklang'.

Synopsis of 'Viklang'

The title of the original story, in Urdu, by Suraj Sanim is 'Apaahij'. However, my source text is the Hindi translation of 'Apaahij' titled 'Viklang; by M. Shahbaz, which I have then chosen to translate into English. I have mostly referred to the Hindi translation and not to the original Urdu story both in this chapter and for my translation since I have no expertise in Urdu to be able to do so. The plot of 'Viklang' develops around a friendship between the narrator who is from a well to do family and a boy named Bhushan who comes from an underprivileged background. The story hinges on this difference in their monetary and social status. The narrator teaches drawing to students at a school where Bhushan and the narrator's brother Pradeep study. Struck by Bhushan's exceptional drawing skills, the narrator invites him home. Bhushan sells newspapers and magazines to support his studies and hopes that education will help him overcome his poverty someday. He is extremely well read and articulate, and the narrator starts meeting him regularly. Their conversations leave the narrator very impressed but also threatened by the boy's intellectual prowess. The narrator, who is preparing to appear for the Indian Administrative Services exam at the beginning of the story, clears it eventually, gets married and is posted away from his hometown Simla. He loses touch with Bhushan. Many years pass and he is posted back to Simla where he meets Bhushan once again at an officer's club where the narrator is the guest of honour. Bhushan is working as a waiter there. His dreams of making it big have obviously not been realised.

The story revealed several points of interest when examined through the lens of disability as well as translation studies. I have tried to address three in particular through this chapter and my translation. The title of the story 'Viklang' posed the first challenge. How should I translate this? Since the title of the story usually provides a crucial entry point to the narrative, I needed to carefully think through how I wanted to go about this. The second point of interest lay in the use of disability as an 'opportunistic metaphorical device', a term used by Mitchell and Snyder, and the third lay in examining the eugenic gaze that the story seems to employ in order to validate this metaphorical usage. I attempt to address each of these in the following.

Translating the title

It is not very clear why the translator, Shahbaz M., chose not to retain 'Apaahij', the original title of the story in Urdu, as the title of his Hindi translation. *Viklang* seems like an attempt at Sanskritisation of the word *Apaahij*. In fact, apart from the title, many other words commonly shared in Hindustani are translated to a standardised form of Hindi in Shahbaz's translation of the story. For example, *mulaqaat* is translated as *bhent* and more tellingly, *Hindustan* as *Bharat*. However, my concerns, while considering how to translate the title came from a different quarter. The story does not really have a character with any kind of impairment which is the general sense that both the titles, 'Apaahij' and 'Viklang', carry. So is Bhushan to be seen as *viklang* because he is poor? The question is whether the story equates poverty with impairment, seeing each of these as an inherently impoverishing and pitiful state. My first reading of the story seemed to confirm this. Like the medical model of disability, which sees impairment as located in the body and thus as an unfortunate individual circumstance which must be addressed through assimilation or ostracism of difference, *Viklang* also seems to leave the burden of impairment/poverty almost entirely with the individual.

Both *viklang* and *apaahij* may be loosely translated as 'cripple', 'freak' or 'disabled'. However, within a disability studies framework each of these three has vastly different implications. The term *cripple* with its clearly pejorative tone is seen as being reductive of and doing violence to the life worlds of the disabled. Its usage is seen as partaking of a charity model or the medical model of disability, which lays the burden of impairment entirely on the individual. In this sense, a cripple is seen as somehow chained to her biological make and deserving only of pity, cure or erasure. However, there are sections of Disability activists who have strategically reclaimed the word *crip* as an empowering term just as some lesbian, gay, bisexual and transgender activists have reclaimed the word *queer* or Mad Pride activists have reclaimed the word *mad*. *Freak* is again seen as largely pejorative in its usage today. It carries a violent history of the disabled being displayed for commercial purposes, as human curiosities in the 19th century and 20th century in the West, particularly in the U.S. and the U.K. The term disabled (within the social model of disability) is seen as applying to someone who is deprived of a full participation in life due to infrastructural and attitudinal barriers within society and not due to her impairment.

The story seems to fall into the normative mode of evoking pity for Bhushan, the 'poor boy' (literally as well as metaphorically), who is fated to be what he is. Given this, translating the title 'Viklang' as 'Cripple' seemed the right thing to do. However, a nagging doubt remained. Did I as a translator want to be 'true' to the overarching tone of pity in the story, or did I want to highlight the moments of what Spivak has called 'frayages' (qtd. in Spivak 1993: 180) in the story, which disrupt this tone and thus open up other spaces of interpretation? While discussing the two aspects of language, 'logic' and 'rhetoricity', Spivak writes that although every act of reading or communication carries a bit of the risk of fraying, or 'disruptive rhetoricity' (Spivak 1993: 180), 'our stake in agency'(Spivak 1993: 180) keeps this down to a minimum. She writes that the translator's task is to facilitate this fraying and pry open the gaps already present in the text rather than follow mere logic of language. 'Cripple' as a title, seemed to too quickly seal these gaps. It was at this point that I decided to make the title interrogative – 'Cripple?' In doing this, my intention was to keep the pejorative tone visible and yet, through the insertion of the question mark, trouble it. I wanted to thus highlight the few but important moments in the story when the authorial voice seems to detach itself from the pitying gaze of the narrator thereby problematising any direct equation constructed between poverty and impairment. I will return to these moments of frayages towards the end of this chapter.

Disability as an opportunistic metaphorical device

Mitchell and Snyder in a chapter titled 'Narrative Prosthesis and the Materiality of Metaphor' in their book, *Narrative Prosthesis: Disability and the Dependencies of Discourse*, contend that 'stories rely upon the potency of disability as a symbolic figure, they rarely take up disability as an experience of social or political dimensions' (Mitchell and Snyder 2011: 48). They speak of stories doing this in two main ways, first, by using disability as 'a stock feature of characterization' (Mitchell and Snyder 2011: 47) and, second, by using it as a 'metaphorical signifier of social and individual collapse' (Mitchell and Snyder 2011: 47). It is the second that is used frequently in 'Viklang'. Let me now elaborate on the idea of 'materiality of metaphor' as discussed by Mitchell and Snyder. They observe that while a theorist such as Antoine de Baecque has written about material metaphor and how it harnesses the corporeality of the body to give substance to intangible political ideals in editorial caricatures leading up to the French Revolution, he has ignored another important aspect of this metaphorical usage of the body. They write

> While de Baecque's theory of material metaphor argues that the attempt to harness the body to a specific ideological program provides the text with an illusory opportunity to embody Truth, he overlooks the fact that the same process embeds the body within a limiting array of symbolic meanings: crippling conditions equate with monarchical immobility, corpulence evidences tyrannical greed, deformity represents malevolent motivation and so on.
>
> (Mitchell and Snyder 2011: 63)

The metaphor in the case of 'Viklang', does not take shape as a recalcitrant fleshly and impaired body that might illuminate Bhushan's poverty through its corporeal presence. Bhushan has no impairment. He is poor. But his working-class background and probably his caste (though not explicitly mentioned in the story), certainly seem to hold the burden of the metaphor and may be read as a symbol of or reason for his 'failure'.

I would like to briefly list here, some instances in the story when disability is used as a metaphor of destitution and failure. The first instance, as I have discussed earlier, is in the very title of the story, which is 'Viklang'. The next occurs when the narrator goes looking for Bhushan in order to apologise to him for having dismissed him as a worthless scholar just because he can't afford to buy his own books. To the narrator's apology Bhushan makes the following reply, 'If you call a blind person *Surdas*, it can make no difference to him. I am aware of my poverty every moment of the day'. The story ends with yet another instance. Bhushan's dreams of making it big are not realised and he resolves not to get married or raise a family. To justify this decision, he says to the narrator at the very end of the story, 'A cripple like me has been given no right or means to bring a child into this world.'

The metaphor also extends to equate the disabled and the working class with commodities that need to prove their worth and create enough demand to be able to survive the capitalist framework. So when the narrator tries to assure Bhushan that one day he will make it big despite his poverty, Bhushan remarks, 'The value of a commodity is judged by the demand there is for it in the market'.

The repeated use of different kinds of disability, like blindness (Surdas was a 14th-century blind poet, saint and musician) and physical impairment, as metaphors of poverty and failure, seem to push the reader to adopt an uncritical acceptance of the 'inherent' incapacity attributed to these 'afflictions'. It also seems to write off the social and political reality of the disabled and in the same breath does likewise with the poor and the lower castes – I attempt to elaborate on this obvious disregard of structural oppressions that form the ground for Bhushan's 'failure' in a later section of the chapter. Instead, there is a naturalisation of social and structural oppressions as fate or destiny. This is made clear when at the end of the story Bhushan himself remarks that 'if the gardener does not know how to protect what he has planted, he must not plant at all'.

But the tone and the frequency with which these metaphors are doled out by Bhushan, the poor protagonist, trouble any such conclusive analysis. Bhushan goes on mouthing these spurious truisms with a disarming self-effacement but faint yet palpable sarcasm that puts the narrator in an increasingly uncomfortable space of becoming aware of his own position as the privileged other/oppressor. The figure of the narrator becomes increasingly pompous and vacuous as the story develops, and this also tilts the scale more in favour of Bhushan. The exaggeration of the metaphorical usage, especially through overused proverbs/aphorisms, undercuts the authority with which they are spoken, and here is where I am tempted to read language as becoming performative and playful rather than merely representative in the story. This frayage, caused by the too-frequent use of debasing metaphors employed by Bhushan to describe himself, does not allow for a casual reading and compels the reader to reflect on the lingering soreness left by this writerly tactic. It is not easy to see the metaphorical usage of disability here as simply a 'signifier of social and individual collapse'.

The eugenic gaze

Lennard Davis has traced the development of the term *normal* to 19th-century empirical sciences and technological innovations such as statistics, fingerprinting, physiognomy, phrenology and eugenics in conjunction with the rise and consolidation of the middle class in the West. He contends that it was at this time that the 'loose association between what we would now call disability and criminal activity, mental incompetence, sexual license, and so on' (Davis 2006: 9) was established as against 'the middleness of life, the middleness of the material world, the middleness of the normal body' (Davis 2006: 11). While describing statistical aims and methods in the West in the early 19th century, Davis speaks of the need for newly formed nations to administer populations in order to strengthen national unity as well as productivity. Statistics and eugenics are deeply implicated in the ideal of liberal political economy adopted by the newly emergent nations. He observes that many of the early statisticians like Quetelet, Malthus and Babbage were also eugenicists:

> While this coincidence seems almost too striking to be true, we must remember that there is a real connection between figuring the statistical measure of humans and then hoping to improve humans so that deviations from the norm diminish – as someone like Quetelet had suggested. Statistics is bound up with eugenics because the central insight of statistics is the idea that a population can be normed. An important consequence of the idea of the

norm is that it divides the total population into standard and nonstandard subpopulations. The next step in conceiving of the population as norm and non-norm is for the state to attempt to norm the nonstandard – the aim of eugenics.

(Davis 2006: 6)

The disabled still face trouble living down this legacy. In the post-independence Indian context, what gets constituted as the norm or the 'unmarked modern' (Pandian 2002: 1738) is the well to do, upper-caste, able male body. For the rest, modernity mostly comes as a deeply stigmatising and paradoxical experience.

In 'Viklang', the eugenic gaze is rather apparent. When the narrator marks Bhushan's drawing higher than Pradeep's saying that he has all the makings of a good artist, Pradeep retorts, 'Sure he will become a good artist! Can't even afford to buy paper and pencil!' suggesting a direct association between poverty and incompetence. Bhushan himself seems to confirm this later, when he says with some sarcasm to the narrator, 'Sir, you are right, it is a long established fact – only the one who can afford to buy books can be a true scholar.'

However, throughout the story, Bhushan's powerful intellect debunks these suspect associations made among disability, poverty and incompetence. The author lets Bhushan's erudition shine forth until it threatens to eclipse the narrator himself. It is in the face of this threat that Bhushan is finally shown his place. The narrator humiliates him for daring to speak with him as an equal. The benevolent mask falls to reveal an insecure oppressor, and given the post-independence Indian context, the oppressor is most likely an upper-caste one – 'It had become necessary to let this worthless newspaper vendor know that I was doing him a favour by treating him as an equal. This was beyond belief! He actually had begun to think that he was my equal'.

In one of the many conversations between the narrator and Bhushan, there is also mention of the word *vikaas* (Shahbaz 2011: 95) in the context of envisioning the promise of a future to come. Bhushan excitedly shares, with the narrator, the vision of a future that nature, as interpreted through modernity, the theory of evolution and technological development, holds in store for *mankind*. When the narrator asks him 'So what does nature really want to sublimate?' Bhushan replies in a voice full of mystery, 'perhaps an existence which is complete in every sense, someone who has no lack of any kind, a person . . .'.

Bhushan leaves the sentence unfinished. This trailing off suggests that Bhushan knows very well that the future he is speaking of (based on evolutionary logic and the promise of modernity), has no place for the likes of him. I chose to translate *vikaas* as 'evolution' rather than 'development', keeping in mind this sense of a eugenic gaze and its oblique critique in the text. The future, seen in the light of modernity and its 'universal narrative of capitalism' (Pandian 2002: 1737) only always disempowers someone like Bhushan whose neither class nor caste fit the norm of the modern Indian nation state. For the narrator, however, this same vision fills him with a sense of purpose and he declares rather pompously, 'I will work toward achieving the grand purpose which nature has chosen for me to accomplish'. It is interesting to note how the active support and privileges that the liberal political-economic structure provides for an upper-class and upper-caste individual like the narrator, are naturalised in one sweeping sentimental declaration and the narrator can dream of fulfilling 'the grand purpose which *nature* [emphasis mine] has chosen' for him to accomplish. Bhushan remains outside of this grand project of modernity. While Bhushan's friendship and erudition have opened a whole new world for the narrator, Bhushan himself does not profit in any way through his association with him. At the end of the narrative, he remains where he was despite the promise of social and economic mobility offered by modernity.

Moments of frayages

Although Bhushan appears to remain largely pitiable and meek in the story, he is not rendered entirely devoid of agency. As we have seen, his deliberate and repeated self-abasement, coupled contrastingly with his outstanding intellect that defies this effacement, threatens to upset the status quo that the narrative tries to hold together. I would like to take the role here, of Spivak's reader as translator, and locate, as well as widen, some more of these gaps that betray the apparently coherent logic of the narrative.

There are two moments of silence in the story which are full of interpretative possibilities. The first such instance, which I described earlier, occurs during the discussion on evolution. Bhushan dare not give words to the entity that will emerge as a result of eugenic manipulation of the world and the developmental project of post-independence India – 'perhaps an existence which is complete in every sense, someone who has no lack of any kind, a person . . .'. This refraining from giving shape/name to the future is an important silence/gap in an otherwise dense and overwhelming argument based on *commonsense* notion of development and progress associated with modernity. This gap leaves the surety of the eugenic dream and the developmental project of modern India in doubt. Should we really look forward to what this kind of a dream of a future that portends to silence and even actively decimate difference by labelling it as merely individual/personal lack or misfortune?

The other important gap is when the narrator, insulted by Bhushan's superior intellect, snubs him and later, feeling guilty, apologises to him. Bhushan tells him that there is no need for the apology, as he is used to being shown his place all the time. 'I am aware of my poverty every moment of the day. But I have never ever begged for help. And so. . . '. Again he trails off. The pause sets us thinking. Does Bhushan really hope to beat the unjust capitalist framework by continuing to follow the unrewarding and misleading ethics it advocates to the poor, the disabled, the lower castes – that of individual struggle and self-reliance in the face of obvious exploitation? Shouldn't he rather break with its code of conduct which seems to apply only to the already oppressed groups? Or perhaps look to fickle chance to help him get out of this cycle of exploitation? The narrator tries to fill this potent silence by quickly offering a weak platitude: 'Perhaps a blind man cannot get back his sight but a poor man can certainly leave behind his poverty'.

But the question remains, lingering. M.S. Pandian has observed how the idea of common good within the 'democratic ideal elbows out the politics of differ- ence based on inferiorised identities and sports the interests of the powerful as that of the society as a whole'(2002: 1738). He contends that in a postcolonial country like India, even as modernity holds out a promise of equality for one and all, there is a simultaneous reinforcement of old lines of power (he speaks, in particular, of the validation of elite upper-caste culture through 'so called' (Pandian 2002: 1737) sovereign culture of the emerging nation and the simul- taneous denigration of the lower castes as 'inadequate citizens in the making' (Pandian 2002: 1737). In this sense, women, the disabled, the lower castes and classes always fall outside of the pale of modernity. Bhushan is painfully aware of this paradox of a simultaneous promise and a betrayal. In fact, by the end of the story, while the narrator has made considerable progress in the world, becom- ing a chief guest in a club which was earlier reserved only for the colonisers, all Bhushan is able to manage is to become a waiter in the same club serving drinks to the narrator. The hierarchies of pre-independence India are maintained, only in a different guise.

Conclusion

Davis has observed that in order for it to perpetuate itself, the idea of normal, is in constant need of reinforcement within the social and cultural sphere through various means. He locates these means in all kinds of cultural production, such as popular media, literature and art. My attempt, in choosing to critically examine and translate 'Viklang', has been to understand the story in the light of this collusion between the social and literary sphere in reinstating the hegemony of the nor- mal (read male, elite upper caste, able). The narrator of 'Viklang' is a non-disabled, upper-middle/upper class and most likely an upper-caste male. Since the reader tends to identify with the character from whom the first-person narration ema- nates, it would seem that the author is keen to affirm the life world of this particu- lar class of reader. But this seeming privilege is gained at a cost for any discerning reader who, after reading the story, is most likely to squirm in his or her seat for holding this self-same privilege. The editors of the volume which carries the Hindi translation of 'Viklang' write that they wanted to bring together a collection of sto- ries written in Urdu post the 1970s decade, since these seem to mark a significant break from earlier Urdu writing. They note how most of these stories forgo the idealism and belief in the possibility of transformation which post-independence Urdu writing carried. Many of the stories have a central figure of the anti-hero who is full of disenchantment, cynicism even hopelessness. It is through this very figure of the anti-hero that 'Viklang' poses a very subtle, yet palpable challenge to the hegemonic norming of much literary production.

References

Davis, Lennard J. 2006. *The Disability Studies Reader*, 2nd ed. New York, NY: Taylor and Francis.

Mitchell, David T. and Sharon L. Snyder. 2011. *Narrative Prosthesis: Disability and the Dependencies of Discourse*. Ann Arbor, MI: University of Michigan.

Pandian, Mathias Samuel Soundra. 2002. 'One Step Outside Modernity: Caste, Identity Politics and Public Sphere', *Economic and Political Weekly*, 37(18): 1735–1741.

Shahbaz, M. 2011. 'Viklang', in Ram Lal and Izahar Usmani (eds) *Urdu Ki Nayi Kahaniyan*. New Delhi: National Book Trust.

Spivak, Gayatri Chakravorty. 1993. *Outside in the Teaching Machine*. New York, NY: Routledge.

16

TRANSLATING STIGMA IN THE POSTCOLONIAL CONTEXT

An analysis of Bharat Sasne's short story 'Mai Dukh Ki Lambi Raat'

Rohini Mokashi-Punekar

Situating Bharat Sasne in Marathi short fiction

As with other Indian languages, the short story has had a long history in Marathi literature and has been one of its most significant forms of expression. From the early decades of the 20th century to contemporary times, writers have represented the complex tangled realities of their times in short fiction that arrests the reader with its novel and profound ways of seeing the world. Encompassing writers from several diverse political and artistic persuasions, the Marathi short story has reflected the changing contours of literary sensibility and taste of modern Marathi literature in general. The earliest attempts at short fiction in the first few decades of the last century were based on characters' emotional conflicts as seen in the short stories written by writers such as V.S. Khandekar, N.S. Phadke, Kusumavati Deshpande and Vibhavari Shirurkar amongst others. In the years following Indian independence, there was a new wave in Marathi literature marked by the modernist movement of the West which was also reflected in the genre of short fiction. Short story writers such as Gangadhar Gadgil, P. B. Bhave, Arvind Gokhale and Vyankatesh Madgulkar presented the human predicament with fine subtlety in a realistic and/or surrealistic manner and experimented with the linguistic capacities of the Marathi language (Rasal 1992). One of the greatest short story writers in the Marathi language, G.A. Kulkarni, belongs to this period, though like all great writers, he is not contained by it. His stories reflect multiple layers of reality, shuttling between the apparently obvious to the imperceptible, though haunting, reality of the subconscious. Focusing on the inherent limitations hemming and oppressing the human being, his stories attempt to represent the sadness and alienation intrinsic to human existence.

From the 1960s onwards the momentum provided by the mass conversion of the Dalits to Buddhism under the leadership of Dr. Ambedkar as well as the linguistic reorganisation of the Indian states leading to the creation of Maharashtra resulted in the efflorescence of new literature, written, more often than not, by first-generation literates. Dalit literature addressed the lives of the working castes in rural and urban landscapes, and in the hands of several writers reflected a Marxist bent. Quite clearly therefore, Marathi literature from the 1960s onwards changed its focus from the primarily middle-class, upper-caste milieu and brought into the mainstream representations and the concerns of the socially marginalised and excluded. Although caste and poverty as social stigma found attention in most literary genres, yet it is difficult to identify a Marathi literary text that focuses on disability or disabled character(s) with any degree of substantial consideration.

In more recent times, Bharat Sasne, the well-known contemporary Marathi short story writer, carries the tradition of G. A. Kulkarni's short fiction forward, even as this legacy in his hands shows a negotiation with both Marxist and Dalit literary influences. Writing after the 1980s, Sasne reveals in his work a piquant blend of the traditional and the experimental: the novel and the unusual hold his interest even as he presents these in a realistic/naturalistic manner, securely anchoring them to the social and material base but within an existential framework. Besides urban lifeworlds, his stories show sustained engagement with rural and tribal worlds and the different social sections therein and, at times, with Muslim cultures. Issues of social stigma, including disability, find representation in his work. In his layered and complex short fiction, Sasne explores the human psyche encased as it is in social convention: not only does he document social reality; he also attempts to recover the subjectivity of his characters in all their psychological and metaphysical complexity. Sasne, therefore, is acutely interested in exploring the links between the human psyche and its material and social location. Collected in a number of volumes, his short fiction explores with philosophical profundity, experiences that fall outside the general ambit of quotidian middle-class preoccupations.

In his story 'Mai Dukh ki Lambi Raat' ('The Dark Night of Sorrow' in my English translation), the focus of the present chapter, Bharat Sasne presents stigma resulting from disease, disability and marginalised existence on the edges of modern urban India in unflinching, almost naturalistic detail. The author portrays disability emerging from a combination of natural and systemic factors, and my analysis of the story attempts to explore the challenges involved in recuperating material reality and the subjectivity of the disabled person, on one hand, and translating stigma and acute deprivation into an elite linguistic register such as English, on the other. Towards this end I have made use of a few theoretical perspectives that emerge from a number of different disciplinary domains such as Disability Studies, Urban Geography and Translation Studies. Although these conceptual ideas seem very diverse, their deployment may prove to be extremely useful in the analysis of the text under consideration and its English translation. The next section attempts a discussion of Sasne's story with the help of a few seminal perspectives from contemporary theoretical discourse in the areas mentioned earlier.

A reading of 'Mai Dukh ki Lambi Raat'

In his illuminating introduction to *The Disability Studies Reader* (2013), Lennard Davis dwells on the inescapable presence of the norm and its centrality in understanding contemporary culture and the national life during modern times. Asserting that there is no area of contemporary life in which some idea of a norm, mean or average has not been calculated, he proposes that the study of disability could be premised on the construction of the normative. Tracing the birth of statistics in the early decades of the 19th century and its growing deployment for an industrial nation, Davis also sees its twinning with eugenics in the work of key figures in the eugenics movement such as Francis Galton, Karl Pearson and R. A. Fisher (Davis 2013: 1–3). If the realistic novel/short fiction as a literary genre also emerges from the same set of political, economic and social developments in Western history, it may be rewarding to examine how the novel/short fiction as a form 'promotes and symbolically produces normative structures', wherein 'the plot and character development of novels tend to pull toward the normative' arising as these do 'as part of the project of middle-class hegemony' (Davis 2013: 9). Disability therefore rarely forms the central preoccupation of works of fiction, even when these are produced in postcolonial cultures outside Western metropolitan locations, since even here they veer towards the normative, with the caveat that the idea of the norm in the developing world may differ from the one prevailing in highly developed political economies.

It is very important therefore to take into consideration 'the cultural location of disability' as expressed in Sharon Snyder and David Mitchell's formative work, where the authors assert that 'the definition of disability must incorporate both the outer and inner reaches of culture and experience as a combination of profoundly social and biological forces', emphasising in equal proportions both culture and experience in the definition of disability (Snyder and Mitchell 2006: 7). This direction of thought has been usefully exploited by theorists who seek to bring together the intersections between Disability Studies and Postcolonial Studies. While there is some momentum already in place within Disability Studies to globalise its outlook and methodologies, there is an understanding that it must exercise caution about an uncritical transfer of theories and methodologies developed within the Western academy to other cultural locations. At the heart of both Disability Studies and Postcolonial Studies lies the implicit interrogation of power. However there is need for Disability Studies to 'undo the over rigid models and vocabularies' through which it often functions and develop approaches that focus on 'situated analysis, cultural difference, environments of disability and representational practices' in order to 'include and respond to postcolonial locations of disability' (Barker and Murray 2013: 63).

It may be a truism to acknowledge that the inherent cultural differences and social stratification within the erstwhile colonised societies together with colonial processes, anticolonial nationalism and postcolonial resistance have produced, at least within the context of India, vast and complex systems of cultural representation. However, even within the growing corpus of postcolonial literatures available in the several language cultures of India, if one were to move away in the context of Marathi literature, from the more mainstream literature marked by the hegemony of the middle class to literature born out of protest, such as Dalit literature, which is inscribed with the experience of being doubly oppressed and discriminated and which attempts to represent social stigmatisation, one would see that even this literature largely operates on the idea of the able as the normative, even if the able is perceived and represented as socially stigmatised.

Bharat Sasne's story 'Mai Dukh ki Lambi Raat' (henceforth 'The Dark Night of Sorrow'), however, challenges the normative in a number of ways. By means of deploying a structural strategy: that of a story within a story, Sasne is able to portray two starkly divergent worlds that coalesce on a small-town railway platform. In postcolonial, post-independence India railway platforms are sites where space is *produced*: they transform into shelters for the migrant, the poor and the orphaned; they are also typical sites of modern societies that produce anonymous meetings and chance interactions. The two binaries which Sasne brings together within this space are the world of the able-bodied, which though mediated by stratifications of class and gender, exercises hegemony over the other world: that of the disabled which exists, literally in this story, on the margins. Sasne employs two narrators that become representatives in a way of these two worlds: the normative and the disabled. The yawning abyss between the experiences typical to these two worlds is bridged briefly during the short time it takes for the disabled Babruvan, the second narrator, to narrate a real story from his own past for the entertainment of the first narrator. The two narrations exist one within the other, the first enveloping the second story. The first narrator is unnamed and able. He is obviously middle class and secure in his careless assumption that the world generally fulfils his expectations of it. Babruvan, the second narrator is clearly disabled and diseased and obviously expects nothing better than suffering from the world.

The first omniscient though unnamed narrator encapsulates the second narrator Babruvan who speaks to the first as well as to the reader at the same time. The outer story opens on a wind-swept stormy night with the unnamed first narrator stranded on the platform of an unknown station and describing to the readers his aimless wandering of a typical railway platform deserted in the small hours of the morning save for the huddled up throng of fellow passengers waiting in the rain and cold for a delayed train. He attempts to find some company in the anonymity of his surroundings for he is bored and hungry for a story, to hear a good yarn from someone with whom he would like to smoke together companionably. Sauntering up and down the platform in his raincoat, hands in his pocket, he is at his ease, at once in command of the space and an observer, examining and describing to the reader one by one, the passengers waiting for the train in various states of drowsiness. After a while he discovers Babruvan or, rather, is made aware of Babruvan staring piercingly at him from a dark corner of the platform. As he walks towards Babruvan, drawn by the yellow eyes burning redly in his direction, the first narrator is gradually made aware that he is seeing a disabled vagrant beggar who is perched on his little wheeled wooden plank, his hands bound in rags and sitting a little below, hidden behind the dark edges of the platform.

At this initial and only extended encounter between the two narrators which forms the plot of the story, what arrests the reader is the first narrator's lack of discomfiture in his appraisal of Babruvan and a rather *easy* acceptance of his physical, social and stigmatised *difference*. His interest in the meeting is still to elicit a story and to smoke together over its narration. It is puzzling that Sasne should allow his middle-class and able narrator to betray little trace of unease or social anxiety or pity on beholding Babruvan's wretched and disabled body arguably the more 'standard' set of responses to one so stigmatised by disability, disease and destitution. The thought and quotation 'what man has made of man' does flit across his mind, and he confesses to a feeling that his spirits are undergoing a meltdown, but he continues to gaze on Babruvan's diminutive person, wondering if he could be made to tell a story in exchange for a cigarette. In his superb examination of literary modes of representing disability, Ato Quayson offers the phrase 'aesthetic nervousness' that is seen 'when the dominant protocols of representation within the literary text are short-circuited in relation to disability' (2013: 202). The primary level in which it may be seen, says Quayson, 'is in the interaction between a disabled and nondisabled character' (2013: 202). The ease of interaction between the two narrators of his story: Is it Sasne's political correctness, a determination not to admit difference that is on display here, or is it an 'aesthetic nervousness' in the face of representing disability? Amongst the many levels of aesthetic nervousness, Quayson also includes in his list the reader's possible responses of unease and discomfiture on reading a given text. In this case, is it the reader's (the present author!) inherent biases and predilections, whose social attitudes to disability forms the filter of aesthetic nervousness through which this particular representation is viewed? One may only ponder and surmise.

We must come back to the story. Upon being persuaded and bribed with a cigarette, the much longer second story is narrated from memory by Babruvan to the first narrator. This story from his past which he titles 'The Snarl of Justice and Injustice' is based on the destitute inhabitants of a shanty near the railway station in a northern town caught in the deathly chill of a severe winter. Babruvan's family, comprising his wife and a brood of children, lives on the pavement under a makeshift awning of plastic covers and is freezing to death. A rich merchant donates a blanket to each of the impoverished families, but a single blanket cannot keep the chill at bay: his children are close to turning blue. Babruvan attempts to take away his disabled and aged neighbour Bholashankar's new blanket, which has been tightly anchored to splints driven into the mud floor for fear of theft, and is angrily berated. Driven to desperation he goes in again with a plan to kill him if he must but discovers that Bholashankar has, in fact, loosened the ends of his blanket, enabling Babruvan to easily flick it away. The family is saved from the cold by this act, but it is discovered the next morning that Bholashankar has died sometime during the night. Babruvan's wife has been a silent instigator and witness to the act but does not say anything. Nor is the theft which has, in all possibility, led to the old man's death discovered.

In some time, Babruvan's wife leaves him for another man and, taking their children with her, leaves him alone. He pretends to be asleep when she attempts to take leave of him. Babruvan is left alone to brood over questions of justice and injustice and whether, in fact, he was the author of Bholashankar's death and his own present condition. Had he forcibly stolen the blanket and so caused the old man's death or had Bholashankar himself facilitated the theft and so killed himself voluntarily? Was he the cause of the old man's death or was his death a premeditated act? Did his wife abandon him, or did he set her free by not remonstrating with her when she went away? These are the questions that now haunt Babruvan and which he, through the narration of his story, places before the first narrator and the reader.

It is important to note at this point Sasne's introduction of an additional angle to the story. Babruvan's narration makes brief reference at the very beginning of his story to the gradually growing symptoms of his affliction without ever mentioning the name of the disease. At the point in his narration when the wife leaves, he only indicates that symptoms were growing and his face had begun to look strange and distorted. The unnamed first narrator and the reader have to infer that it is leprosy that has him now, at this present time of narration, in full capture. The story ends with the stunned silence of the first narrator looking down at Babruvan's diseased and disabled body wrapped in Bholashankar's now-ragged blanket and the tangled snarl of existential questions which no one can answer.

The brief summary of the story narrated above raises interesting points for debate and analysis. It is intriguing that Sasne should give an existentialist and not an overtly political slant to this story of want and deprivation. Babruvan, impoverished, diseased and disabled as he is, is portrayed as asking fundamental philosophical questions about the circumstances into which he has been thrown. While this is not unusual in itself, it is interesting that a writer like Sasne, who presents to his readers that segment of the population which the middle-class gaze has trained itself not to see, should precipitate such questions through his character. Babruvan reveals a political understanding of poverty: note his rather ironical reference to the rich merchant donating the new blankets as a remedy to forestall misfortunes of fate or to the uproar in the assembly over the many deaths of the poor exposed to the cold wave. However, his preoccupation is with his own action and agency. He ponders over its results and questions what is the just or the unjust act given a certain set of circumstances and whether the justice of an act must be measured by its consequences. This is a profoundly philosophical direction and Sasne enables the reader to wonder and probe simultaneously political and philosophical questions emerging from Babruvan's narration. By refusing to sacrifice the profoundly metaphysical in questions of justice, Sasne is, in fact, enabling the older forms of storytelling to merge with the new directions interested in exploring political aspects which is the foundation of Dalit and Marxist texts in recent Marathi literature. However, by positioning his story within the locale of a railway station and its immediate surroundings, Sasne, in fact, enables a thorough grounding of the philosophical in the material base which the next section hopes to examine.

Disability, marginal existence and the politics of space

An aspect of Sasne's story that has interesting implications for analysis is the spatial location of the railway station and the slums adjoining its precincts that form the sites of the two narrations in the story and connect them. In his path-breaking work on human geography and space in the context of modern cities, Henri Lefebvre (1974) postulates that space is the product of social relations in urban metropolises:

if human relations are shaped by space, so too is space 'produced' by human relations. The city as a geographical space, suggests Michel de Certeau, is not only constituted by its citizens but is also inclusive of the 'ordinary practitioners of the city' who 'live "down below", below the thresholds at which visibility begins' (1988: 93). Thus, the city encodes power relations that are manifested in the spatial locations of its legitimate citizens as well as the de-centred subjects who form an essential part of urban life and services but are erased from visibility. The mainstream and the marginal exist together in a pattern of the visible and the invisible. Such erasures are more accentuated in the urban worlds of the erstwhile colonised regions that now fall within the category of developing nations. Postcolonial perspectives have a significant influence on contemporary work emerging from urban studies: they have interrogated normative assumptions and attempted to reveal the dynamics of power and hierarchies of caste, class and patriarchy inherent in the representations of urban space. For instance, Partha Chatterjee (2004), in his book *The Politics of the Governed: Reflections on Popular Politics in Most of the World*, examines the phenomenon of slums and squatter settlements in the rapidly growing urban networks of the developing world. Such burgeoning, unplanned urban conglomerations in contemporary global South mock the classic ideal of the city as the space for civil discourses.

Fictional representations of urban life by postcolonial writers undergo both an appropriation and a modification of urban themes suitable to their geographical locations. As seen in the foregoing section, a railway platform and a shanty adjoining a railway station form the sites of the two narratives of Sasne's story under consideration in the present study. Indian railways: the running trains, the platforms, the over-bridges or the grimy corners under their steel girders are home to the destitute poor and disabled. In a developing nation like contemporary India, cities are swollen with rural immigrants in the wake of the distress in the countryside. Despite the overcrowding, the filth and the perpetual paucity of deliverables promised by the state and the depletion of services that mark most Indian cities, their urban modernity promises the possibility of employment and some livelihood to the rural destitute. The migrant poor constitute the bulk of the daily-wage casual urban labour which is lucky if it finds some shelter in slums and squatter settlements, displaced as it is from more secure rural communities. Forced into begging for a living, the weaker members of these populations such as the infirm and disabled often live on roads by the traffic signal or in shanties by the railway stations in the urban landscape. These are familiar sights. The appropriation of these spaces speaks of political and social relations of power in a postcolonial society, such as the one described in Sasne's story. These habitations of real spaces become representative of social relations of power and are a dynamic testimony to the everyday reality of socially differentiated populations.

Translating disability in a multilingual context

It is a truism to note the vast linguistic diversity that characterises India and the multilingual competencies of a majority of Indians. Uprooted from their social milieu and language cultures, the migrant and marginalised populations are also forced to acquire the language spoken on the streets in the specific urban locations of which they eke out a marginal existence. This is frequently a working-class language register. In India this feature is further complicated by the existence of caste/class/regional registers of several languages which the writer may employ to suit the social background and identity of his or her characters. In public spaces such as railway stations this register may see a substantial increase in loan words from Hindi or specific varieties of Hindi may find currency as these are places where diverse sections of populations from different linguistic regions aggregate.

It is possible to present this vast linguistic variety with great felicity in a regional language text like the present story under discussion. Sasne's focus on marginalised existences is reported first hand through dialogue involving subaltern characters along with the contrapuntal voice of the middle-class narrator describing his setting and the people. Sasne employs the standard upper-caste/middle-class colloquial Marathi for the voice of the first narrator, who narrates the outer shell of the story. In his attempts to strike up a conversation, he interacts with working-class characters initially in Hindi, and they reply in the working-class urban register of Hindi and/or Marathi. There is liberal use of swear words too in various language registers. The code-shifting from one language and register to another are perfectly possible within the cultural domains of a contemporary regional language text like Sasne's story.

References to movies and songs from the Hindi film industry located in Bombay, pejoratively but popularly known as Bollywood, run throughout the story. No public space in India can be devoid of posters from Hindi films and Sasne dwells with some affection on a typical poster with its formulaic themes of sex and violence. More significant, Sasne pictures both his narrators sharing the lyrical and melodic strains of an invented Hindi film song 'Mai Dukh Ki Lambi Raat', translated as 'The Dark Night of Sorrow' here, which is also the title the author chooses for his story. The author deliberately titles his Marathi story with a Hindi poetic phrase that plays around with a fictitious snatch of an invented lyric of an apparently popular Bollywood number: these are very inventive and self-reflexive postmodern narrative strategies that are cleverly adapted by Sasne to represent the multilingual setting of his story.

While these linguistic variations form a skilled writer's tools that help delineate aspects of a character or the nuance of a situation, a translator working in English is forced to make some difficult choices. She can choose to either borrow native English/American colloquialisms in order to indicate class registers, running the risk of sounding embarrassingly fake, or deploy more accentuated forms of Indian English. This second choice may work in some places. Discussing the Indian English novel, G.J.V. Prasad asserts in his excellent study that the Indian novelist writing in English 'is creating a language as well as creating in it'. Given the challenge of representing a very different cultural reality,

> the act of writing in English is not 'merely' one of translation of an Indian text into the English language, but a quest for a space which is created by

translation and assimilation and hence transformation of all three – the Indian text, context and the English language.

(Prasad 1999: 42)

If this is the case of Indian English literature what is the creative process involved in the translation of bhasha literature(s) into English? What does a translator do in the context of translating an Indian text which depicts polyglot situations and multi-lingual characters who code-switch and code-mix fluidly? It is close to impossible to indicate in English, Indianised or otherwise, whether the translation indicates a working-caste/-class Hindi or Marathi or a combination of both. In letting go these differences or not attempting to indicate the different cultural registers inter-woven into a given situation of the literary text, the translator runs into the danger of flattening and sanitising the fascinating multilingual and cosmopolitan vibrancy that marks anonymous interactions in the modern public places of contemporary urban India. In translating these complex linguistic situations of the story, I have simply used the strategy of reporting the language/register in which a particular character speaks in addition to Indianising parts of the English syntax to translate certain speech characteristics.

In connection with the above discussion, it is significant to note a point of departure in Sasne's linguistic structuring of 'The Dark Night of Sorrow'. This concerns a marked liberty which Sasne takes in the way the subaltern Babruvan narrates his story. While Sasne is very particular in showing the class/caste differ-ences between the first and second narrator in the initial and later conversations between the two within which his story is sandwiched, Babruvan narrates his own story not in the linguistic register which the author has himself marked out for him, but in standard Marathi. This is surprising not only because it sacrifices in some measure the naturalism that Sasne so painstakingly attempts to establish; it also does not permit Babruvan the use of his own voice for the extended nar-ration, which fidelity to character and political cause would demand. These are important aspects of authorial intervention in the apparently 'authentic' represen-tation of stigma and disability. However, it is difficult to represent this authorial decision in the English translation, where the difference of register is impos-sible to capture. In English translation, what we have quite clearly is an erasure of the evidence of this aesthetic choice exercised by Sasne. The reader cannot but surmise that this authorial choice could be in consideration of the largely middle-class readership and its familiarity with established modes of narrative and reading strategies. Another departure that marks Sasne's narration is the deliberate underplaying of details in imparting information about Babruvan's illness. Sasne only hints at the symptoms of the disease on Babruvan's face and outlook with-out naming it as leprosy in any of the words available in Marathi. These hints are provided with great economy and subtlety at just two junctures in the story but are culturally loaded, therefore making it challenging for the translator to enable the cultural transfer into English.

How do we understand these two choices exercised by Sasne discussed in the foregoing paragraph? Is it possible to see these authorial decisions also as forms of 'aesthetic nervousness'? As discussed in an earlier section, Ato Quayson refers to the writer's aesthetic nervousness in the representation of disability. Are Sasne's narrative choices underpinned by unease and trepidation? Do these narrative quirks point to signs of writerly and readerly forms of 'aesthetic nervousness'?

Much of the above discussion concerns issues of translating social stigma and marginalisation, and by implication disability, since Sasne's central character is afflicted with a disease that induces impairment. As Lerita Coleman Brown suggests, stigma results in a special kind of downward mobility which is perceptible in Babruvan's increasing deprivation and gradations of erasure from the normative world (2013: 149). This then has bearings, as has been seen in the foregoing analysis of the story, on linguistic representations of culturally uprooted and traumatised lives that pose a challenge to the translator. As Davis suggests, narrative fiction is, by and large, the play of the norm or the normal which marginalises the disabled or the non-normal insofar as it indicates the hegemony of the normal in any given culture or nation. Sasne's story focuses largely on the spaces and cultural worlds in which the deprived, the disabled and the stigmatised carry on with their lives. It casts an ironic, even satiric, light on the normative world of the middle-class narrator and, by extension, the reader. However, by exercising an important choice in the selection of the linguistic register in the narration apportioned to the marginalised disabled character, Sasne may have perforce lost an opportunity to represent stigma and disability in a manner that challenges the power of the normative.

References

Barker, Clare and Stuart Murray. 2013. 'Disabling Postcolonialism: Global Disability Cultures and Democratic Criticism', in Lennard J. Davis (ed) *The Disability Studies Reader*, pp. 61–73. New York, NY: Routledge.

Chatterjee, Partha. 2004. *Politics of the Governed: Reflections on Popular Politics in Most of the World*. New Delhi: Permanent Black.

Coleman Brown, Lerita. 2013. 'Stigma: An Enigma Demystified', in Lennard J. Davis (ed) *The Disability Studies Reader*, pp. 147–160. New York, NY: Routledge.

Davis, Lennard J. 2013. 'Introduction: Disability, Normality and Power', in Lennard J. Davis (ed) *The Disability Studies Reader*, pp. 1–16. New York, NY: Routledge.

deCerteau, Michel. 1988. *The Practice of Everyday Life*, Vol. 1. Trans. Steven Rendall. Berkeley, CA: University of California Press.

Lefebvre, Henri. 1974. *The Production of Space*. Trans. D. Nicholson-Smith. Cambridge, MA: Blackwell.

Prasad, G.J.V. 1999. 'Writing Translation: The Strange Case of the Indian English Novel', in Susan Bassnet and Harish Trivedi (eds) *Post-Colonial Translation: Theory and Practice*, pp. 41–57. London and New York: Routledge.

Rasal, Sudheer. 1992. 'Marathi', in Karimpumannil Mathai George (ed) *Modern Indian Literature, an Anthology: Volume One, Surveys and Poems*, pp. 264–284. New Delhi: Sahitya Akademi.

Sasne, Bharat. 2009. 'Mai dukh ki Lambi Raat', in Pradeep Karnik and Chandrakant Bhonjal (eds) *Tapt Pravaha: Nivdak Bharat Sasne*, pp. 108–122. Mumbai: Lokvangmaya Griha.

Snyder, Sharon L. and David T. Mitchell. 2006. *Cultural Locations of Disability*. Chicago and London: University of Chicago Press.

Quayson, Ato. 2013. 'Aesthetic Nervousness', in Lennard J. Davis (ed) *The Disability Studies Reader*, pp. 202–213. New York, NY: Routledge.

17

TRANSLATING RHETORICITY AND EVERYDAY EXPERIENCES OF DISABLEMENT

The case of Rashid Jahan's 'Woh'

Shilpaa Anand

> *First, then, the translator must surrender to the text. She must solicit the text to show the limits of its language, because that rhetorical aspect will point at the silence of the absolute fraying of language that the text wards off in its special manner.*
> – Gayatri Chakravorty Spivak (2008: 205)

The epigraph has often been taken, along with her essay 'The Politics of Translation', as instructive to translators of third world women's texts. Spivak, stating that 'language is not everything' (2008: 202), argues for finding what we can 'beside language, around language' (202) to not restrict ourselves to the more logical tasks of translating for meanings of words and phrases. To translate the rhetoric and silence in the original text one needs to 'surrender to the text' (205). In the present chapter, I want to redraw our attention to the observations Spivak makes about translating rhetoricity and adapt her essay to enable a critical understanding of another range of corporeal differences that have come to be known under the catchall category of disability. Rashid Jahan's Urdu short story 'Woh' and three translations of the story into English provide a suitable opportunity to examine how the facial disfigurement of a woman plays out within a context that has its own ways of knowing and going about disablement. The English translations of the story examined here include those by M.T. Khan, Rakshanda Jalil and a third by Aneesa Mushtaq and me. The phrases *disablement* and *disability*, for the purposes of this chapter, are adopted as placeholder terms that indicate forms of corporeal difference. One of the primary intentions, then, is to investigate how translation may benefit disability studies as the latter, a field of inquiry that emerged in the UK and US contexts, develops a more global line of investigation.

What translation can bring to disability studies

Disability studies, as a field, enables an epistemic re-orientation that puts the experience and discourse of being disabled at the centre of the discourse by destabilising the epistemic authority standardly ascribed to the status of being 'normal'. This is done by critically evaluating institutions and experts that have traditionally assigned to themselves the roles of knowing and designating who is disabled, what disability is and how the two can be treated. The inherent logic of this epistemic re-orientation emerged in the West which has had a long and known history of prioritising 'the normal', 'the healthy', 'the sane' and 'the norm', to name only a few concepts. As disability studies moves beyond the West, it has unfortunately carried with it an intense sense of that historical development even as it finds a place in contexts whose epistemic, social and cultural environments may not have followed the same or similar trajectory. As a result, we have before us a growing body of scholarship produced about non-Western contexts, conceptualised and carrying the same inflexion as scholarship about disability in the West. This chapter works with the premise that disability is only one conceptualisation of corporeal difference and other conceptualisations of difference are still in the process of being explored. Spivak's essay, referred to in the early part of this chapter, which is a response from the standpoint of what she calls 'third-world' women to the feminist discourse that is dominated by Western women's experiences, may be instructive for the purposes of investigating 'disability' in the non-Western contexts through acts of translation.

Context-sensitive examination and translation of literary narratives would reveal or, at least, enable us to become acquainted with other ways of knowing and engaging with corporeal difference that are specific to distinct ways of going about the world. Translation practices could be reinvigorated by attending to disablement experiences more closely by attending to some of the critical insights that the field of disability studies has offered us in recent times. While disability as a trope of being and experience may be drawn from the West, the field itself has opened a range of methodological avenues that could be explored further if our object of inquiry is to know diverse ways of knowing difference.

What is a 'disability' text?

A significant point of departure for this paper is a series of dilemmas that came to the fore directly and indirectly in the papers that were presented at the 'Translating Disability Across Cultures: The Translation and Representation of Disability in the Modern Indian Short Story' conference in Jawaharlal Nehru University in September 2016. Participants at the conference were expected to find short fiction in different Indian languages that had a disability element, translate them into English, and discuss their experiences of translating disability-related content. The following dilemmas, which all pertain to the issue of finding a 'disability text', explicate further the question related to knowing disability in non-Western cultural context:

a   Disability is everywhere in literature: Participants at the conference expressed wonder at the fact that they had rather easily found short stories that related to disability. Their wonderment was due to their initial anxiety at having to look for stories that would appropriately fit the expectation of the conference. The range of stories chosen by participants at the conference to translate into English from various Indian languages revealed that one does not have to look very hard to find a 'disability' text. In stating so, participants were pointing to the fact that disability, which is a familiar category had become unfamiliar through the process of literary defamiliarisation. They may, however, have been saying that 'disability' was not a trope in which they had previously known these texts in their own languages and that they had now found a concept with which to think of and relate to these texts.

b   It is tedious to find disability texts in Indian languages: Contrary to what in fact emerged, as outlined earlier, another common experience shared by participants was that they had difficulty finding a short story in their language that contained a disabled character or a disability experience. This response revealed that there was some compulsion to identify disability as an already known category, as familiar in certain ways, probably in terms of impairment groups that are standardly known as disabilities, for instance, blindness, deafness, loss of limb and so on. What was being stated perhaps was 'We are familiar with what disability is, but is this thing that we see in the text really the same?' This dilemma perhaps relates to the issue of how ways of knowing and going about bodily difference are specific to each context; it is probably a dilemma of conceptual differences.

c   The case of over-representation of papers on 'Subha': Of the short stories that were translated as disability short stories, there appeared to be a predominance of Tagore's short story 'Subha'. This fact coincides with the previous point that most scholars present at the conference had identified a text as a 'disability' text that contained all the known markers of disability. In their papers on this short story, however, participants reflected on the problem of self-evidentiality of disability, expressing in diverse ways that what we know as disability, the normatively defined category, turned out differently in the process of translating the short story.

d   And fourth, the interesting case of identifying conditions that would not normatively be identified as disability: The conference also reflected the presence of 'disability' texts that did not qualify in the familiar way, those referred to in points (b) and (c) as 'disability' texts. Here, it was the interpretative or hermeneutic tradition of literary studies that came in handy. But the dilemma was somewhat resolved by expanding the range-of-reference of disability.

The preceding dilemmas, in fact, help clarify the fact that while adopting disability studies within the Indian context, it would be restrictive to employ what this field constitutes as disability (loosely, as a sociocultural-political lived experience) as a prescriptive category. At best, disability studies may offer those of us working in literary and cultural studies, a critical framework that serves well as an approach to reading and translating texts.

A brief detour to explicate this fact in a set of English texts of Indian contexts may not be out of place. Brit in Fridaus Kanga's *Trying to Grow* (2008), Malini in

Girish Karnad's *Broken Images* (2005) and Animal in Indra Sinha's *Animal's People* (2007) are all characters who in the normative sense would be identified as disabled but each of these texts offers us, ways of rethinking disability conceptually keeping in mind the cultural context. To illustrate, in the first text, Brit has osteogenesis imperfecta, what is better known as brittle-bone syndrome but what the narrative reveals is the way in which the condition is conceptualised socially in terms of its physical manifestation, that his diminutive stature carried more social meaning and resulted in his being treated as a little child, the essence of which experience is best exemplified in the title of the novel, 'trying to grow'. In conjunction with Karnad's and Sinha's texts, Kanga's novel enables us to examine the complex relations that the English language has in relation to the modern category of marginalisation, 'disability'. While Karnad's and Kanga's texts reflect the way in which prowess in the English language enables disabled people of the middle-class, Sinha's novel demonstrates how the modern emergence of disability politics in India does not extend to a rural class of disabled people whose impairments were acquired through congenital disabilities caused by industrial disasters limits (Anand 2015). Disability studies, it may be argued, serves us better as an approach or methodology rather than as a prescriptive framework.

Facial disfigurement in Rashid Jahan's 'Woh'

Rashid Jahan's short story 'Woh' is often contextualised within the discourse of women's writing considering that it was notably anthologised in Susie Tharu and K. Lalita's *Women Writing in India*. This story, nevertheless, enables us to sharpen questions previously outlined in the introduction: How can we uncover culture-sensitive concepts of knowing and going about corporeal difference through a study of literature in different languages? How can translating the rhetoricity and silence, of the story reveal something about how difference is conceptualised?

A quick outline of the story reveals the following – Safia, the narrator, meets the protagonist, 'that one'/'woh', by chance in a hospital which they both have visited for treatment. All accounts the narrator provides tells us that it is unbearable to look at 'that one' because her face is disfigured – she has two holes for a nose and one eye, which to use she has to strain her neck. Safia controls her disgust and smiles at the woman. When she meets the woman again at the counter where medicines are dispensed, the woman asks Safia for her address and leaves. The compounder who dispenses medicines tells Safia that the woman is a wretched prostitute and expresses his disdain for the doctor who insists on treating the woman with little regard for her fallen social status. The woman begins to visit Safia at the girls' school where the latter works. She enters the staffroom once classes are over and places a jasmine flower before Safia, who then asks her to sit down and leaves after a while. Safia places the flower in her hair in front of the woman. Conversation is minimal between them, but speculation is rife in our narrator's mind. Why does she come here? Who is she? Why was she the way she was? Was she just another woman before she became afflicted with this disease that attracts such social boycott? Safia's unspoken speculation is influenced by the comments and barbs made by her co-teachers and by Naseeban, the non-teaching assistant's refusal to even touch the chair that the woman sits on. On one occasion, the woman, while leaving the staffroom, wipes the snot from her nose on a wall and thus attracts the wrath of Naseeban. Naseeban hits her with a slate and lashes out at her verbally accusing her of being a slut and beneath disgust. Safia rushes to help the woman to her feet, and in a gush of tears, the woman says to Safia, 'Now you know who I am.'

The short story, it is important to note, opens the second volume of Susie Tharu and K. Lalita's historic two-part anthology *Women Writing in India*. Rashid Jahan was infamously known as 'Angareywali' given her role in the groundbreaking Urdu writing anthology *Angaaray* that was published in 1932. Given Rashid Jahan's commitment to communist politics it is not difficult to identify the short story as a narrative that wishes to underscore class differences and the inherent problems. Rashid Jahan has also become a well-known name within feminist writing considering her literary explorations of Muslim women's lives at a time when colonialism and communalism had successfully silenced any discourse of hardships of women who belonged to a minority. Tharu and Lalita's anthology showcases the story as an instance of the social awakening of the middle-class woman, in this case, Safia, as she encounters a prostitute, the representative of a *sui generis* class of women. In their introduction to the second volume the editors explicitly note that the narrative voice is one that belongs to the centre and the narrated object, that woman with facial disfigurement, a social outcast, clearly belongs to the margins.

The object of everyone's gaze, the woman in the story draws our attention, quite centrally, to social responses to her disfigured face. We are drawn not only to the indescribable and unspeakable disability of the woman but more robustly to the reactions and responses of her onlookers. The readers are called on, even if only indirectly, to sympathise with her. Readers, it is most likely, aspire to identify with the narrator, to overcome disgust, to share social spaces and to be sociable with 'that woman'. It is important to note that the narrator identifies herself, in a somewhat self-deprecatory manner as a woman who belongs to a privileged class. Within this class, responses of disgust are a significant part of disability experience and **as** important as pity and fear, the other two standard responses, that has been severally documented in literary presentations of disability experiences. That disability is an experience constituted by the response to the disabled individual, primarily formulated within the visual gaze of the onlookers is explicit in the story. No one can look at the woman without feeling disgust, and their disgust is normalised, it seems, because it is shared. In the responses of disgust evident in the underprivileged classes portrayed in the text, the dispenser of medicines in the clinic and the maidservant at the school, aspirational qualities are writ large. It is through the expression of similar disgust for the woman, a feature of morality specific to the middle class that these classes of people aspire to transition to. Responses to certain forms of disablement, one can say, contribute to the making of social classes and their aspirations. The expression of disgust in the text constitutes facial disfigurement as a classed disability. Bill Hughes discusses how pity, fear and disgust are "building blocks of the emotional infrastructure of ableism 'that serve in creating and exacerbating 'social distance between disabled and non-disabled people' (2012: 68).

Disgust as a reaction to facial disfigurement or physical disability appears to have been inscribed into class relations rather consistently. Susan Schweik's compelling work *The Ugly Laws: Disability in Public* (2009) traces the normalisation of aesthetics pertaining to appearances in the US context by examining vagrancy laws that penalised 'unsightly beggars'. City laws oriented towards urbanisation seem to have dictated bodily aesthetics as well as imposed a limitation on human diversity (Schweik 2009). The study describes legal and social discourses in late 19th-century and early 20th-century America that constituted disability in terms of aesthetics thus marking people who were blind, had clubbed feet and so on as 'street obstructions' (Schweik 2009: 1). The people affected by these city laws were often beggars, not involved in any 'productive labour', reminding us of the persistent argument forwarded by international development agencies, that disability and poverty exacerbate each other. Disgust, in the context of the American ugly laws, we can say, frames structural exclusion of disabled people and creates a normative equation of economic worth and corporeal aesthetics.

In another sense, the story attempts to recover the woman, who is fast spiralling into a vortex of moral diagnosis, by focusing on her disease condition. One of the struggles among the onlookers, primarily Safia, the narrator, is to know her medical diagnosis. Rashid Jahan's professional training as a medical doctor had also probably demonstrated to her that people readily classified skin-related conditions as immorally contracted through unacceptable sexual relations. In Rashid Jahan's short story, the entire focus appears to be on Safia's reactions to the woman as well as the reactions of all the other onlookers. Her disfigurement tests all the people around her, and it is only Safia who begins to pass the test; the woman, however, is never transformed; she finds only a temporary companion. Ato Quayson, in his work on the typology of disability narratives, identifies 'the moral test' as a common pattern that is prevalent in myths, legends and other literature of the West that has a disabled character (2007). A common feature in myths and fables, a character with a hunchback or facial disfigurement is introduced to test the responses of the other character. Depending on the nature of the response, the character is either rewarded or punished; disgust and horror often constitute the common stock of negative responses that are punished while compassion and kindness are rewarded. In such situations, it often occurs that the disabled characters, due to the actions of the other characters, are transformed back to their original non-disabled/heroic/attractive selves. Disability serves as a guise that tests the morality of the other characters (Quayson 2007).

Safia's struggle in her responses to the woman is a struggle to overcome both compassion and disgust and attain a kind of indifference. Rashid Jahan's story doesn't quite fit the category of 'disability as moral test' but instead could be read as a modern intervention in the vein of *nirvicikitsa*. In his study on South Asian history, M. Miles recommends moving beyond the Western model's framework of disability theorising to incorporate other cultural contextual experiences of disablement. And it is within this approach that we could locate what occurs in the story 'Woh' by focusing on how disgust works within the context of the story, primarily in relation to the narrator's responses to the woman with facial disfigurement. In his paper 'Disability on a Different Model: Glimpses of an Asian Heritage' (2000), Miles dwells on epistemic frameworks and narrative structures that are used in diverse cultural contexts to know oneself and the world around. Miles asks whether the model's framework, a template forwarded within disability scholarship (primarily the medical model and the social model), is necessary at all to the writing of disability history of diverse cultural contexts. His question is based on his findings that Asian historical instances and conceptual paradigms cannot adequately be characterised as 'religious', 'bio-medical' or 'social'. One such paradigmatic instance he draws on is taken from the Jaina tradition, where there appears to be a concerted effort to root out revulsion expressed by a person at another's disfigurement. His study of the Jaina tradition reveals that one who wishes to qualify for being an advanced Jaina would have to attain the quality of *nirvicikitsa*. The practice of *nirvicikitsa* would enable one to feel no revulsion at the sight of disease, deformity or disfigurement of any kind in another human being. This ability to be indifferent, Miles cautions must not be confused or conflated with the modern-day commitment of disability advocates to 'piss on pity'. The Jaina form of indifference adhered to the idea of detachment which meant 'all passion spent and all compassion absent' (Miles 2000: 607) and thus diverges significantly from the modern-day disability activism that emphasises compassion which is framed within the human rights discourse. What we have in 'Woh' is a way of knowing disability, better still corporeal difference that is inherent to that context which is embedded in the very rhetoric of the story.

Safia is tormented by the dual pressures of wanting to be helpful to the woman whom everyone else hates and wanting to stay away from her to draw less attention to herself. If we assume, as many critics tell us, that Rashid Jahan pictured herself in her stories quite consistently, it could then be argued that the writer of this story assumes multiple roles, moving intermittently from one to the other – usually as the contented middle-class narrator, then as the repulsed but somewhat tolerant doctor probably symbolic of the Nehruvian ideal of an unbiased modern medical establishment and as an onlooker who suppresses her revulsion. It is this last role that the narrative successfully emphasises with its use of personal and demonstrative pronouns, *woh, uski, meri, yahan* and so on. The pronouns serve two purposes: (a) to distance the woman from the society that looks at her and (b) as euphemisms for the profession she belongs to as well as the disease that she has contracted. Rashid Jahan's narrative exposes the idiosyncrasies of how an elite society speaks of the unspeakable and crafts a linguistic barrier that socially distances her from us. The pronouns used are invested with evaluative force as evident in 'Must **she** come **here**?' where the emphasis is on *she, that one* who is disgusting, and *here*, this sacred place which is a school for girls. Later, the narrator muses, 'How had she become like **this**?' and the evaluative emphasis on the sentence-ending *this* refers to the noseless-ness and its connotations of that which cannot be spoken. Priyamvada

Gopal has rightly pointed out while referring to Rashid Jahan's other works that her literary pieces are better understood as speech acts (2002). The author, in this case, succeeds in employing the pronouns to emphasise the harmful effect of rhetoric that frames our social experience of disabling diseases.

Translating rhetoricity

The use of pronouns denoting distance is fundamental to the narrative, and this is recognised by M.T. Khan who translated the story for *Women Writing in India* and Rakshanda Jalil, whose translation of the story is included in her book, *A Rebel and her Cause: The Life and Work of Rashid Jahan* (2014). Khan retained the Urdu title for his English translation, thereby indicating that the rhetorical work done by that word is not matched by any word or phrase in English. Jalil translates the title as 'that one', once again, emphasising the significance of the rhetorical weight borne by *woh* and how it means what it means, something akin to Walter Benjamin's idea of the 'mode of intention'. While both translators take care to retain the rhetoricity in the title of the story, their translations of the text of the story proceed differently. The Urdu words *woh* and *yeh* that appear repeatedly through the text, are both translated as *she* into English by Khan and Jalil. Their translation then gives into what Spivak calls the 'logical' mode: 'Logic allows us to jump from word to word by means of clearly indicated connections. Rhetoric must work in the silence between and around words in order to see what works and how much' (Spivak 2008: 202–203).

The reason for invoking Spivak's distinction between a translation that attends to logic and one that attends to rhetoric in the context of Rashid Jahan's story is because there is a shift in the rhetoric of Safia's thoughts that makes a compelling case for her *nirvicikitsa*. There is, change in the use of pronouns towards the latter part of the story, from *woh* to *yeh* perhaps reflective of a turn in the torment that Safia undergoes in trying to decide how to proceed in her relations with her new-found admirer. Safia's wonderment about the woman is presented in the story as a series of questions that appear in two or three clusters, but there is a gentle shift in the use of pronouns from the early to the later clusters. The pronoun *woh* (that one/ that woman) is replaced by *yeh* (this one/this woman), suggesting a shift in terms of proximity and a new way of knowing the woman. To Safia, the woman had become, in due course, almost unbeknownst to herself if one follows the narrative, a familiar mystery or a known mystery rather than a distant or unknown one.

The new translation of the story, one undertaken by Aneesa Mushtaq and me attempts to retain the rhetorical shift in Safia's response to the woman by translating *woh* in most cases as 'that woman' and *yeh* as 'this woman'. The translation also makes a distinction between the two rhetorical uses of *woh* evident in the text. While the dominant use of *woh* in the text indicates a distancing that facilitates a communally desired dissociation, a second use of *woh* appears in the Urdu text when Safia's colleagues pretend to chide her about her visitor. Here the use of the term *woh* connotes 'special person' in the way that one would be teased about a person of romantic interest. For this second use of *woh*, we have retained the Urdu word just to distinguish it from the other distal pronoun *woh*. The dominantly used pronouns in the Urdu original, capture the materiality of the woman's everyday disablement experience as well as Safia's transition from one who suppresses her disgust first by being able to distance her and then by becoming her acquaintance. She appears to have overcome her disgust of the woman by coming to terms with it.

Approaching Rashid Jahan's story from the framework that Miles uncovers would require us to re-focus our attention on the writer's experiences and insights as a medical practitioner in 1930s'/1940s' India, particularly how her life as a gynaecologist treating women in purdah informed her literary writings. During her medical work, Rashid Jahan discovered that women were poorly informed about their medical health and were susceptible to different forms of domestic violence and trauma due to which they had malnutrition or sustained injuries and remained silent about them. Biographers tell us that a significant part of Rashid Jahan's later years were dedicated to educating women about their health by offering free medical check-ups. Her writing is replete with narratives of encounters with her female patients.

The euphemisms used in the story to talk about her unspeakable condition strongly suggest that what the woman may have is a sexually transmitted disease. What disease does the woman have? The compounder, while calling her a 'whore' and a 'wicked woman', states that she has a disease that is rotting her away, of which she is possibly dying. In another moment, Safia, trying to unravel the mystery of the woman, wonders if the woman does not know that she is bearing the fruits of her misdeeds. The phrase used in the Urdu text is *'gunahon ka phal bhugatna'* (literally bearing the fruits of one's crimes) referring to the facial disfigurement, thereby identifying the disease as a consequence of her whoring. Later Naseeban, the assistant in the school, while lashing out at her in anger and calling her a *'haramzadi randi'* (literally, horrible whore) and one who used to frequent the 'chowk', describes her disease as one in which her flesh is falling off piece by piece – *'kat-katkar gosht gir raha hain'*. Drawing on David Mitchell and Sharon Snyder's theory about narratives of disability, it could be argued that the woman's condition in the story is narrated, even if euphemistically, to prostheticise the normalcy of the social and moral universes that the characters belong in. Mitchell and Snyder in their essay 'Narrative Prosthesis and the Materiality of Metaphor' (2000) argue that the dominance of disability as metaphor in language serves to occlude material aspects of disability as a lived experience.

Syphilis, a historically maligned disease condition, is apparently also known, medically, as 'the great imitator' because it imitates other diseases, in this case it appears to be imitating leprosy. Or has she contracted leprosy? We do know that nerve damage caused by leprosy bacteria leads to loss of sensation in the extremities and often results in damage to the nose, fingers and toes. Sociocultural histories of leprosy reveal that the disease had long been associated with sexual misdemeanours, both Judaic and Hindu texts characterise it as a punishment that befalls those who have committed sexual transgressions. Nevertheless, in the case of the woman in the story, it could be that she had contracted leprosy which was mistakenly believed to be sexually contracted, as is the case in this story. The connection between sexually transmitted diseases, skin conditions and visual disgust has a long cultural history. Rashid Jahan *may* have been fairly aware of this. Her story lays bare the problems caused because of this quick equation people made upon encountering someone with a skin condition that caused visible disfigurement. The disease in the story, at one level, works as a metaphor for the woman's so-called immoral actions.

Safia's musing in the Urdu text, '*Kya yeh samajhti hai mein isko sirf ek bimari samjhti hoon?*' (Shakeel 2006: 46) is translated as 'Does she actually believe that I consider her only another sick person?' (Jahan 1995:121) in M.T. Khan's text and as 'Does she really think that I merely regard her as an ill person?' (Jahan 2014:119) in Rakshanda Jalil's text. It is worth considering that the use of *bimari* in the Urdu text is a reference to prostitution as a social ill or a social disease. When Safia is wondering about this woman, she is also reflecting on her own responses to her and trying to make sense of their interactions. She is conflicted. While she wonders, what may have made this woman this way and whether she was once like her, she also can't help wondering what the woman thinks that Safia thinks of her. Does the woman think that Safia only thinks of her as a social malaise? It is more likely, then, that Safia's use of *bimari* is metaphorical and has been translated as such in the recent translation. The translation of the rhetorical use of *bimari* not as 'ill person' but as 'disease' or 'malaise' captures the momentary anger that Safia feels when she thinks that the woman thinks that even Safia thinks of her as a social ill, considering the speculation that is rife that she might be a prostitute.

Coming to disability metaphors and how they assume material roles in the text, it would be pertinent to turn to Rashid Jahan's biography. When *Angaaray*, the infamous short story collection, was published and criticism started to pour in, the writer received threats that her nose would be cut off (Jalil 2014: 45). A metaphor that appears to work out materially in the text concerns the noseless-ness of the woman. The woman in the story has lost most of her nose, we are told, she has two holes that suggest the erstwhile existence of a nose. Let us momentarily consider the metaphorical uses of 'losing one's nose' which implies losing one's honour, and how it takes a material form in the context of the story. Just as those who were threatening to punish the Angareywali by literally chopping off her nose, the woman in Rashid Jahan's story manifests the material aspect of an otherwise metaphorical usage. If we think about it, the idiom, *naak-katana* which uses the metaphor of one's nose being cut as an act of shaming is turned into a material experience in the story. Could it be that the woman's noseless-ness in the story stands as a reflection of other people's shameful behaviour towards her? If we hold onto this interpretation then Rashid Jahan can be recovered as a writer who put her medical experience to use by highlighting the lived experience of disablement. Rashid Jahan's short story unsettles us by emphasising the materiality of being noseless and resists the linguistic compulsions, or logical compulsions as Spivak would have it, to use disability only as metaphor.

Conclusion

While Tharu and Lalita's criticism of the story is that the woman with the facial disfigurement does not represent herself and that she is spoken for by Safia, what a disability-focused translation has revealed, is that, the story is more about Safia's *nirvicikitsa* and can only be narrated by the one struggling with it. Tharu and Lalita's critique harps on the aspect of subjectivity and agency which are inherent to a feminist reading of the text. In examining the story for culturally specific responses to disablement one finds that it, in fact, reveals a way of going about and a way of knowing. Translating the rhetoricity of Jahan's short story draws our attention to the discursivity that attends everyday interactions of bodily differences. Recognising that Safia is the centre of disability subjectivity, helps us realise that all ways of knowing disability (culturally distinct ways) may not be centred on the corporeality of the disfigured individual but some cultural contexts may know or make sense of disability through the individual who relates to the disfigured individual. The title of the story, 'Woh'/'That One', is better comprehended as ironic; the focus of the narrative seems to reveal not so much the details of the objectifying implied in the title but the process of objectifying that centrally implicates the actors around the woman. The plot draws more attention to the conflicting responses to specific kinds of disfigurement that frame everyday experiences of disablement. The woman in the story is not privy to Safia's thoughts but only to her actions. Safia's actions may be perceived as enabling from the perspective of the woman, we can say she even develops a bond that propels her to rush to the hurt woman at the end. This temporary bond probably provides a kind of reprieve to the woman who is only otherwise maligned. But Safia's responses to the woman, we as readers know, is fraught with the struggle to attain a kind of indifference towards the woman, it is not as if Safia's initial reactions have not consisted for repulsion and at times pity but that she's comfortable expressing neither. What the story captures best is the complexity of our social responses to corporeal differences that consist of thought, speech and action where none of them may be aligned or intertwined. These responses cannot be precisely fixed as medical model, moral model or social model but suggest that a serious study of literary narratives of the Indian context may uncover conceptualisations of corporeal difference that are yet to be theorised. The task of translating this story has helped realise the weight of Spivak's critical insights into translation that attending to the rhetoricity of the original text enables the agency of the translator.

References

Anand, Shilpaa. 2015. 'Disability and Modernity: Bringing Disability Studies to Literary Research in India', in Shridevi Rao and Maya Kalyanpur (eds) *South Asia and Disability Studies: Redefining Boundaries and Extending Horizons*, pp. 246–262. New York, NY: Peter Lang.

Gopal, Priyamvada. 2002. 'Sex, Space, and Modernity in the Work of Rashid Jahan Angareywali', in Crystal Bartolovich and Neil Lazarus (eds) *Marxism, Modernity and Postcolonial Studies*, pp. 150–166. Cambridge: Cambridge University Press.

Jahan, Rasheed. 1995. 'Woh ('That One')', in M.T. Khan (trans) and Susie Tharu and K. Lalitha (eds) *Women Writing in India*, Vol. II, *The Twentieth Century*, pp. 119–122. New Delhi: Oxford University Press.

Jahan, Rashid. 2014. 'That One', in Rakshanda Jalil (trans and ed) *A Rebel and Her Cause: The Life and Work of Rashid Jahan*, pp. 117–120. New Delhi: Women Unlimited.

Jalil, Rakshanda. 2014. *A Rebel and Her Cause: The Life and Work of Rashid Jahan*. New Delhi: Women Unlimited.

Kanga, Firdaus. 2008. *Trying to Grow*. New Dehli: Penguin Books India and Ravi Dayal Publisher.

Karnad, Girish. 2005. 'Broken Images', in Girish Karnad (ed) *Collected Plays*, Vol. II, pp. 261–287. New Delhi: Oxford University Press.

Miles, M. 2000. 'Disability on a Different Model: Glimpses of an Asian Heritage', *Disability and Society*, 15(4): 603–618.

Mitchell, David T. and Sharon L. Snyder. 2000. *Narrative Prosthesis: Disability and the Dependencies of Discourse*. Ann Arbor, MI: University of Michigan Press.

Quayson, Ato. 2007. *Aesthetic Nervousness: Disability and the Crisis of Representation*. New York, NY: Columbia University Press.

Schweik, Susan M. 2009. *The Ugly Laws: Disability in Public*. New York, NY: New York University Press.

Siddiqui, Shakeel. 2006. *Rashid Jahan Ki Kahaniyan*. New Delhi: Vani Publications.

Sinha, Indra. 2007. *Animal's People*. New York, NY: Simon and Schuster.

Spivak, Gayatri Chakravorty. 2008. 'The Politics of Translation', in Gayatri Chakravorty Spivak (ed) *Outside in the Teaching Machine*, pp. 200–225. New York, NY: Routledge.

18

DISABILITY AND THE CALL FOR PRAYER

Translating Khalid Jawed's short story 'Koobad'

Sania Hashmi

Khalid Jawed's story 'Koobad' begins with two quotes, one in English, and the other in Urdu. The English quote states: 'The story may psychologically support the resolution but it does not logically justify it'. The other quote in Urdu reads: *Hum keechad ke saney jooton ke saath hi behishht ki sarzameen par qadam rakh sakte hain* (It is only in our mud-stained shoes that we can step onto the surface of heaven)[1] (Jawed 1999: 35). With the two seemingly incompatible quotes setting the tone for the narrative, one is left with the task of finding the connection between the self-awareness of the story's moral relativism as conveyed in the prelude and the non-negotiability of the mud-stained shoes. Consequently, the translator is left with the task of identifying this self-assertive resolution of the story that it so pointedly supports but does not dare to justify while communicating how the tragedy of the mud-stained shoes came about therein. Analysing the nature of the difficulties faced in translating Khalid Jawed's short story 'Koobad', the first part of the chapter places disability in the theological framework of Islam to understand what is expected of a disabled individual for her to lead a faith-sanctioned successful life. The second part highlights the role played by the story in exploring the idea of 'disability and guilt' in the theological framework established previously while the third part of the chapter tries to understand the task of the translator by highlighting the limitations of translating the translated. The fourth part argues how Urdu as the source language does not require an identification of the nature of disability through its reliance on a poetic-descriptive analysis, despite making it the cornerstone of the protagonist's existence not just as a failed Muslim in this world but also as determining his destiny in the Hereafter. In conclusion, this chapter argues that the amused tone of the narrator as a righteous and ableist Muslim presenting to us the tragic life of the protagonist in contradistinction to his own normative understanding is one which is reflective of the opening quote in English and therefore ends up binding the translator to the task of psychological support sans logical justification.

'Koobad' is a story about an aged man with a hunched back and a disproportion-ate body who has been literally and metaphorically woken up from his apostasy by the voice of a *fakir* on his way to waking people up for *sehri* during the holy month of Ramzan. The story spans the distance covered by the unnamed protagonist, who, having recently found faith, is in search of a mosque where he can offer his Eid prayers for the first time in his life. As he is covering the distance to the mosque with great difficulty in the hope of forgiveness from God, he recounts instances from his life where he had made it a point to forgive not just people but all living and non-living beings for their injustice to him during his lifetime. The idea of forgive-ness dominates the narrative wherein the narrator observes with great amusement just how much care the protagonist had taken to not only forgive everything and everyone he ever came in contact with but also to remember and reiterate the fact that he had forgiven them. There is just one question that haunts most parts of the story, namely, what is it really that he seeks forgiveness for? The answer to which is provided by the narrator who speaks for the disabled protagonist when he says,

> He wasn't aware of his sins, but what difference does the knowledge of one's sins make anyway? The fact remains that they consider you a sinner because the very form of your eyes, your lips, your head, the structure of your bones, are akin to that of a sinner. You also appear as alert as a sinner and that is just about enough reason.

There has to be a reason why God in his divine wisdom would give him the body that he did, and it is for that incontestable reason that he must now seek forgiveness. This is but an instance of the involved-yet-removed position adopted by the narrator, and by extension the translator, in communicating the aporia faced by the protagonist where psychological support and logic cannot coexist. In translating the original line '*Aur tum mujrim ki tarah chaukanne bhi nazar aate ho, bas itna kaafi hai*' (Jawed 1999: 38) to 'You also appear as alert as a sinner and that is just about enough reason', the idea is to communicate the fact that when the narrator is calling out the shallowness of the society he is also accepting the fact that there is something awry about the protagonist. He may be counting himself out of the list, but he is at the same time testifying to the empirical proof on which their deduction is premised. And this, by and large, is the position adopted by the narrator throughout the story. The gaze of the narrator not only originates in the normative but also derives its legitimacy from it. In addition to this, since the very being of the story is located in a theological framework, the norma-tive that the narrator espouses is also one of normative religiosity such that the narrator by virtue of being able is apparently a superior Muslim and therefore legitimised to draw judgements on the accuracy of the protagonist's attempts at redeeming himself.

The spectre of the disabled Muslim

> Believers, when you rise to pray, wash your faces and your hands as far as the elbow, and wipe your heads and your feet to the ankle.
>
> (Qur'an 5: 6)

The preceding lines from the Holy Qur'an give directions as to how one must cleanse him- or herself before he or she can offer his or her *namaz*. In an exercise that is bound by strict rules and a 'rigidly defined choreography'(Dokumaci 2011: 129) where it can be performed only during specific time slots during the day while facing the *qibla* – predefined for people across the world based on the direction of their respective locations from Mecca – one of the quintessential prerequisites for someone to be able to offer the *namaz* is cleanliness, which is obtained through a process of ablution or *abdest/vuzu*. One cannot offer one's prayers unless one has performed the *vuzu* first and has therefore become clean or *paak*. This procedure includes the rinsing of various parts of the body which presume a physical ability which allows one to stand, sit, and bend at will even before the actual *namaz* begins, which in its performativity betrays the assumption of its subject being an able-bodied individual. Additionally, *namaz*, or daily prayer, is one of the five *farz* in the Islamic tradition, *farz* being those acts which are mandatory for every human being. Arseli Dokumaci points out,

> The first *rekàt* and following ones have some slight variations, but the main movements remain as described. Throughout the performance of *namaz*, communicating with the outside world, making movement that is not part of the choreography, and uttering any sound other than the recitations are strictly forbidden. Should any occur, the *rekàt* must be repeated. The prescribed formulas for *abdest* and *namaz* require a functional body that can kneel down, stand up, lie prostrate, and raise arms.
>
> (2011: 130)

What then is the scope for the disabled Muslim in the larger scheme of religiosity especially when his or her fate in the Hereafter is contingent on her conduct in this world?

Beginning from the very beginning, Vardit Rispler-Chaim returns to the Qur'an to understand how it addresses disability and what sanctions have been made for it in a scripture that essentially lays out the codes of conduct for all of humanity till the end of time. She writes:

> Turning now to examine Arabic terminology, we may often come across labels for bearers of specific disabilities such as the *a'ma* (blind), the *asamm* (deaf), the *abkam* or *akhras* (dumb, mute), the *a'raj* (lame), the *majnun* (insane) and the *khuntha* (hermaphrodite). There are also feminine forms for the same adjectives, such as *'amya'* (blind), *'arja'* (lame), *majnuna* (insane), etc., to indicate that the disabled person is a woman. In classical Islamic sources I could not identify any single general term that would combine all people with disabilities as a group. . . . The fact that no single term in Islamic law encompasses all disabilities might in itself teach us something about attitudes to the disabled in Islamic societies. . . . It is only in contemporary literature that we find somewhat generalized terms, such as *ashab al-'ahat* or *dhawu al-'ahat* ("owners" or bearers of impairments, defects), *mu'awwaqun* or *mu'aqun*

(literally, those held back by difficulty and limitations on their mental or physical functions), and *'ajaza* or *'ajizun*, pl. of *'ajiz* (a weak person, unable to do things, like the old).

(Rispler-Chaim 2007: 4)

What are the possible conclusions one can draw from the fact that a language's vocabulary does not have a word to signify disability as a larger umbrella term for a range of conditions? It is important to distinguish between the significance given to specific conditions and the need to have a general term that encompasses all disabilities. Does the absence of a general term end up excluding the disabled population while reinforcing the hegemony of the able majority? Or does it exclude those minority disabilities that fall outside the ones that are most commonly found? Is there really a binary therein or is it simply a double marginalisation of the disabled Other? Perhaps one can understand these contentions better by analysing the concessions, if any, that are made for the disabled population in the established codes of conduct which demand strict physical tasks to be performed with maximum accuracy.

Since the central idea is to remain clean at all time, those with incontinence – whether temporary or permanent are advised to keep purifying themselves and find ways to stop the leakage by blocking or sealing the concerned orifices. On the question of physical ability and performing the *namaz*, there are varying rulings made by the different schools of thought which highlight the nature of exemptions made for those who are absolutely incapable of performing the rituals. However, the only thing agreed upon is that one must push oneself to the limits to reach the standard as much as possible. About the different interpretations, Rispler-Chaim writes,

> The ruling with regard to prayer is that anyone who is Muslim, sane, and mature, is obliged to pray, or make up with prayer at a later date for the missed prayers (*qada'*). According to another Shi'i jurist, a man who testified that he had been sick for four months, and therefore could not pray, was told that he need not repeat the missed prayers, because "*al-marid laysa kal-sahih*" (the sick person is not like the healthy one). In other words, the requirements from each regarding the religious duties are different. But generally, the Shi'i jurists require that the sick pray similarly to the healthy, as long as they are sane. The Hanafis too exempt the unconscious and the insane from praying, if their health condition exceeds five prayer occasions. If it lasts less than that, and the person regains consciousness or sanity, he or she has to make up for the missed prayers. The Hanbalis require the belated completion of a prayer if *junun* (insanity) and *ighma'* (unconsciousness) occurred after the beginning of that service or just before its ending time.

(2007: 23)

It is important to notice the conflation in this citation between sickness and disability. And it is in this difference that the importance of linguistic signification assumes greater prominence. Wherever these and other concessions are made, they have been done while keeping the sick and the old in mind. The primary and most obvious difference between them is the simple fact that while sickness is temporary, disability is not. Consequently, the concessions do not address people like the protagonist in 'Koobad' who have endured the process of disablement over an extended time.

The primary reason behind this ambiguity is the fact that there is no word for disability in the Qur'an which could have clarified the issue, assuming that the disabled is on par with the able subject. Rispler-Chaim concludes that the word *marid* (sick person) or *marad* (sickness) can be taken to qualify both sickness and disability. However, this chapter argues that the preceding assumption on part of scholars like Rispler-Chaim, Bazna and Hatab (2005) display not only an excessive simplification but also perhaps a disloyal translation of the word *marad* (Persian/ Urdu: *maraz*) which is essentially characterised by its curability and temporariness. The etymological meaning of the word clearly states that it signifies disease. To use *disease* and *disability* synonymously is also an extension of ableist sensibilities as a diseased individual would be as removed from the lived experience of the disabled as the dominant able individual.

Disability at the limits of spiritual awakening

In the short story 'Koobad', the protagonist had spent his whole life having nothing to do with either God or godliness. However, on that fateful night when the *fakir*'s voice woke him up, the narrator tells us that up until that moment the protagonist had assumed a certain companionship between his soul and his body and that it was only in that moment that his soul had abandoned his body and followed after the trailing voice of the *fakir*. While the companionship lasted, the body had steered clear of all such painful rituals that constitute religiosity and the soul was at peace with the same. However, with the soul's betrayal of the body to the voice of religious conscience, the protagonist is forced to inflict on the body all such normative processes that he had erstwhile avoided. However, despite all his attempts at learning how to perform *vuzu* or the process of cleansing oneself, and his repeated attempts to memorise the many verses that constitute the *namaz* as he walks to the mosque on Eid on the road to salvation, the road for him remains an unending one. No matter how assiduously he learnt the *vuzu* rituals, as he walked to the mosque, he was aware of the fact that he had forgotten most of it and that he was therefore impure, invoking, more than anything else, disgust in the narrator. As Hughes points out, '[d]isgust is a moral tribunal that is used to judge others, to assign them to an inferior status and at the same time make a compelling case for 'our' superiority, 'our' place above the herd, 'our' purity. In its judgements, disgust is harsh and invalidating' (Hughes 2012: 32). The cumulative effect of all the misery and pain he had brought upon his body following his turn to religion is manifested in the acute difficulty he faces in walking to the mosque. However, what he had planned wasn't meant to be. Just as he could not cleanse his impurity, he realises that he can never really arrive at a moment when he can actually offer his prayers. In trying to understand at what point the 'calculus of disability' begins in the process of disablement, Dokumaci writes:

> Bodies appear able to the extent that they can conform to preordained social routines and appear disabled to the extent that they cannot conform to social routine. Because of internalizing social impositions, disabled people may feel compelled to perform *namaz* in the same way that everyone else is performing *namaz*, compelled to embody the same material gestures that everyone else is embodying, even to the degree that such efforts result in physical pain and discomfort. The ability to wash one's feet during *abdest* without asking for help, the capacity to attend communal prayers without using a chair, or the performance of any taken-for-granted material gesture is where the calculus of disability begins to manifest itself.
>
> (2011: 138)

Despite his sincerest efforts, he cannot be co-opted into the normative because he is always already condemned, always already an Other. For instance, when his wife tells him, "No matter how hard you try, your face always looks dirty", he is immediately reminded of the girl he had liked as a young man who had told him the same thing. The only two women he had ever been interested in had told him the exact same thing. Again, the only emotion he invoked in them was disgust. As William Ian Miller argues, '[disgust] . . . judges ugliness and deformity to be moral offences', and 'it knows no distinction between the moral and the aesthetic, collapsing failures in both into an undifferentiated revulsion' (1997: 21). This interaction, which inevitably ends in invalidation in every facet of his life, is a cycle that the protagonist cannot escape. It is not for lack of trying that he must step on to the surface of heaven in his mud-stained shoes, he is condemned to it.

It is this condemnation that becomes the bone of contention in identifying the story's resolution. The impossibility of psychological support to coexist with logical justification is manifested in the narrator's take on the everyday experiences of the disabled protagonist. Therefore, the narrative has no dearth of sympathy for the protagonist but no grounds for empathy. When the protagonist prepares to present himself before God, the narrator records the proceedings in a tone of utter amusement. For instance, for the first time in his life, when the protagonist has religiously deprived himself of food and water during the Ramzan fasts, the narrator acknowledges the same while also highlighting how pointless and inaccurate his efforts were. He is quick to dismiss his fasts as mere *faakas* for the simple reason that he had not offered his prayers during those fasts, and the able narrator has no qualms in casually letting it slip to the reader that these fasts don't mean anything anyway. The narrator says, '*Zaahir hai uske ye rozey sirf ek qism ke faaka hi the*', translated as 'Obviously these fasts were nothing more than *faakas*', the focus of the translation was not so much on the type of *faaka* it was but on the obviousness of it being one. According to Hughes, '[i]n the specific case of disability, the tragic object – the impaired body – is judged to be, relative to the non-disabled self, an unfortunate and broken being' (2012: 72). In addition to this, there is also a constant infantilisation of the protagonist wherein all his attempts at redemption are compared to a child's enthusiasm for new toys. Thus, while the narrator pities the protagonist's troubles, he does not share them.

The sympathetic stance of the narratorial witness finds culmination in the climax of the story when the wandering protagonist arrives at the graveyard mosque after having failed to find any congregation where he could have joined everyone else for the Eid prayers that he had so eagerly been planning for. As he collapses outside its shut door, he can only hear the *azaan* (the call for prayer) from every direction. Before he dies a most poignant death, he says to himself, "*Zaroori nahi hai ki har insan ko eid ki namaz padhne ka mauka mil sake, magar yakeenan Allah bada hai. Apni tareef mein di gayi azaan se bhi bada*" (Perhaps not everyone gets to offer the Eid prayers. God is indeed great. Greater than these *azaans* sung in His praise) (Jawed 1999: 42). The narrator bears witness to his death only to remark how

> [w]hen they tried to straighten his stiff body in the morning, his forefathers' cap fell to the ground, the hump was more prominent than ever, and the coins in his *shervani* filled the air with their clattering against the cold and silent graveyard floor.

The narrator, who had passionately participated in determining the legitimacy of the protagonist's attempts to reconcile with his faith, ends up as a dispassionate witness to the latter's failure. What remains is the tone of obviousness at the course of events which had to culminate in failure and death.

The translator's task of psychological support sans logical justification

What then is the task of the narrator's translator? If disability is the central character of the narrative, the narrator is once removed from the lived experience. If the translator must re-communicate the words of the narrator, she is twice removed from the same. Every single event mentioned in the story is a consequence of the protagonist's disability and it is these consequences that the narrator narrates. Since he is a witness, the disability is always already in the realm of perception, and therefore any information about it is descriptive. As a result, we do not know what the hunched back has to do with the inability of the protagonist to consummate his marriage, or why did his backbone give him so much pain. We just know that it did. Apart from the dehumanisation that it unwittingly entails, it also contributes to creating a sense of sympathy sans understanding.

What then are the feelings that the disabled Other invokes in the ableist Self? Bill Hughes argues that

> [t]he object of compassion and pity in 'the real world' is always a victim, the other whose shoes one does not want to be in, the one who invokes the pity-ing response, 'there but for fortune go I', the one whose invalidity is redemption and validation for the valid. The charitable attachment to the disabled other is saturated with selfishness because it sustains one's sense of ontological security and wholeness.
>
> (2012: 71)

Thus, while the narrator would never want to be in the mud-stained shoes of the protagonist, he will point out the stains to his fellow able and religious members of the community, if only in a charitable fashion. The protagonist then becomes a manifestation of what-could-have-been and what-should-never-be. 'In the non-disabled imaginary', Hughes argues,

> impairment/disability is equivalent to ruin, a blighted life, a life not worth living. Disability is a collapse in one's human currency, the destruction of one's social, emotional and cultural capital. It is an irretrievable stumble into a dark and negative existence, a gateway to ontological invalidation. All light and positivity is extinguished.
>
> (2012: 72)

In 'Koobad', the disabled protagonist is not only the representation of a 'blighted life' in respect of this world but also with regard to the Hereafter. Apart from being 'ontologically invalidated', the disabled protagonist is also condemned to be a failed Muslim whose every attempt at redemption must therefore also end in failure. There is a reason why the most common adjective used to describe him is *ganda* (dirty) when the first thing Islam requires of him is cleanliness. Rispler-Chaim points out,

> Al-Ghazali, the Shafi'i jurist turned Sufi who died in 1111, quotes several prophetic hadiths which encourage purity: 'Religion is based on cleanliness'; 'The key for prayer is purity'; 'Purity is one half of the belief', and two Qur'anic verses in which it is recommended to keep pure because 'Allah loveth the purifiers' (**9**, 108) (Pickthall) and 'He would purify you and would perfect His grace upon you, that ye may give thanks' (**5**, 6).
>
> (2007: 19)

Throughout the story, the narrator makes it a point to highlight every instance where despite making an effort, the protagonist ends up becoming dirty. In the particular instance, when he was returning from work and lost his balance because of a live electric wire, it is not on the road but in the drain that he must fall to reunite with the sewage that he is compared to. Even on his way to offer the Eid prayers, he must walk through mud and soil in the clothes he took so much care to put together. In his very being, he cannot be a good Muslim because he is condemned to live with an impurity he cannot shake off. And it is the narrator's disgust at that impurity that the translator must endorse and communicate lest she deprives the text of the religious framework in which it is situated.

Translating disability from Urdu

One of the difficulties faced in translating from Urdu to English in general and with questions of disability, in particular, is the nature of the source language which is essentially poetic. It is not with a sense of false pride but as a matter of fact that one must establish the inherently poetic vocabulary of Urdu prose. Analogous, and not by chance, to the position of Muslims in India, the fate of Urdu was deeply entwined with the many vulnerabilities felt by the minority population. Shamsur Rehman Faruqi argues that around the close of the 18th century, attempts were made to separate Urdu from the common language and anoint it as over and above the crassness of the common tongue (Faruqi 2003: 850). Arguing how the motive of these purist tendencies was to create an elite class, he writes:

> Within this new system, codes of conduct and protocols of behaviour – such as the *mushā'sirah*, or literary gathering – were developed. These were mostly in place by the 1760s, soon spreading to all Rekhtah/Hindi centres: Lucknow, Benares, Allahabad, Murshidabad, Patna, Aurangabad, Hyderabad, Surat, Rampur, Madras, and so on. One important manifestation of this new Urdu literary culture was its almost morbid obsession with "correctness" in language. Undue – and sometimes even almost mindless – emphasis on "correct" or "standard, sanctioned" speech in poetry and prose, and even in everyday converse, has been one of the most interesting and least understood aspects of Urdu culture from the mid-eighteenth century onwards. Persian's immense prestige . . . may account for a part for this emphasis.
>
> (Faruqi 2003: 850)

The extensions of the purist tendencies can be seen in the highly compact vocabulary of the language which does not boast of great representational potential, as can be seen in the case of disability in general and specific conditions in particular which are often clubbed together under umbrella terms signifying a range of conditions that lie outside the normative. When the idea is to cultivate a cultured and elite community, its imaginary hinges on the fantasy of seeing itself as *embodying* the very invincibility that it aims for. And it is this imaginary which has no space for the disabled Other who is always already outside the 'hegemony of ableist sensibilities' (Campbell 2010: 105). As Margrit Shildrick argues,

> [g]iven the explicit privileging of wholeness, independence and integrity demanded of the able-bodied subject, the cultural imaginary is highly

invested in fantasies of an invulnerable body. Yet, in the face of disability that threatens always to claim its identity in the selfsame, such fantasies generate a normative anxiety that cannot be allayed.

(2005: 757)

Consequently, the disabled is not named because his disability falls outside the said imaginary.

Essentially the language of Ghalib and Zauq, it was only in the early decades of the 20th century that Urdu prose arrived at the literary scene through pioneering contributions of people like Premchand, Manto, and the Progressive Writers' Association. The first Urdu-to-English dictionary, compiled by Maulana Abdul Haq, was published in the 1930s from Aurangabad. The only other reputed dictionary to have come after that was the recent *Oxford Advanced Dictionary*. The point one is trying to make here is that with its springs firmly rooted in poetry, the vocabulary of Urdu prose is overwhelmingly limited, and the repercussions of these limitations are clearly felt during the process of translation. This is particularly relevant in the current context because the entire story is premised upon the protagonist's troubles with his *reed ki haddi*. However, when the translator – acquainted with the wide taxonomy of human biology in the target language – has to identify and describe the ailment, he or she is spoilt for choice at the risk of his or her fidelity to the source language. *Reed ki haddi* in Urdu is generally used to denote two things, the spine and the metaphorical lack of one. It refers to any, every, and all the parts along one's backbone while also used to call someone spineless in idiomatic Urdu.

Therefore, one is aware of the many connotations implied by the writers in choosing *reed ki haddi* as the main site of the protagonist's tryst with disability. While it can be translated as the tail bone, the vertebrae, the backbone and so on, I knew I had to go with spine because the pun at work in the original must also be communicated. Therefore, in its poetising of the prosaic, what is actually undermined is the nature of the protagonist's disability which is never really identified. It is for this reason that the reader will never know the possible and probable interconnectedness of the protagonist's many biological and behavioural traits. The story strives to establish the form of the protagonist as an Other on which is projected the many abjections of the Self, as a result of which the remainder is greater than the sum of its parts. For instance, why was he incapable of sexual activity even as a young man? If it is a consequence of his hunched back or his disproportionate body, as is only suggested in the story, one can never know the connection therein for the simple reason that the nature of his disability has not been identified because the vocabulary of the source language does not allow it.

Conclusion

In a story dominated by the poesy of its language and the rhythm of the *azaan*, the protagonist is condemned to a prosaic existence which is therefore always already rootless. As he is bombarded with the *azaan* from every corner of the sky in the story's climax, his abject Self is analogical to his disability as a character in the story. Just as he can never really arrive at a point where he can finally offer his *namaz*, the disability is disallowed by the source language to emerge at the forefront of the discourse despite being its centre. And because this centre is situated outside the linguistic structure of the story, the translator, too, is thrown into a quagmire of deference. What follows is a constant undermining of the actual disability which is always already absent in its presence and present in its absence. This is further established through the lack of any investment on part of the narrator in finding the source of the protagonist's troubles. We know about all the miserable things that happened to him because of the body that he had, but we are never told the actual reasons behind it. Just as the protagonist is too soiled and smeared to be co-opted into normative religiosity, his disability is too prosaic to be taken up by a language that is so pompously poetic.

Since the posture of the narrator is one of translating for the general physically able and religiously righteous reader the many troubles of the disabled and irreligious protagonist, the task of the story's translator is therefore one of translating the translated. When the narrator dismisses the protagonist's attempts with an audacious degree of amusement, he is sharing a story, a joke if you will, with the majority, the translator is condemned to communicating that fascination. The translator is bound to lending psychological support sans logical justification. Just as it is only in his mud-stained shoes that he can step on to the surface of heaven, it is only with the same degree of muddled amusement as the narrator that the translator must traverse along and between the lines of an ableist, normative, and righteous testimony.

Note

1 All translations are mine.

Works cited

Campbell, Fiona Kumari. 2010. *Contours of Ableism: The Production of Disability and Abledness*. Basingstoke: Palgrave Macmillan.

Dokumaci, Arseli. 2011. 'Performance of Muslim Daily Prayer by Physically Disabled Practitioners', in Darla Schumm and Michael Stoltzfus (eds) *Disability in Judaism, Christianity, and Islam: Sacred Texts, Historical Traditions, and Social Analysis*, pp. 127–140. New York, NY: Palgrave Macmillan.

Faruqi, Shamsur Rahman. 2003. 'A Long History of Urdu Literary Cultures, Part 1; Naming and Placing a Literary Culture', in Sheldon Pollock (ed) *Literary Cultures in History; Reconstructions from South Asia*, pp. 805–863. Berkeley, Los Angeles and London: University of California Press.

Hughes, Bill. 2012. 'Fear, Pity and Disgust: Emotions and the Non-disabled Imaginary', in Nick Watson, Alan Roustone and Carol Thomas (eds) *Routledge Handbook of Disability Studies*. London and New York: Routledge.

Jawed, Khalid. 1999. 'Koobad', *Shabkhoon Urdu Monthy*. Allahabad. 32(232): 35–42.

Miller, William Ian. 1997. *The Anatomy of Disgust*. Cambridge, MA: Harvard University Press.

Rispler-Chaim, Vardit. 2007. *Disability in Islamic Law*. Dordrecht: Springer.

Shildrick, Margrit. 2005. 'The Disabled Body, Genealogy and Undecidability', *Cultural Studies*, 19(6): 755–770.

INDEX

Note: Page numbers in *italics* indicates figures and **bold** indicates tables respectively.

Ability Unlimited 61–62, 66–68
able-bodied 37, 42–43, 45, 47, 49, 100, 108,
    110–112, 142, 161, 168–169, 176, 178,
    189, 195, 208, 223, 245, 251
'able-bodied', norm of 174
'able-bodied normalcy' 178
able-bodied-reader-specific texts 45
'abled-disabled' 43
ableism, cultural notions of 22
ableism, emotional infrastructure of 128
activism 3, 19, 45, 55–56, 61, 67, 103,
    109, 237
adolescent dreams 113
aesthetic nervousness 11–12, 224, 229
aesthetics, reconceptualisation of 68
afterlife 51n2
Agarwalla, Jyotiprasad 127
Agha, Sohail 104
Ahom kingdom 122
Alam, Fakirul 108
Allan, Julie 48
alternative aesthetics 19, 47–48, 51, 55,
    61, 68
alternative cultural production 47
alternative vision of humanism 166
Altieri, Elizabeth 44
Alvarez, Román 56
American Baptist Missionaries 126
Anand, Shilpaa 23, 231–232, 234, 236,
    238, 242
Anderson, Philip M. 45

Andha Yug (The Blind Age) 89
Andrew, Dudley 77
Angareywali 235, 240
animal metaphor 31
Animal shelter 182
Animal's People 234
Appiah, Kwame Anthony 40
Apter, Emily 42
archaisms 41
Asch, Adrienne 190
asexual objectification of women 190
aspirational qualities 235
Assamese culture 122, 125–126
Assamese literature 126–130
'assistive' or prosthetic technologies 170
Aubrecht, Katie 35

Baecque, Antoine de 214
Bagchi, Jatindra M. 162
Baker, Mona 55–56
Bandyopadhyay, Manik 135
Bandyopadhyay, Tarashankar 133–135
Bargohain, Rajashree 20, 119–120, 126, 130
Barker, Clare 9, 85, 88–89, 125, 222
Barounis, Cynthia 69
Bashir, Vaikom Mohd 1
Bassnett, Susan 41, 73, 80, 105, 119, 123,
    125, 133, 135
Beckford, James 12
Beethoven 119–131; analysis of 120, 125;
    disability and 124–125; disability in

126–130; figure projection 130; mental image of 128; narrative structure 124; nature of language 122; as a postcolonial narrative 129; revolves around an autobiographical episode 121; tale-within-a-tale structure 124, 126; translation of 123; treatment of disability 125; Western material 123
Beloved 162
Bengal Renaissance 134
Benjamin, Walter 19, 38, 51n1, 115, 136, 142, 238
Berger, Ronald J. 97
Bermann, Sandra 52n5
Bérubé, Michael 2, 162
Bezborooah, Lakshminath 126
Bhabha, Homi 105
Bhagavad Gita 19, 55, 61, 63–64
Bhagavad Gita on Wheels 19, 55, 61, 63; form and content 63; Krishna's *Vishvarupa* 65; Narasimha 66; representation of Vishnu *64*; representative images of the *Dashavatar* 65; text and performance 64–66; wheelchairs as 'chariots of war' 61–63
Bhagwat Purana 187
Bhambani, Meenu 174
Bhandarkar Oriental Research Institute 56
Bharati, Dharamvir 22, 89, 186
Bharatiya Janata Party (BJP) 9
Bharatnatyam 61–63, 67
'Bharatnatyam on Wheels' *62–63*
bhasha literature(s) 228
Bhattacharjee, Ritwick 198, 200, 204, 208, 210
Bhattacharya, Ritwick 22
Bhave, P. B. 220
blindness, philosophical implications 168
body language 14, 33
Bollywood 227
Bolt, David 10, 26–27, 35
BORI Mahabharata 56
boundedness of a translation 38
Brahma Vaivarta Purana 188
Bṛhadāraṇyakopaniṣad 168
bride-price agreement 57–58; *see also* Ramayana
brittle-bone syndrome 234
Broken Images 234
Brown, Lerita Coleman 229
Buranjis 122
Burhi Air Sadhu (Grandma's Tales) 126

Cahir, Linda Costanzo 80–81
'calculus of disability' 248
Campbell, Fiona Kumari 251
caregiving, idea of 179
Cassia Tora plant *see* Thakara
caste divides, critique of 28
Central Board of Secondary Education (CBSE) 20, 85, 90–92, 94–95; *see also* Goongey
centrality of activism 183
Certeau, Michel de 226
Chakravarty, Radha 19, 25, 28, 32, 36, 108
Chaliha, Saurabh Kumar 119–122, 124, 129–130, 131n3
Chamberlain, Lori 104
Chāndogyopaniṣad 168–169
Chandran, Abhilash 13, 153, 155
'characterization' stock feature of 213
characters with physical disabilities 109
charity model 174
Chasie, Charles 125
Chatterjee, Partha 134, 226
Chaturvedi, Mukul 21–22, 186, 188, 190
Chellappanasari 74–76, 78–80
Chitra Harshvardhan 19, 37–38, 44, 48, 52, 54
Cilappatikaram 148
cinema adaptations 67
Clark, Laurence 93
code-mixing 22
codes and conducts of 'normalcy' 135
code-shifting 227
code-switching 22, 41
collaborative translation 41–42
collective authorship 41
collective social prejudice 30
colonialism 123, 125, 131, 235
common language 160, 170, 251
communalism 235
communicative through gestures 46
conceptual ideas 221
Concerto for the Left Hand: Disability and the Defamiliar Body 5
Conroy, Colette 68
context-sensitive examination 23, 232
conventional beliefs 21
corporeal difference, theory of 2, 23
Couser, Thomas G. 196
crawling 156
critical avoidance 10–11; *see also* Bolt, David
Critical Disability Studies (CDS) model 43
cross-cultural dialogue 180
cultural alterity 37–38
cultural belief 174

cultural borders 33
cultural communication 141
cultural stereotyping 150
cultural transmission 37
Culture and Imperialism 137
culture-specific terms 193
Cummins, Robert A. 79

Dagut, Menacham B. 182
dalit-centric texts 97
dalit literature 114, 190, 221–222
dalit text 104, 147, 153
dalit woman's resistance 152
Das, Shilpa 21, 173, 178, 180
Dasa, Sarala 55–56, 59
Dashavtar 63
Davidson, Michael 5
Davis, Lennard J. 3–4, 7, 10, 45, 47, 75, 177,
    215–216, 218, 221–222, 229
Davis, Lionel 12
Davison, Claire 37
de-centred subjects 226
deconstruction theory 182
defamiliarising 158
de Man, Paul 181
'depressive effect' 111
'de-provencialising' 40
Derrida, Jacques 199–201, 207
Deshpande, Kusumavati 220
desire and disability 109–112
Devi, Mahasweta 25, 28–29, 34
Devy, G. N. 41
Dharwadkar, Vinay 41
Dignani, Vanda 175
directive principles 9
disabilism 135, 139, 182
disability activists 213
disability-as-disaster narrative 175
disability-as-translation 180
disability-centric text 190, 192, 196
disability dance 68
disability movement 47, 170
Disability Studies 2, 4, 6, 11–12, 19–21,
    23–24, 42, 72, 97, 221–222
Disability Studies Reader, The 221
disability studies scholars 3, 5, 205, 209n5
disability terms 14
Disability Theory 5
disabled Muslim 244–247
disabledness 50
disabled women, oppression of 177
'disciplinary normalisation' 164
Discipline and Punish 177
disfigurement-as-disability 28

disruptive style 41
divine reprisal 174
Dokumaci, Arseli 245, 248
Doll's House, A 42
Doniger, Wendy 116
double radicalism 26
dream sequence 209n6
Drishtidaan 107–109, 113, 116
Dubey, Shubhra 20, 84, 86
Dusi, Nicola 68
dysfunctionality 25

economic deprivation 22, 153
Eliot, T. S. 209n4
Elizabethan comedy 115
emancipatory socio-literary practice,
    dualistic model 26
encouragement for disability awareness 163
Enforcing Normalcy 3–4, 7
English/American colloquialisms 227
English textbooks 92
Enlightenment thinkers 160
epistemic re-orientation 232
Essential Tagore, The 108
ethos and ethics of translation 37
euphemisms 14, 47, 237, 239
European Enlightenment thought 160
Even-Zohar, Itmar 51n4
existentialist crisis 182
experience of disablement 2, 4–6, 8, 10–12,
    21, 240
Extraordinary Bodies 4, 29
Ezekeil, Nissim 94

facial disfigurement 234–238
facial expressions 48
Famished Road 88
Faruqi, Shamsur Rehman 251
Faruque, Yasmin 108
Faulkner, William 8
female disabled body 176
female experience 186, 189, 196
feminine sexual being 194
femininity 188–190; normative assumptions
    of 189
feminist disability, theme of 179
feminist movement 14
feminist translation practice 14, 194, 196
feminist translation strategies 22, 186, 191
feminist translation theories 22, 186
fictional representations 226
Film and Television Institute of India 76
Film Finance Corporation 76
Fine, Michelle 190

Fisher, R. A. 222
Flotow, Luise von 191
footnote 34
forgiveness 23, 149, 244
Foucault, Michel 164, 177–178
Freakery: Cultural Spectacles of the Ordinary Body 32
French, Sally 174, 178
French Revolution 214
full citizenship 43

Gadgil, Gangadhar 220
Gallagher, D. J. 5
Galton, Francis 222
Gandhi 17, 86
Ganguly, Somrita 20, 107–108, 110, 118
Ganjefa 98–100, 104
Garland-Thomson, Rosemarie 3–12, 29, 32, 42, 44–45, 47, 49, 177–178, 188, 190
Geertz, Clifford 41
gender-caste matrix 152
gendered dimension 186
gender ideology 165
gender-specific constraints 150
Gentzler, Edwin 38, 111
Ghai, Anita 10, 26, 43–44, 174–175
Ghalib 252
Ghosh, N. 6
Ghoshal, Ananya 21, 159–160, 162, 164, 170
glossary 34
Goffman, Erving 11, 178
Gokhale, Arvind 220
Goongey 20, 84–87, 89–95; critical refraction 91–92; empathy for *goonga* 94; geographical or linguistic markers 87; imagined public 89; impact of word *goonga* 93; introductory scene 86; lexical register of Khari Boli 87; narrative techniques 87; part of the CBSE curriculum 94–95; problematic text 90; in translation 92–94
Gopal, Priyamvada 237–238
Goswami, P. 122
Grimms' Fairy Tales 125
Grosz, Elizabeth 159
Gulki Banno 22, 186–196; anger and spirited defence 195; appearance as bride 189; coy gestures 195; cross-cultural translation 190; double standards and hypocrisy 193; effort to live life 187; farewell ritual 191; gendered experience of disability 192; humanity and indefatigable 193; identity crisis 195; normative sexual objectification 190;

performative aspect of surrender 194; revulsion, amusement and scorn 189; subjected to compassion and kindness 187; suffering 188; trials and tribulations 187; womanhood and femininity 190
Gupta, Jagadish 133–134, 142

Hahn, Harlan 190
Halmari, Helena 114
Handbook of Disability Studies 89
hand movements 48
Hans, Asha 174
Haq, Maulana Abdul 252
Harijan 17
Harini, Maheswari 142
Hashmi, Sania 23
Hassan, Bilquis Zafirul 98
Hatim, Basil 137
Heidegger, Martin 198
helplessness 88
Hermans, Theo 40, 57
heterogeneity, recognition of 26
'hijacking' 41
Hindi–Awadhi belt 191
Hindi film industry 227
Hindu gods, visualisation of 18
Hola, Malathi (para-athlete) 46
Holmes, James 51n3
Homel, David 41
host language (HL) expression 179
Hughes, Bill 74, 89, 97, 104, 109–110, 111, 128, 187, 235, 247, 249–250
'human morphology' 139
'Hunchback Bride, The' *see* Gulki Banno
Hutcheon, Linda 81

images and metaphors, innovative use of 41
immoral actions 240
impairment and able-bodiedness 160–161
'inclusive genius' 109
inclusive otherness 37
Independent, The 143–144n3
Independent Living Movement (ILM) 3
Indian disability movement 165
India–Pakistan partition 89, 201–202
Ingstad, Benedicte 125
intellectual disability 79
inter-semiotic translation 55–57, 68, 77, 80; *see also* translatability
inter-wars period 133
intra-cultural relationships 138
involved-yet-removed position 244
Iruttinte Aatmavu 73

Jahan, Rashid 2, 23, 231, 234–241
Jain, Shefalee 22, 211, 216
Jakobson, Roman 56, 77
Jalil, Rakshanda 231, 238, 240
Jawed, Khalid 8, 243–244, 249
Jedamski, Doris 121
Jnaneshawar 56
Johnson, Mark 204
Jordonova, Ludmilla 166
Joyce, James 209n4

'Kafka of Lucknow' 98
Kalliney, Peter 135
Kalyanpur, Maya 174
Kama, Amit 67
Kamala, N. 14
Kanga, Firdaus 234, 233
Kanna Panna 46
Kapoor, Himani 19, 55–56, 62, 68
Karnad, Girish 234
Kaṭhopaniṣad 168
Katkatha Puppet Arts 59–60, 69n4
Katkatha Puppet Arts Trust *30*, 60
Katkatha Puppet theatre 55
Kaushik, Sunil 8, 199, 206, 209
Kesavadev 76
Kesey, Ken 8
Khan, M.T. 231, 238, 240
Khora (Bengali register) 137
Khora Sheikh 137–138
Kinnarathumpikal 80; *see also* Thakara
Kleege, Georgina 114
Koka Deuta Aru Nati Lora 126
'Kona Aru Kuja' 126
Koobad 8, 243–244, 247, 250; protagonist
   in 247
Kothari, Rita 114, 117n10, 135, 190
Krebs, Katja 77
Kristeva, Julia 77
kulin 27–28, 34, 35n2
Kulkarni, G.A. 220–221
Kumar, Gulshan 61

Lackoff, George 204
Lal, Purushottama 41–42, 193
Lalita, K. 234–235
language: able-ist Language 205;
   of disability discourse 158; disabling language 203; fundamental
   comprehension of 22; of gestures 48;
   hegemony of 72; homogenising tendency
   of 206; lexical elements of 200; niche
   of 198; primal nature of 199; propriated
   Truths 199; role of 19; regional languages

133; 'singularity' of the structures 200;
   supplementary duality 200
Layanam 80; *see also* Thakara
Lee, Harper 8
Lefebvre, Henri 225
Lefevere, André 39, 73, 80, 84–85, 91,
   94–95
linguistic compulsions 240
linguistic hospitality 19, 40
linguistic transformation 28
literary activism 26
literary defamiliarisation 233
literary representation 16, 44, 72, 120,
   124–125, 162; cultural imaginary of 44;
   rich diversity of 51
lived experience of a disabled person 156
locating disability 42–44
Lohini Sagai 173–182
Lotbiniere-Harwood, Suzanne de 194
love–hate relationship 124
luminescence 102–103
lunacy 32

Madgulkar, Vyankatesh 220
Mahābhārata 2, 19, 55–57, 59, 61, 109, 162,
   188; dominant versions 59; Katkatha's
   interpretation of 59; retellings of 61;
   Sarala's version 59; Shakuni from *60*
'Mai Dukh ki Lambi Raat', reading of
   221–225
Mairs, Nancy 47
Maitrāyaṇīya Upaniṣad 168
Malayalam literature 73
male-oriented movies 80
Mangalam, B. 21, 146, 150, 152, 156, 158
Manimekalai 148
Manjapra, Kris 134
Man, Paul de 181
Manto, Saadat Hasan 1, 8, 98, 252
Marathi language, linguistic capacities
   of 220
Marathi literature 220–222, 225
Margolis, Howard 45
Marsh, Stephen 93
Marx, Eleanor 42
Masefi, Paddy 68
Mashi and Other Stories 108
Masood, N. 8
mass conversion of Dalits to Buddhism 220
Masud, Naiyer 98, 103–104
materiality of metaphor 127, 214
Matiyani, Sailesh 199, 201–202
Mc Cabe, Marita P. 79
McDowell, Linda 167

mediating 158
medical model of disability 178
Mehrez, Samia 136
Mehrotra, Arvind Krishna 109
Mehrotra, Nilika 43–44, 67
Melville, Herman 8
mentally retarded 76, 184
metaphorisation 88–90, 93
Midnights Children 88–89
Miles, M. 12, 23, 236–237, 239
Miller, William Ian 248
Millet-Gallant, Ann 109, 111
minority model 43
mirroring 147, 158
mirroring the "other", 147–148
Mishra, Vinod Kumar 45
Mitchell, David 8–9, 13, 44, 100, 102,
    110–113, 116, 126–127, 129, 131, 141,
    164, 205, 211–214, 222, 239
Mizrachi, Nissim 17–18
mobility 58, 98, 123, 139, 154–155, 169,
    181, 217, 229
modernity and liberation 141
modular translation 17–18
Mohanty, Prafulla Kumar 59
Mokashi-Punekar, Rohini 22, 220, 224,
    228, 230
Mooppan, Mathu 73, 75, 78–79, 81
Morrison, Tony 162
motherhood, ideal of 179
'motherland', corporeal attractiveness
    of 135
Mukherjee, Sujit 42, 116
Mukhopadhyay, Balaichand 135
multi-layered translation 140
Mulvey, Laura 80
Muṇḍaka Upaniṣad 168
Murderball 62
Murray, Stuart 222
Mushtaq, Aneesa 231, 238
'muteness', metaphor of 91
mythology 44, 187–188

Nair, M. T. Vasudevan 76
Nakshathrangale Kaaval 81
narrative prosthesis 44, 101, 126, 164
*Narrative Prosthesis: Disability and the
    Dependencies of Discourse* 213
narrative, regressive nature of 143
narratives and translation 149–151
narratorial witness 249
Nathan, Archna 60
National Council for Education, Research
    and Training (NCERT) 85–86

National Film Archives 76
national language debate 87
'natural human variations' 43
Natyashastra 67
Navajbai Ratan Tata Trust 46
NCERT curriculum 90; *see also* Goongey
Neog, Maheswar 122
neologisms, use of 41
*New India: A Weekly Record and Review of
    Modern Thought & Life* 162
Nietzsche, Friedrich 111
Nimati Koina, ('The Silent/Mute Damsel')
    126–127
Niranjana, Tejaswini 117n11, 122–123, 196
nirvicikitsa 236–238, 241
Nondi Natakam 148
non-disabled translation theories 21
non-speech-sounds-tongue 48–49
nonverbal sign 56
normative femininity, privileges of 188, 194
normative religiosity 244, 253

objectification and exploitation 30
objective translation 107, 129
O'Brien, Eugene 39–40
Oedipus Rex 162
Okri, Ben 88
Oliver, Mike 174, 178
one-armed man 100–102
opposite sex, interactions with 155
oral narratives 68n1
'ordinary conceptual system' 204
Orientalism 137
orthography, unconventional usage of 41
orthopedically challenged, experience
    of 156
Otherness, counter-discourse of 40–42
otherness of the world 11, 21, 169–170
Ottha 151–153
overlapping identities 148, 153, 157

Padmarajan, P. 8, 72, 74–77, 81
Pal, Joyojeet 188
Pandian, M. S. 216, 218
panic-driven desire 102
Panja, Shormishtha 108
Papadimitriou, Christina 97
partition, trauma of 202
partition of Bengal, colonial decision 143n1
Pasha, Syed Sallauddin 61–66, 69n5
Paterson, Kevin 102
patriarchal communities 175
patriarchal culture 176
patriarchal norms 30, 80

patrilineage, cultural legacy of 174
Pauwels, Heidi R.M 188
Paz, Octavio 140
Pearson, Karl 222
performance and disability representation 57–61
personal tragedy model of disability 174; *see also* charity model
Persons with Disabilities (Equal Opportunities, Protection of Rights and Full Participation) Act 1995 9
Petlikar, Ishwar 8, 173
Phadke, M. S. 220
Phukan, Nilamani 122
poetics and the politics, translating 13–18
poetics of the politics 7–13
politicising translation 206–209
politics of disablement 2–6
'politics of disavowal' 2
Politics of Friendship 136
Politics of the Governed, The 226
polysystem 39
Postcolonial Fiction and Disability 88
postcolonial writers 89, 120, 226
'post-disability' approach 27
post-structuralist notions 4
practice of translation 18–24, 119
Prakṛti 171n19
Prasad, G. J.V. 6, 8, 10, 14, 16, 20, 22, 24, 120, 227–228
Prasad, R. C. 58
prejudiced distinction 58
Premchand 252
problematisation of presentation 205
'productive labour' 236
progressive literary, translation of 19
Progressive Writers' Association 252
prosthetic 50, 170
'protocols of the text' 39
psychological support 23, 243–244, 248–251, 253
public spaces 155
punishment-oriented authoritarian teaching 85
purist tendencies 251

Quayson, Ato 3, 11–12, 125, 224, 229, 236

'rabid segregation' 111
Radha and Krishna, myth of 140
radical conceptualisation 8
radical disruption 199
radical textual practices 19, 35
Raghav, Rangeya 20, 46, 84–86

Rahman, Rizia 25, 32–33
Rajendran, Sowmya 46
Ramayana 3, 19, 41, 57–58; Ramavtar 66; retellings of 61; stage and televised representations 58
Ramcharitmanas 58
Rangaswamy, K. 175
range-of-reference of disability 233
Rasal, Sudheer 220
Ray, Debes 25, 30–31, 34
Ray, Subhadeep 20, 133–134, 140
reading and writing disability 44–47
Rebel and her Cause, A 238
regionalism 21, 137, 143
religious cosmology 17–18
rhetoricity 195, 213, 231, 234, 238–241
Ribeiro, Antonio Sousa 136
Ricoeur, Paul 19, 39–40
'rift-design' 198
right-oriented positive legitimacy 6
Rights for Persons with Disability Act 2015 6
Rights of Persons with Disabilities Bill 2016 10
Rig Veda 168, 171n16
Rispler-Chaim, Vardit 245–247, 250
Rogers, Chrissie 74
Roland Barthes 77
'rolelessness' 190
Roy, Anurupa 59
Rushdie, Salman 88–89, 120
Russell, Emily 189

Saans Ki Kalam Se 186
Sadhana 161
Sahitya Akademy award 81, 119
Sai, Veejay 66–67
Said, Edward 111, 136–137
Salinger, J. D. 8
Samin, Suraj 11, 22
Sāṁkhya 160, 169, 171n18
Sāṁkhya Kārikā 169
sanctification of labour 4
Sangam era 148
Sangari, Kumkum 57
Santaemilia, José 41
Sarla, Jagmohan 192–193
Sasanein, Bharat 11
Sasne, Bharat 22, 220–221, 223–225, 227–229
Satchidanandan, K. 184
Satyanath, T. S 63
Sawhney, Gunjan 62
Schmiesing 125–126

Schmitt, Carl 199, 206, 209n2
Schweik, Susan M. 236
Seibers, Tobin 5
self-articulation 13, 146–147, 149, 153–158
self-conscious physical distancing 149
self-empowerment, gesture of 33
'self expression' 76
self-portrayal foregrounds the struggle 13
self-representation 103, 150–151
'self-sufficiency' 40
semi-divine beings 168
Sen, Amartya 33
Sengupta, Mahashweta 111
sensitisation and awareness 67
sentimentalism 135, 142, 191, 195
'sentimental narratives' 45
sex, role of 111
sexual consciousness 157
Shah, Tanvi 61
Shahbaz, M. 211–212, 216
Shakespeare, Tom 5, 72
Shapiro, Arthur 45
Sharon Snyder, L. 8, 141, 222, 239
Shildrick, Margrit 12, 43, 98, 100–101, 103, 138–139, 251
Shirurkar, Vibhavari 220
'shock value' 67
Shubha, discourse of gender 165–168
Singh, Manmohan 9
Sinha, Arunava 108
Sinha, Indra 234
Skidmore, D. 5
Snyder, Michelle 12
Snyder, Sharon L. 8, 13, 44, 102, 110–113, 116, 126–127, 131, 213–214, 222
social consciousness 147
social discrimination 42–43, 67, 139, 141, 150
social exclusion 11, 19–20, 128, 148, 153, 165
social fabric of disability 169
social malpractices 28
social marginalisation 1
social model of disability 35n1, 42–43, 213
social stigmatisation 222
societal assumptions 168
societal exclusion 18
societal prejudice and discrimination 50
Sohail, Agha 8, 102
source language (SL) expression 181
Space, Place and Gender Relations 167
speech impairment 86, 102, 114, 173, 175, 183
spiritual awakening 247–249

Spivak, Gayatri Chakravorty 22, 28, 39, 136, 186, 190, 193, 195, 213, 217, 231–232, 238, 240
stage performances 57, 60, 67–68
Steinbeck, John 8
stereotyping disability 73–74
stigma, authentic representation of 228
stigmatised 11, 49–50, 223–224, 229
Straus, Joseph N. 129
'strong son-preference' 174
Stuart, O. 5
Subha 21, 107–110, 112–114, 116, 159, 161–168, 233; challenges 162–164; communication with the natural world 163; disability in 161–162; disability narrative in 164; 'domestication' 163; 'foreignisation' 163; impact of tragic event 161; invalidated 165; linguistic signs 164; marginalised 165; narrative style 108; new paradigms 162–164; opportunities 162–164; perceived 165; primary identity 166; usual disability tropes 167
subnormalcy 88
Sukthankar, V. S. 56, 68, 220
'supercrip', narrative of 45
Su SuSudhi Valmeekam 73
Swain, John 174, 178
Synder, Sharon L. 9
syphilis 239

Tagore, Rabindranath 1, 21, 25, 27–28, 34, 107–115, 135, 159, 161, 164–168, 170, 233; child psychology 110; contention 113; exploration of Subha's femininity 166; keen insight into disability 159; narratorial voice 164; portrayal of his women 109; probes into the mind of a guilt-ridden husband 110; vision of the water-nymph 166
tale-within-a-tale structure 124, 126
Tamil dalit writings 147
target language (TL) expression 181
teaching modules 85
textual dynamic 134
textual multifunctionality 137
textual radicalism 25–26
Thakara 19, 72–83; adaptation and Malayalam cinema 76–77; excluded from society 82; exploited by many 82; film's appeal 80–82; 'guinea pig' 75; idea of 'normalcy' and self 74; language, technique and translation 75–76; 'loved as a large doll' 74; 'madness' 79; male gaze

80–82; man–woman relationships 75;
sexual awakening of 78
Thakazhi 76
Tharu, Susie 234–235
themes and craftsmanship 73
'thick description' 41
thick translation 40–41
'third-world' women 232
Thomas, Sanju 19, 72, 74, 76
Thomsen, Mads Rosendahl 136
Thong, Tezenlo 125
thought-provoking interpretations 60
Titchkosky, Tanya 178
Toba Tek Singh 8, 98; *see also* Manto, Saadat
Hasan
Togalu Gombeyaata 55, 59
tongue-in-cheek comments 157
transcreation 41–42, 120–121
transformative needs of the real 7
translatability 56–57
translating literature 116
translational subversion and disruption
48–51
Translation Studies 2, 23–24, 72, 84, 92, 221
translation theory, mantra in 18
translator's choices and political correctness
112
transposition 68n2
Tribute to Tagore 108
Trivedi, Harish 41, 105, 119, 125, 133, 135
Trying to Grow 233
Tymoczko, Maria 38, 107, 111–112,
117n11, 119–122, 142, 184

Ugly Laws: Disability in Public, The 236
UN Convention on Persons with
Disabilities (UNCRPD) 17
Union for the Physically Impaired against
Segregation (UPIS) 3
United Progressive Alliance (UPA) 9
'untroubled fashion' 84
Upaniṣads 159
urban geography 221
Urdu: fiction 98; romanticised perception
of 104; translating disability from
251–252
US Democratic National Committee 14

Usman, Ashiq 67
Usmani, Anjum 8, 100, 104

Vanashree 192
Vedas 159, 168
Venkiteswaran, Chittur Subramanian 76
Venuti, Lawrence 41, 68, 81, 84
Vidal, M. Carmen-África 56
Vidali, Amy 205
'Viklang ' 211–218; eugenic gaze 215–217;
metaphor in the case 214; moments
of frayages 217–218; opportunistic
metaphorical device 213–215; synopsis
of 211–212; tone and the frequency 215
violation of fidelity 150
Vishnu Purana 63
'vulnerable subjects', representation of 196

well-functioning female body 176
Wendell, Susan 174
Western factory system 4
Western model's framework 236
Western powers, hegemonic control of 124
Western theories 12
wheelchair-bound actors 63
wheelchair-bound person 157
Wheelchairs as 'chariots of war' 61–63
Whitaker, Zai 46
Whyte, Susan Reynolds 125
'wicked woman' 239
Wings to Fly 46
womanhood 22, 176, 188, 190, 194, 196
woman's facial disfigurement 28
woman's trauma, male-authored narrative
of 28
Women Writing in India 234–235, 238
World Health Organization (WHO) 160
'writing culture' 41
writing style 209n4
Wynn, Kerry 16, 18

Yajur Veda 168

Zafir, Deeba 20, 97–98, 100, 102, 104, 106
Zama, Margaret 125
Zangwill, Israel 42
Zauq 252

For Product Safety Concerns and Information please contact our EU
representative GPSR@taylorandfrancis.com
Taylor & Francis Verlag GmbH, Kaufingerstraße 24, 80331 München, Germany

www.ingramcontent.com/pod-product-compliance
Lightning Source LLC
Chambersburg PA
CBHW071501110726
47908CB00003B/686